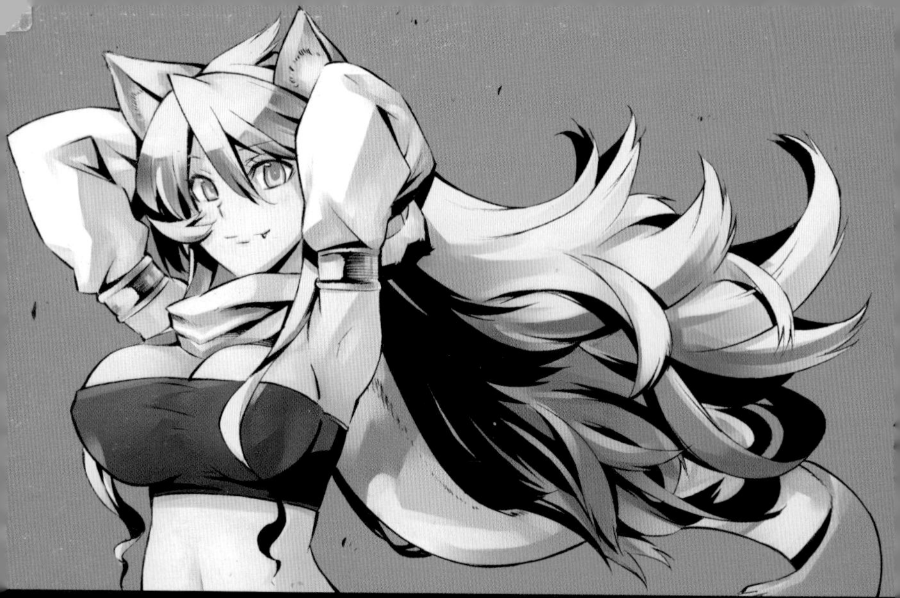

TAKAHIRO × TETSUYA TASHIRO

AKAME GA KILL! II

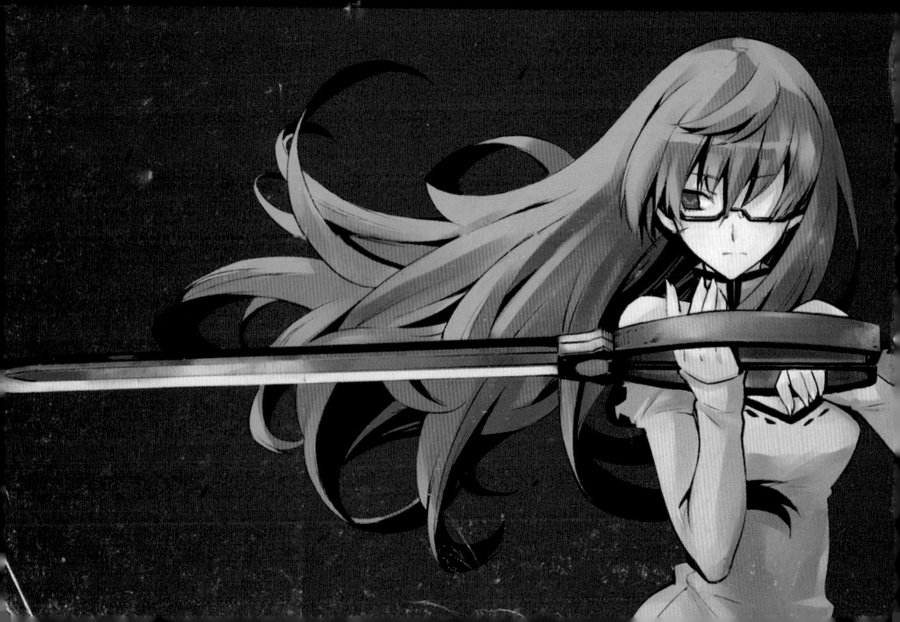

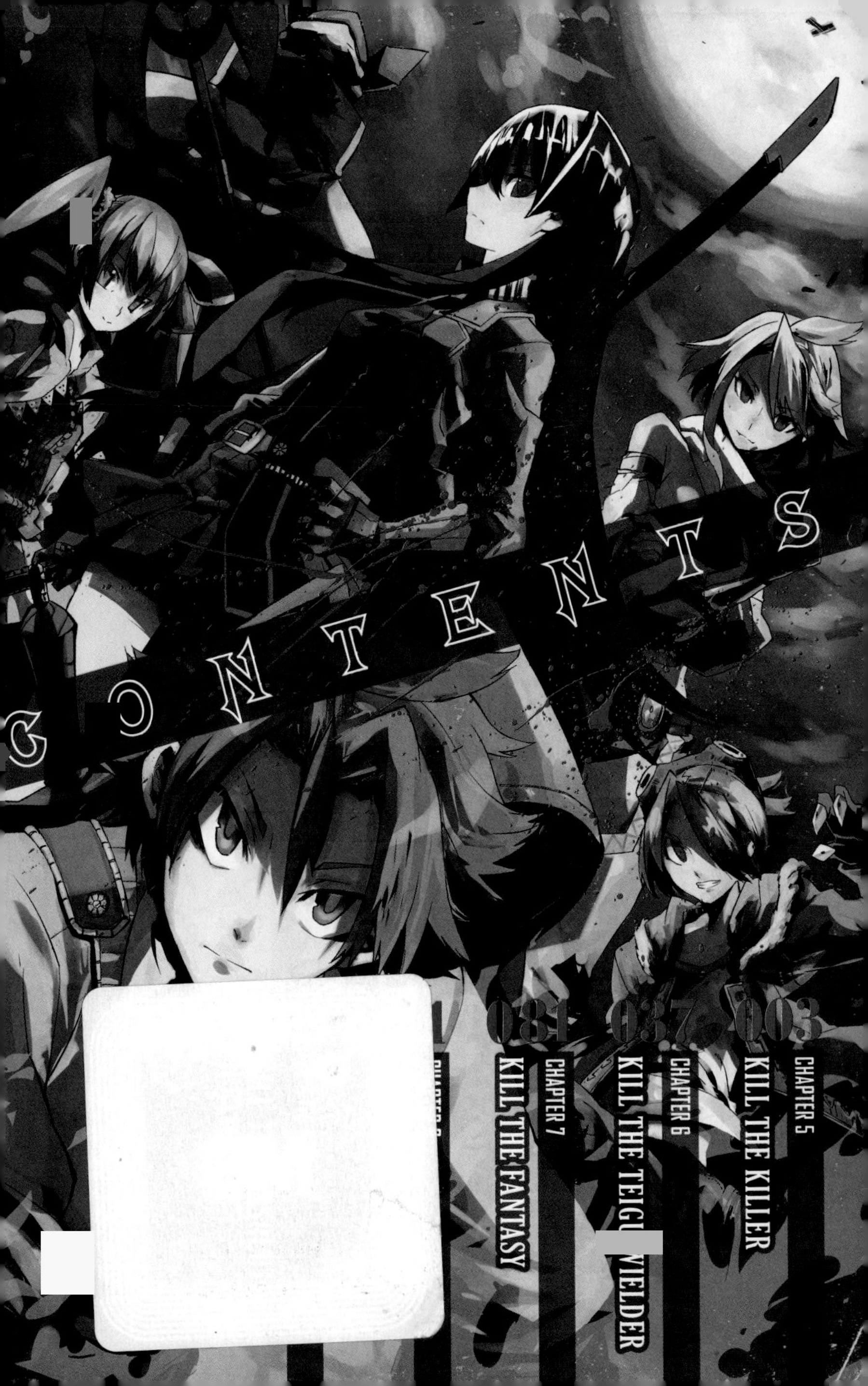
CONTENTS
003 CHAPTER 5 KILL THE KILLER
037 CHAPTER 6 KILL THE TEIGU WIELDER
081 CHAPTER 7 KILL THE FANTASY

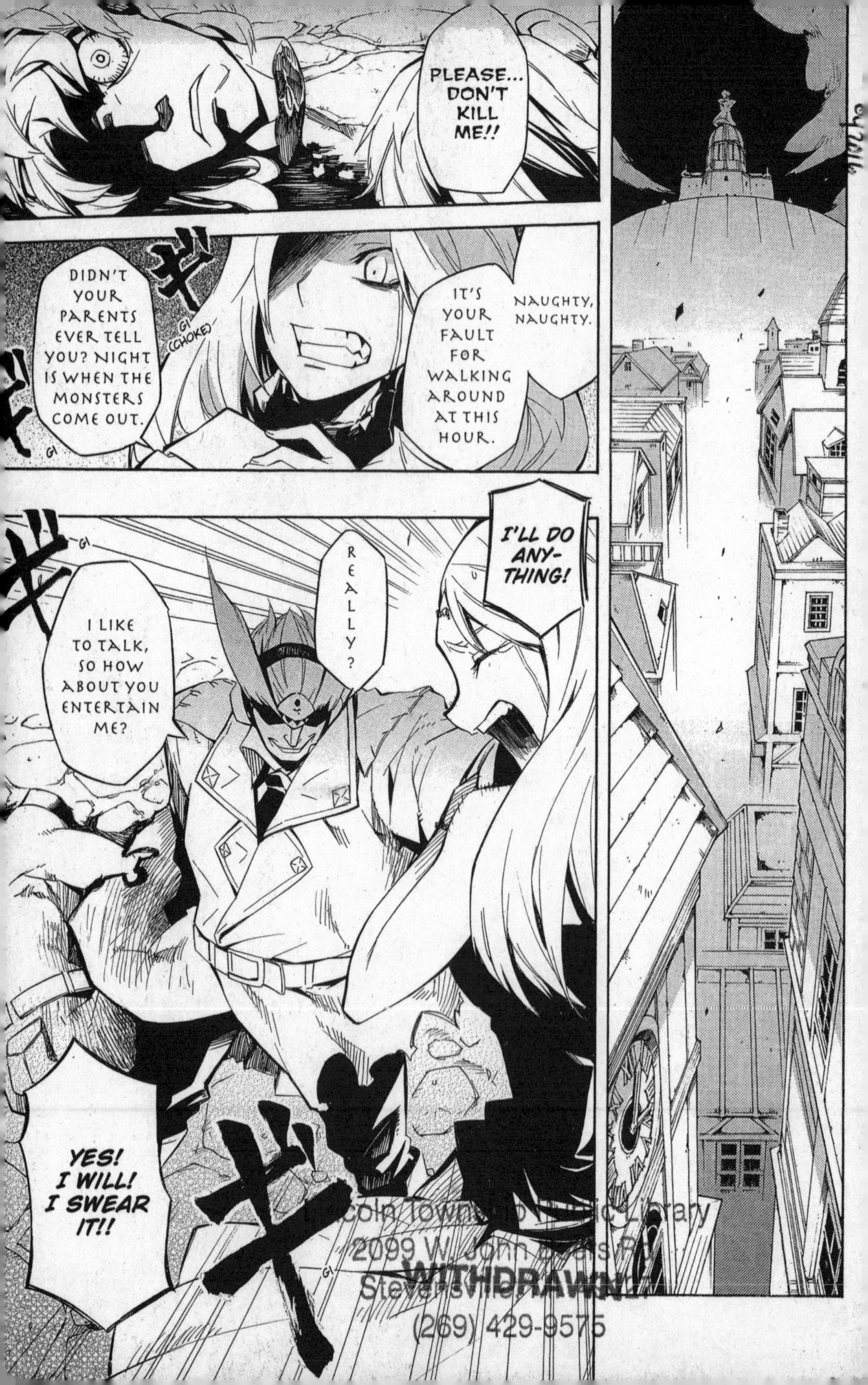
PLEASE... DON'T KILL ME!!
NAUGHTY, NAUGHTY.
IT'S YOUR FAULT FOR WALKING AROUND AT THIS HOUR.
GI (CHOKE)
DIDN'T YOUR PARENTS EVER TELL YOU? NIGHT IS WHEN THE MONSTERS COME OUT.
GI
I'LL DO ANY-THING!
REALLY?
GI
I LIKE TO TALK, SO HOW ABOUT YOU ENTERTAIN ME?
YES! I WILL! I SWEAR IT!!
GI

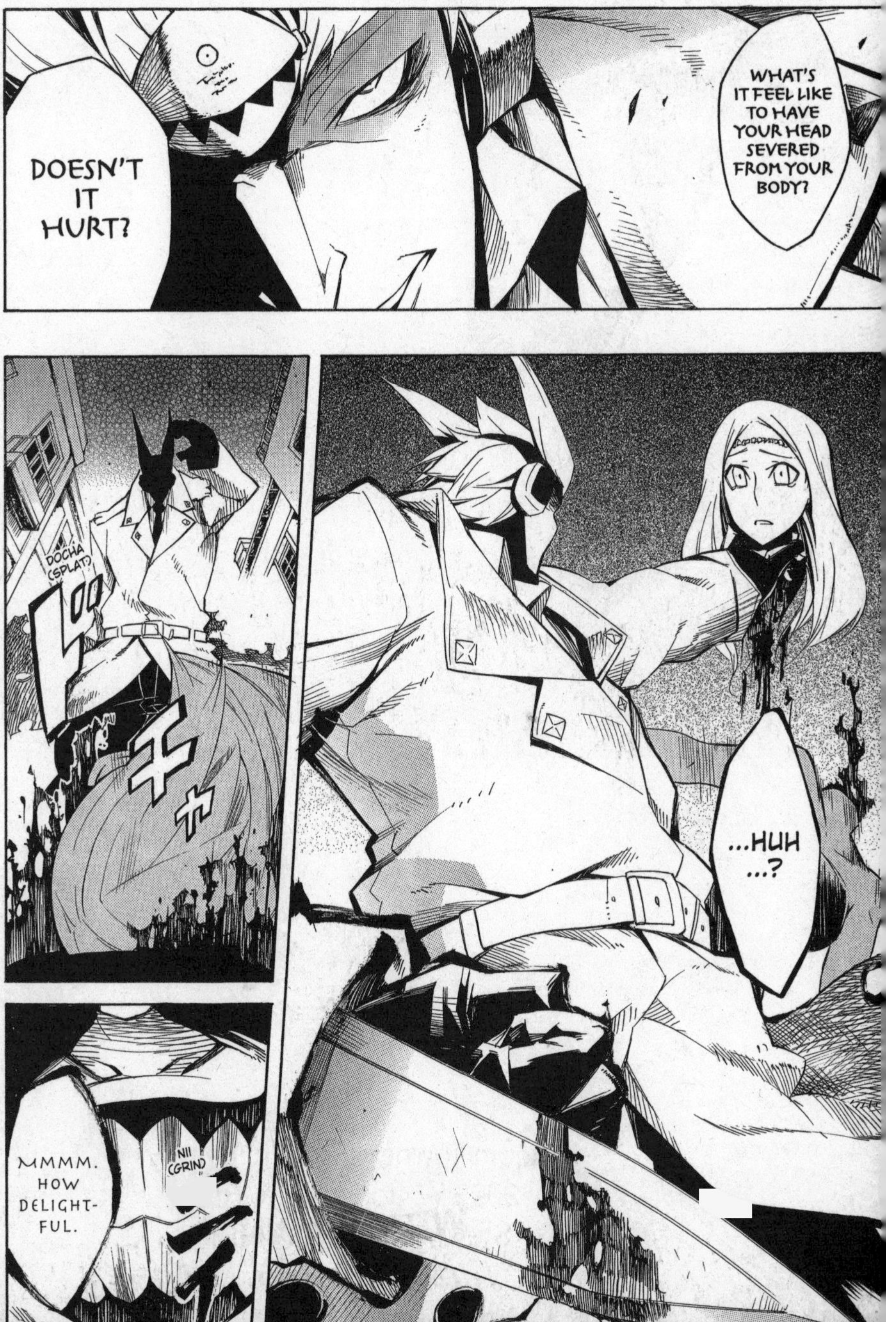
WHAT'S IT FEEL LIKE TO HAVE YOUR HEAD SEVERED FROM YOUR BODY?
DOESN'T IT HURT?
...HUH ...?
DOCHA (SPLAT)
NII (GRIND)
MMMM. HOW DELIGHT-FUL.

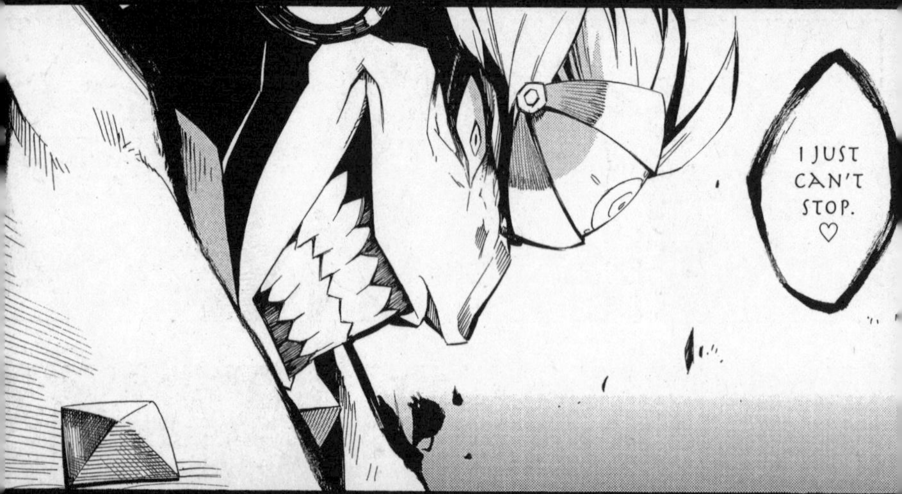
I JUST CAN'T STOP. ♡

CHAPTER 5 KILL THE KILLER

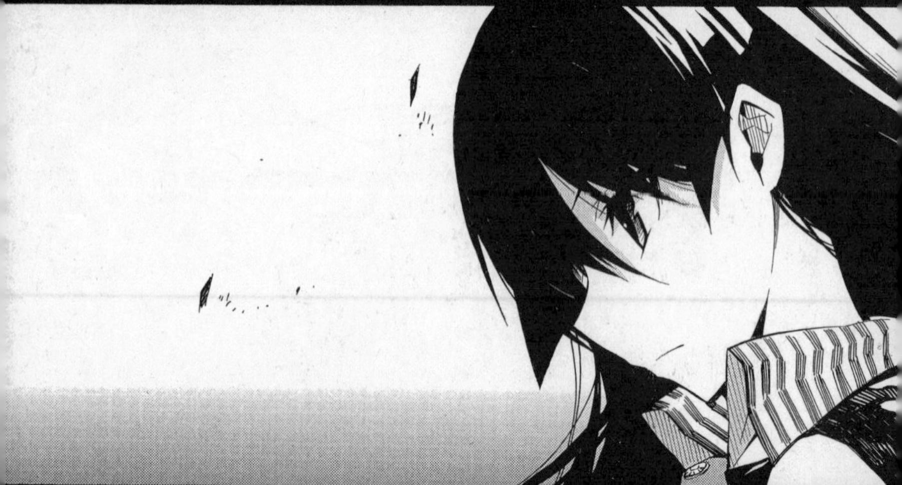

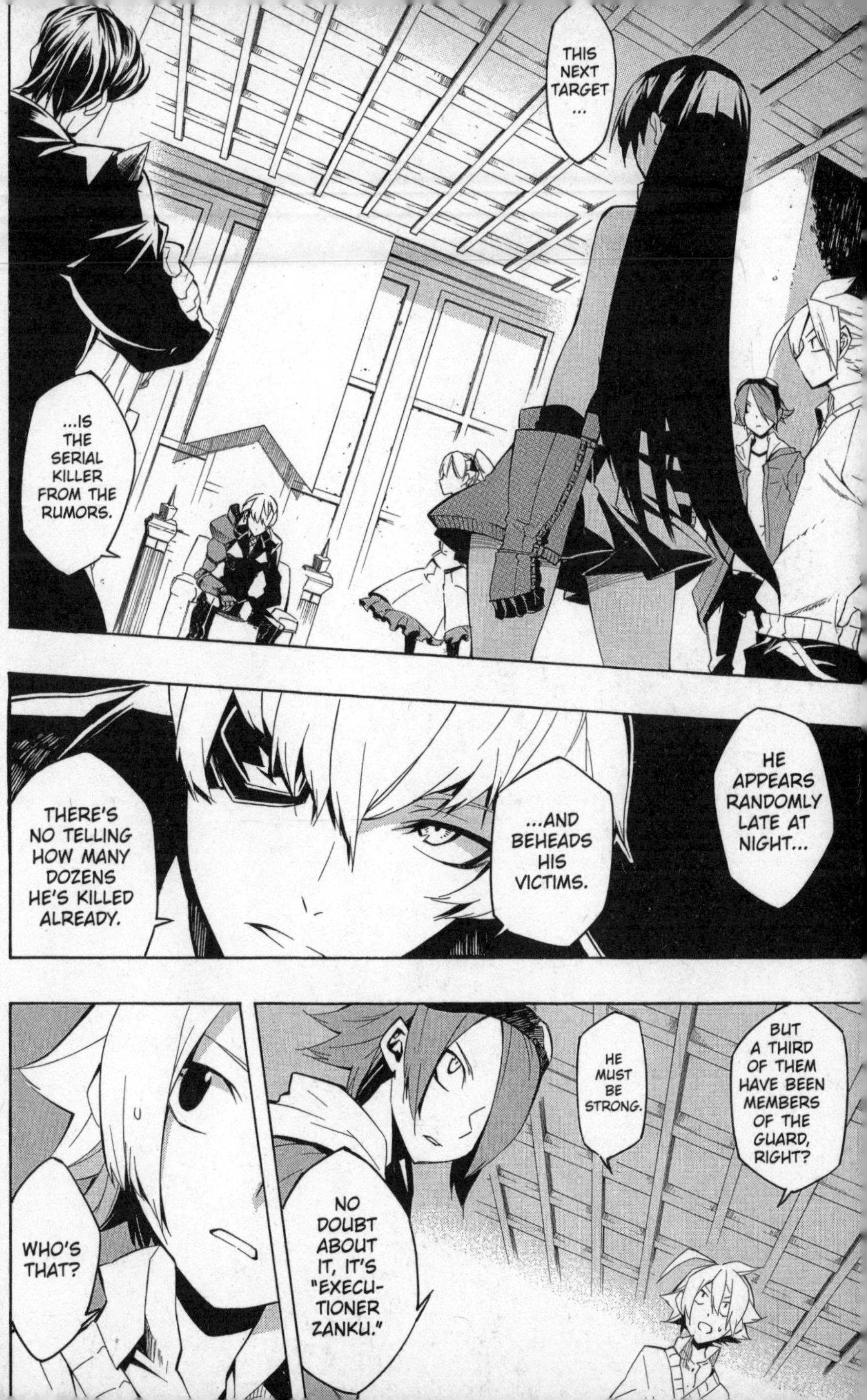
THIS NEXT TARGET...
...IS THE SERIAL KILLER FROM THE RUMORS.
HE APPEARS RANDOMLY LATE AT NIGHT...
...AND BEHEADS HIS VICTIMS.
THERE'S NO TELLING HOW MANY DOZENS HE'S KILLED ALREADY.
BUT A THIRD OF THEM HAVE BEEN MEMBERS OF THE GUARD, RIGHT?
HE MUST BE STRONG.
NO DOUBT ABOUT IT, IT'S "EXECUTIONER ZANKU."
WHO'S THAT?

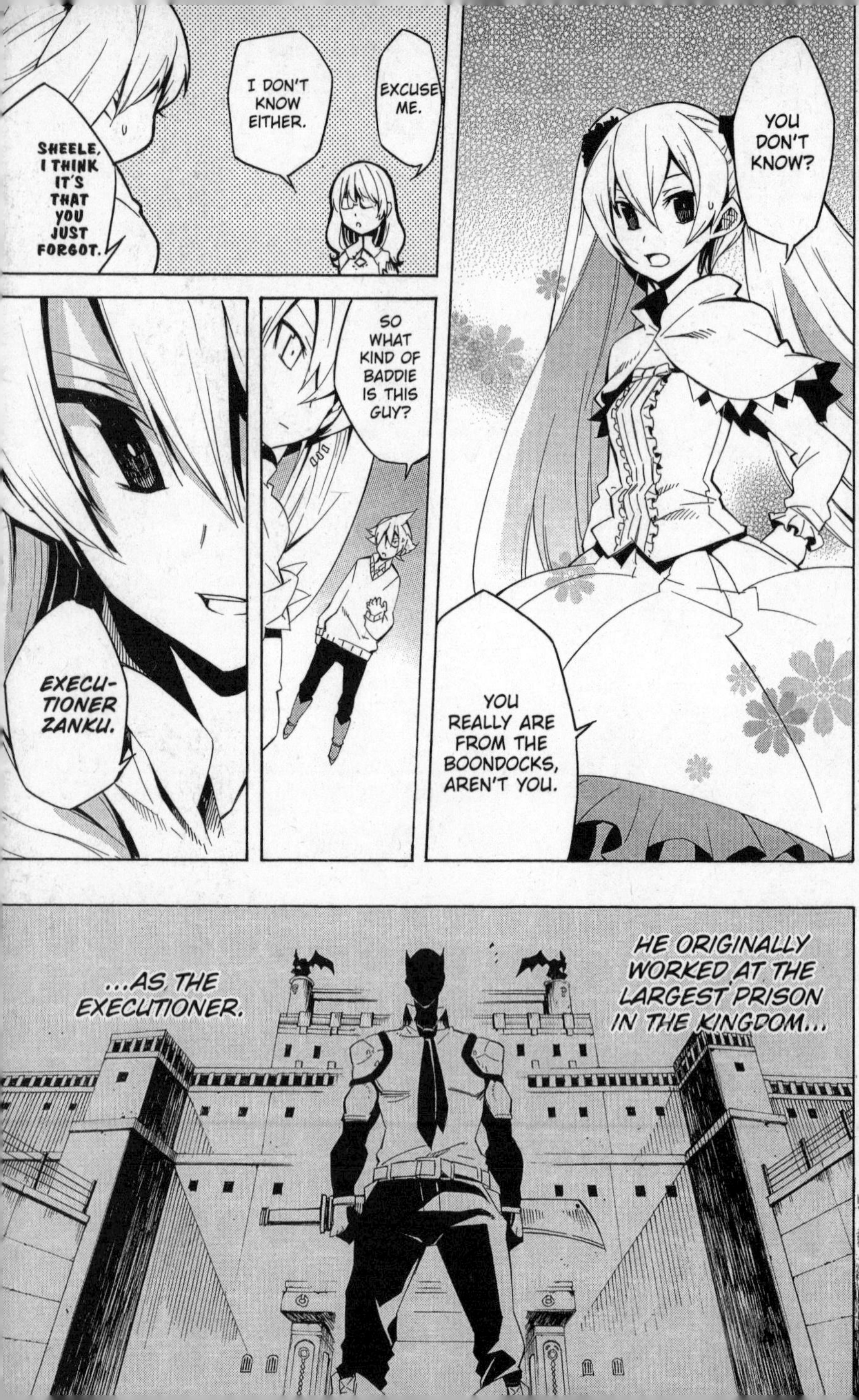
YOU DON'T KNOW?
YOU REALLY ARE FROM THE BOONDOCKS, AREN'T YOU.
EXCUSE ME.
I DON'T KNOW EITHER.
SHEELE, I THINK IT'S THAT YOU JUST FORGOT.
SO WHAT KIND OF BADDIE IS THIS GUY?
EXECUTIONER ZANKU.
HE ORIGINALLY WORKED AT THE LARGEST PRISON IN THE KINGDOM...
...AS THE EXECUTIONER.

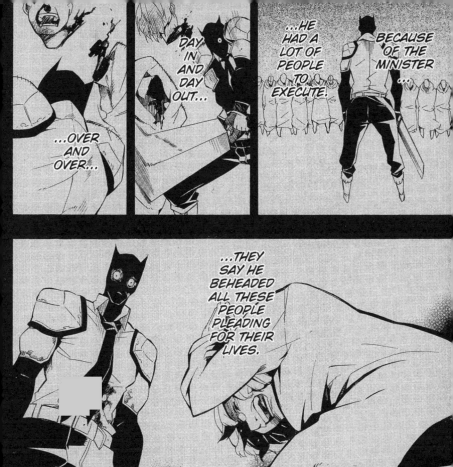

BECAUSE OF THE MINISTER...
...HE HAD A LOT OF PEOPLE TO EXECUTE.
DAY IN AND DAY OUT...
...OVER AND OVER...
...THEY SAY HE BEHEADED ALL THESE PEOPLE PLEADING FOR THEIR LIVES.
AFTER YEARS OF THAT...
...BEHEADING BECAME SECOND NATURE TO HIM.

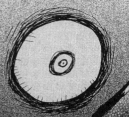

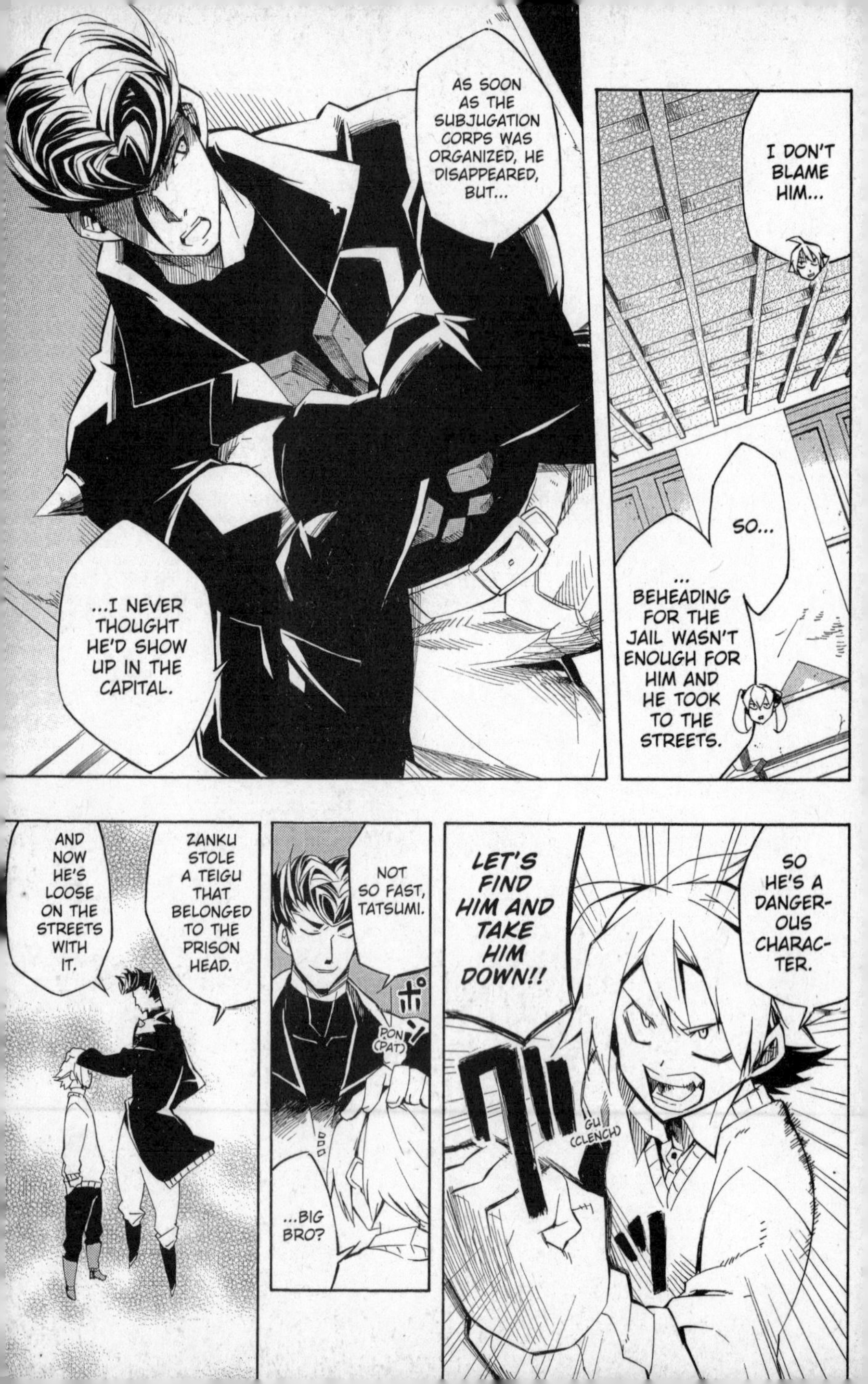
I DON'T BLAME HIM...
SO...
...BEHEADING FOR THE JAIL WASN'T ENOUGH FOR HIM AND HE TOOK TO THE STREETS.
AS SOON AS THE SUBJUGATION CORPS WAS ORGANIZED, HE DISAPPEARED, BUT...
...I NEVER THOUGHT HE'D SHOW UP IN THE CAPITAL.
SO HE'S A DANGEROUS CHARACTER.
LET'S FIND HIM AND TAKE HIM DOWN!!
GU (CLENCH)
NOT SO FAST, TATSUMI.
ポン
PON (PAT)
...BIG BRO?
ZANKU STOLE A TEIGU THAT BELONGED TO THE PRISON HEAD.
AND NOW HE'S LOOSE ON THE STREETS WITH IT.

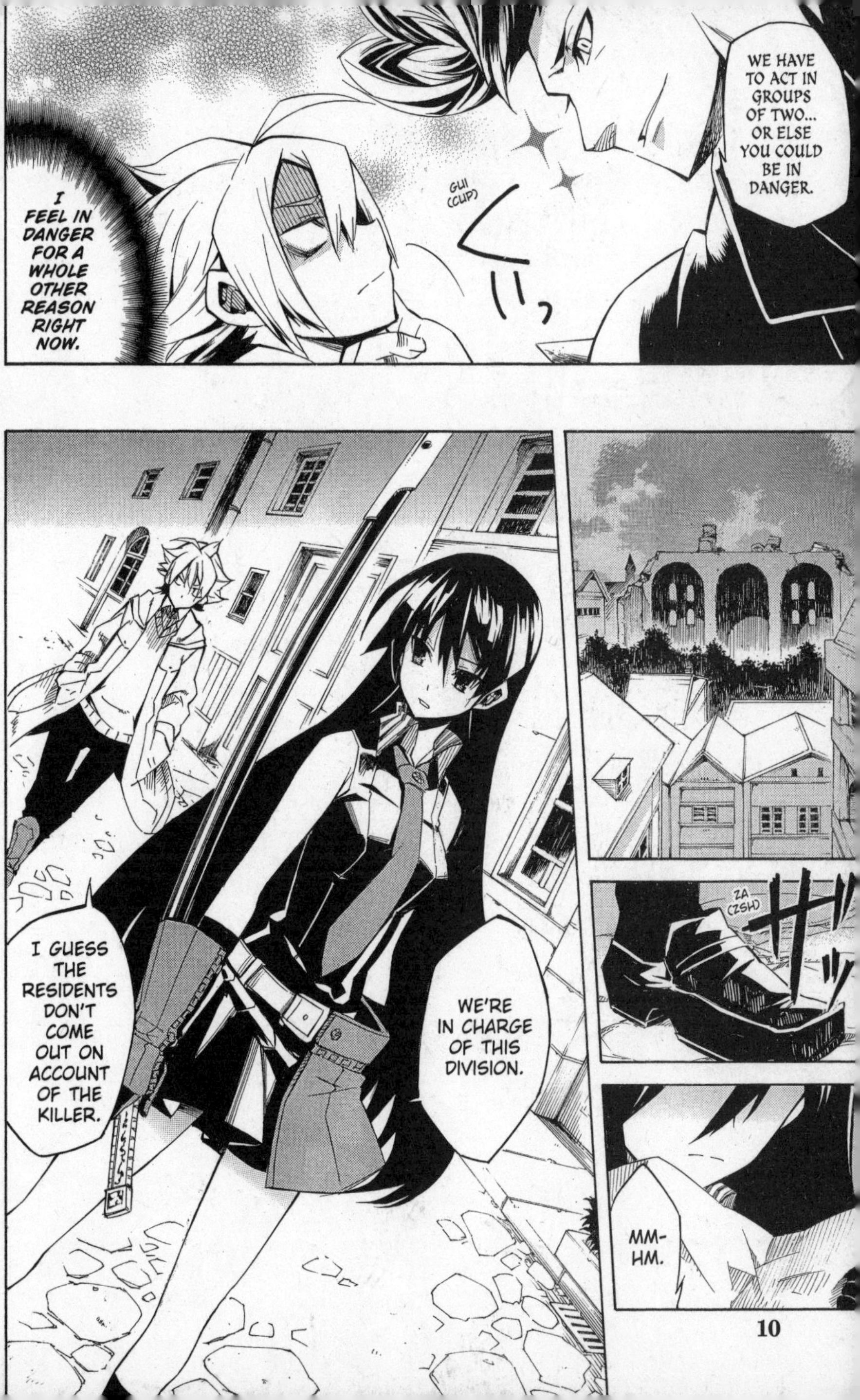
WE HAVE TO ACT IN GROUPS OF TWO... OR ELSE YOU COULD BE IN DANGER.
GUI (CUP)
I FEEL IN DANGER FOR A WHOLE OTHER REASON RIGHT NOW.
ZA (ZSH)
MM-HM.
WE'RE IN CHARGE OF THIS DIVISION.
I GUESS THE RESIDENTS DON'T COME OUT ON ACCOUNT OF THE KILLER.

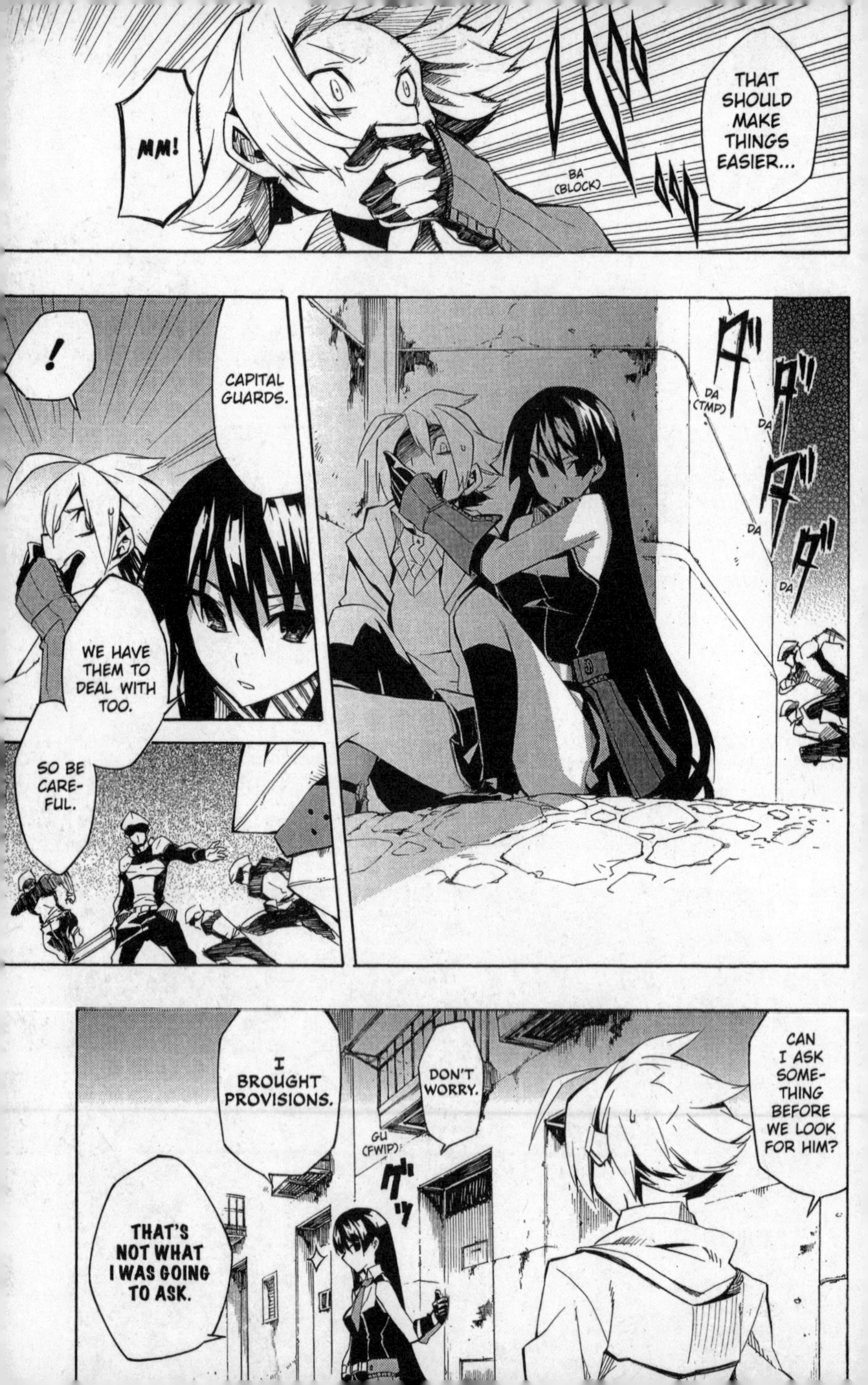

THAT SHOULD MAKE THINGS EASIER...
BA (BLOCK)
MM!
DA (TMP)
DA
DA
DA
CAPITAL GUARDS.
!
WE HAVE THEM TO DEAL WITH TOO.
SO BE CAREFUL.
CAN I ASK SOMETHING BEFORE WE LOOK FOR HIM?
DON'T WORRY.
GU (FWIP)
I BROUGHT PROVISIONS.
THAT'S NOT WHAT I WAS GOING TO ASK.

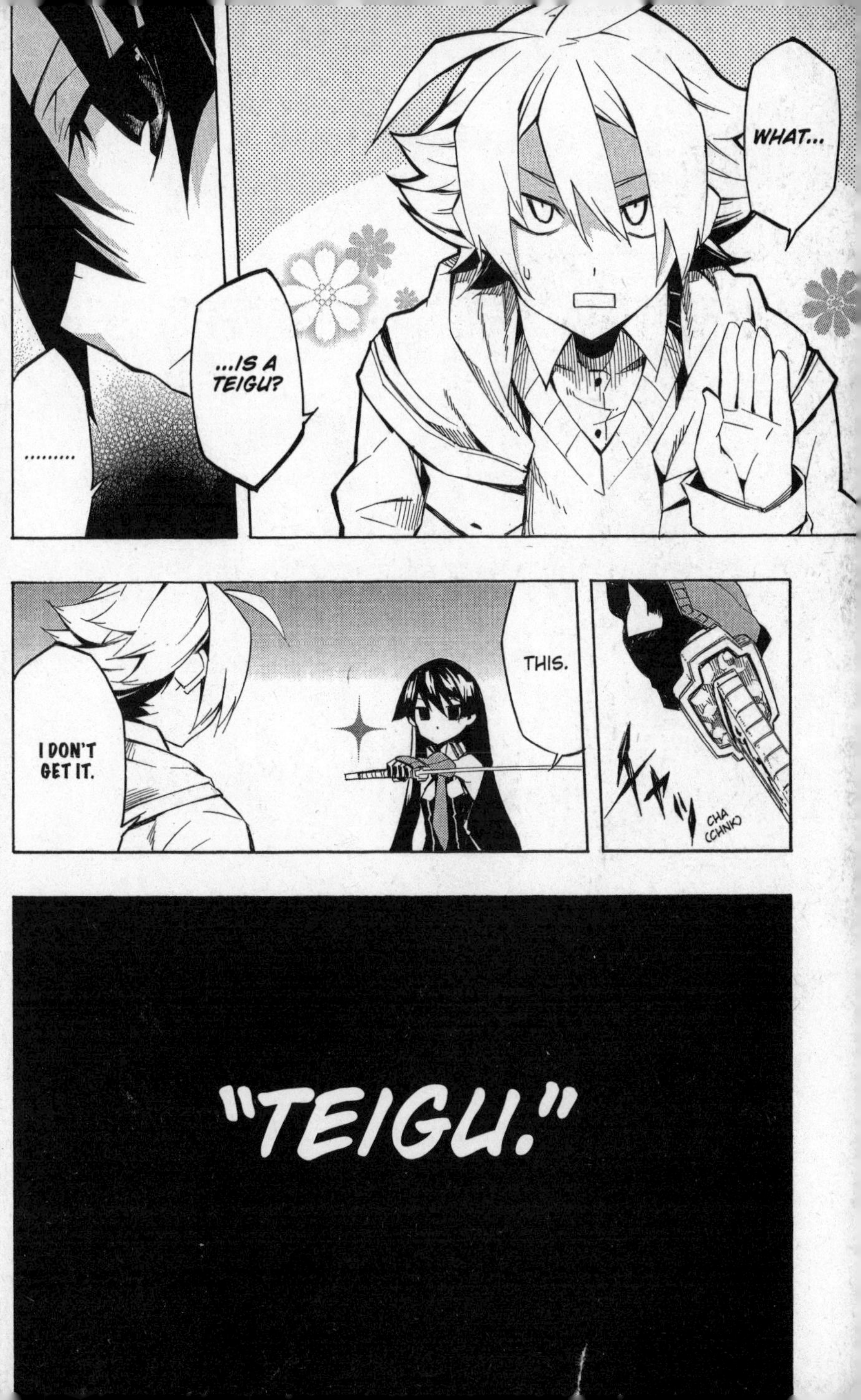
WHAT...
...IS A TEIGU?
....
CHA (CHNK)
THIS.
I DON'T GET IT.
"TEIGU."

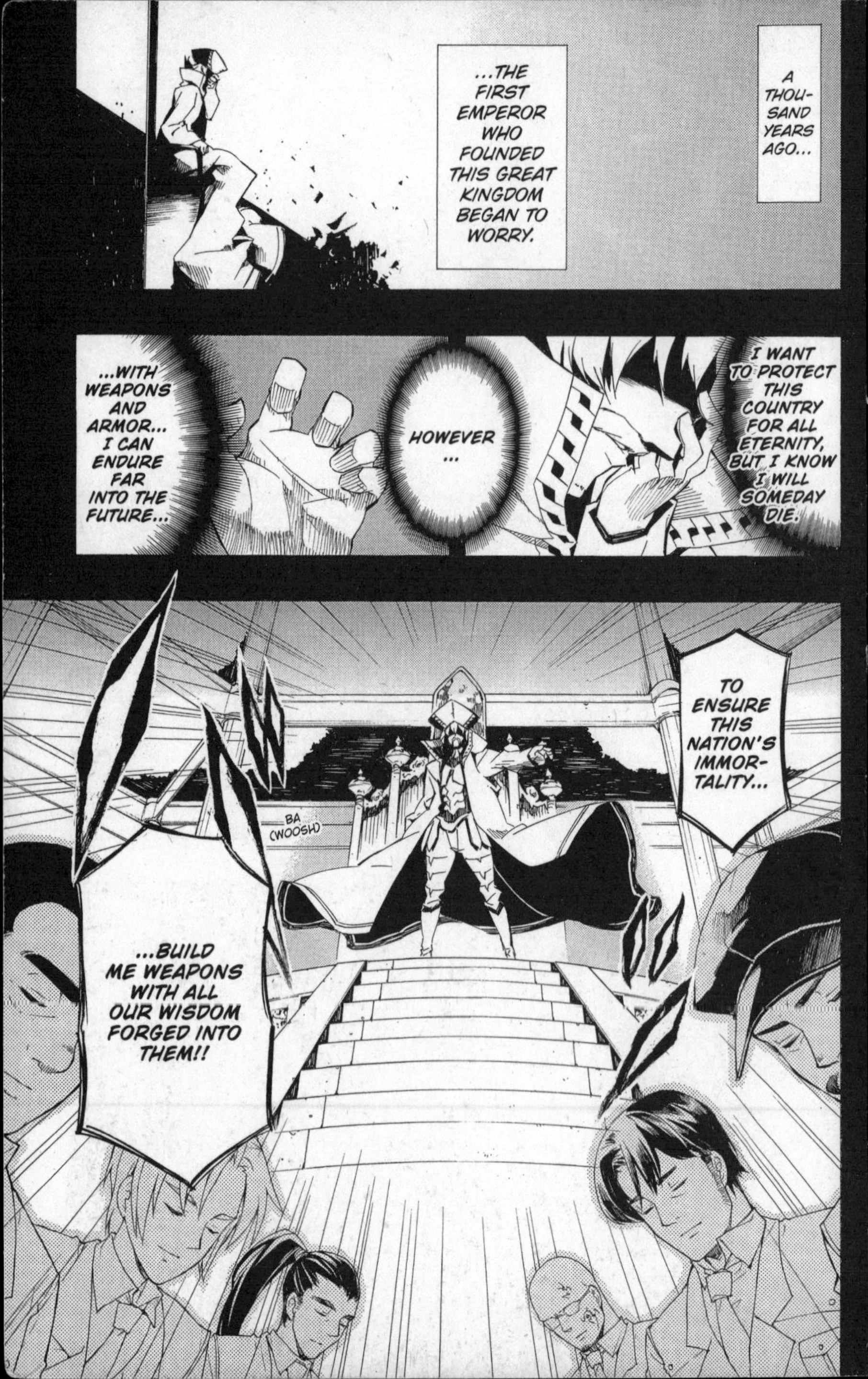
A THOUSAND YEARS AGO...
...THE FIRST EMPEROR WHO FOUNDED THIS GREAT KINGDOM BEGAN TO WORRY.
I WANT TO PROTECT THIS COUNTRY FOR ALL ETERNITY, BUT I KNOW I WILL SOMEDAY DIE.
HOWEVER ...
...WITH WEAPONS AND ARMOR... I CAN ENDURE FAR INTO THE FUTURE...
TO ENSURE THIS NATION'S IMMORTALITY...
BA (WOOSH)
...BUILD ME WEAPONS WITH ALL OUR WISDOM FORGED INTO THEM!!

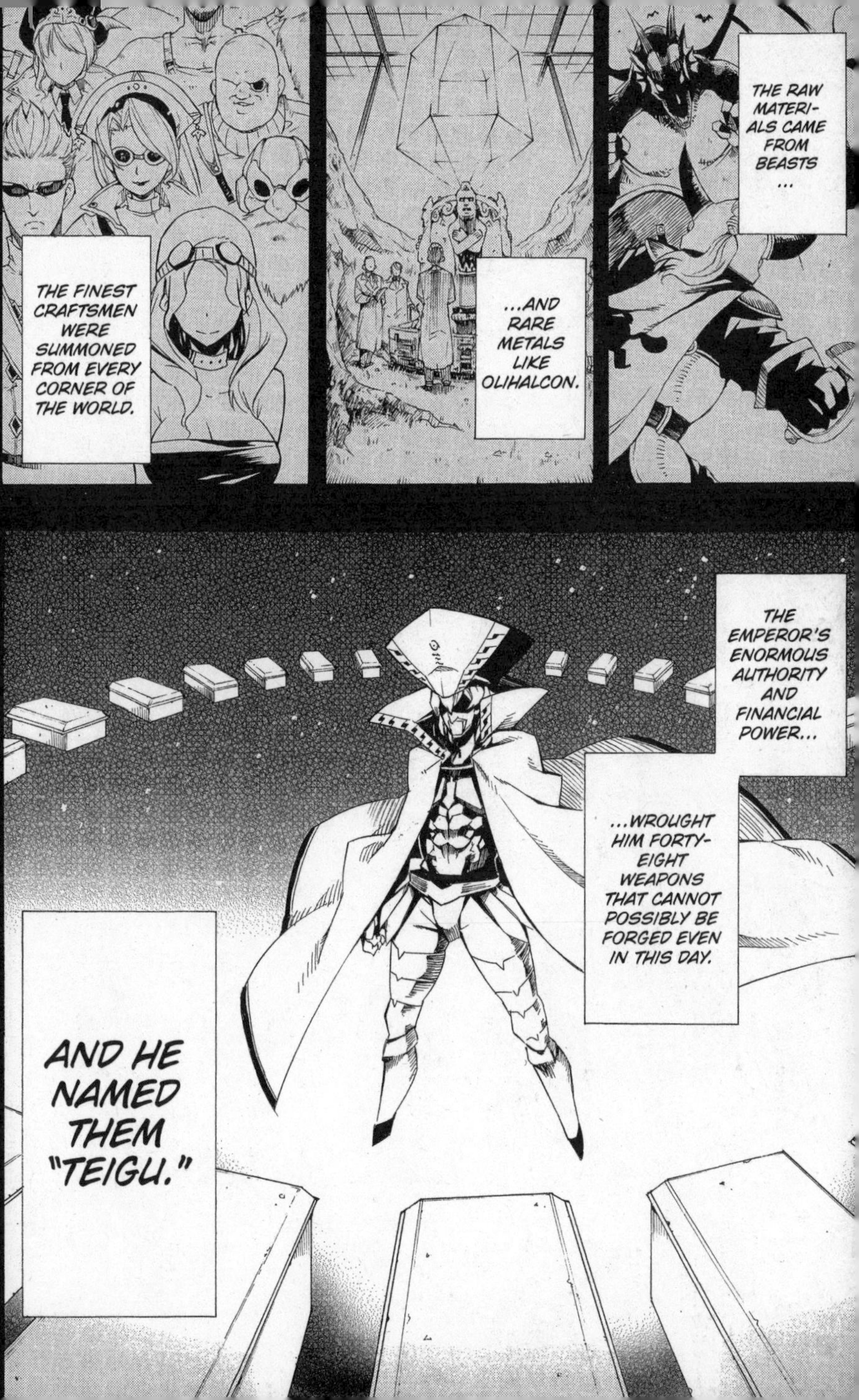
THE RAW MATERIALS CAME FROM BEASTS...
...AND RARE METALS LIKE OLIHALCON.
THE FINEST CRAFTSMEN WERE SUMMONED FROM EVERY CORNER OF THE WORLD.
THE EMPEROR'S ENORMOUS AUTHORITY AND FINANCIAL POWER...
...WROUGHT HIM FORTY-EIGHT WEAPONS THAT CANNOT POSSIBLY BE FORGED EVEN IN THIS DAY.
AND HE NAMED THEM "TEIGU."

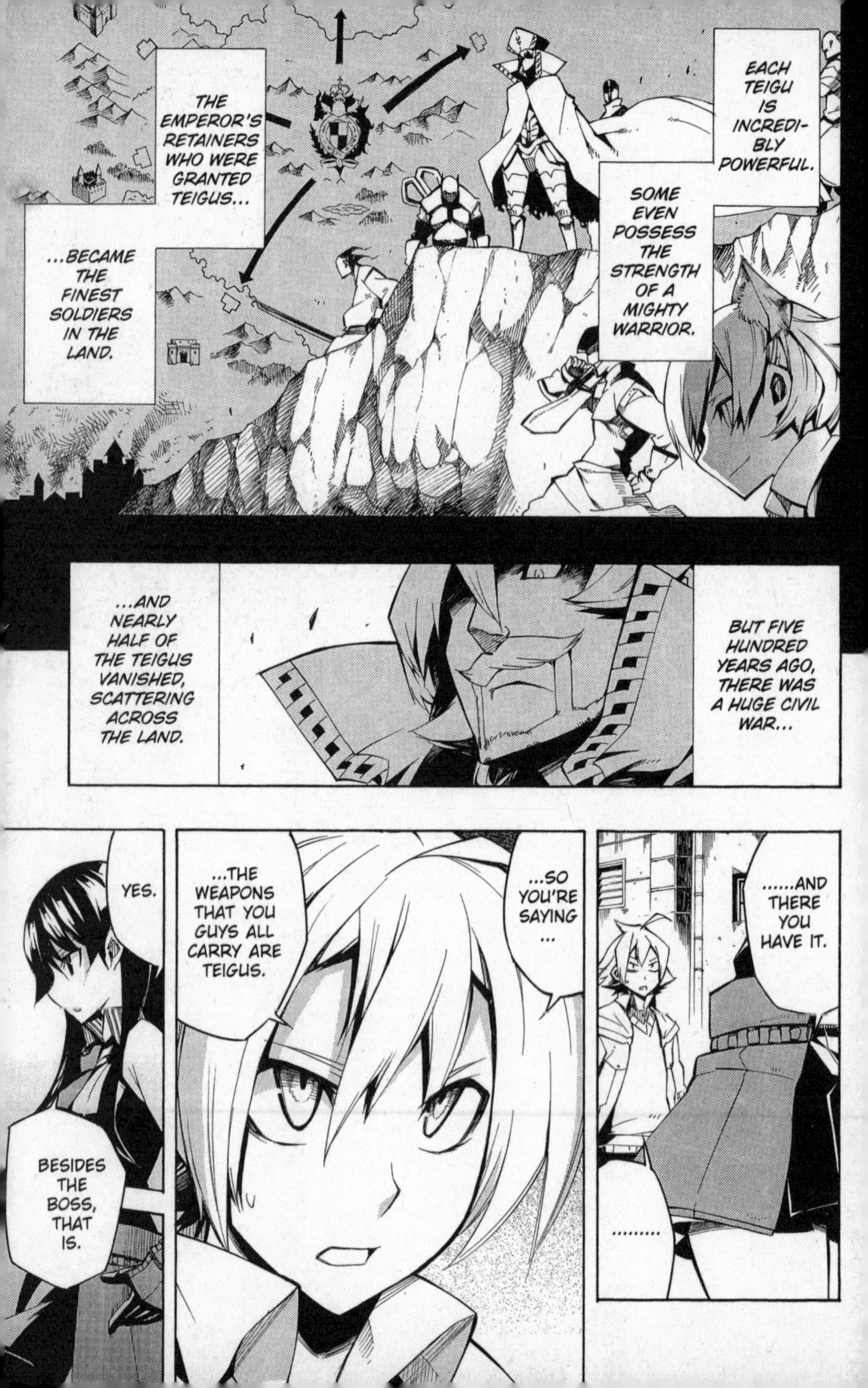
EACH TEIGU IS INCREDIBLY POWERFUL.
SOME EVEN POSSESS THE STRENGTH OF A MIGHTY WARRIOR.
THE EMPEROR'S RETAINERS WHO WERE GRANTED TEIGUS...
...BECAME THE FINEST SOLDIERS IN THE LAND.
BUT FIVE HUNDRED YEARS AGO, THERE WAS A HUGE CIVIL WAR...
...AND NEARLY HALF OF THE TEIGUS VANISHED, SCATTERING ACROSS THE LAND.
......AND THERE YOU HAVE IT.
....
...SO YOU'RE SAYING ...
...THE WEAPONS THAT YOU GUYS ALL CARRY ARE TEIGUS.
YES.
BESIDES THE BOSS, THAT IS.

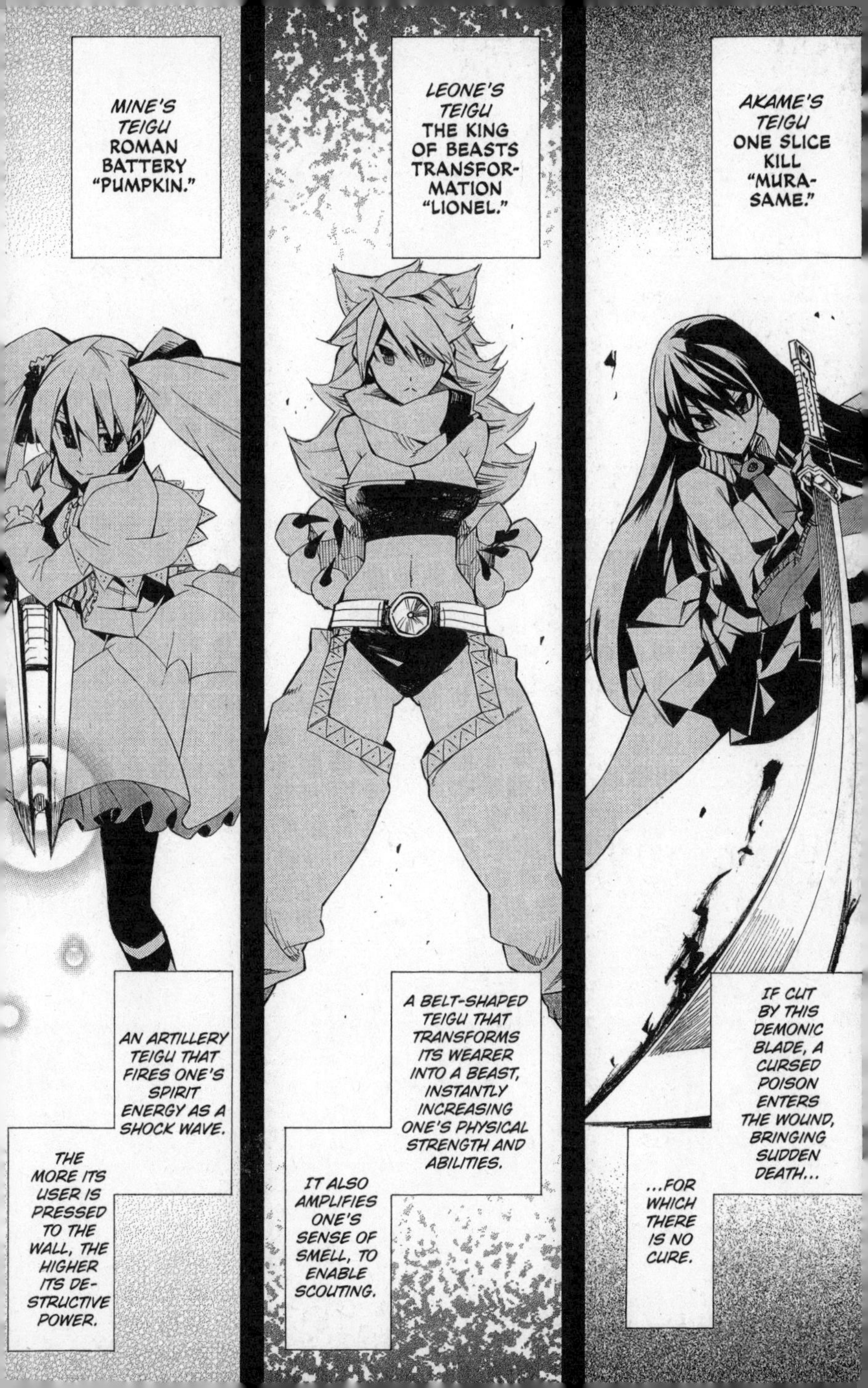
AKAME'S TEIGU ONE SLICE KILL "MURA-SAME."
IF CUT BY THIS DEMONIC BLADE, A CURSED POISON ENTERS THE WOUND, BRINGING SUDDEN DEATH...
...FOR WHICH THERE IS NO CURE.
LEONE'S TEIGU THE KING OF BEASTS TRANSFOR-MATION "LIONEL."
A BELT-SHAPED TEIGU THAT TRANSFORMS ITS WEARER INTO A BEAST, INSTANTLY INCREASING ONE'S PHYSICAL STRENGTH AND ABILITIES.
IT ALSO AMPLIFIES ONE'S SENSE OF SMELL, TO ENABLE SCOUTING.
MINE'S TEIGU ROMAN BATTERY "PUMPKIN."
AN ARTILLERY TEIGU THAT FIRES ONE'S SPIRIT ENERGY AS A SHOCK WAVE.
THE MORE ITS USER IS PRESSED TO THE WALL, THE HIGHER ITS DE-STRUCTIVE POWER.

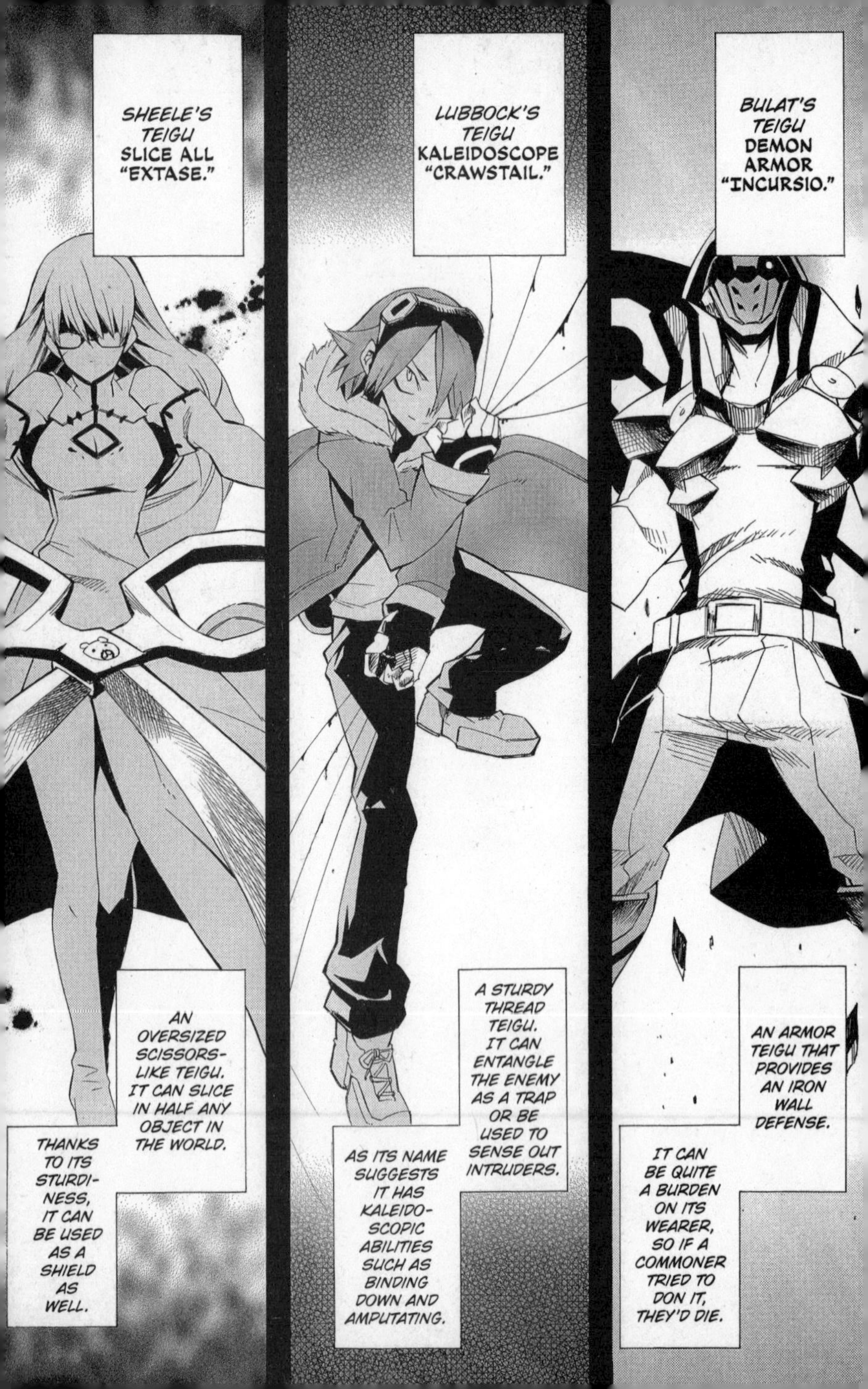
BULAT'S TEIGU DEMON ARMOR "INCURSIO."
AN ARMOR TEIGU THAT PROVIDES AN IRON WALL DEFENSE.
IT CAN BE QUITE A BURDEN ON ITS WEARER, SO IF A COMMONER TRIED TO DON IT, THEY'D DIE.
LUBBOCK'S TEIGU KALEIDOSCOPE "CRAWSTAIL."
A STURDY THREAD TEIGU. IT CAN ENTANGLE THE ENEMY AS A TRAP OR BE USED TO SENSE OUT INTRUDERS.
AS ITS NAME SUGGESTS IT HAS KALEIDO-SCOPIC ABILITIES SUCH AS BINDING DOWN AND AMPUTATING.
SHEELE'S TEIGU SLICE ALL "EXTASE."
AN OVERSIZED SCISSORS-LIKE TEIGU. IT CAN SLICE IN HALF ANY OBJECT IN THE WORLD.
THANKS TO ITS STURDI-NESS, IT CAN BE USED AS A SHIELD AS WELL.

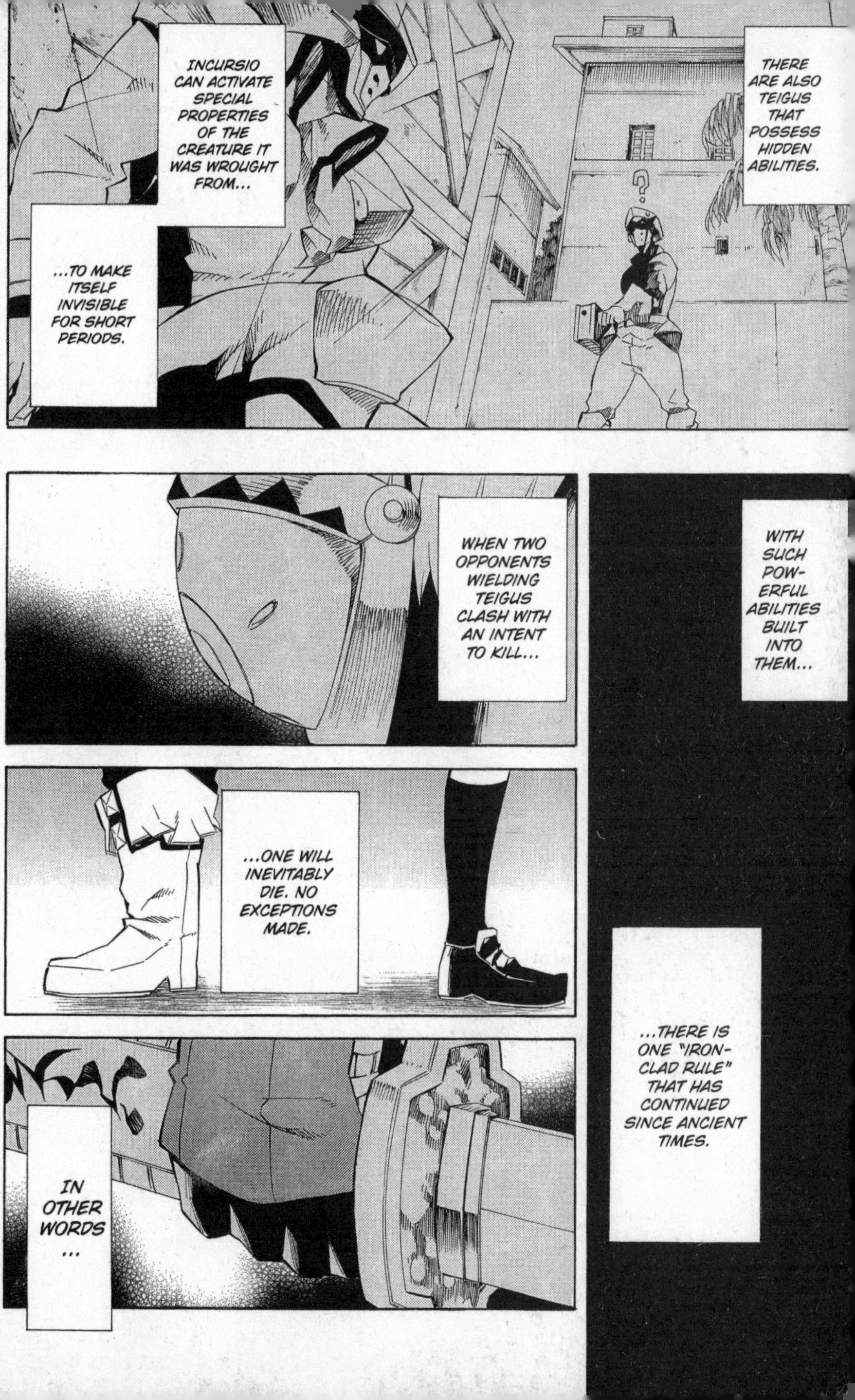
THERE ARE ALSO TEIGUS THAT POSSESS HIDDEN ABILITIES.
INCURSIO CAN ACTIVATE SPECIAL PROPERTIES OF THE CREATURE IT WAS WROUGHT FROM...
...TO MAKE ITSELF INVISIBLE FOR SHORT PERIODS.
WITH SUCH POW-ERFUL ABILITIES BUILT INTO THEM...
...THERE IS ONE "IRON-CLAD RULE" THAT HAS CONTINUED SINCE ANCIENT TIMES.
WHEN TWO OPPONENTS WIELDING TEIGUS CLASH WITH AN INTENT TO KILL...
...ONE WILL INEVITABLY DIE. NO EXCEPTIONS MADE.
IN OTHER WORDS ...

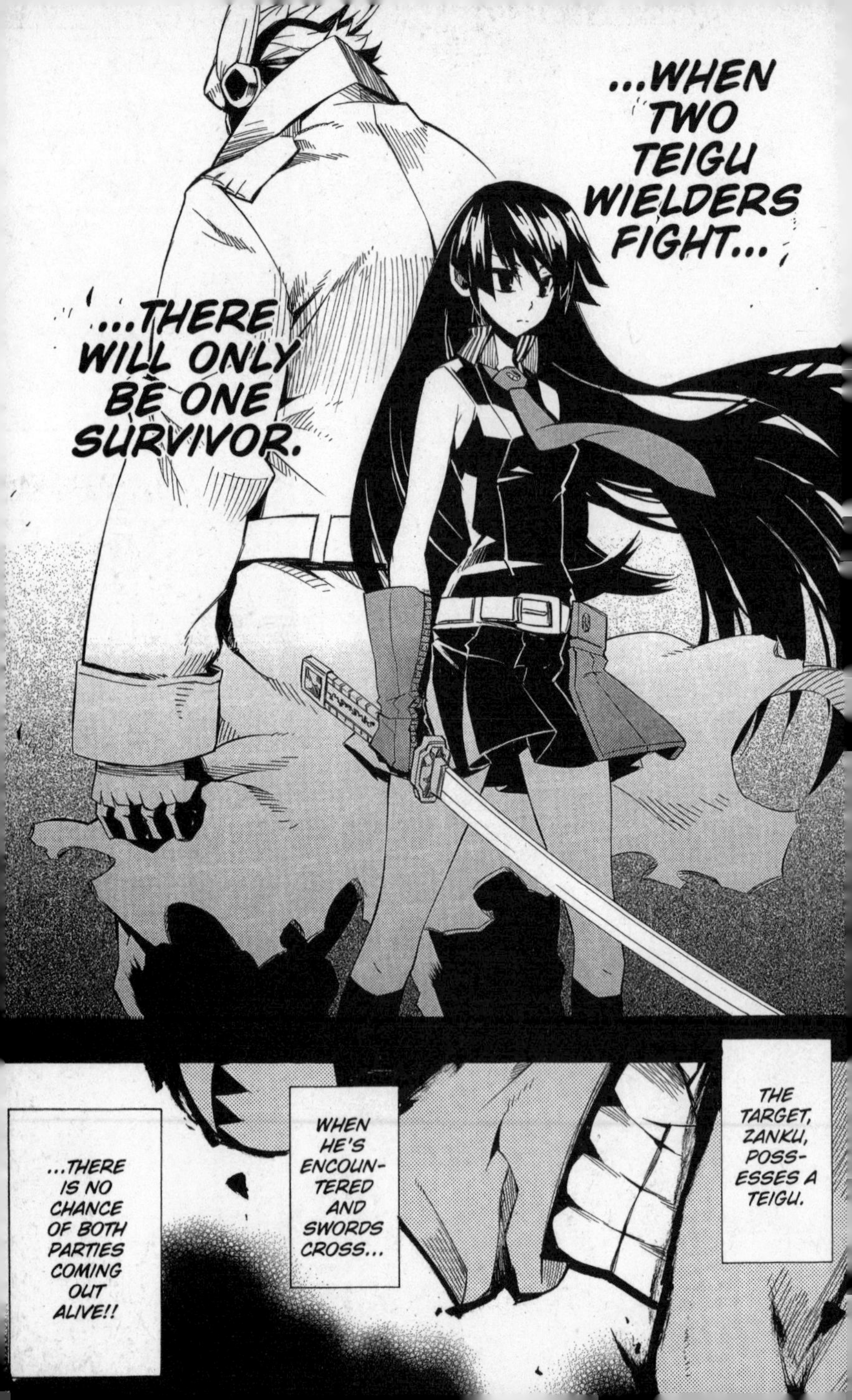
...WHEN TWO TEIGU WIELDERS FIGHT...
...THERE WILL ONLY BE ONE SURVIVOR.
THE TARGET, ZANKU, POSS-ESSES A TEIGU.
WHEN HE'S ENCOUN-TERED AND SWORDS CROSS...
...THERE IS NO CHANCE OF BOTH PARTIES COMING OUT ALIVE!!

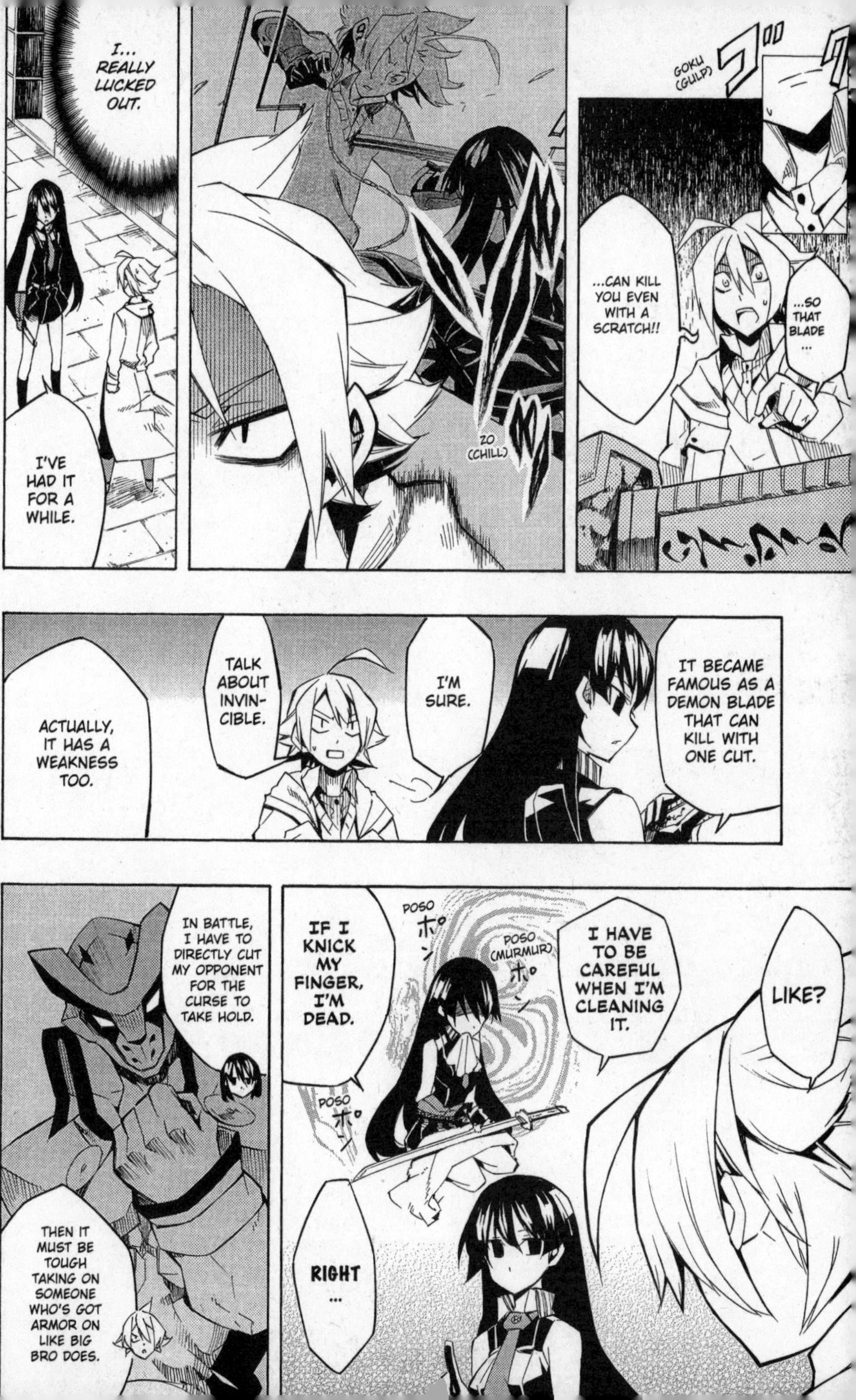
GOKU (GULP)
...SO THAT BLADE ...
...CAN KILL YOU EVEN WITH A SCRATCH!!
ZO (CHILL)
I... REALLY LUCKED OUT.
I'VE HAD IT FOR A WHILE.
IT BECAME FAMOUS AS A DEMON BLADE THAT CAN KILL WITH ONE CUT.
I'M SURE.
TALK ABOUT INVINCIBLE.
ACTUALLY, IT HAS A WEAKNESS TOO.
LIKE?
I HAVE TO BE CAREFUL WHEN I'M CLEANING IT.
POSO (MURMUR)
POSO
IF I KNICK MY FINGER, I'M DEAD.
POSO
RIGHT ...
IN BATTLE, I HAVE TO DIRECTLY CUT MY OPPONENT FOR THE CURSE TO TAKE HOLD.
THEN IT MUST BE TOUGH TAKING ON SOMEONE WHO'S GOT ARMOR ON LIKE BIG BRO DOES.

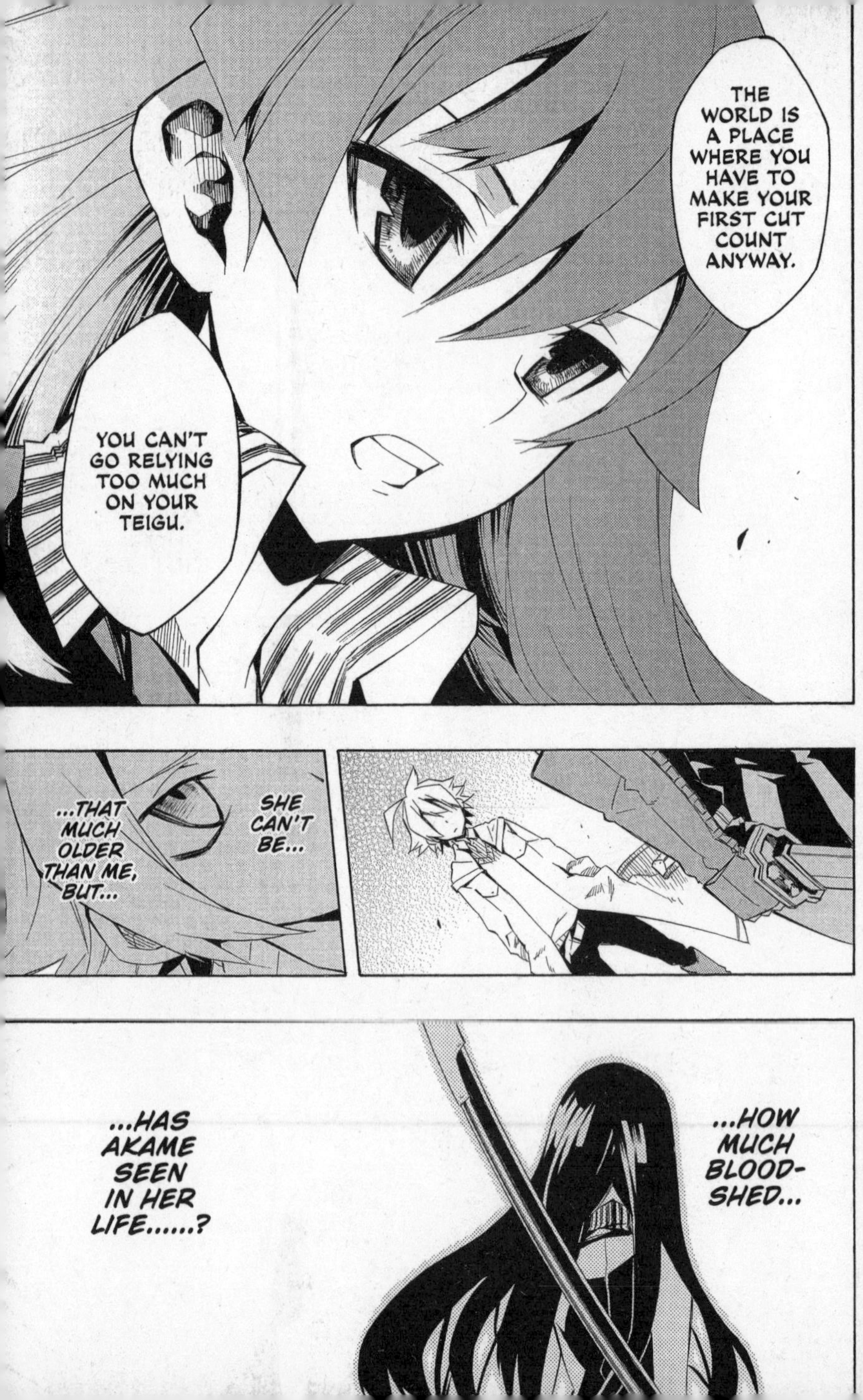
THE WORLD IS A PLACE WHERE YOU HAVE TO MAKE YOUR FIRST CUT COUNT ANYWAY.
YOU CAN'T GO RELYING TOO MUCH ON YOUR TEIGU.
SHE CAN'T BE...
...THAT MUCH OLDER THAN ME, BUT...
...HOW MUCH BLOODSHED...
...HAS AKAME SEEN IN HER LIFE......?

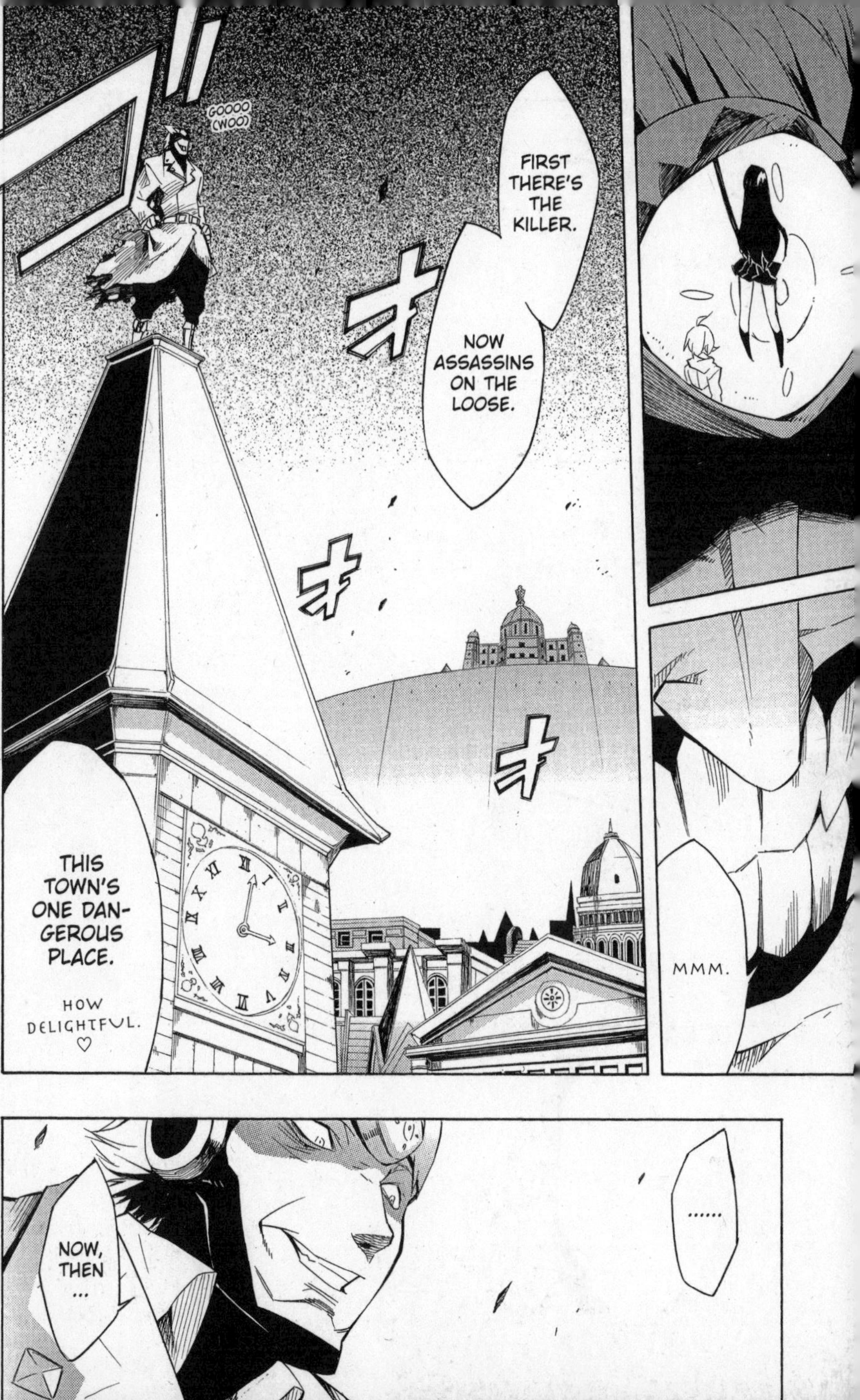
MMM.
GOOOO (WOO)
FIRST THERE'S THE KILLER.
NOW ASSASSINS ON THE LOOSE.
THIS TOWN'S ONE DAN-GEROUS PLACE.
HOW DELIGHTFUL. ♡
......
NOW, THEN ...

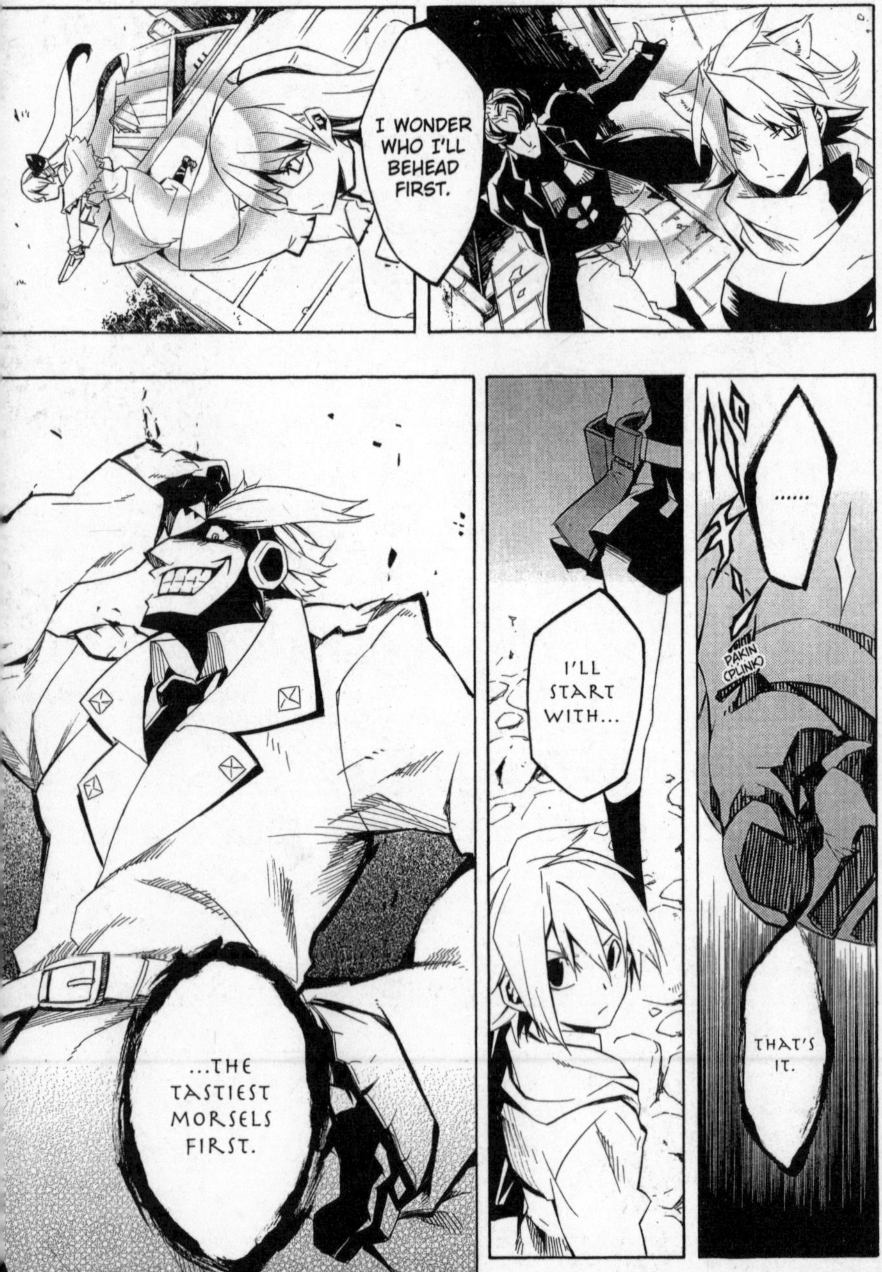
I WONDER WHO I'LL BEHEAD FIRST.
......
PAKIN (PLINK)
THAT'S IT.
I'LL START WITH...
...THE TASTIEST MORSELS FIRST.

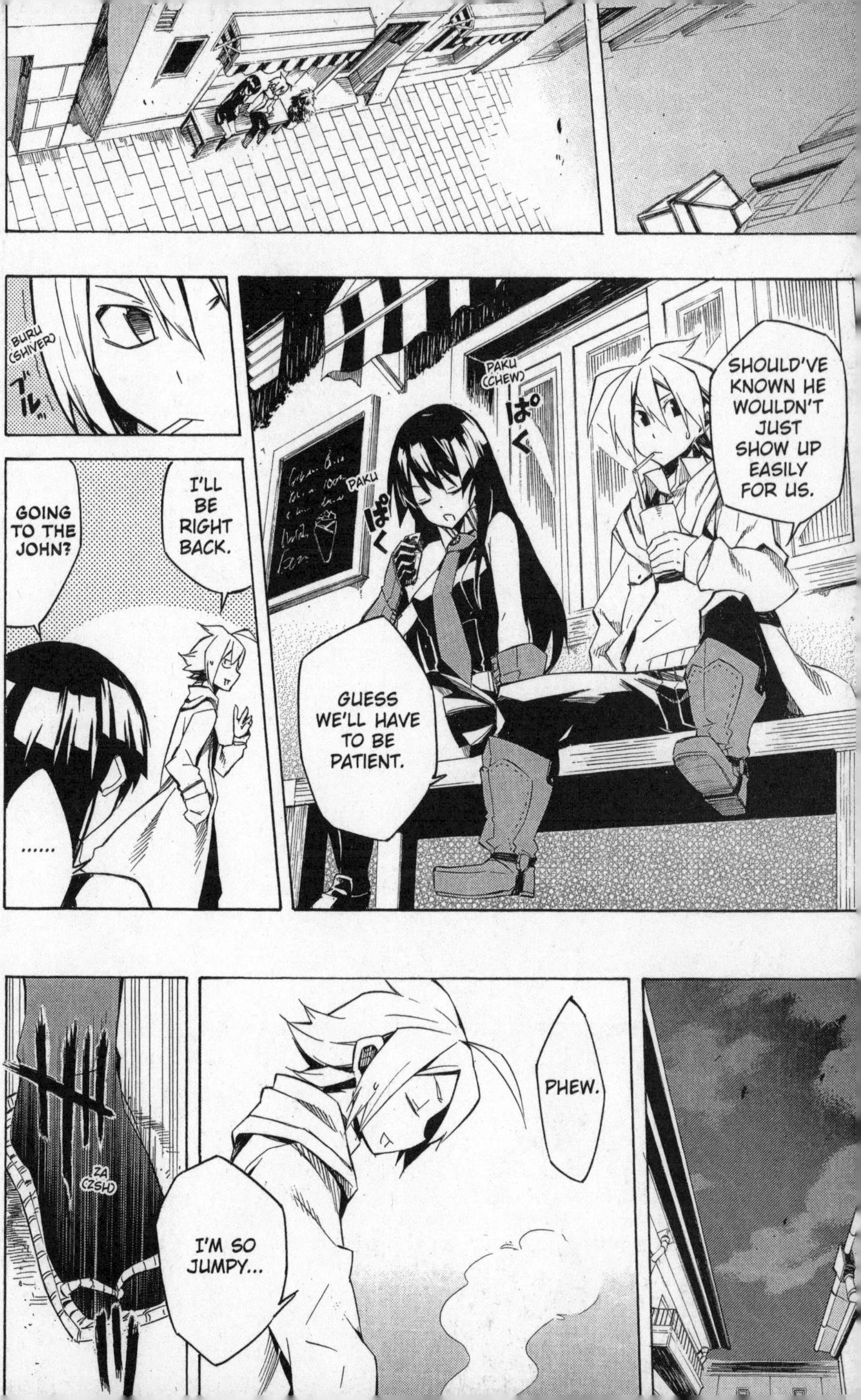
PAKU (CHEW)
ぱく
SHOULD'VE KNOWN HE WOULDN'T JUST SHOW UP EASILY FOR US.
PAKU
ぱく
GUESS WE'LL HAVE TO BE PATIENT.
BURU (SHIVER)
ブル
I'LL BE RIGHT BACK.
GOING TO THE JOHN?
......
PHEW.
I'M SO JUMPY...
ZA (ZSH)

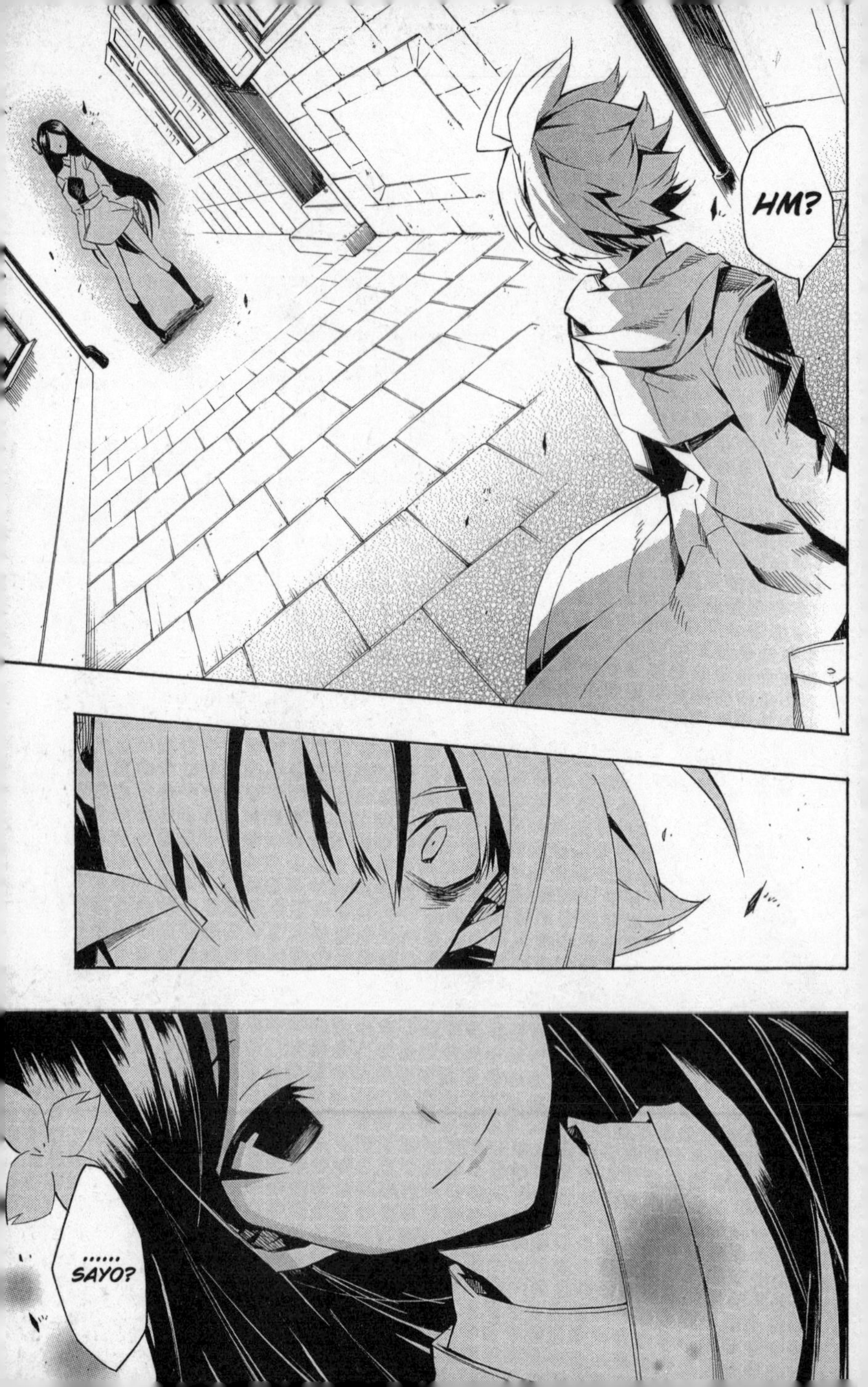
HM?
......
SAYO?

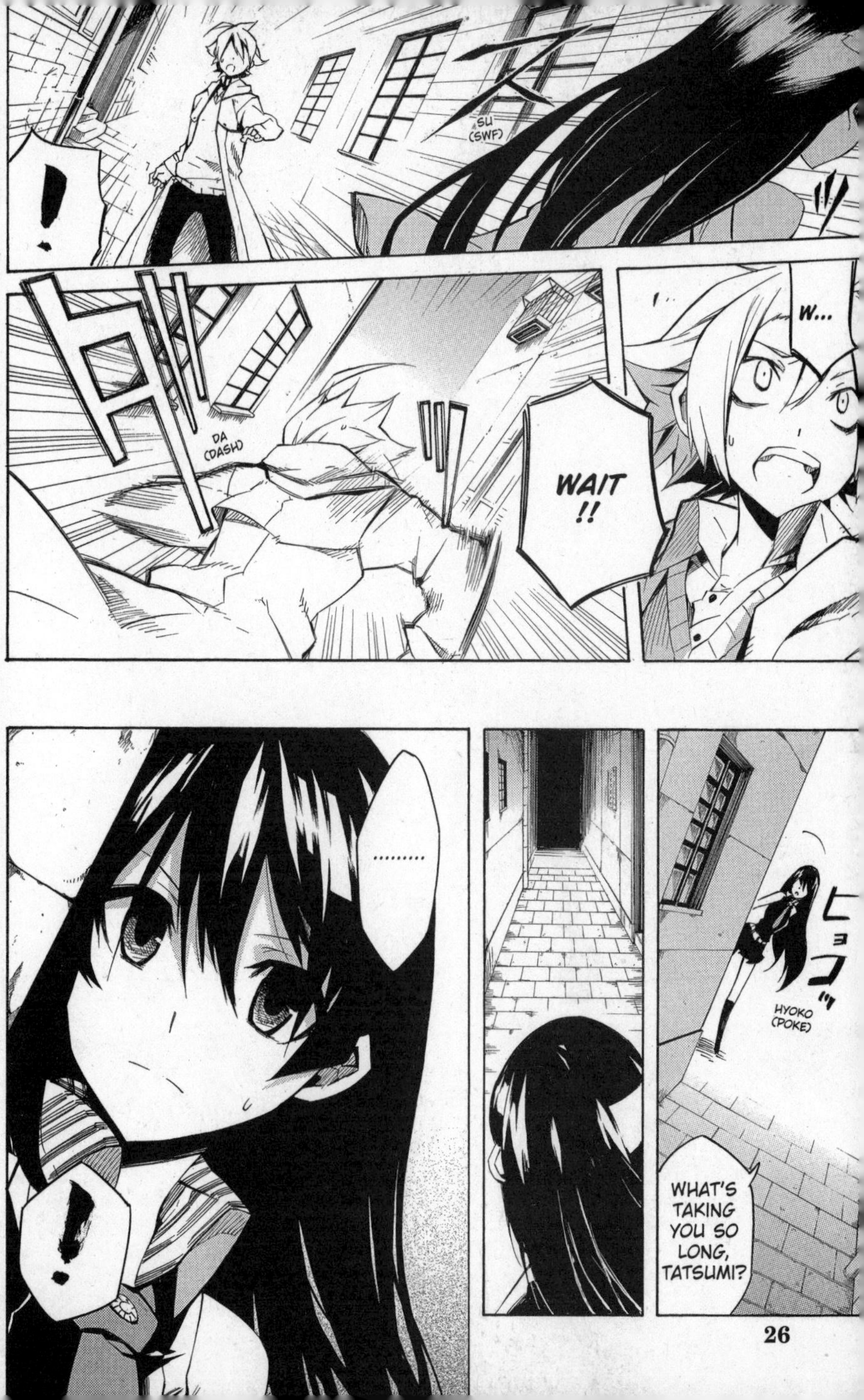
SU
(SWF)
!
DA
(DASH)
W...
WAIT
!!
WHAT'S TAKING YOU SO LONG, TATSUMI?
HYOKO
(POKE)
....
!

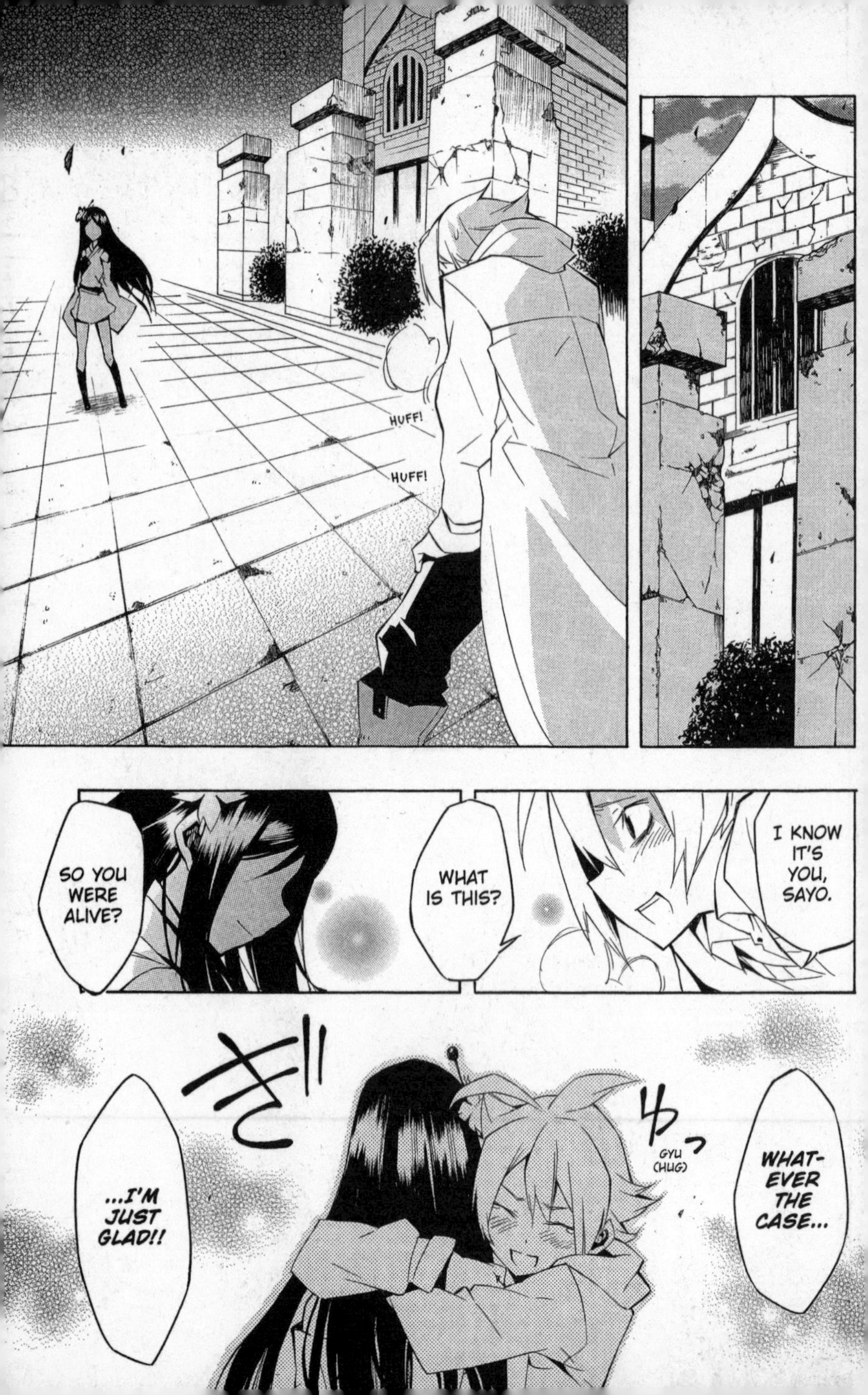
HUFF!
HUFF!
I KNOW IT'S YOU, SAYO.
WHAT IS THIS?
SO YOU WERE ALIVE?
WHATEVER THE CASE...
GYU (HUG)
...I'M JUST GLAD!!

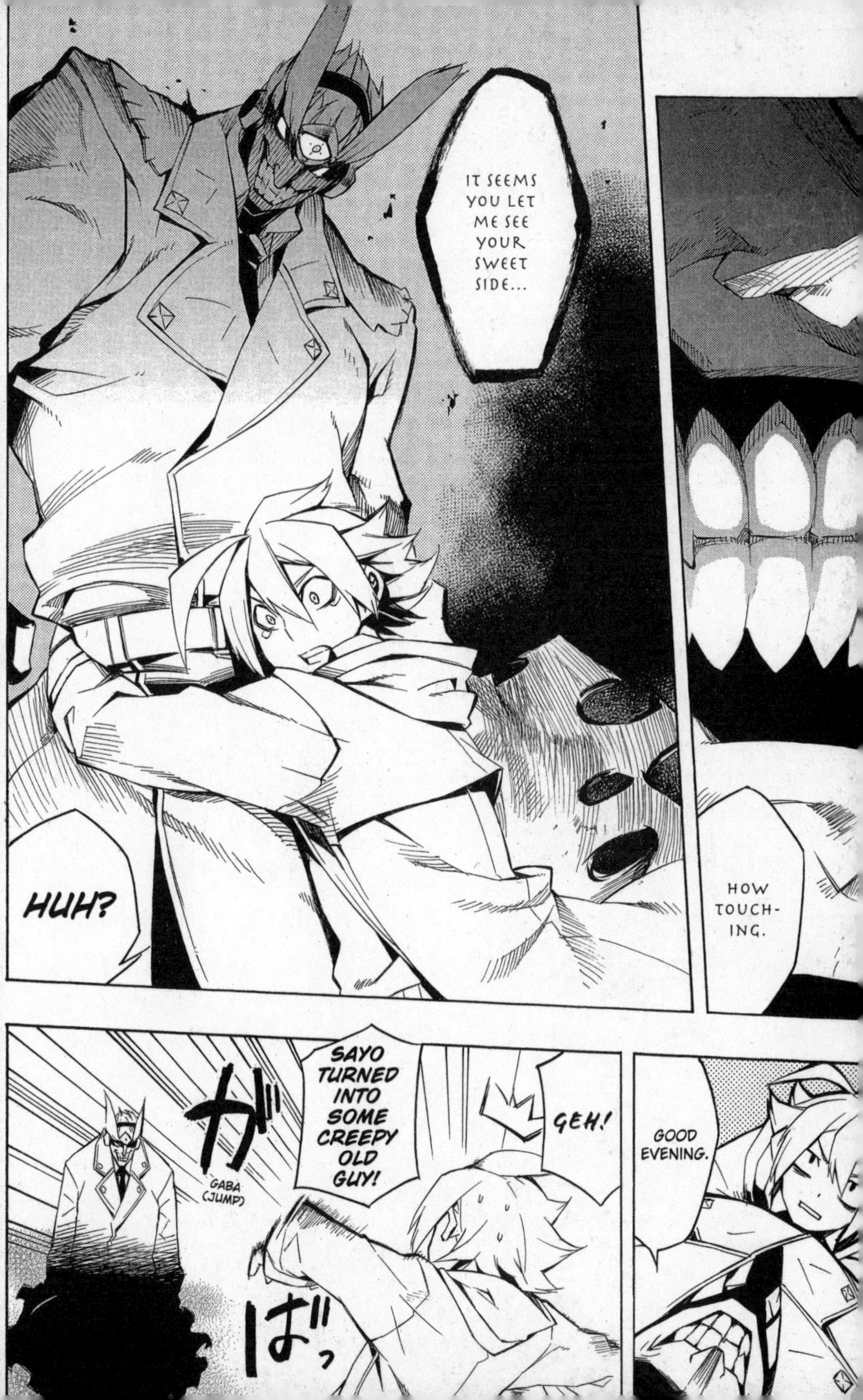
HOW TOUCHING.
IT SEEMS YOU LET ME SEE YOUR SWEET SIDE...
HUH?
GOOD EVENING.
GEH!
SAYO TURNED INTO SOME CREEPY OLD GUY!
ばっ
ガ
GABA (JUMP)

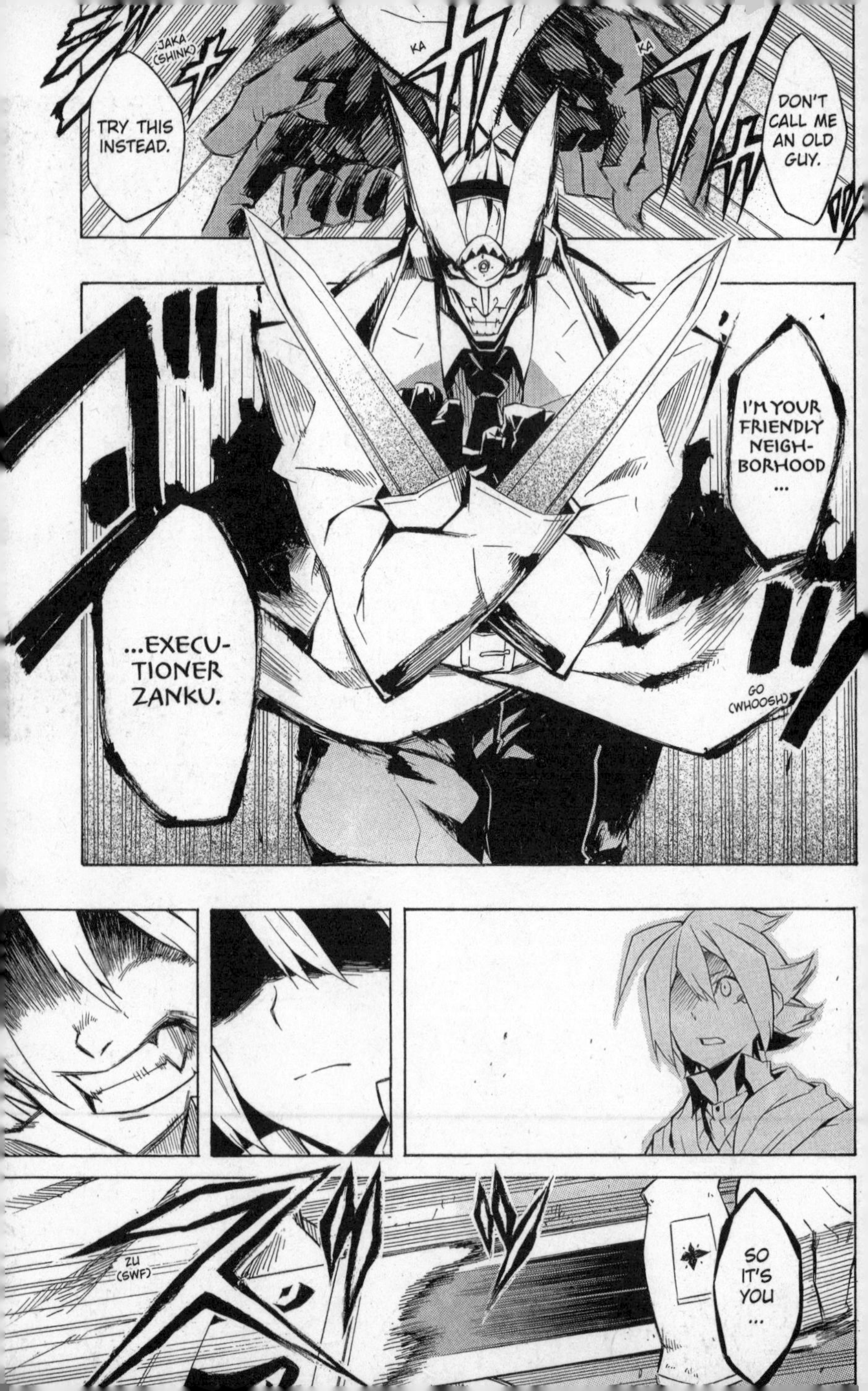
KA
KA
DON'T CALL ME AN OLD GUY.
JAKA (SHINK)
TRY THIS INSTEAD.
I'M YOUR FRIENDLY NEIGH-BORHOOD ...
GO (WHOOSH)
...EXECU-TIONER ZANKU.
SO IT'S YOU ...
ZU (SWF)

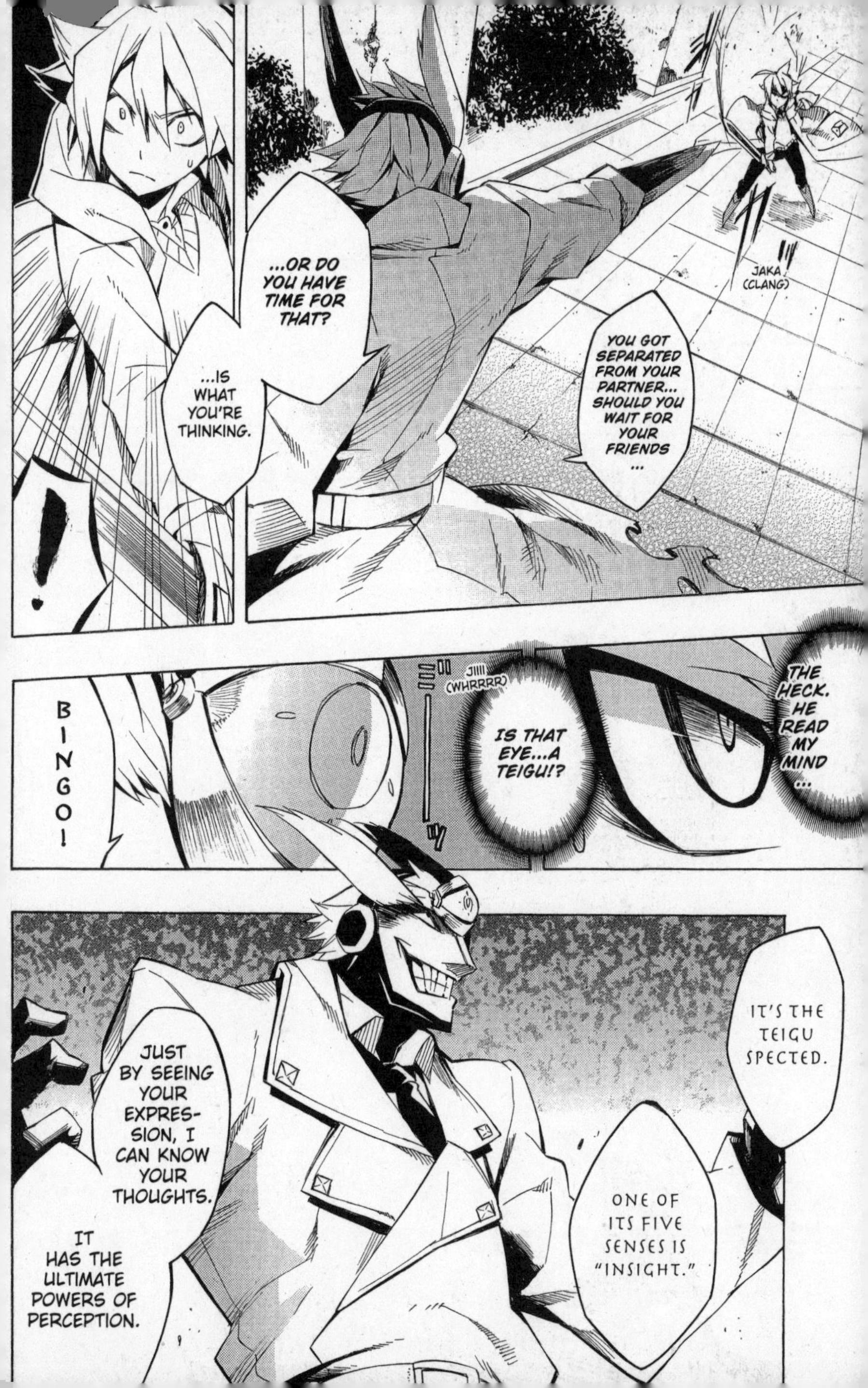
JAKA (CLANG)
YOU GOT SEPARATED FROM YOUR PARTNER... SHOULD YOU WAIT FOR YOUR FRIENDS...
...OR DO YOU HAVE TIME FOR THAT?
...IS WHAT YOU'RE THINKING.
THE HECK. HE READ MY MIND...
JIIII (WHRRRR)
IS THAT EYE...A TEIGU!?
BINGO!
IT'S THE TEIGU SPECTED.
ONE OF ITS FIVE SENSES IS "INSIGHT."
JUST BY SEEING YOUR EXPRES- SION, I CAN KNOW YOUR THOUGHTS.
IT HAS THE ULTIMATE POWERS OF PERCEPTION.

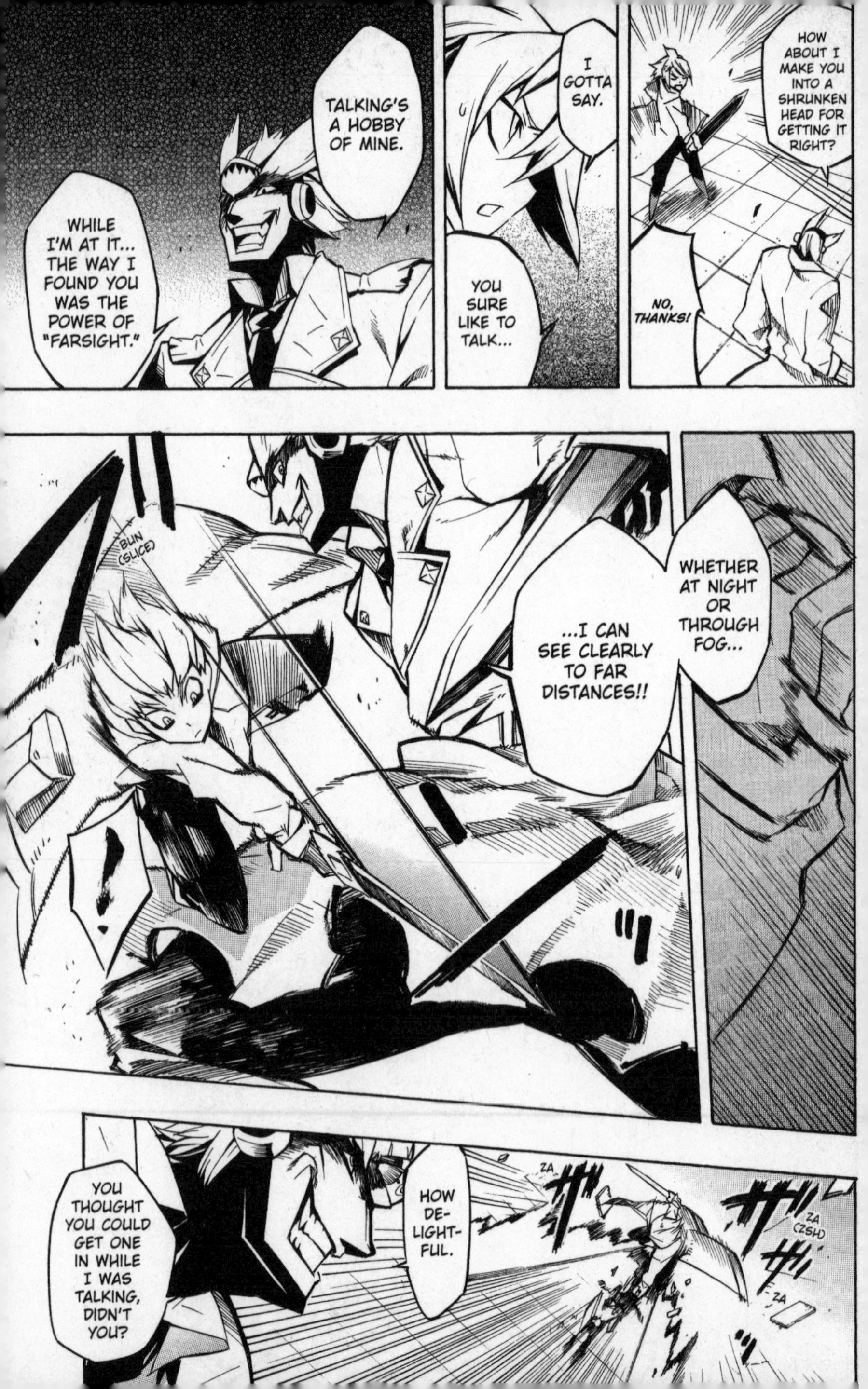

HOW ABOUT I MAKE YOU INTO A SHRUNKEN HEAD FOR GETTING IT RIGHT?
NO, THANKS!
I GOTTA SAY.
YOU SURE LIKE TO TALK...
TALKING'S A HOBBY OF MINE.
WHILE I'M AT IT... THE WAY I FOUND YOU WAS THE POWER OF "FARSIGHT."
WHETHER AT NIGHT OR THROUGH FOG...
...I CAN SEE CLEARLY TO FAR DISTANCES!!
BUN (SLICE)
!
ZA
ZA (ZSH)
ZA
HOW DE-LIGHT-FUL.
YOU THOUGHT YOU COULD GET ONE IN WHILE I WAS TALKING, DIDN'T YOU?

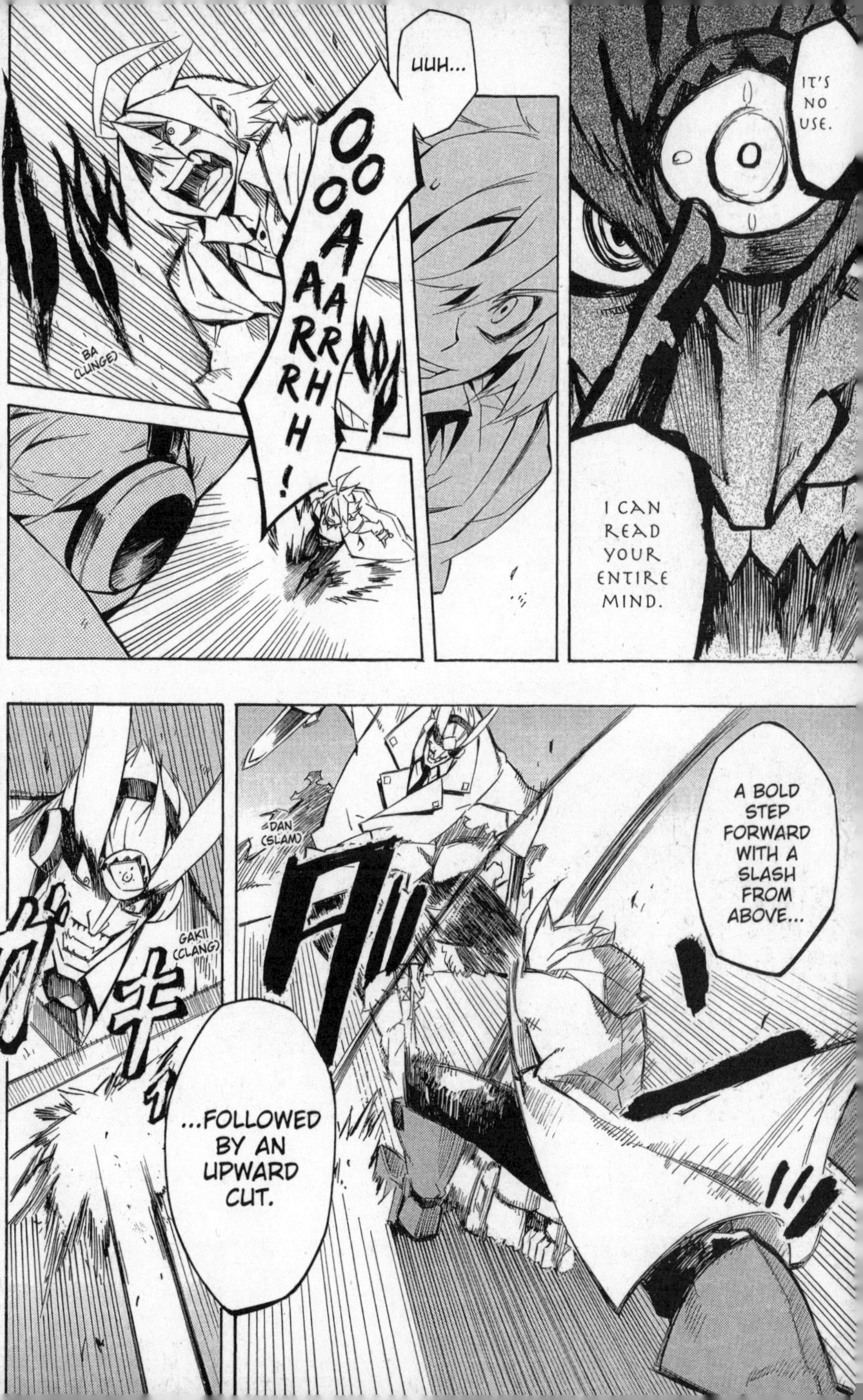
IT'S NO USE.
I CAN READ YOUR ENTIRE MIND.
UUH...
OOOAAARRRHH!
BA (LUNGE)
A BOLD STEP FORWARD WITH A SLASH FROM ABOVE...
DAN (SLAM)
...FOLLOWED BY AN UPWARD CUT.
GAKII (CLANG)

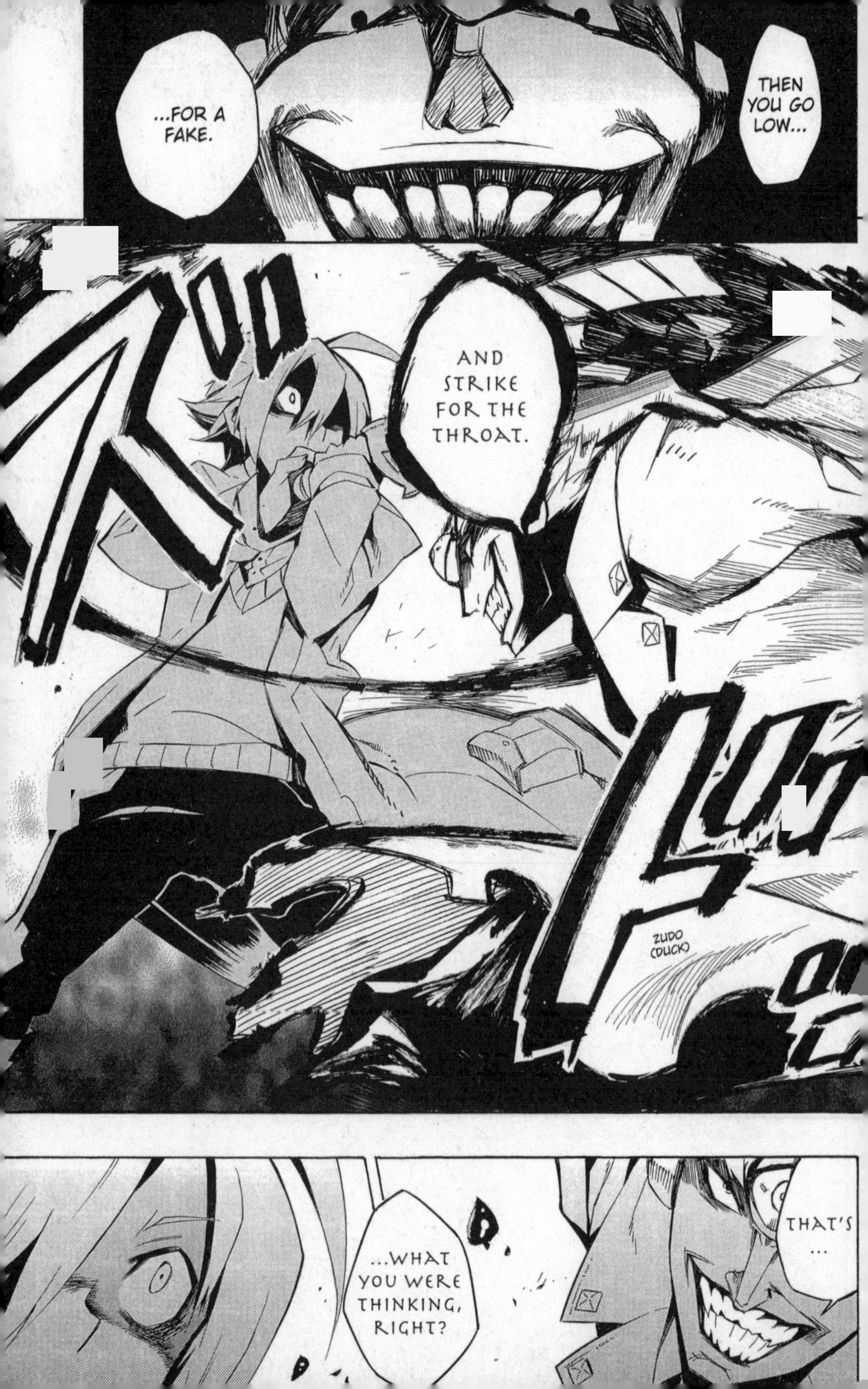
THEN YOU GO LOW...
...FOR A FAKE.
AND STRIKE FOR THE THROAT.
ZUDO (DUCK)
THAT'S ...
...WHAT YOU WERE THINKING, RIGHT?

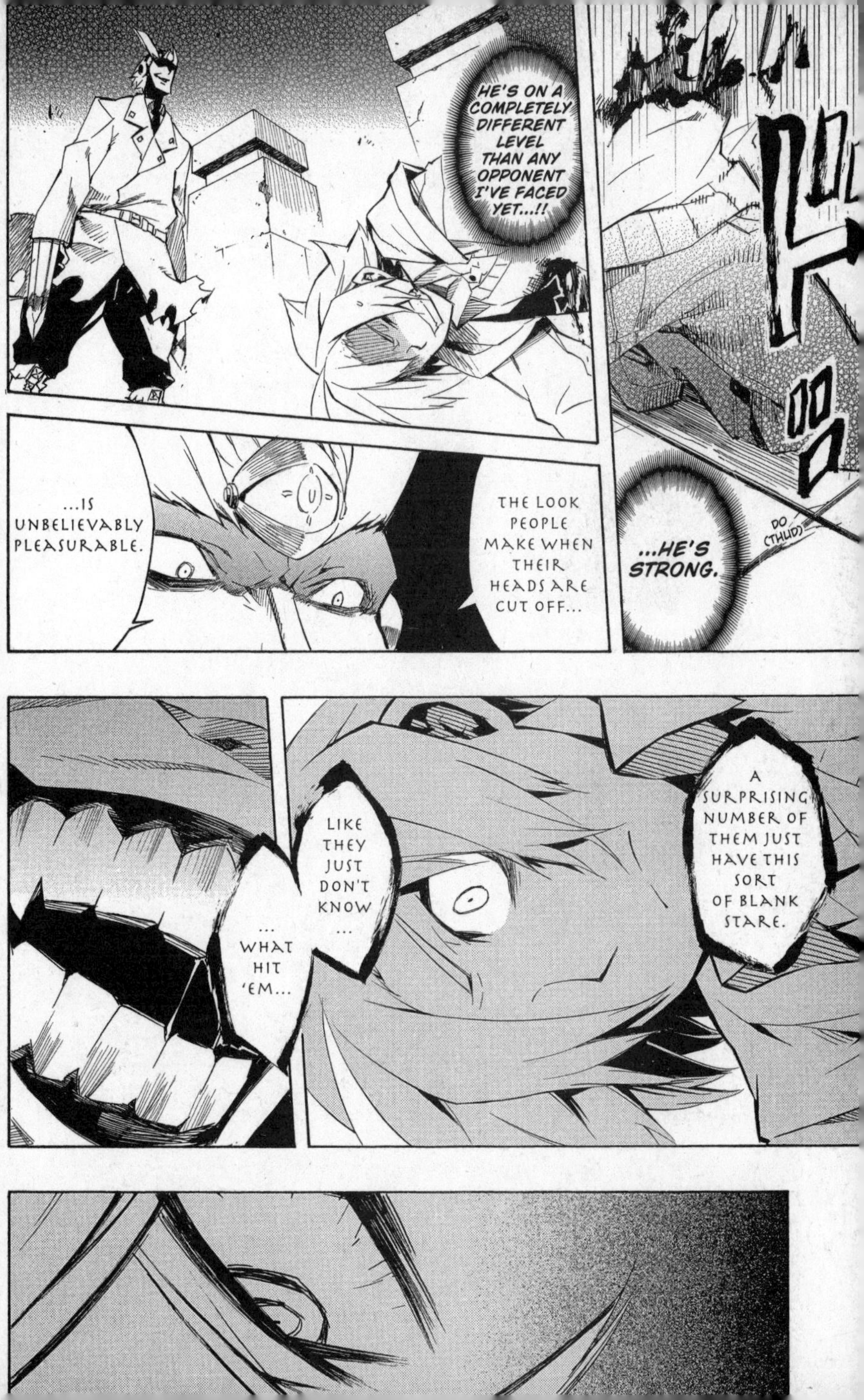
DO (THUD)
...HE'S STRONG.
HE'S ON A COMPLETELY DIFFERENT LEVEL THAN ANY OPPONENT I'VE FACED YET...!!
THE LOOK PEOPLE MAKE WHEN THEIR HEADS ARE CUT OFF...
...IS UNBELIEVABLY PLEASURABLE.
A SURPRISING NUMBER OF THEM JUST HAVE THIS SORT OF BLANK STARE.
LIKE THEY JUST DON'T KNOW...
...WHAT HIT 'EM...

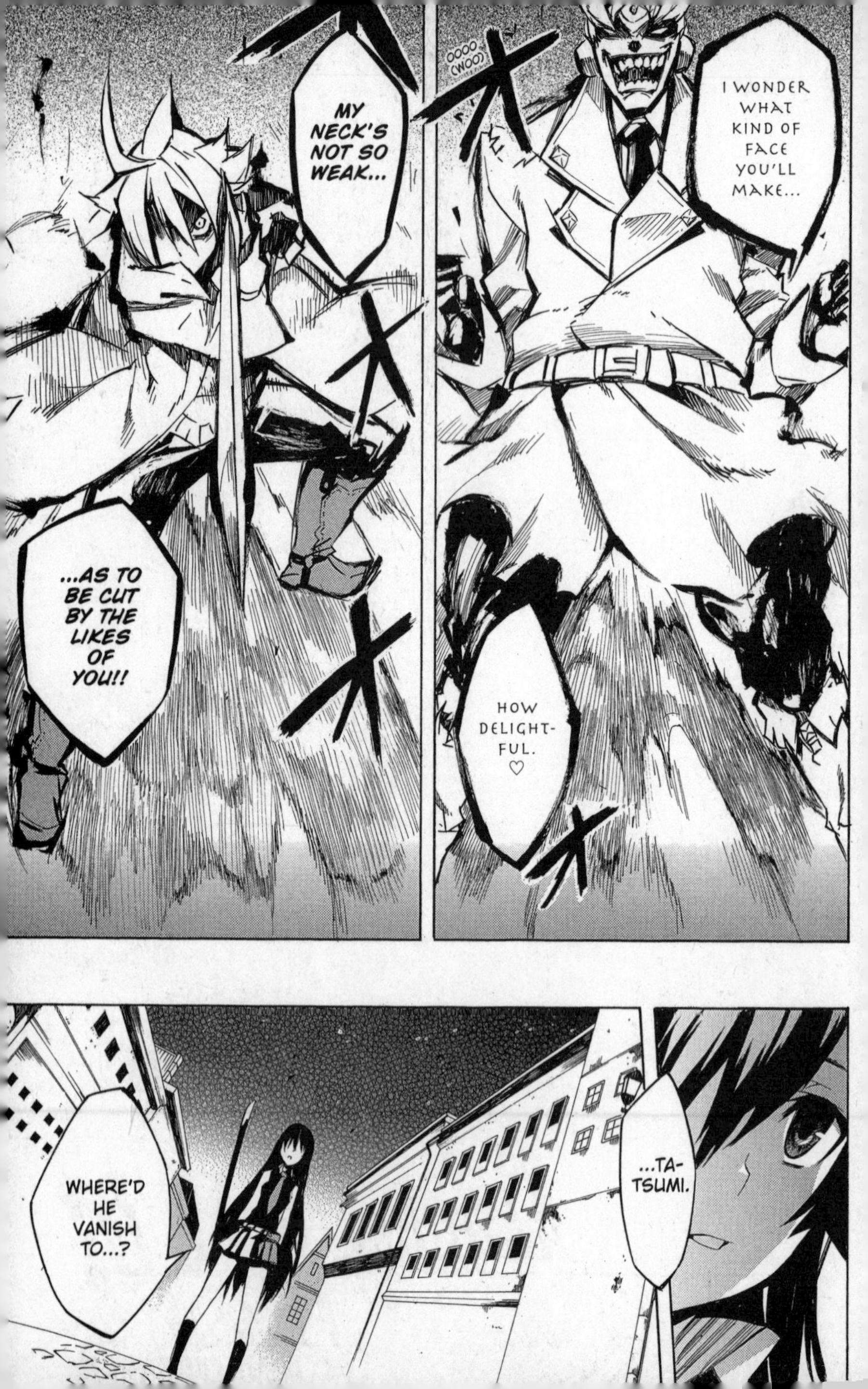
OOOO (WOO)
I WONDER WHAT KIND OF FACE YOU'LL MAKE...
HOW DELIGHT-FUL. ♡
MY NECK'S NOT SO WEAK...
...AS TO BE CUT BY THE LIKES OF YOU!!
...TA-TSUMI.
WHERE'D HE VANISH TO...?

Akame ga KILL!

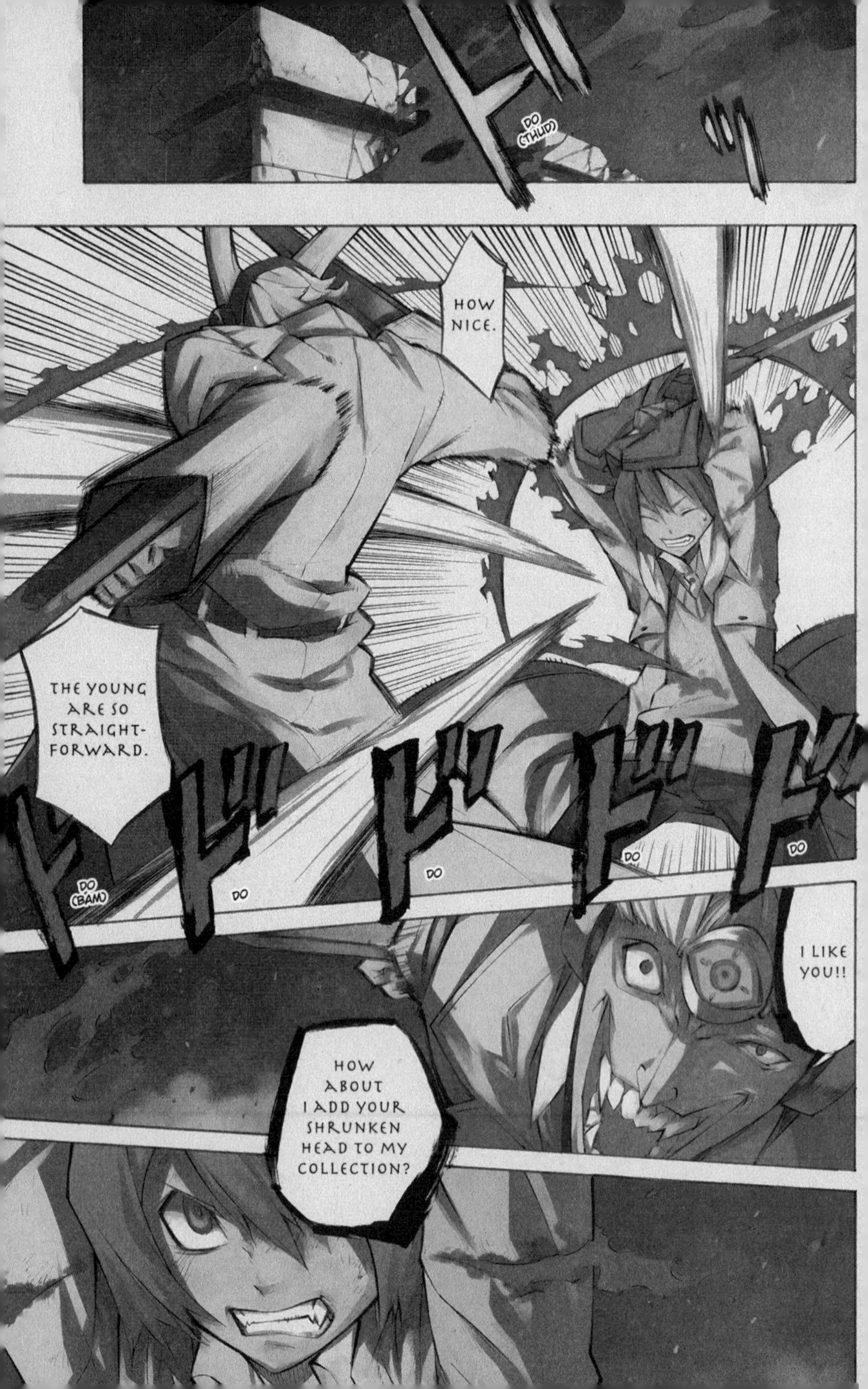
DO (THUD)
HOW NICE.
THE YOUNG ARE SO STRAIGHT-FORWARD.
DO
DO
DO
DO
DO (BAM)
I LIKE YOU!!
HOW ABOUT I ADD YOUR SHRUNKEN HEAD TO MY COLLECTION?

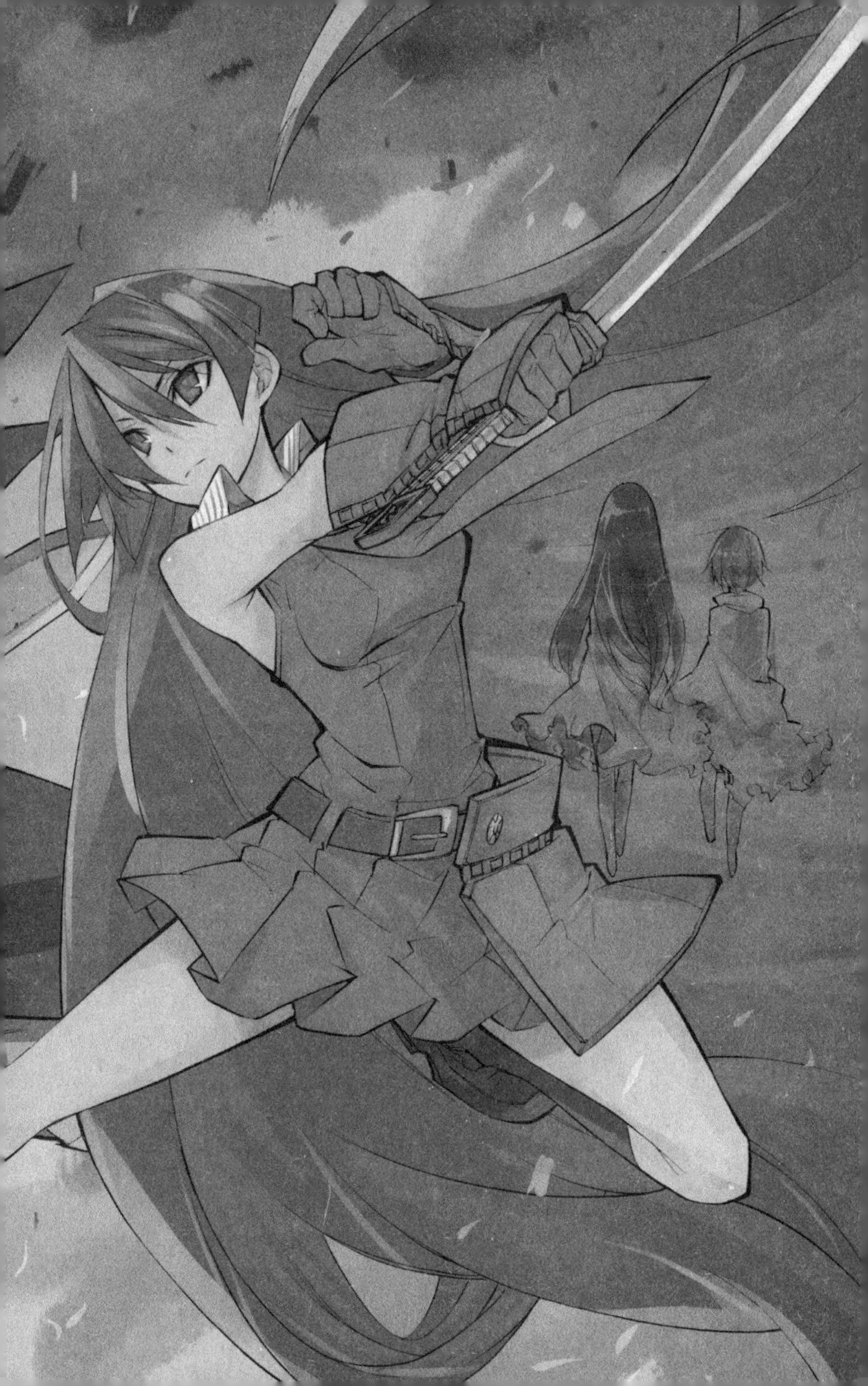

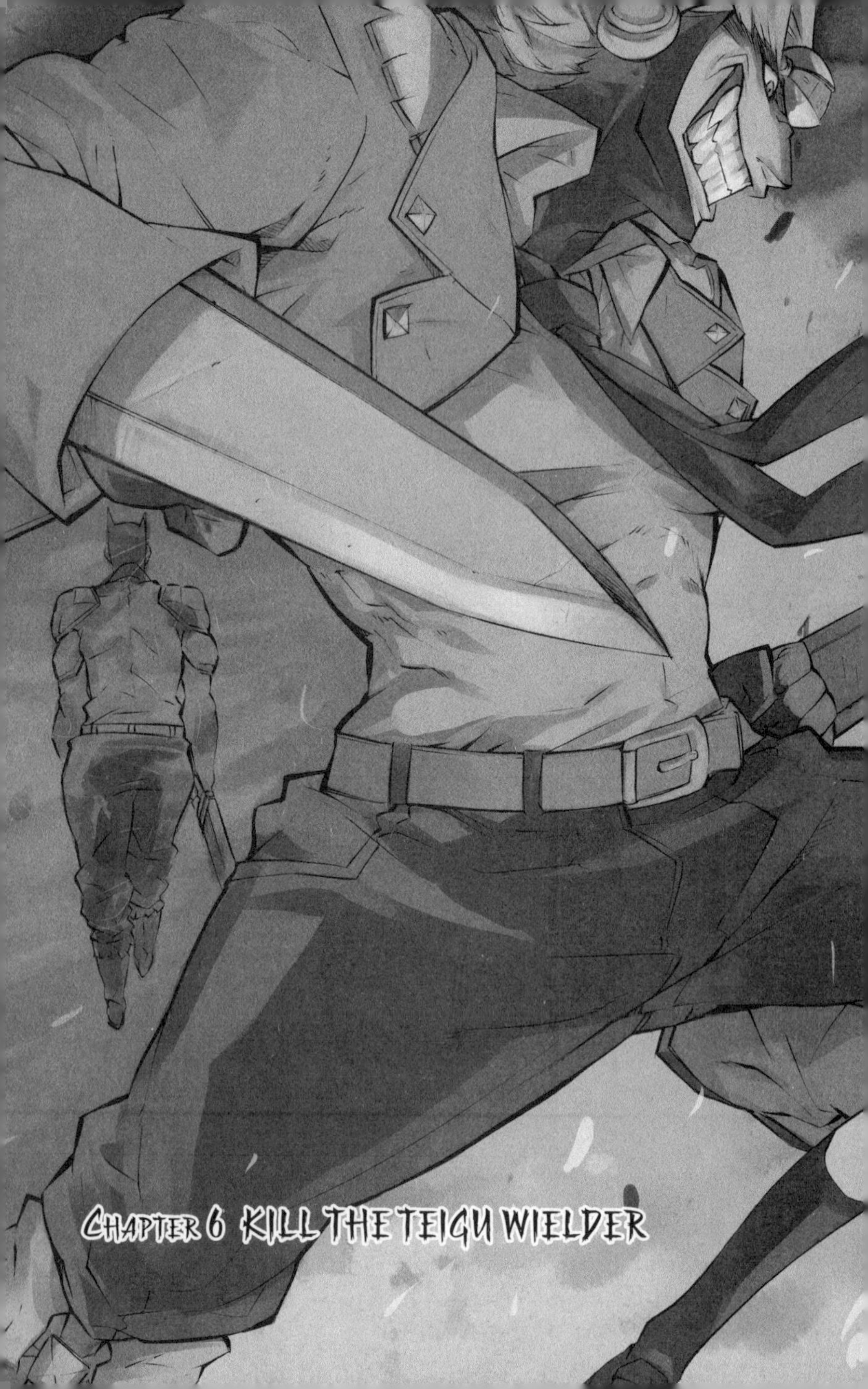
Chapter 6 KILL THE TEIGU WIELDER

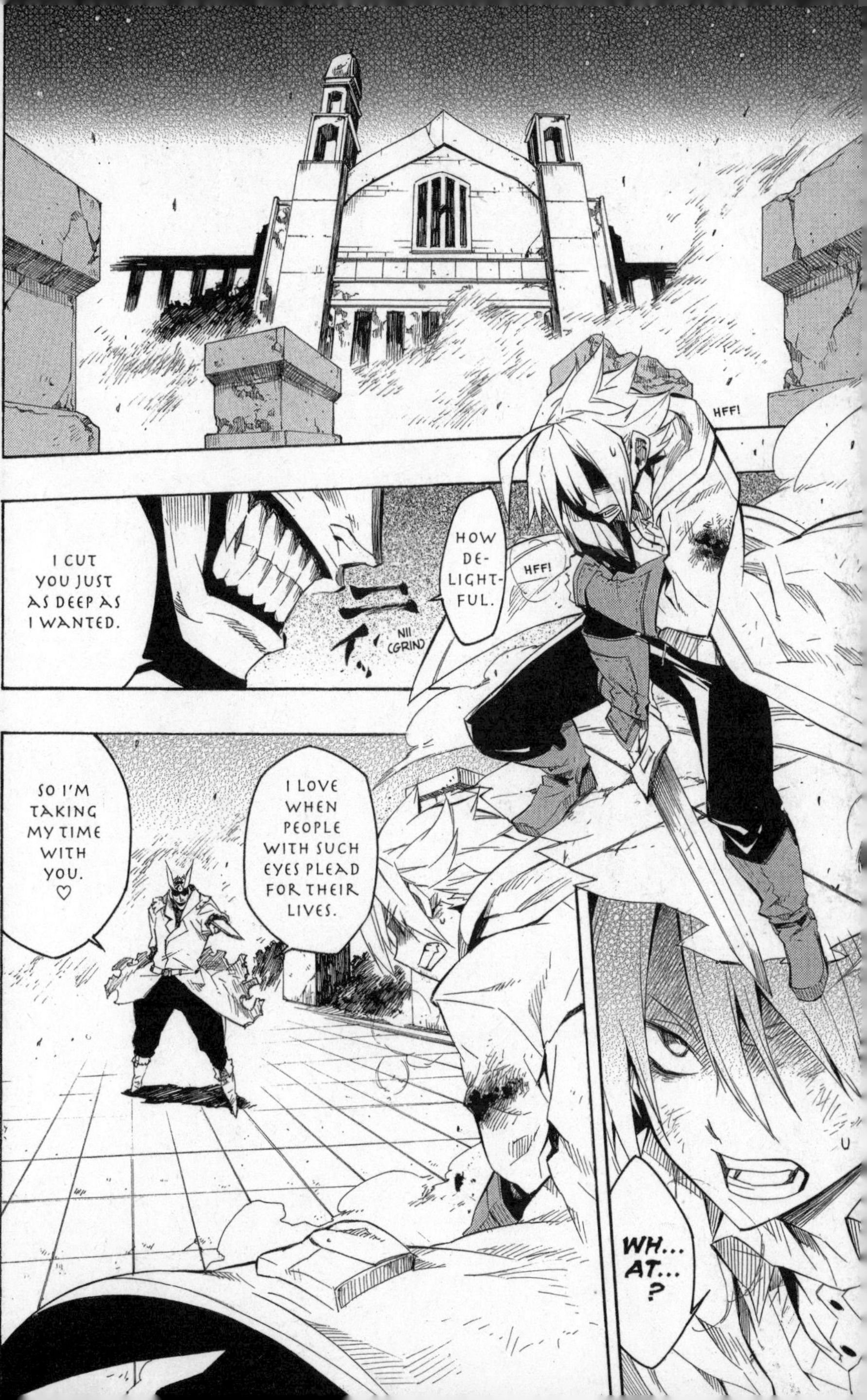

HFF!
HOW DE-LIGHT-FUL.
HFF!
I CUT YOU JUST AS DEEP AS I WANTED.
NII (GRIN)
WH... AT... ?
I LOVE WHEN PEOPLE WITH SUCH EYES PLEAD FOR THEIR LIVES.
SO I'M TAKING MY TIME WITH YOU. ♡

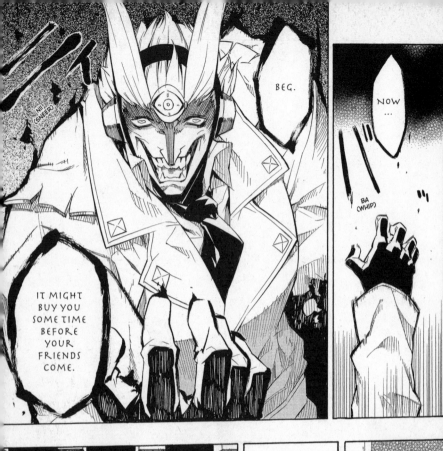

BEG.

NII (SNEER)

IT MIGHT BUY YOU SOME TIME BEFORE YOUR FRIENDS COME.

NOW...

BA (WHIP)

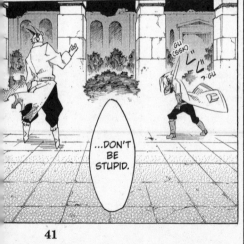

GU (SSK)

?-GU

...DON'T BE STUPID.

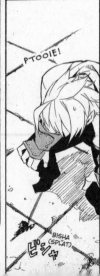

P-TOOIE!

BISHA (SPLAT)

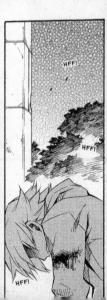

HFF!

HFF!

HFF!

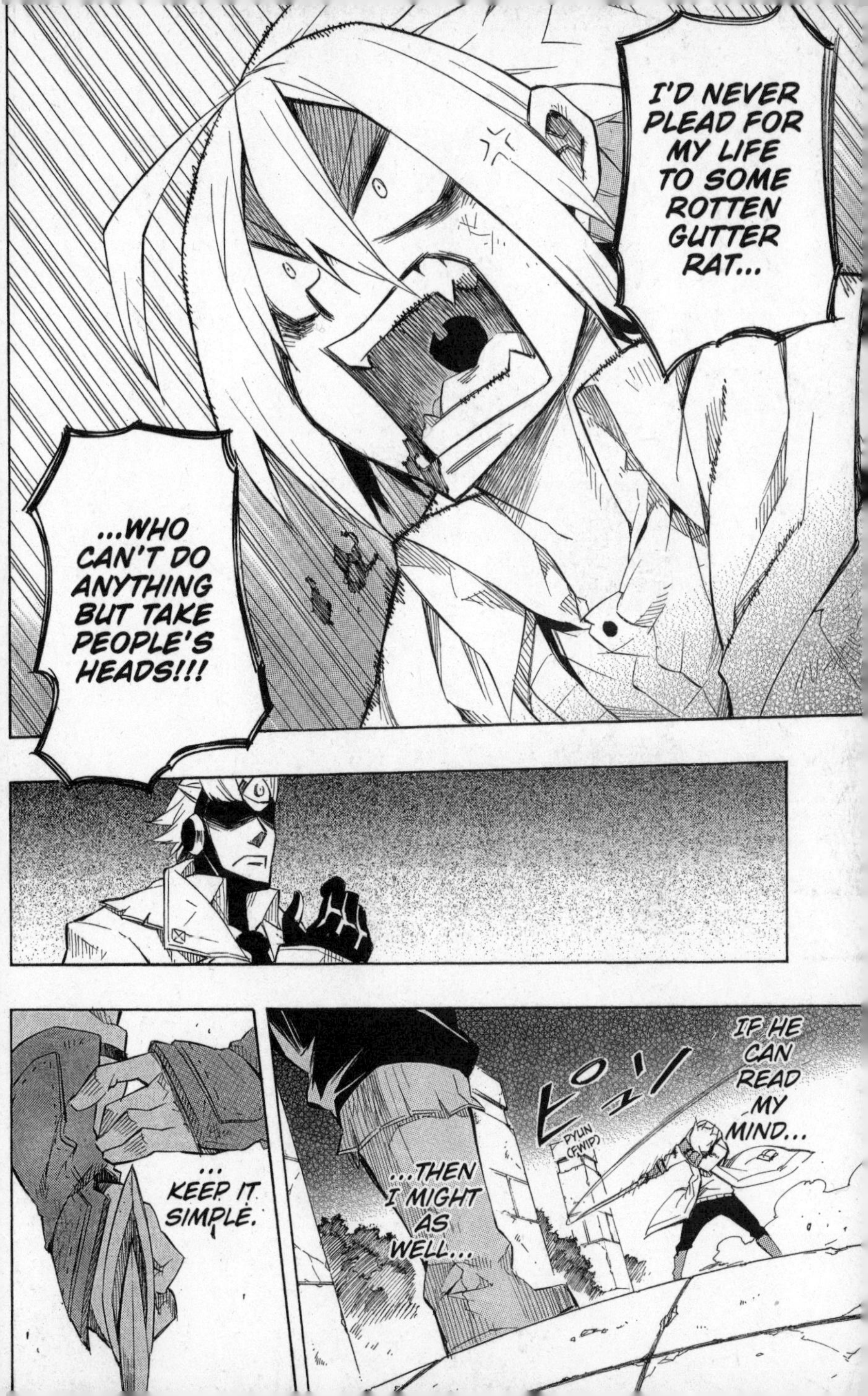
I'D NEVER PLEAD FOR MY LIFE TO SOME ROTTEN GUTTER RAT...
...WHO CAN'T DO ANYTHING BUT TAKE PEOPLE'S HEADS!!!
IF HE CAN READ MY MIND...
ピュッ
PYUN (FWIP)
...THEN I MIGHT AS WELL...
...KEEP IT SIMPLE.

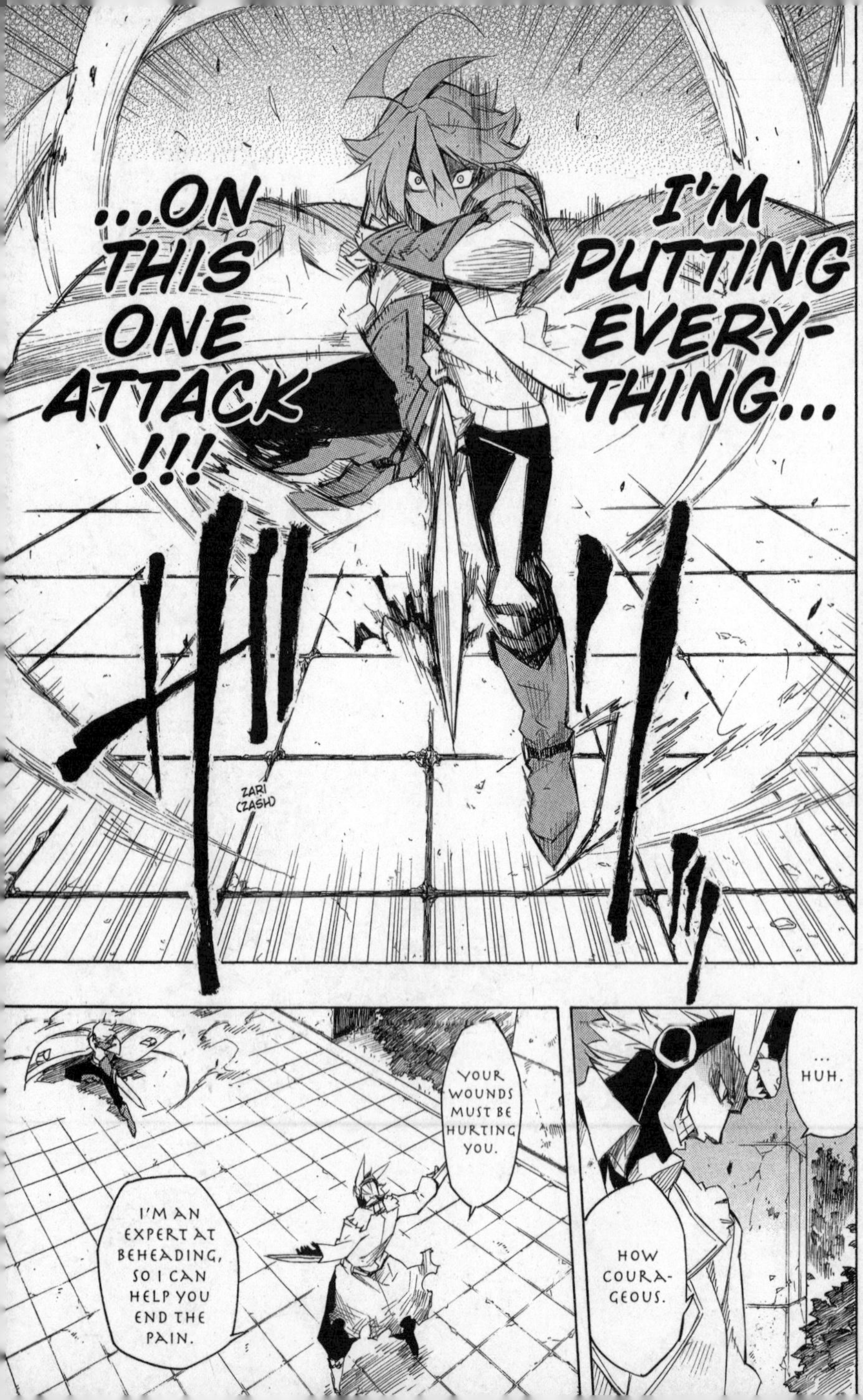
I'M PUTTING EVERY-THING...
...ON THIS ONE ATTACK!!!
ZARI (ZASH)
...HUH.
HOW COURA-GEOUS.
YOUR WOUNDS MUST BE HURTING YOU.
I'M AN EXPERT AT BEHEADING, SO I CAN HELP YOU END THE PAIN.

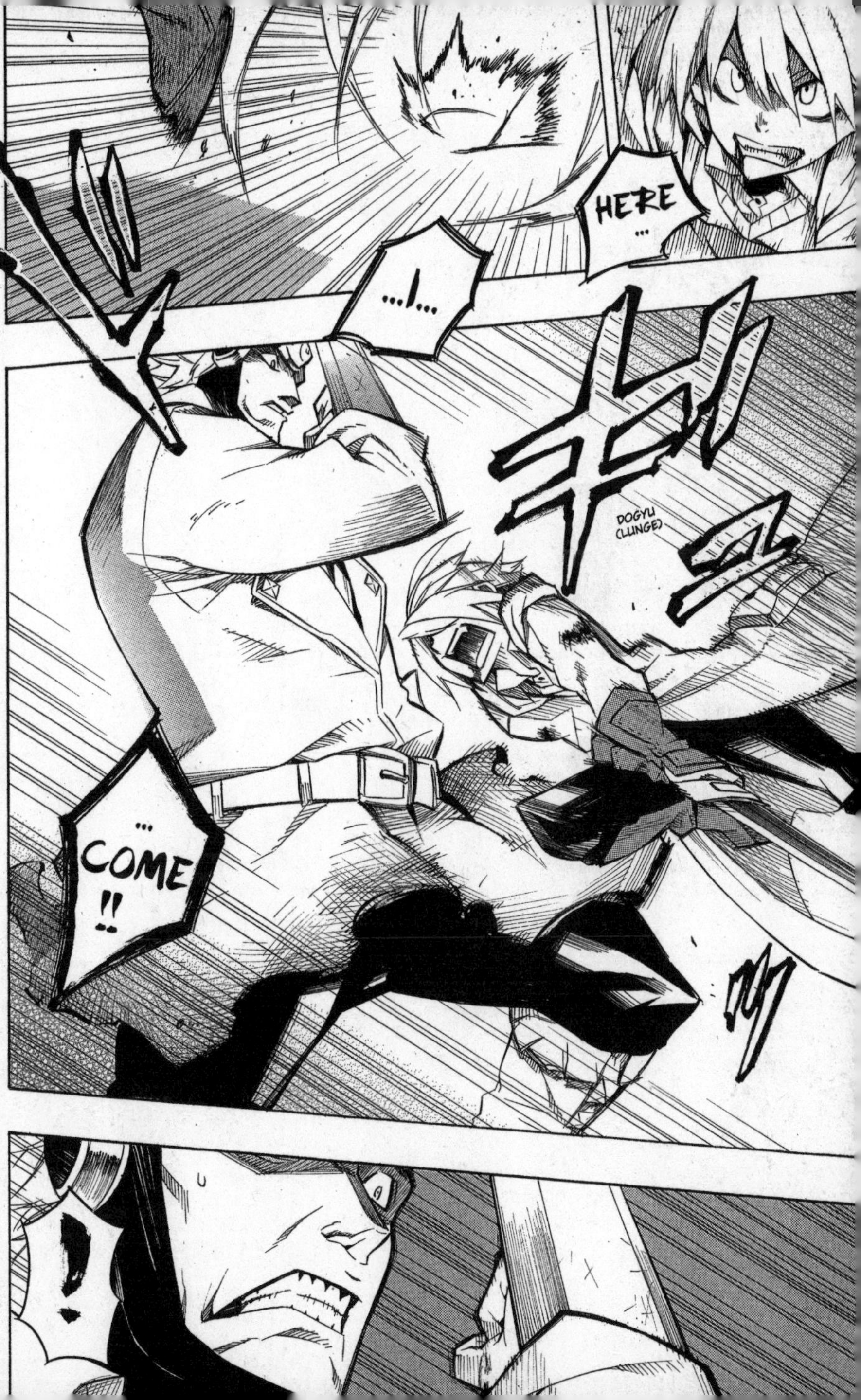
HERE...
...I...
DOGYU (LUNGE)
...COME!!

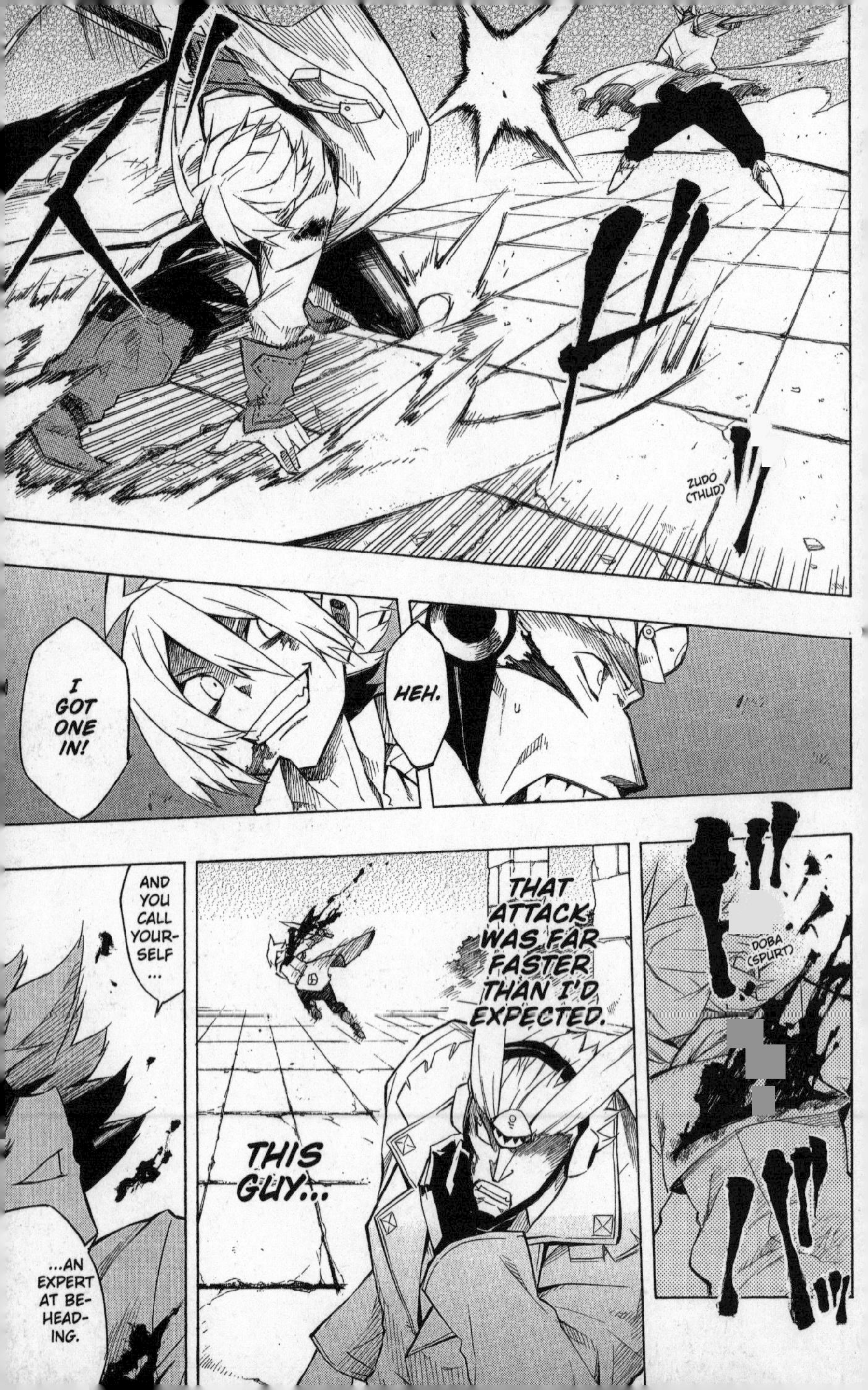
ZUDO (THUD)
HEH.
I GOT ONE IN!
DOBA (SPURT)
THAT ATTACK WAS FAR FASTER THAN I'D EXPECTED.
THIS GUY...
AND YOU CALL YOURSELF...
...AN EXPERT AT BEHEADING.

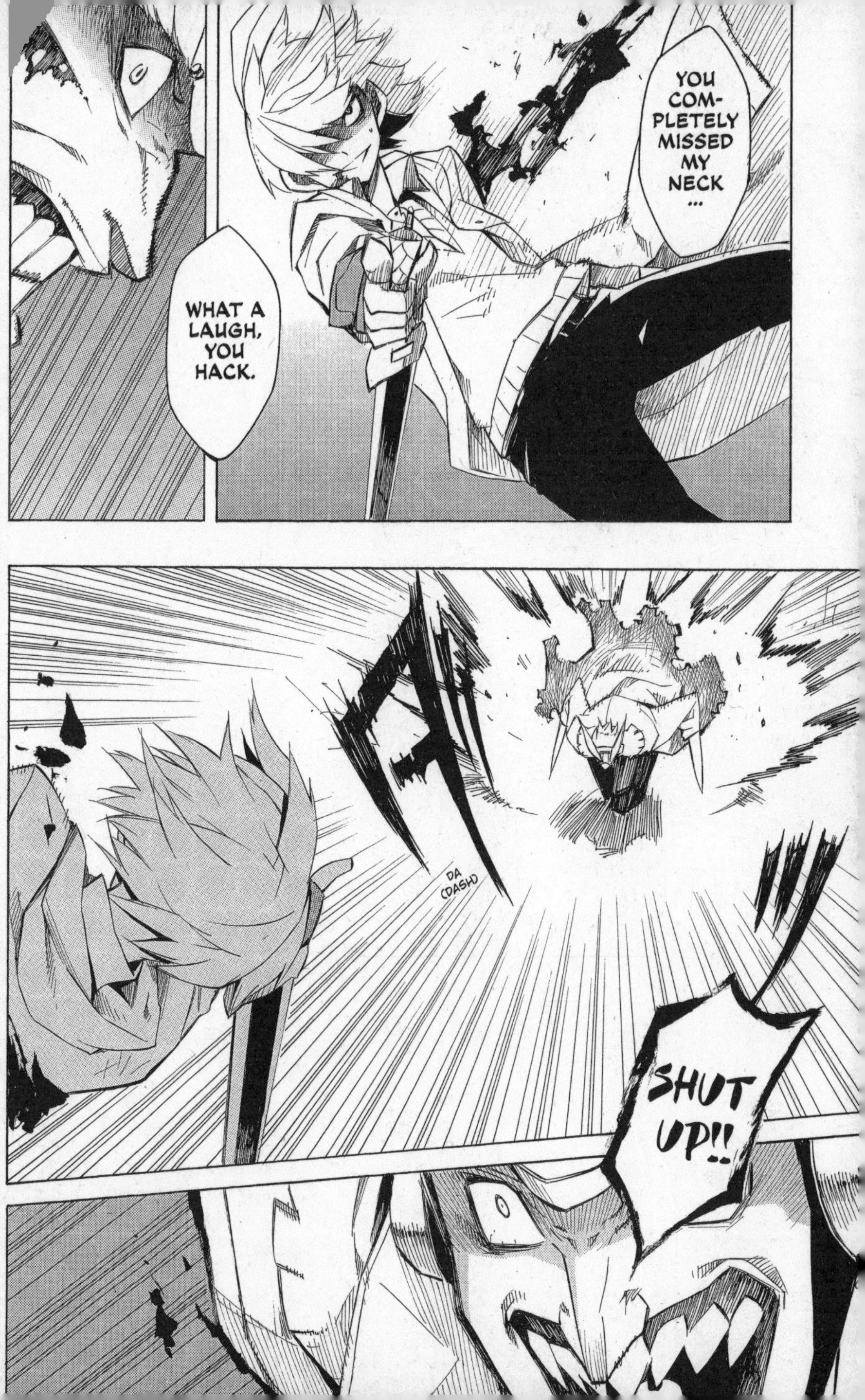
YOU COMPLETELY MISSED MY NECK ...
WHAT A LAUGH, YOU HACK.
DA (DASH)
SHUT UP!!

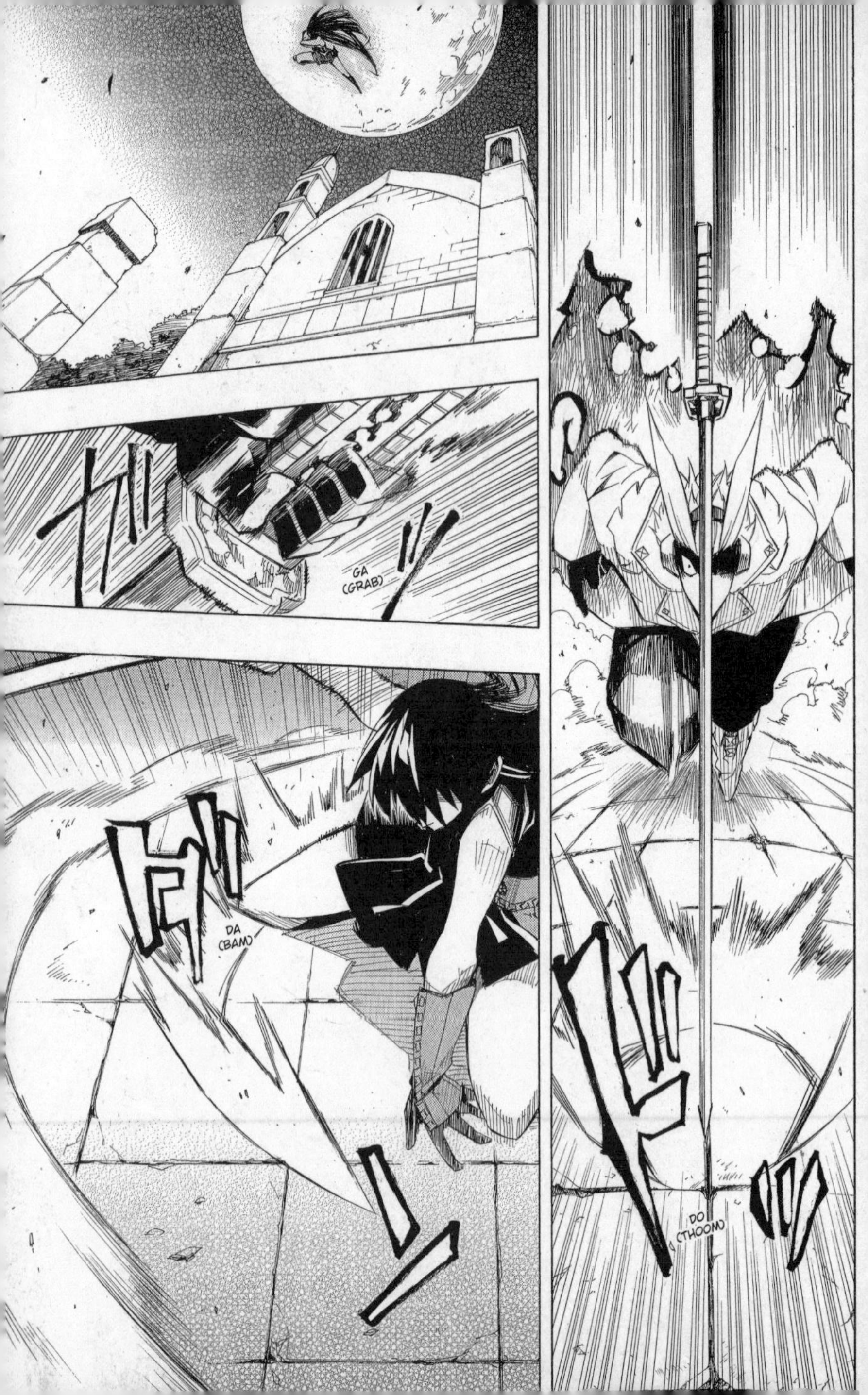
DO
(THOOM)
GA
(GRAB)
DA
(BAM)

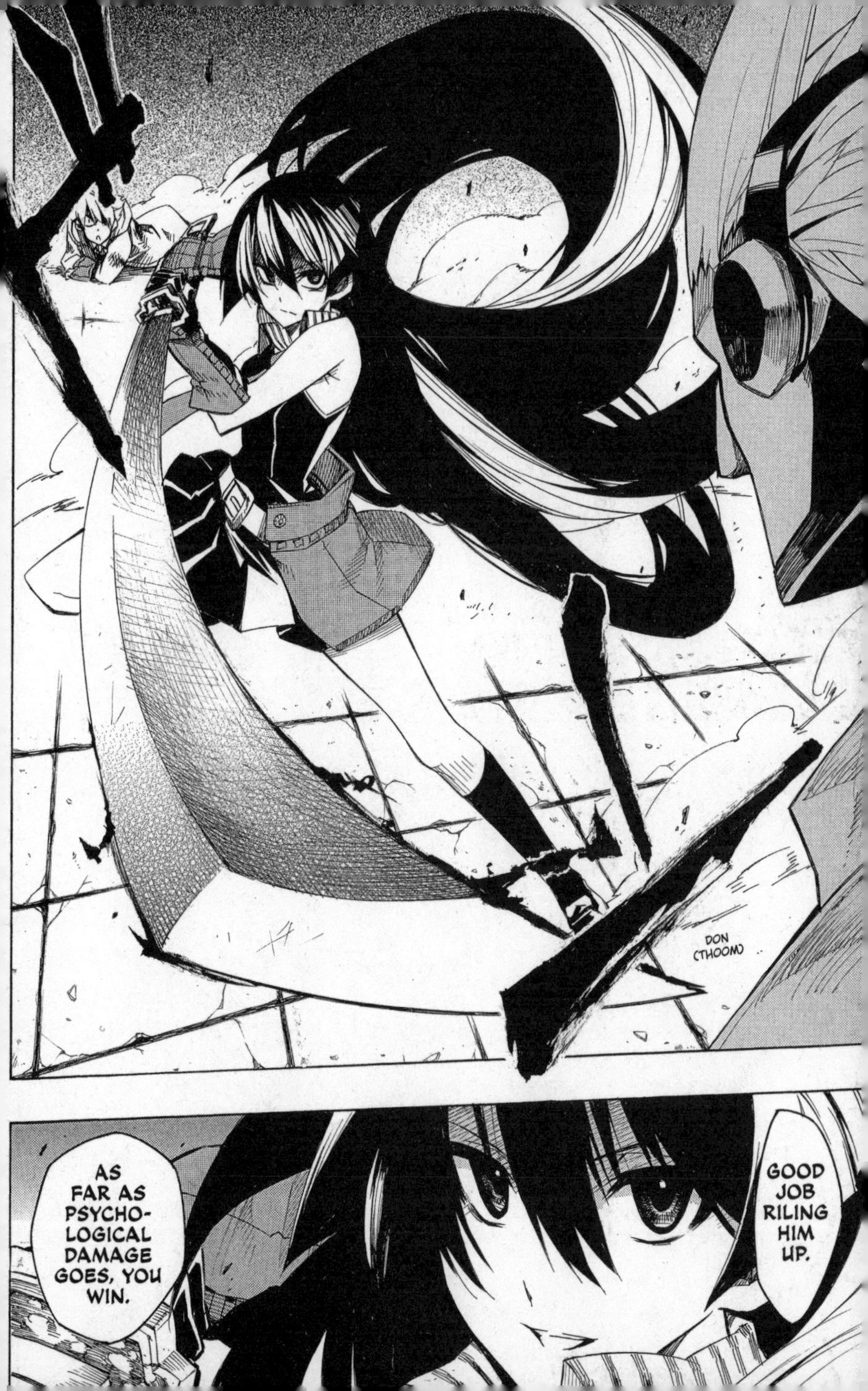
DON
(THOOM)
GOOD JOB RILING HIM UP.
AS FAR AS PSYCHO-LOGICAL DAMAGE GOES, YOU WIN.

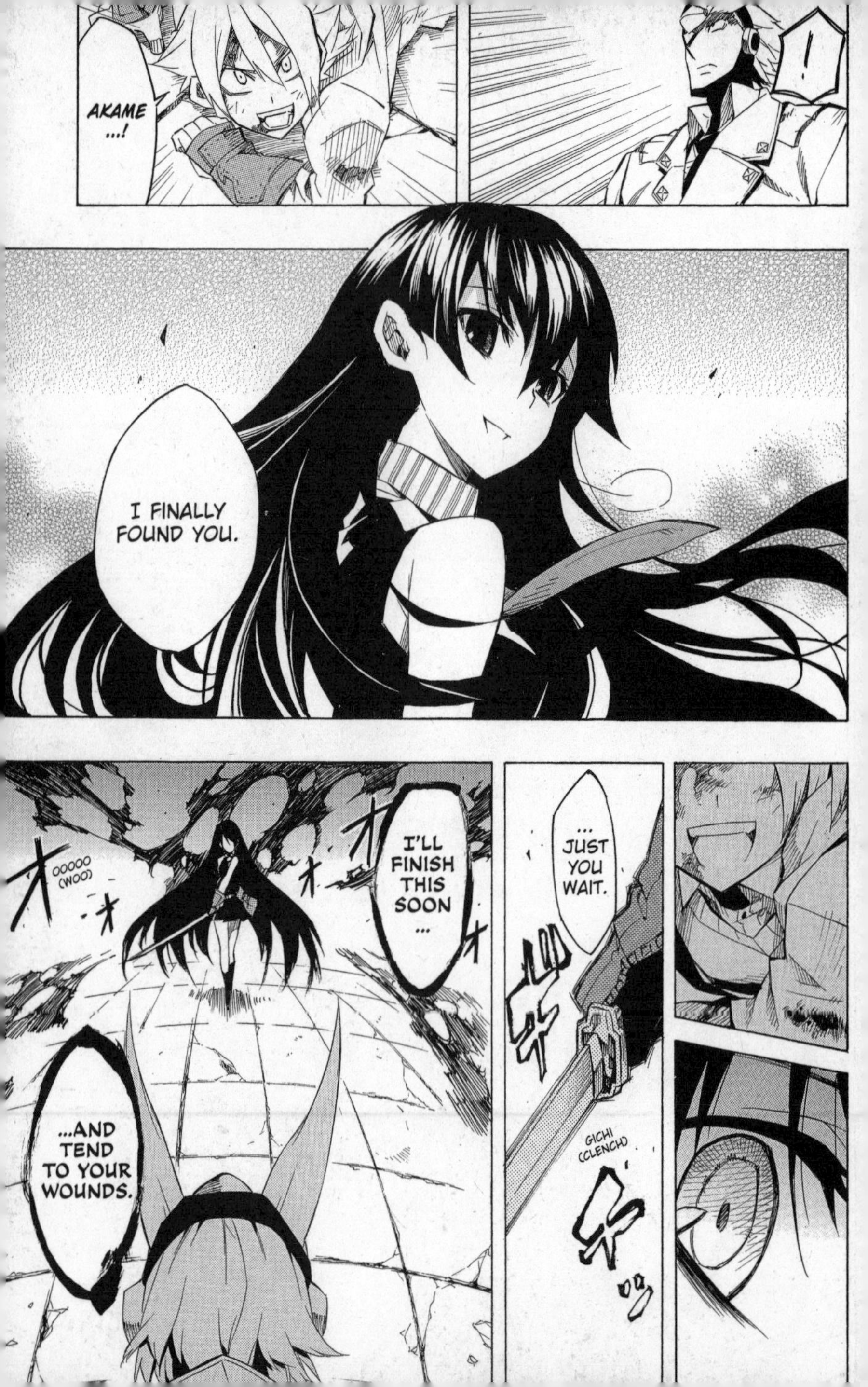
!
AKAME ...!
I FINALLY FOUND YOU.
... JUST YOU WAIT.
GICHI (CLENCH)
I'LL FINISH THIS SOON ...
OOOOO (WOO)
...AND TEND TO YOUR WOUNDS.

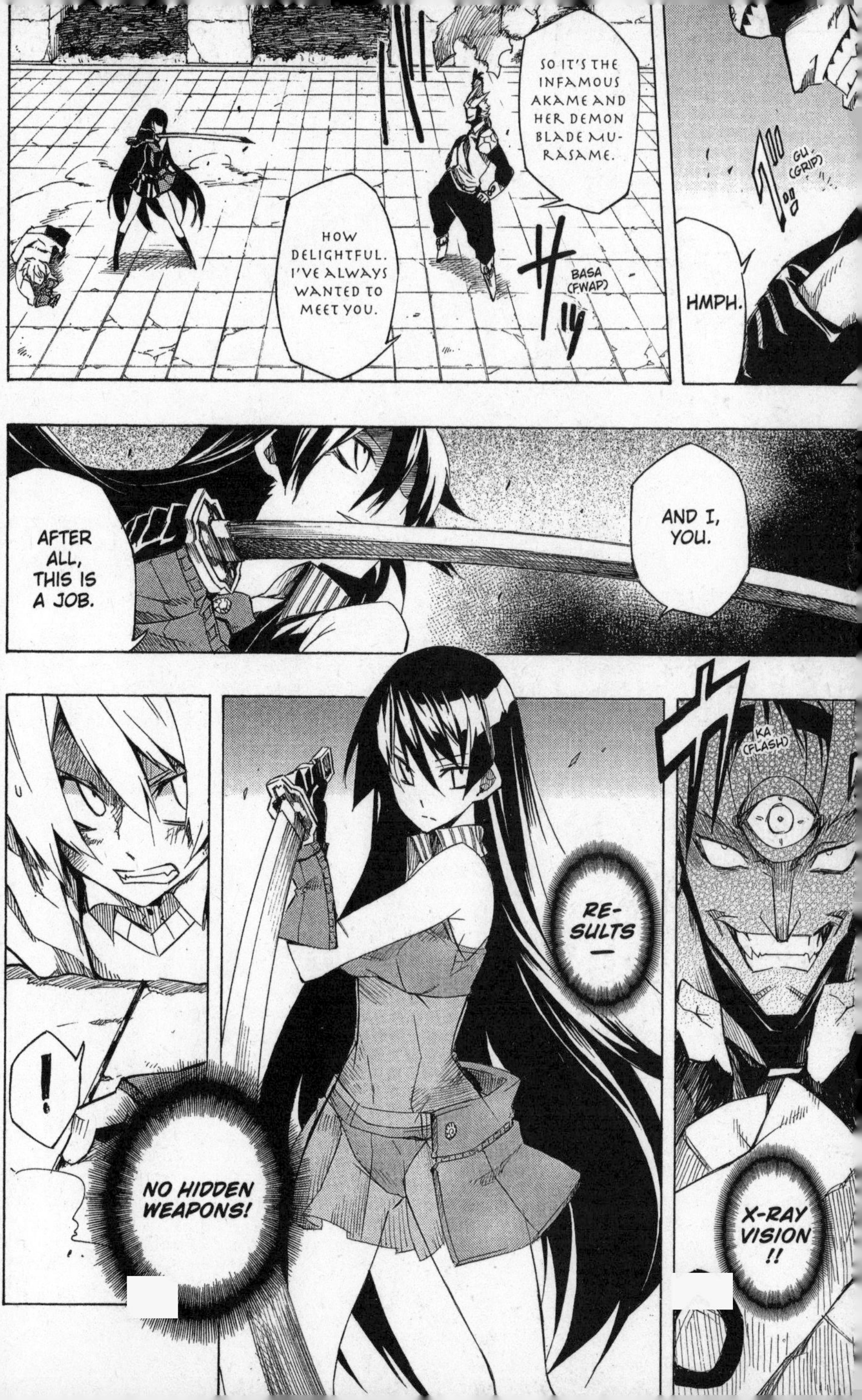
GU (GRIP)
HMPH.
SO IT'S THE INFAMOUS AKAME AND HER DEMON BLADE MU-RASAME.
BASA (FWAP)
HOW DELIGHTFUL. I'VE ALWAYS WANTED TO MEET YOU.
AND I, YOU.
AFTER ALL, THIS IS A JOB.
KA (FLASH)
X-RAY VISION!!
RE-SULTS—
NO HIDDEN WEAPONS!
!

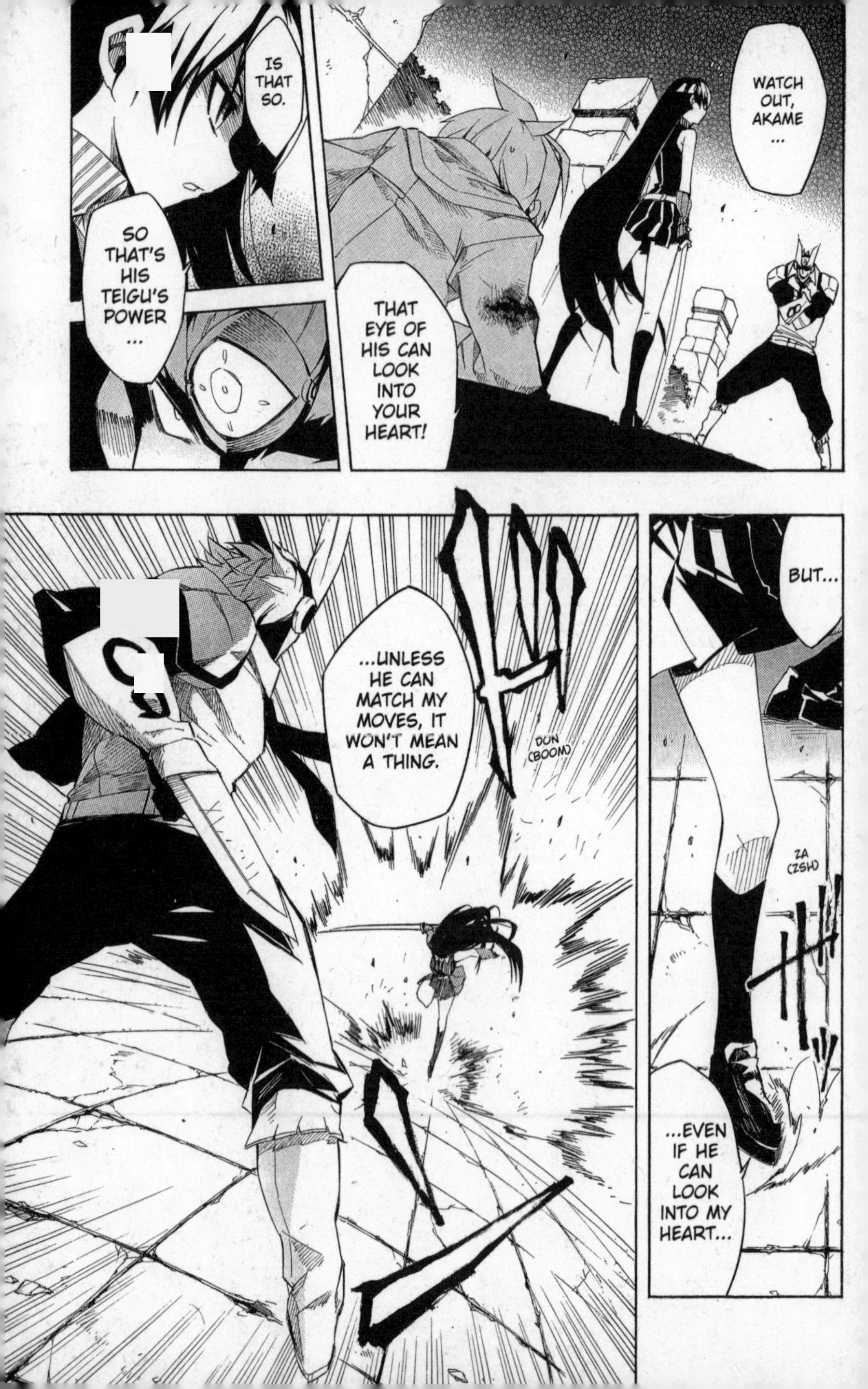
WATCH OUT, AKAME ...
THAT EYE OF HIS CAN LOOK INTO YOUR HEART!
IS THAT SO.
SO THAT'S HIS TEIGU'S POWER ...
BUT...
ZA (ZSH)
...EVEN IF HE CAN LOOK INTO MY HEART...
...UNLESS HE CAN MATCH MY MOVES, IT WON'T MEAN A THING.
DON (BOOM)

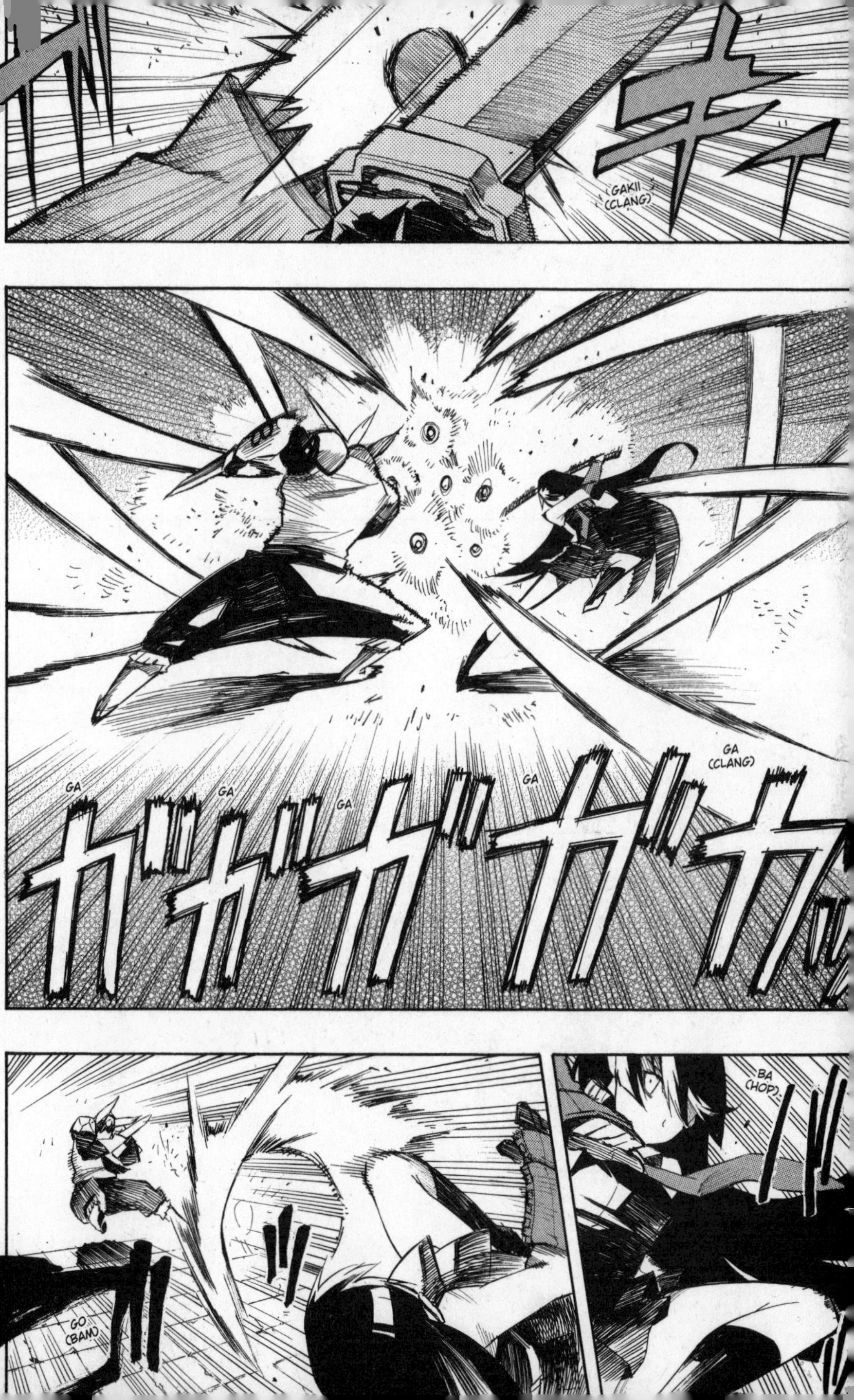
GAKII (CLANG)
GA (CLANG)
GA
GA
GA
GA
BA (HOP)
GO (BAM)

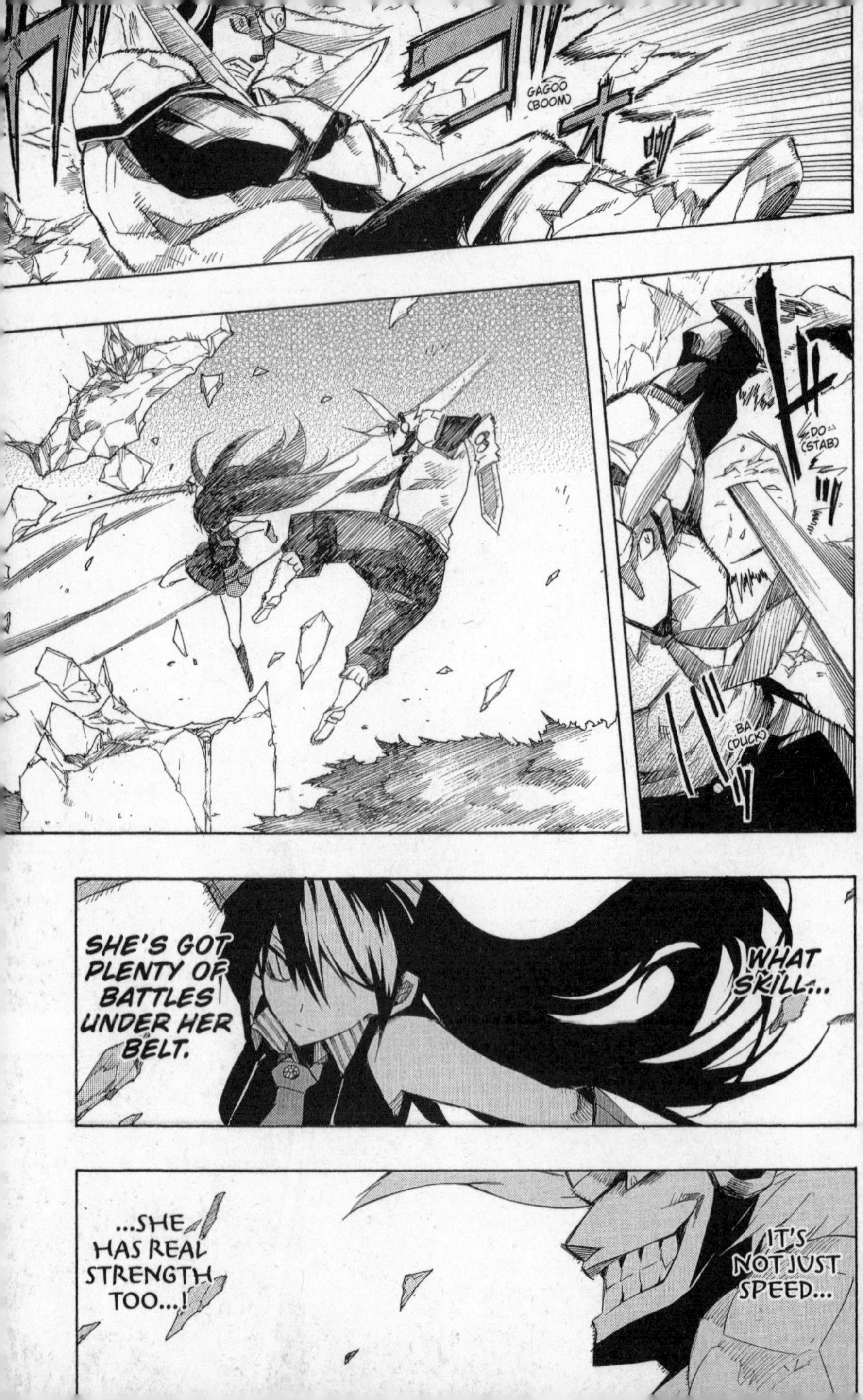
GAGOO
(BOOM)
DO
(STAB)
BA
(DUCK)
WHAT SKILL...
SHE'S GOT PLENTY OF BATTLES UNDER HER BELT.
IT'S NOT JUST SPEED...
...SHE HAS REAL STRENGTH TOO...!

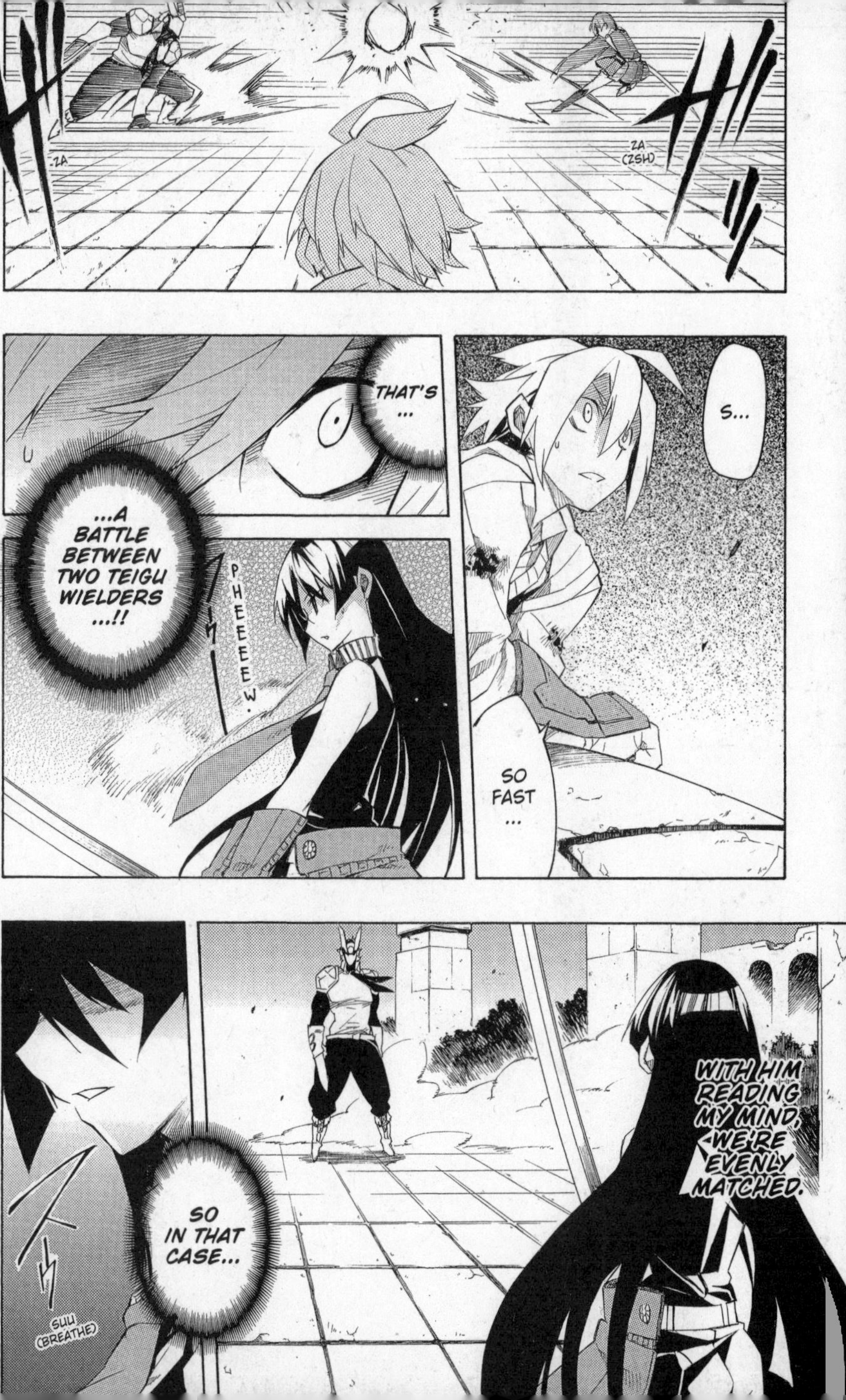
ZA (ZSH)
ZA
S...
SO FAST ...
THAT'S ...
...A BATTLE BETWEEN TWO TEIGU WIELDERS ...!!
PHEEEEW.
WITH HIM READING MY MIND, WE'RE EVENLY MATCHED.
SO IN THAT CASE...
SUU (BREATHE)

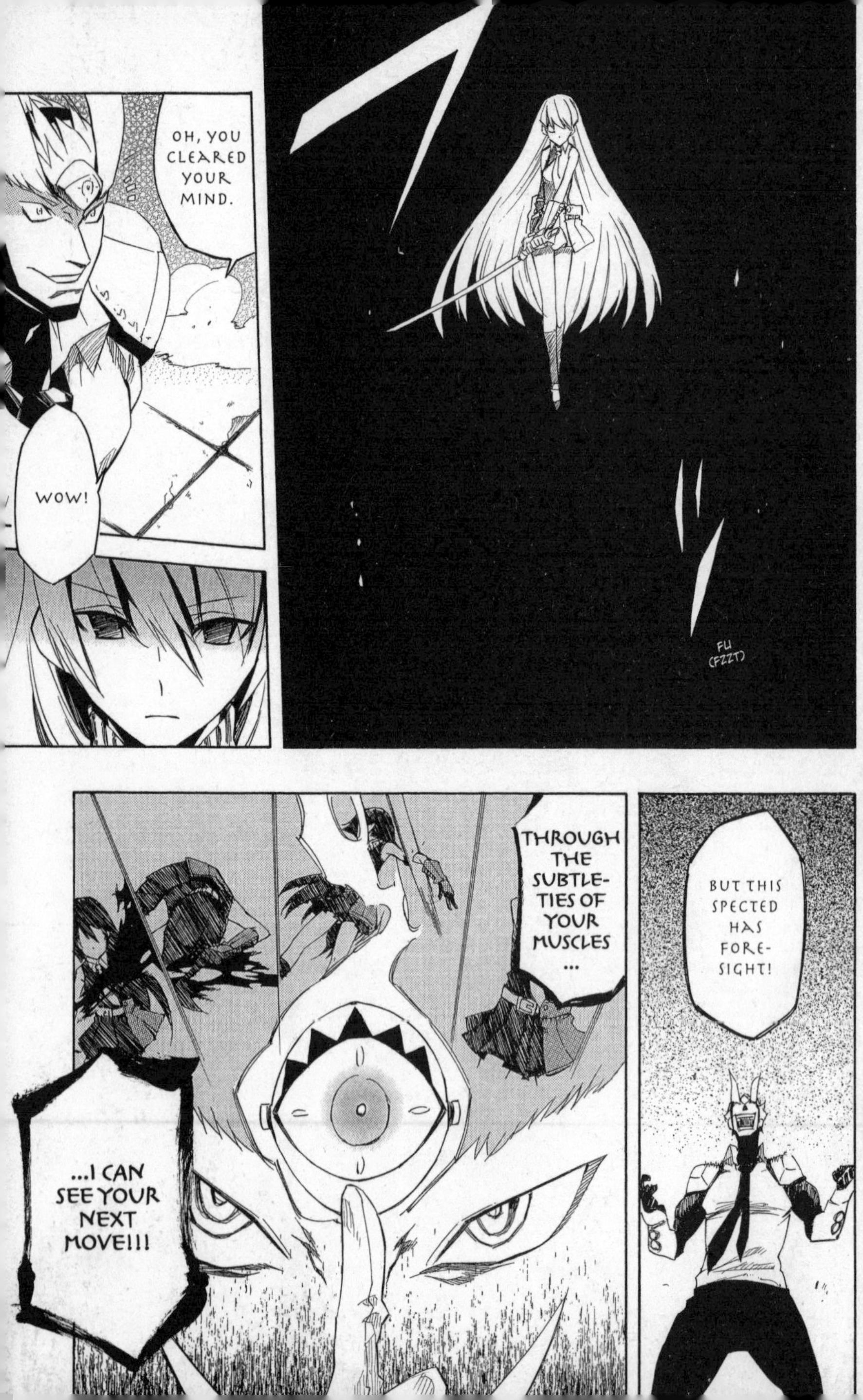
FU (FZZT)
OH, YOU CLEARED YOUR MIND.
WOW!
BUT THIS SPECTED HAS FORE-SIGHT!
THROUGH THE SUBTLE-TIES OF YOUR MUSCLES...
...I CAN SEE YOUR NEXT MOVE!!!

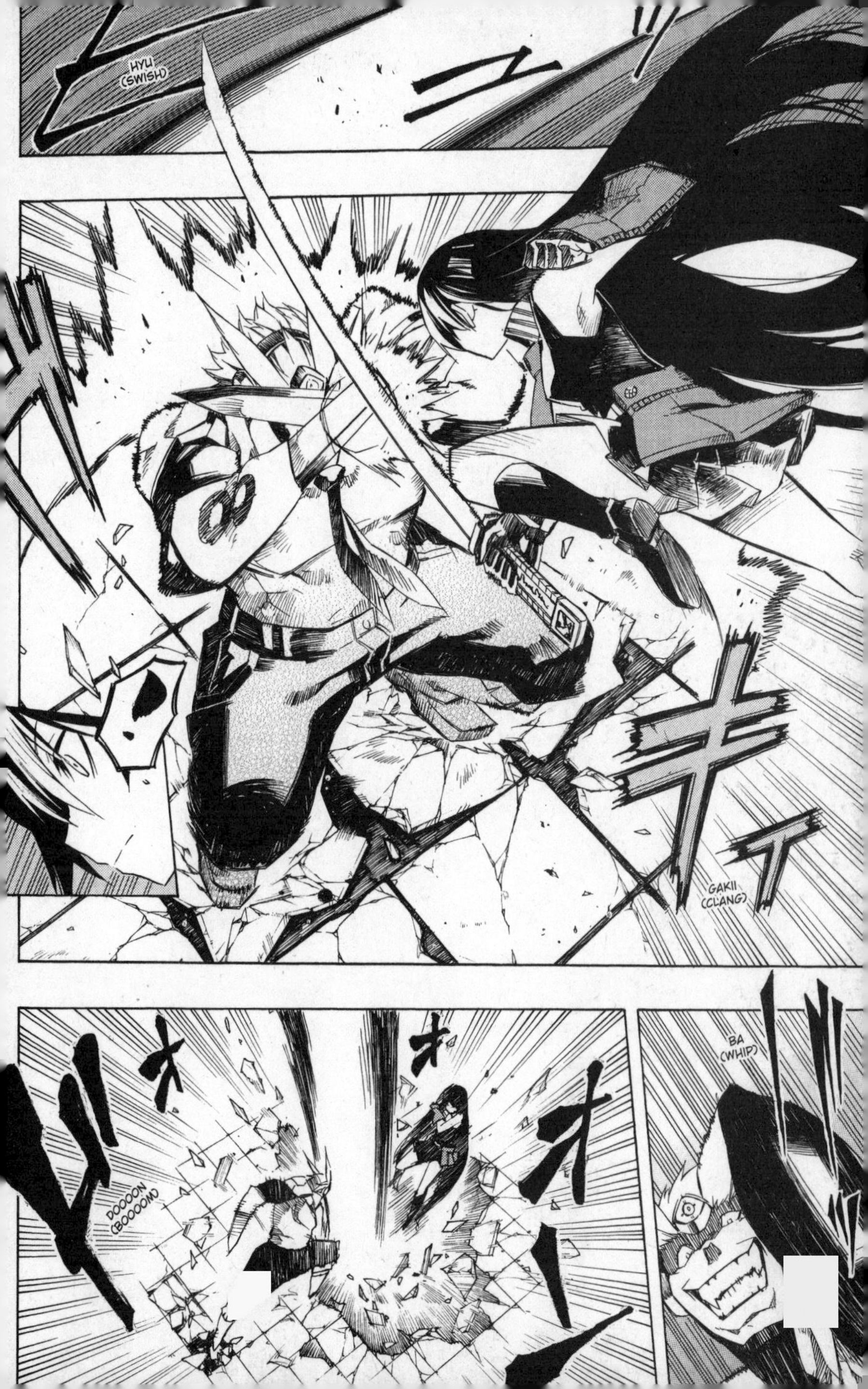
HYU
(SWISH)
GAKII
(CLANG)
BA
(WHIP)
DOOOON
(BOOOOM)

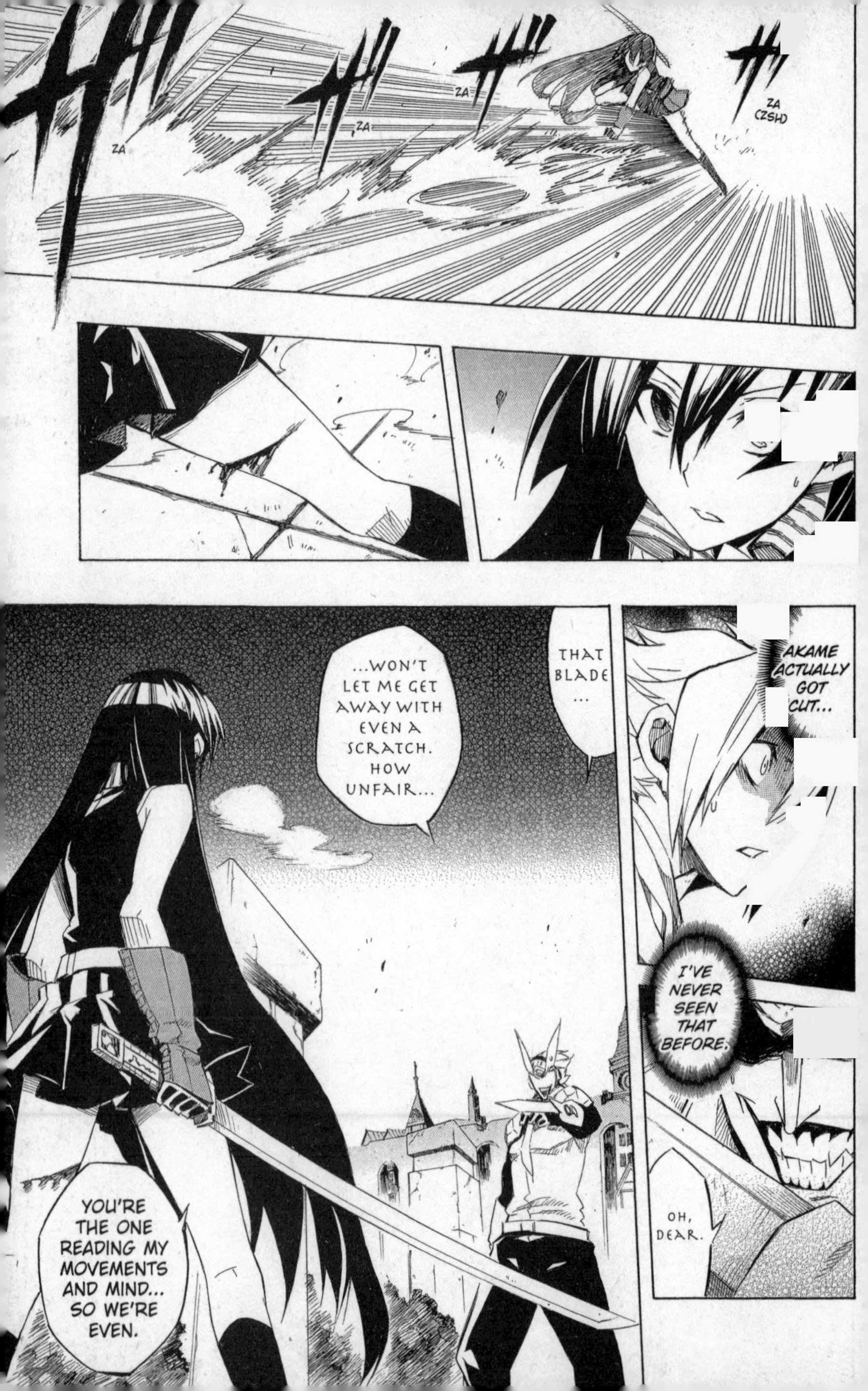
ZA (ZSH)
ZA
ZA
ZA
AKAME ACTUALLY GOT CUT...
I'VE NEVER SEEN THAT BEFORE.
OH, DEAR.
THAT BLADE ...
...WON'T LET ME GET AWAY WITH EVEN A SCRATCH. HOW UNFAIR...
YOU'RE THE ONE READING MY MOVEMENTS AND MIND... SO WE'RE EVEN.

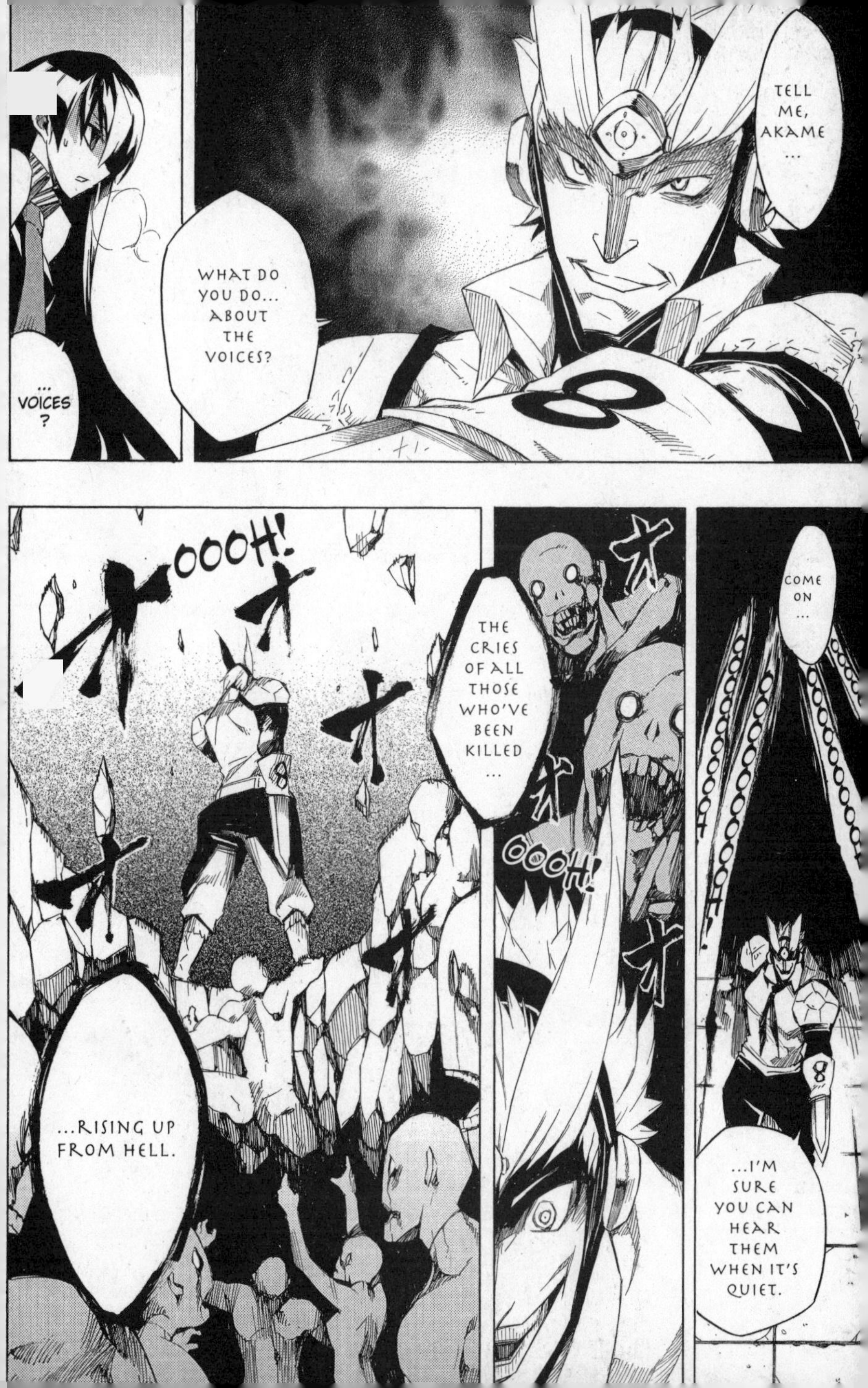
TELL ME, AKAME ...
WHAT DO YOU DO... ABOUT THE VOICES?
... VOICES ?
COME ON ...
...I'M SURE YOU CAN HEAR THEM WHEN IT'S QUIET.
THE CRIES OF ALL THOSE WHO'VE BEEN KILLED ...
OOOH!
OOOH!
...RISING UP FROM HELL.

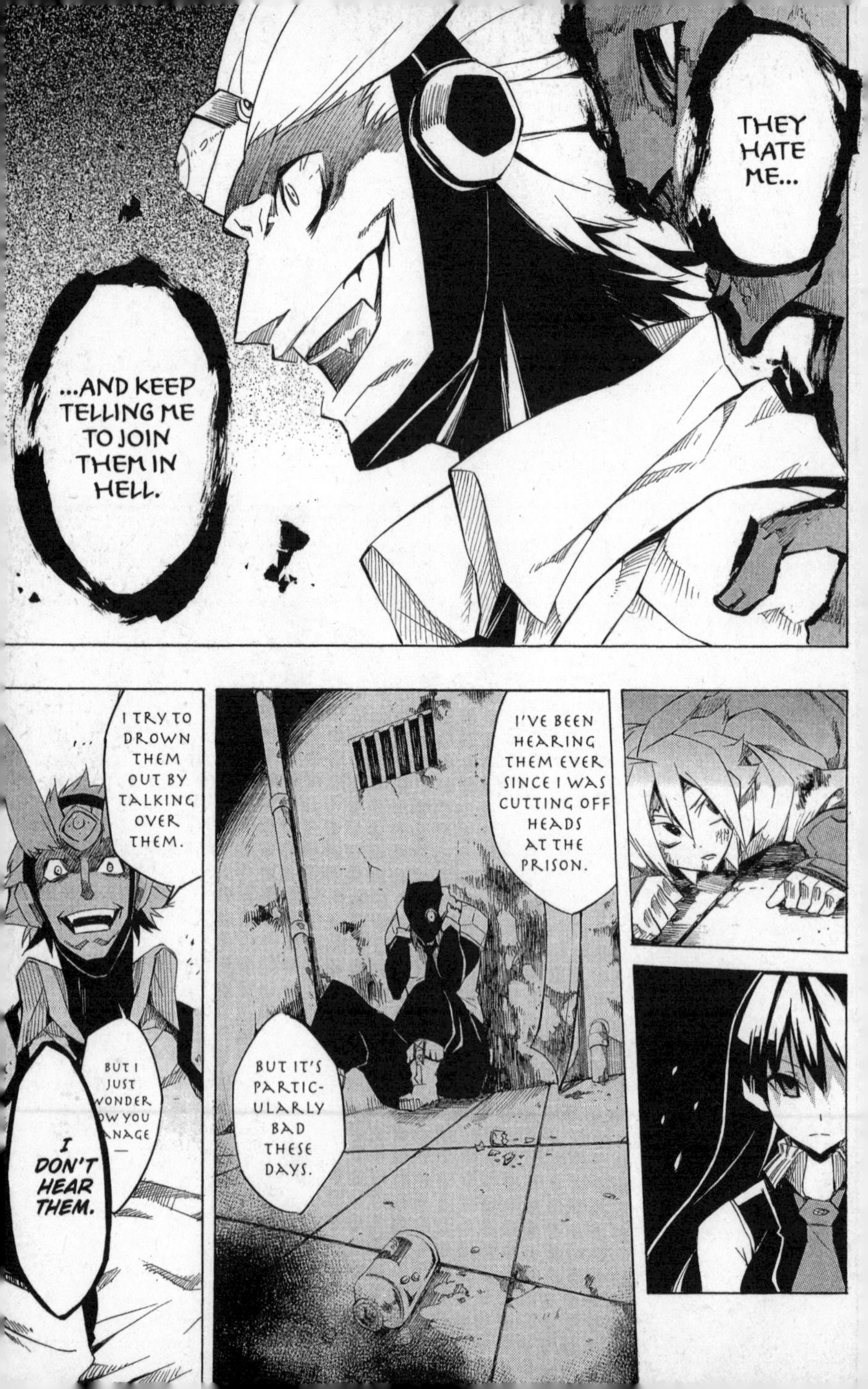
THEY HATE ME...
...AND KEEP TELLING ME TO JOIN THEM IN HELL.
I'VE BEEN HEARING THEM EVER SINCE I WAS CUTTING OFF HEADS AT THE PRISON.
BUT IT'S PARTIC- ULARLY BAD THESE DAYS.
...
I TRY TO DROWN THEM OUT BY TALKING OVER THEM.
BUT I JUST WONDER OW YOU ANAGE —
I DON'T HEAR THEM.

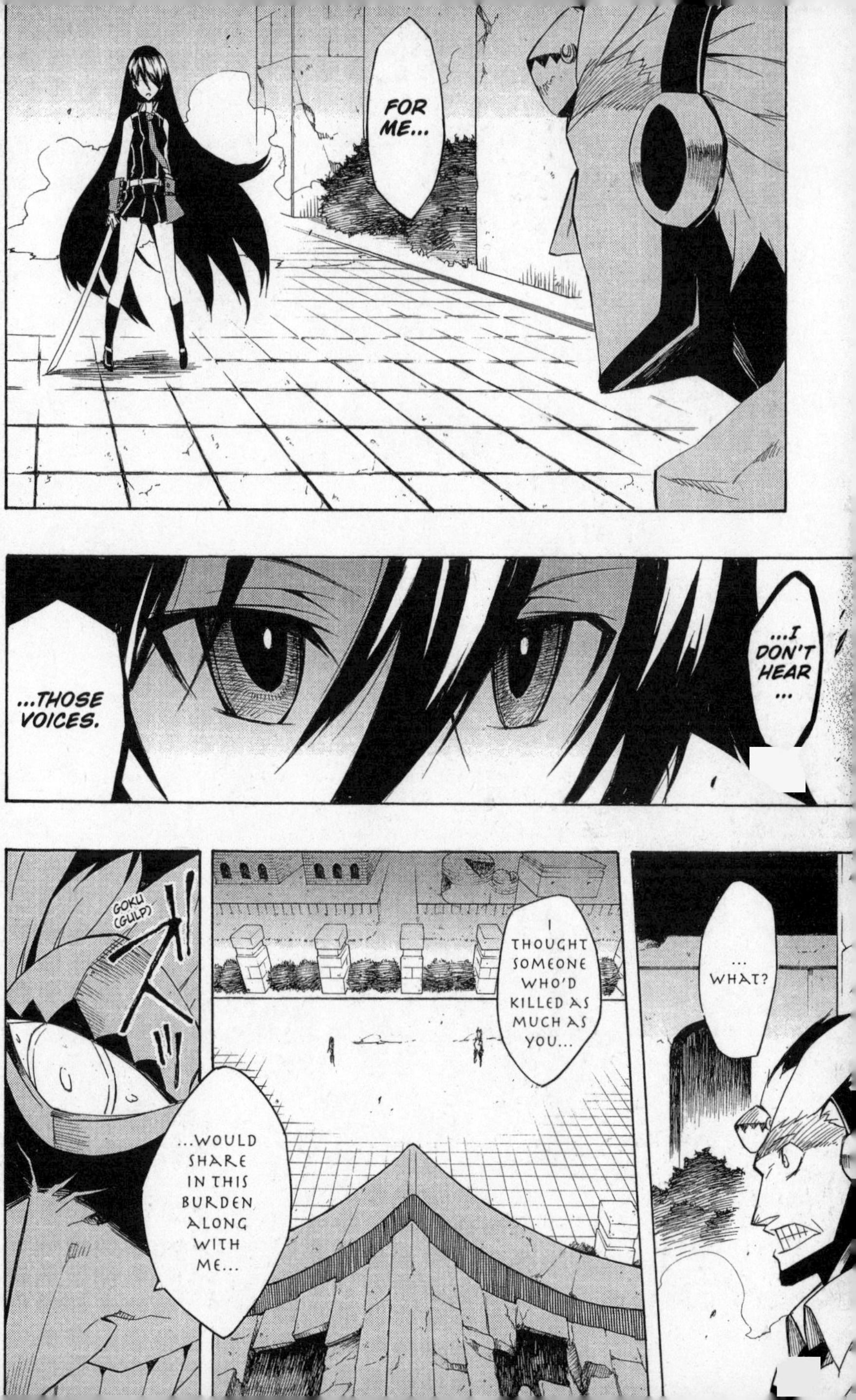
FOR ME...
...I DON'T HEAR...
...THOSE VOICES.
... WHAT?
I THOUGHT SOMEONE WHO'D KILLED AS MUCH AS YOU...
GOKU (GULP)
...WOULD SHARE IN THIS BURDEN ALONG WITH ME...

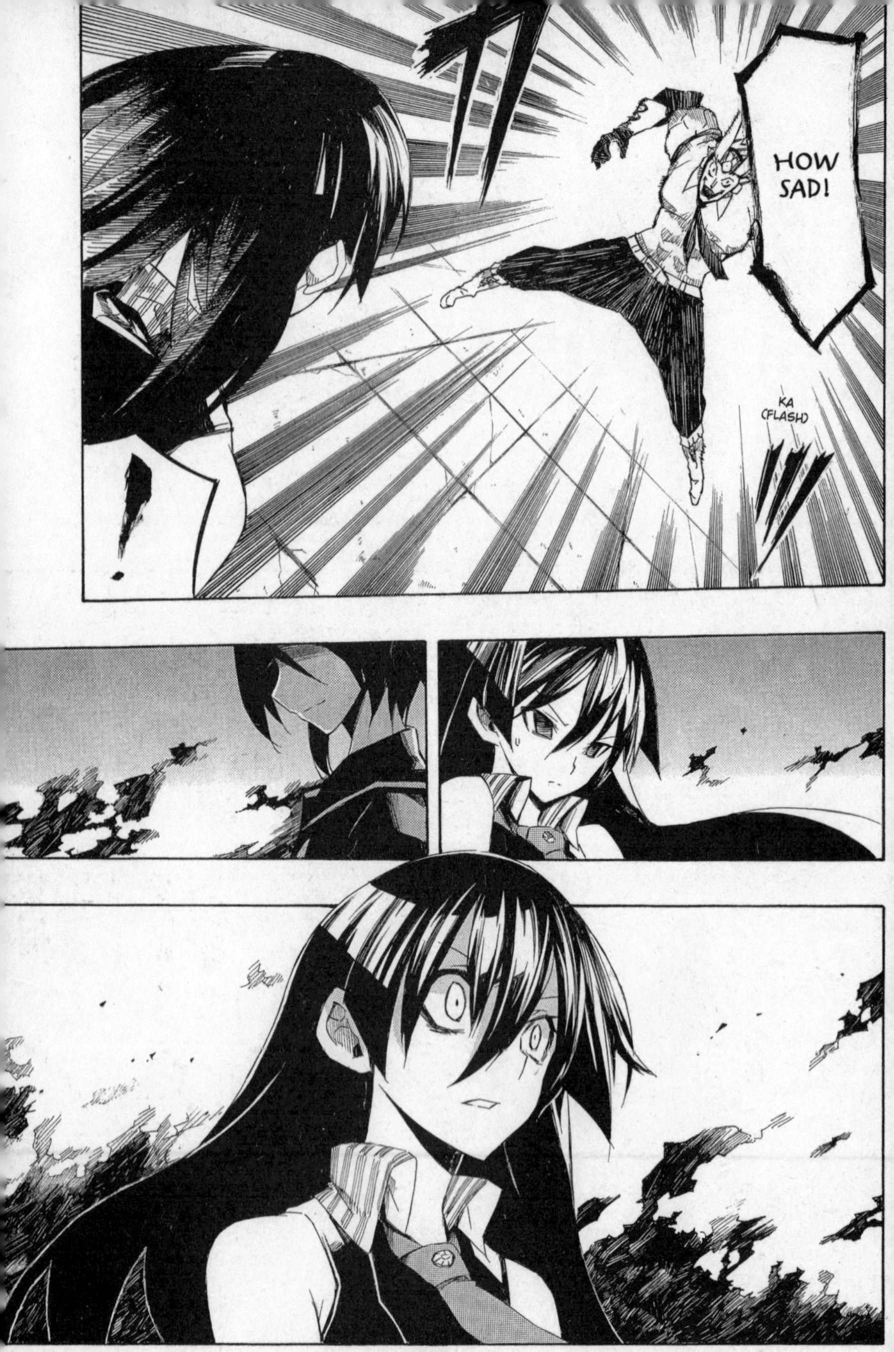
HOW SAD!
KA (FLASH)

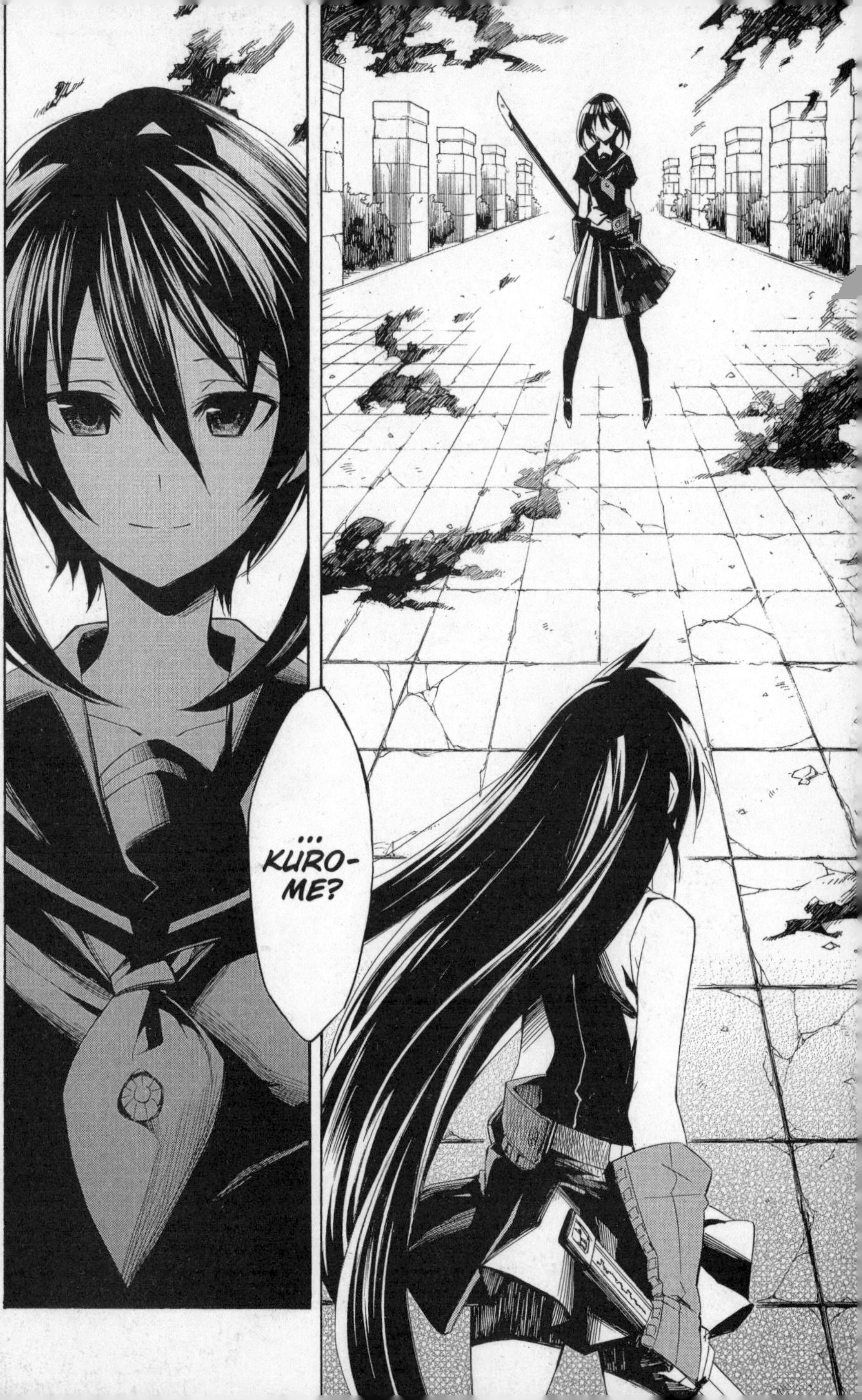
...KURO-ME?

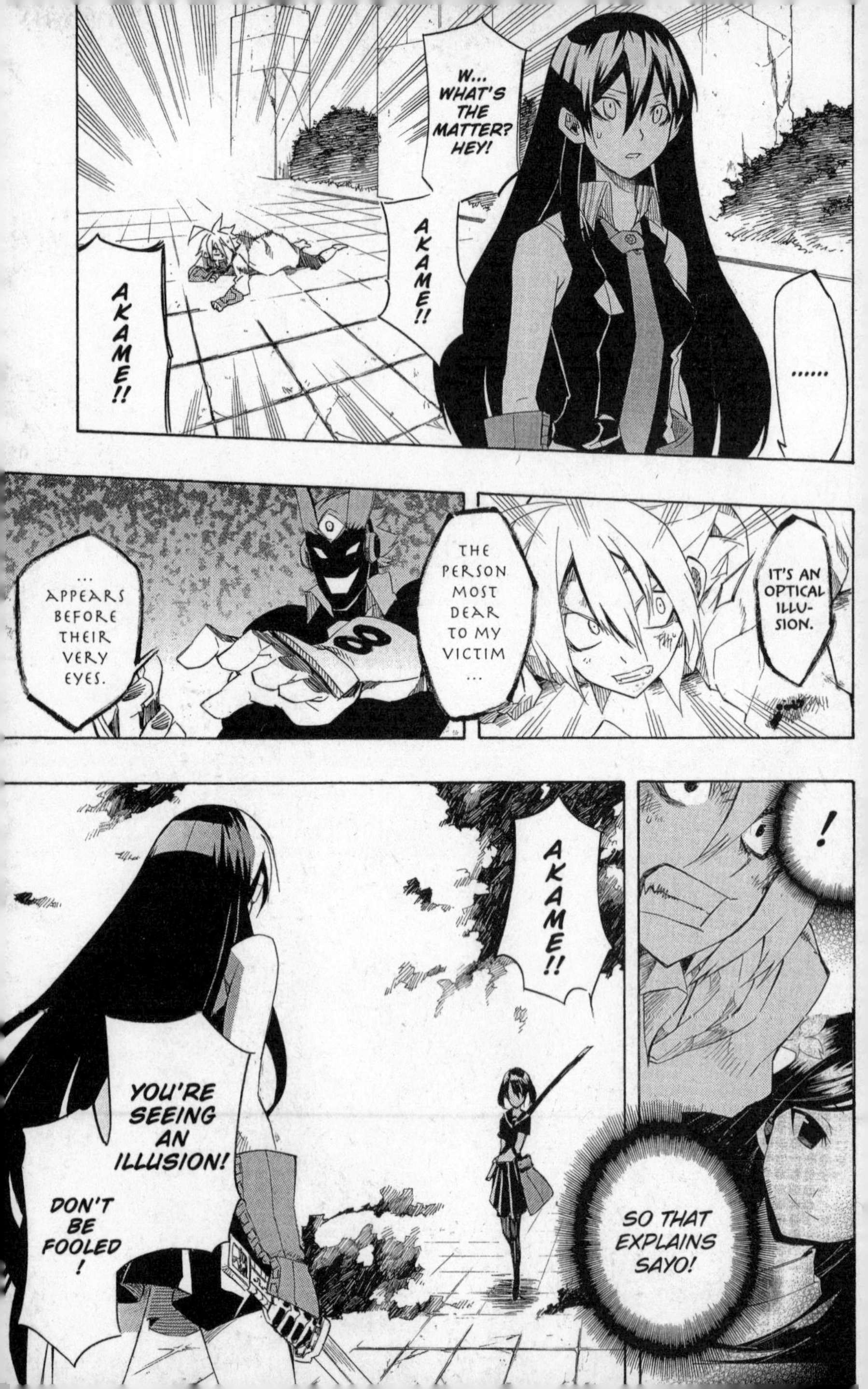
W... WHAT'S THE MATTER? HEY!
......
AKAME!!
AKAME!!
IT'S AN OPTICAL ILLUSION.
THE PERSON MOST DEAR TO MY VICTIM ...
... APPEARS BEFORE THEIR VERY EYES.
!
SO THAT EXPLAINS SAYO!
AKAME!!
YOU'RE SEEING AN ILLUSION!
DON'T BE FOOLED!

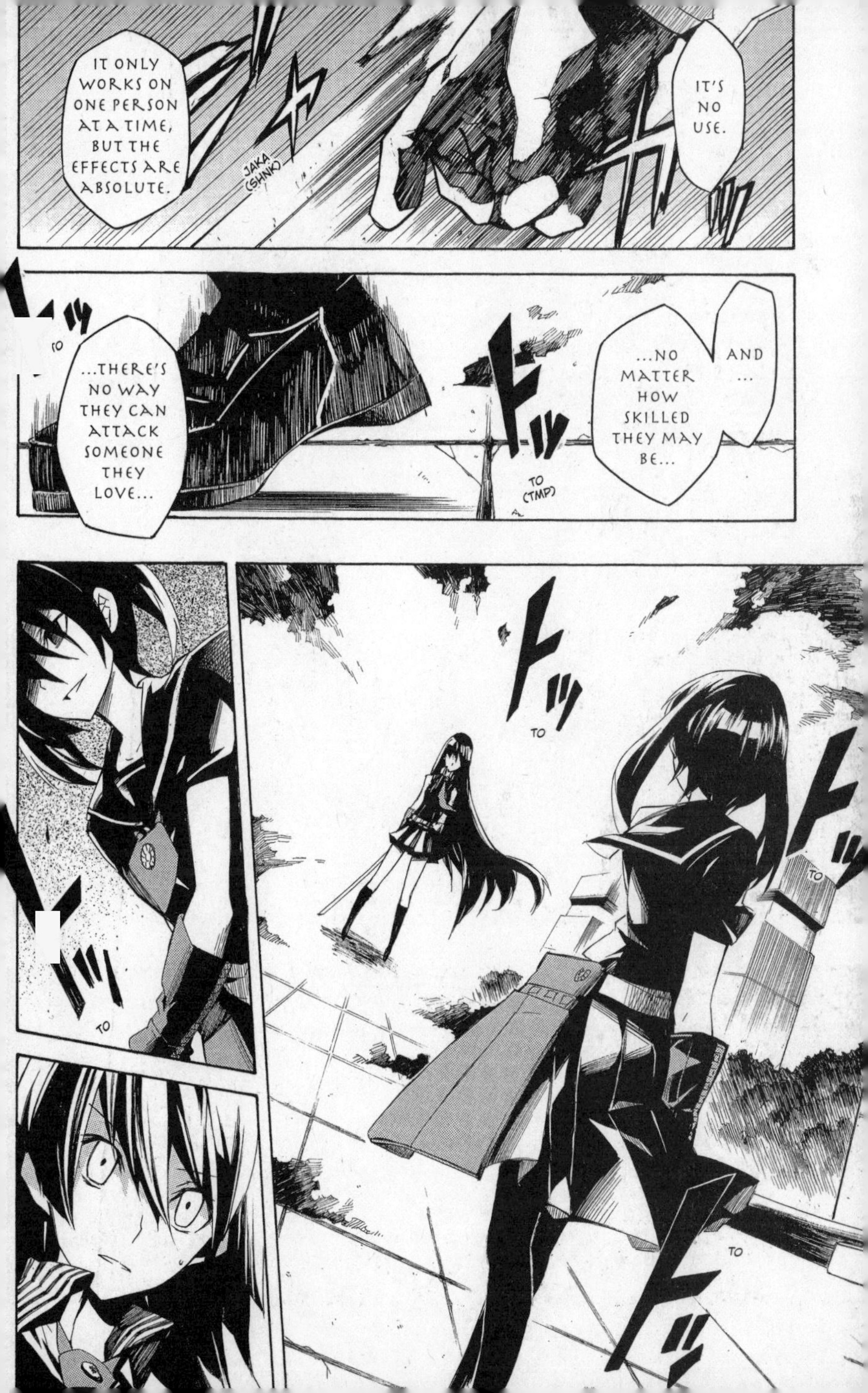
IT'S NO USE.
JAKA (SHNK)
IT ONLY WORKS ON ONE PERSON AT A TIME, BUT THE EFFECTS ARE ABSOLUTE.
AND...
...NO MATTER HOW SKILLED THEY MAY BE...
TO (TMP)
...THERE'S NO WAY THEY CAN ATTACK SOMEONE THEY LOVE...
TO
TO
TO
TO
TO

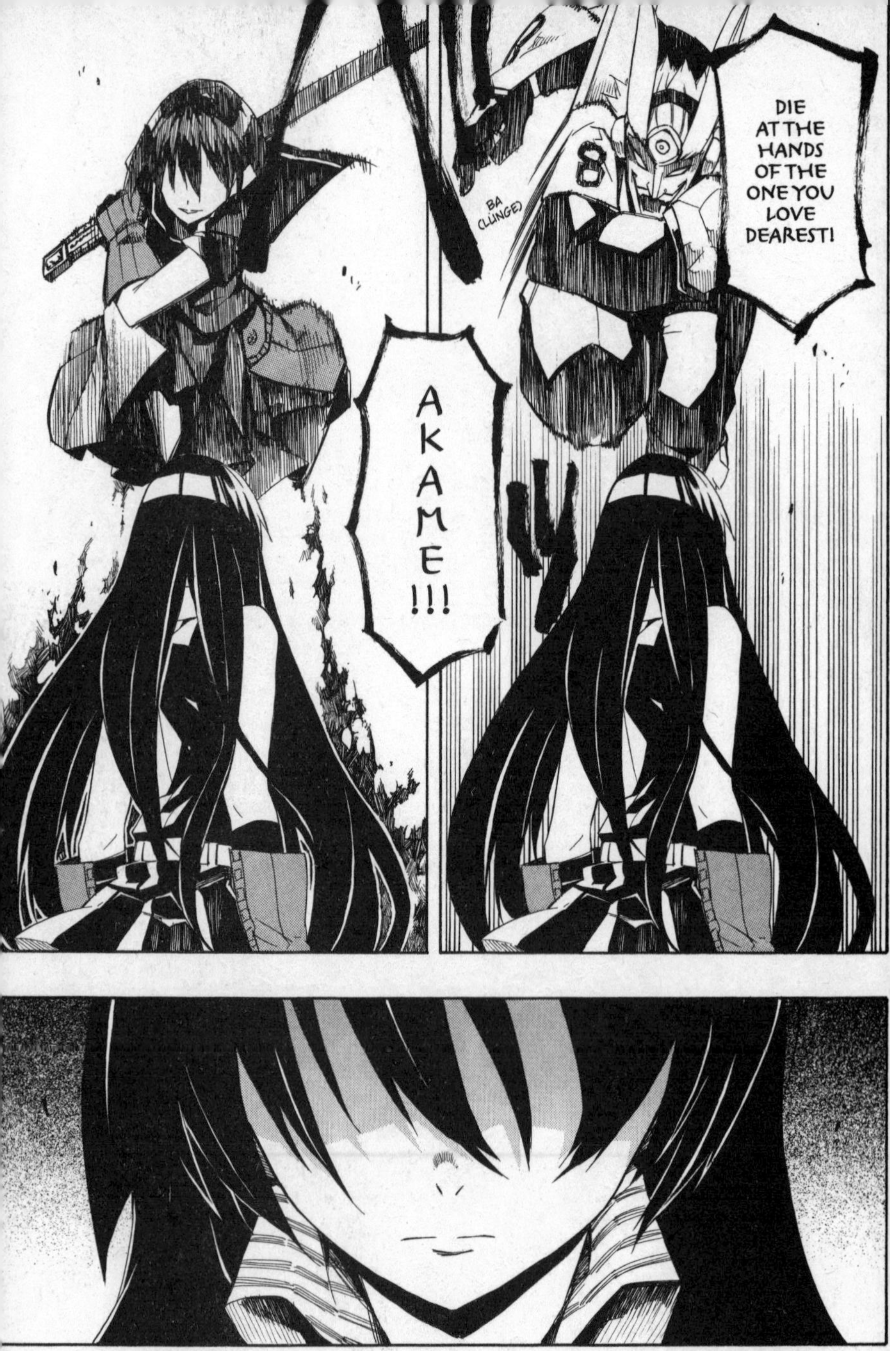
DIE AT THE HANDS OF THE ONE YOU LOVE DEAREST!
BA (LUNGE)
AKAME!!!

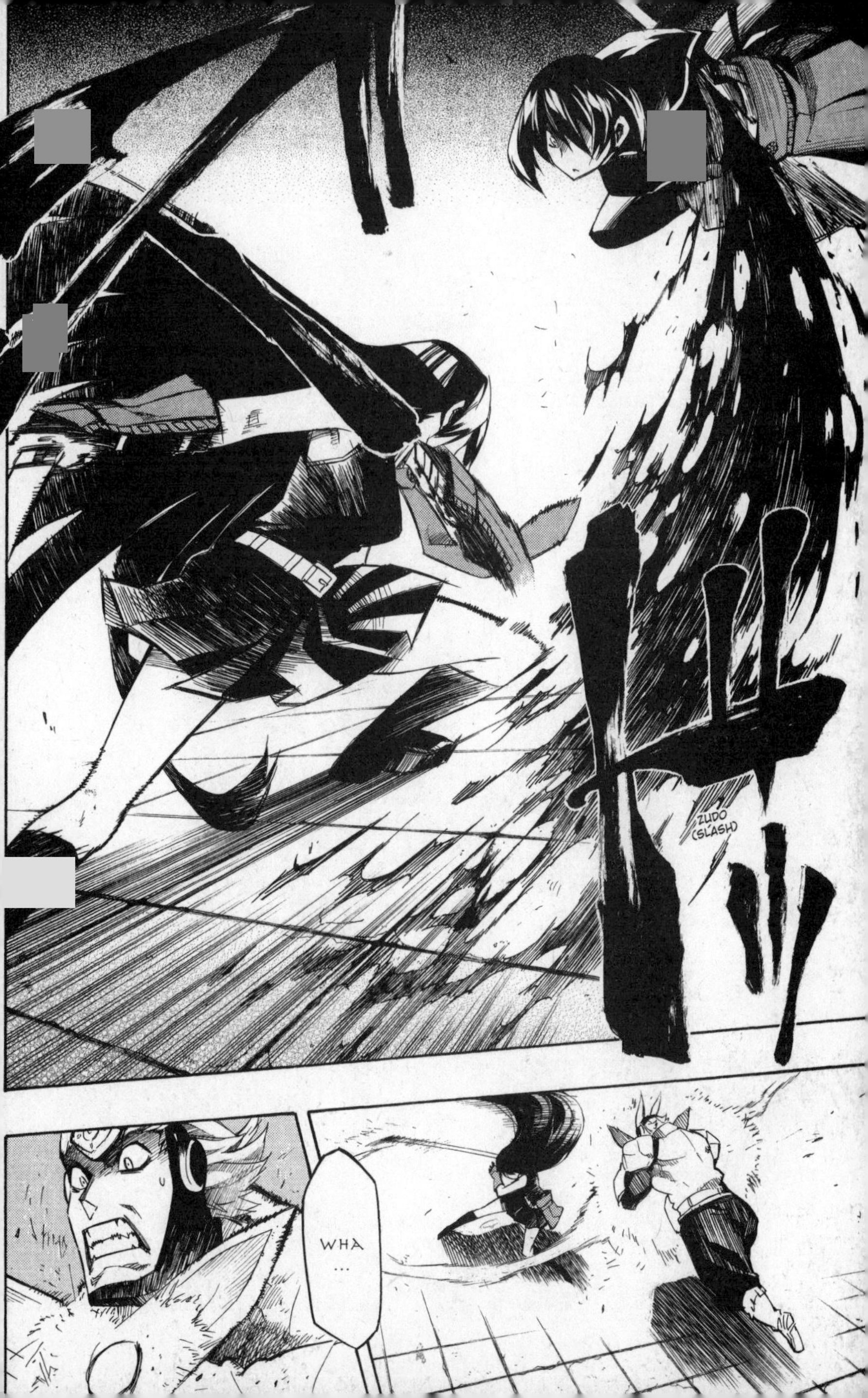
ZUDO
(SLASH)
WHA
...

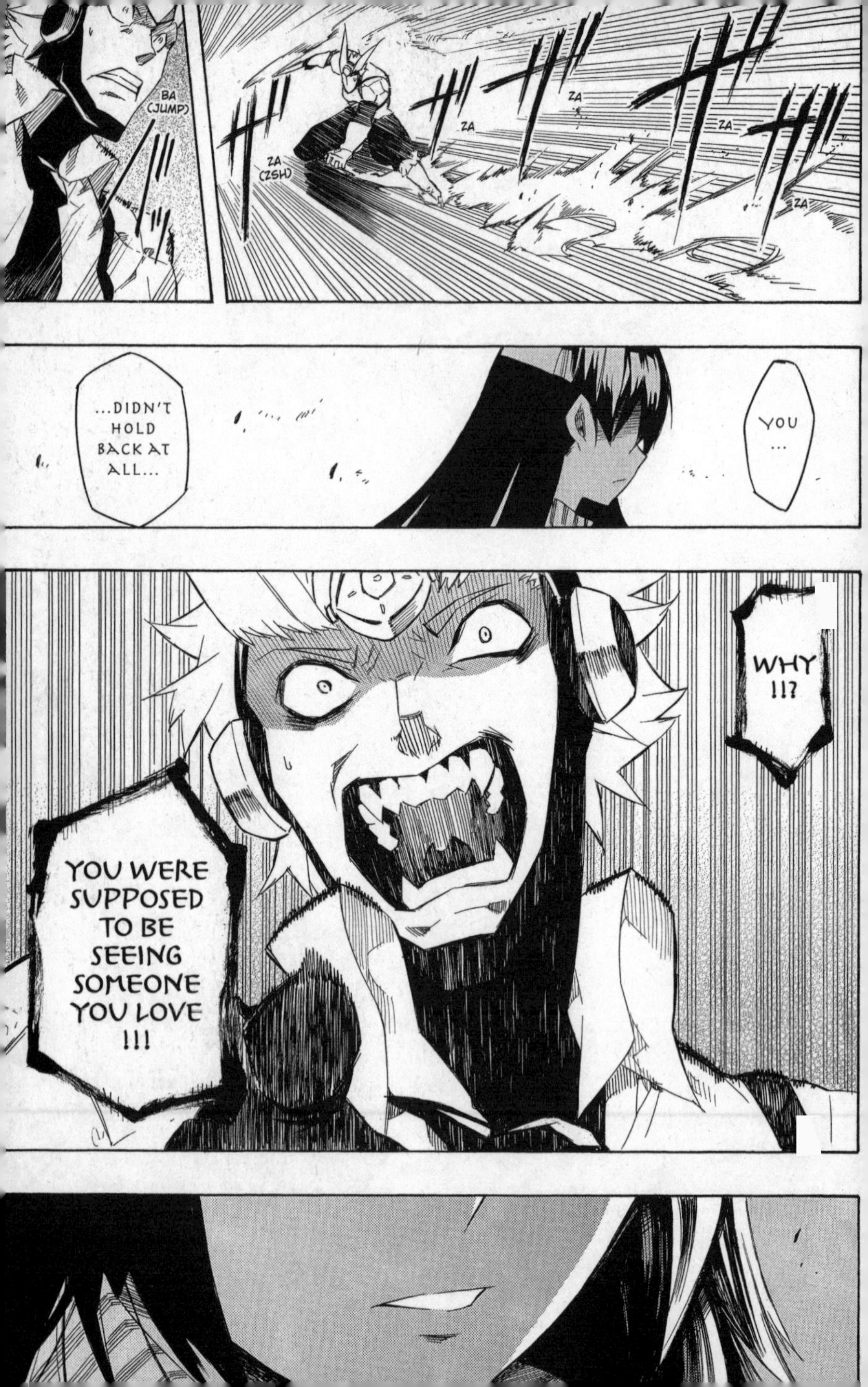
ZA
ZA
ZA
ZA
ZA (ZSH)
BA (JUMP)
YOU ...
...DIDN'T HOLD BACK AT ALL...
WHY !!?
YOU WERE SUPPOSED TO BE SEEING SOMEONE YOU LOVE !!!

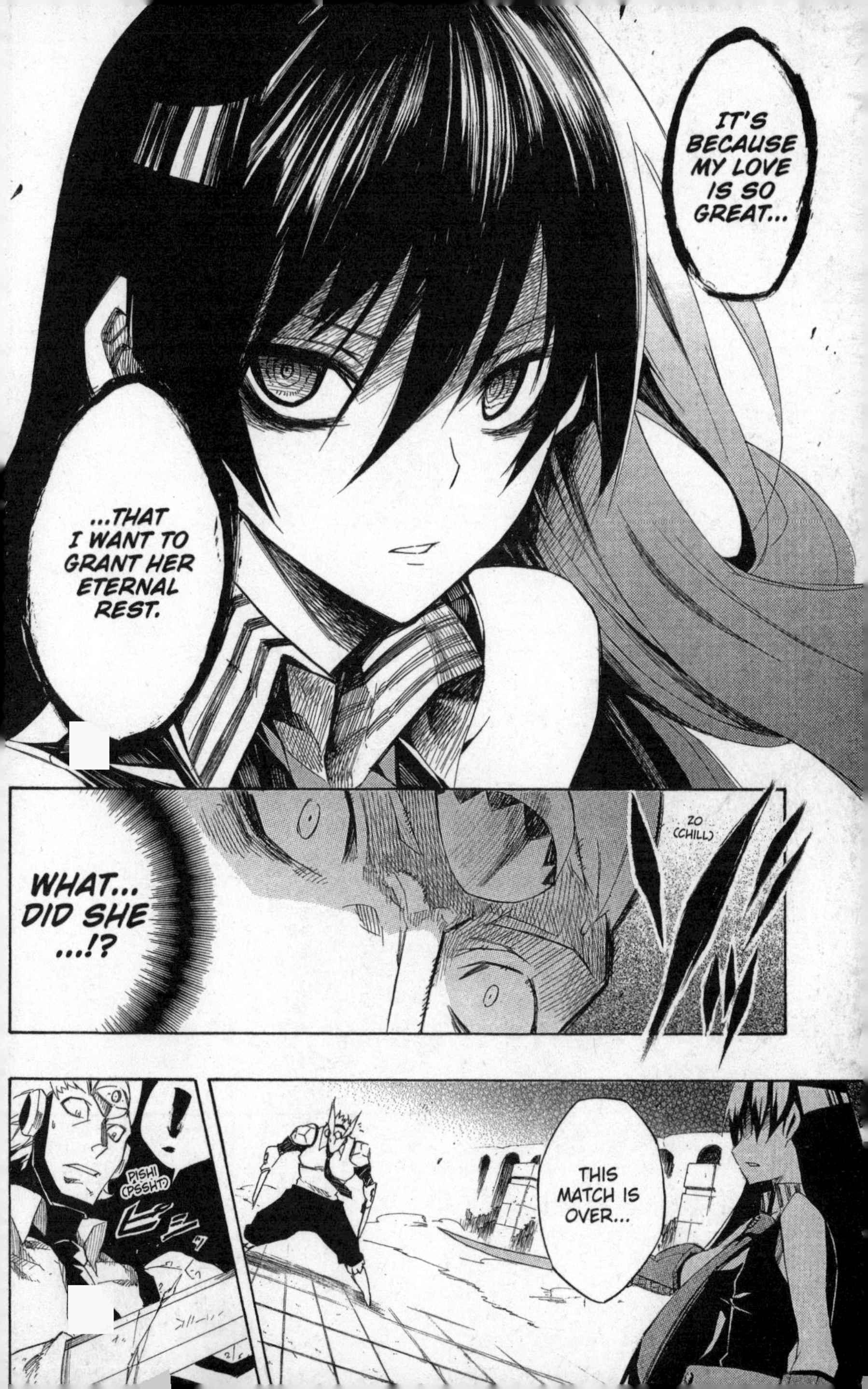
IT'S BECAUSE MY LOVE IS SO GREAT...
...THAT I WANT TO GRANT HER ETERNAL REST.
ZO (CHILL)
WHAT... DID SHE ...!?
THIS MATCH IS OVER...
PISHI (PSSHT)

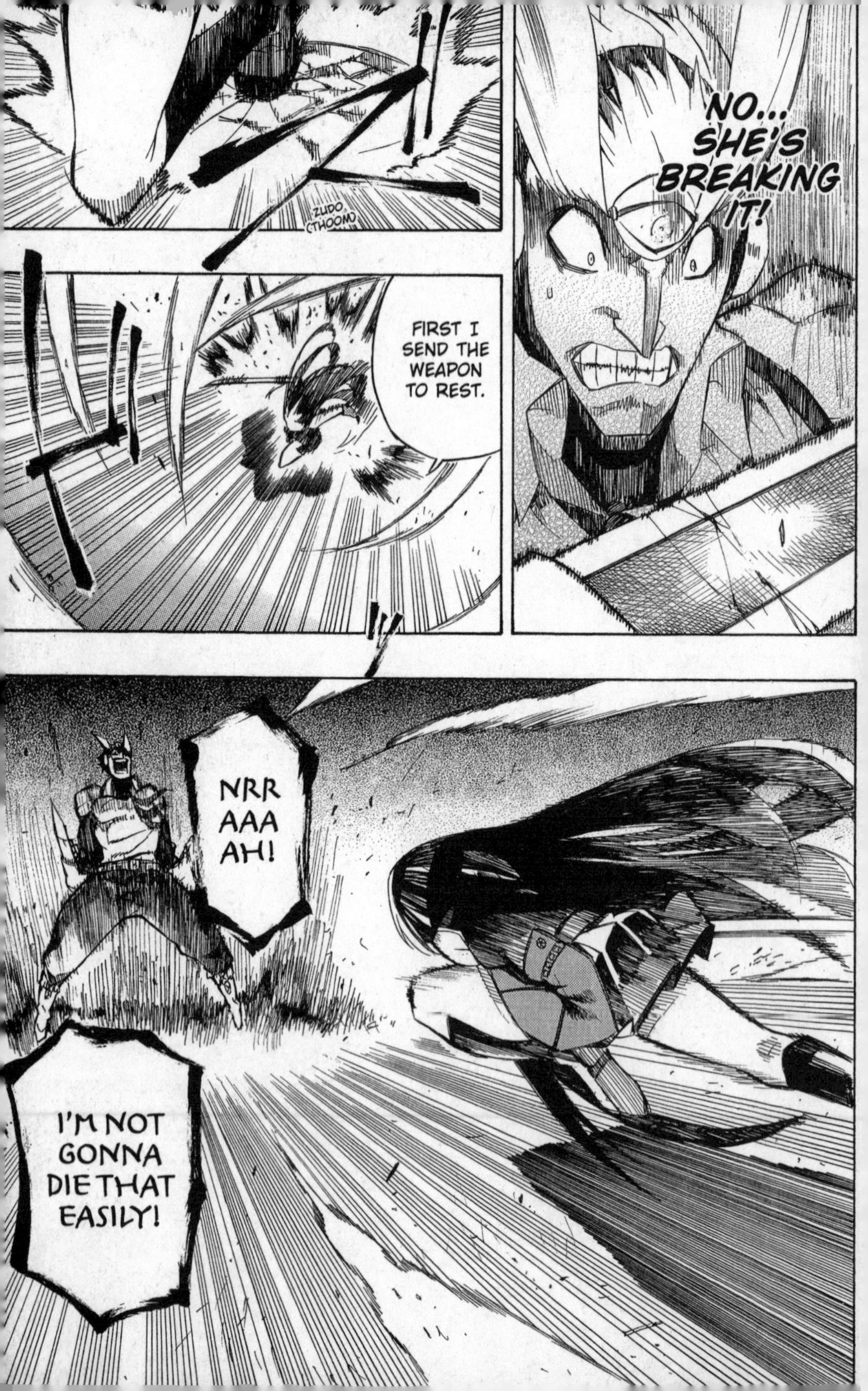
NO... SHE'S BREAKING IT!
ZUDO (THOOM)
FIRST I SEND THE WEAPON TO REST.
NRR AAA AH!
I'M NOT GONNA DIE THAT EASILY!

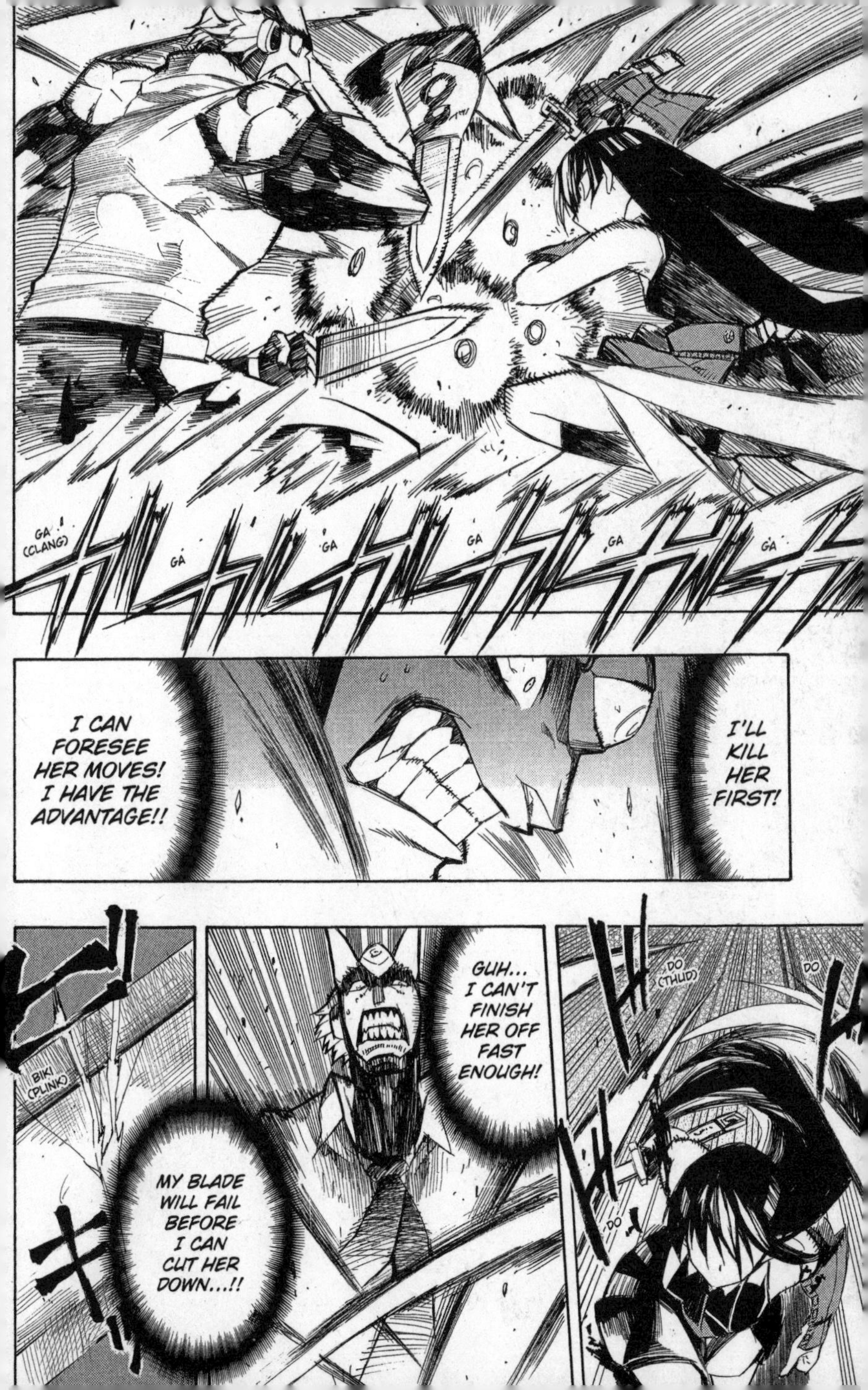

GA
GA
GA
GA
GA! (CLANG)
I'LL KILL HER FIRST!
I CAN FORESEE HER MOVES! I HAVE THE ADVANTAGE!!
DO
DO (THUD)
DO
GUH... I CAN'T FINISH HER OFF FAST ENOUGH!
MY BLADE WILL FAIL BEFORE I CAN CUT HER DOWN...!!
BIKI (PLINK)

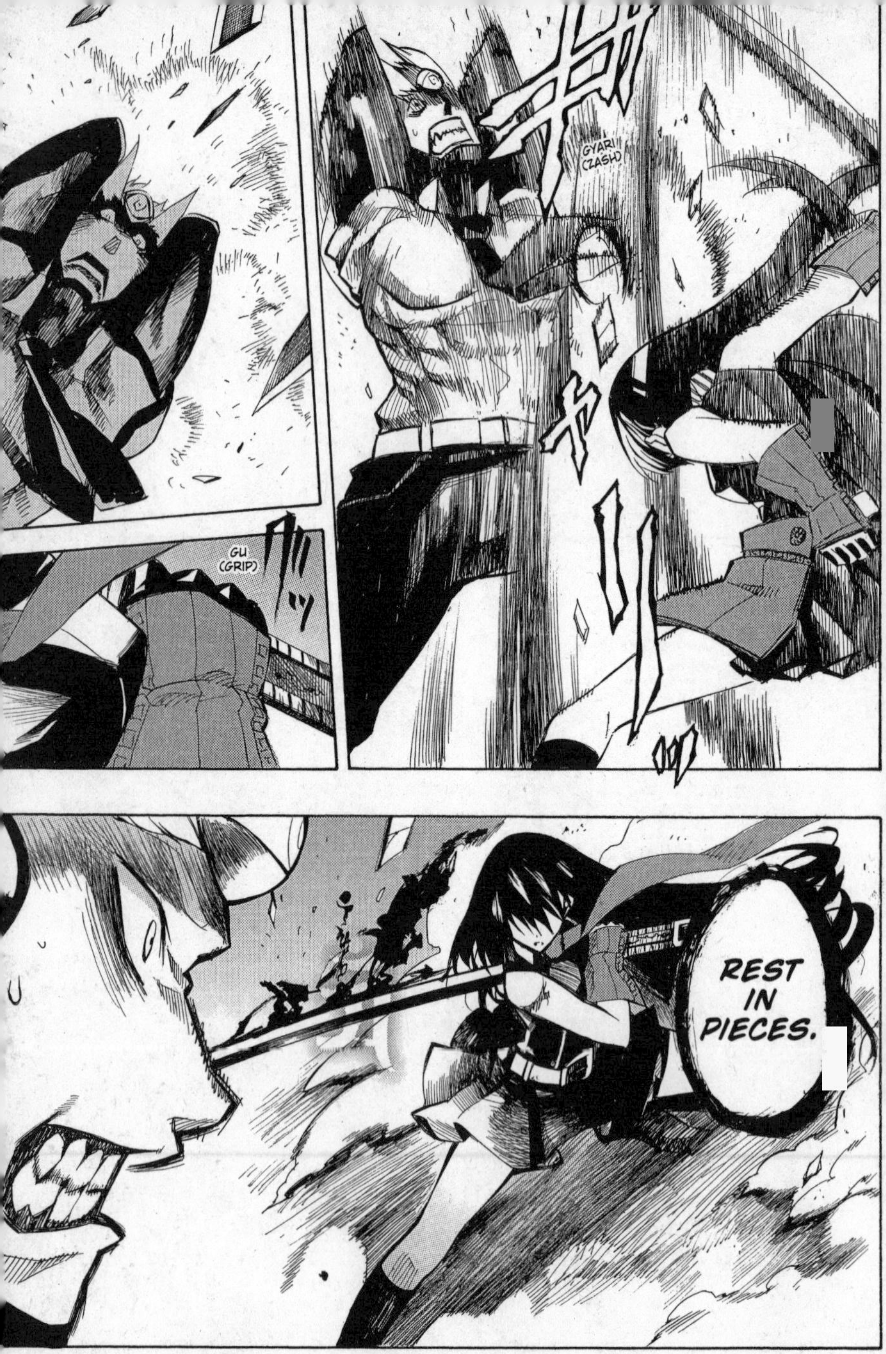
GYARI (ZASH)
GU (GRIP)
REST IN PIECES.

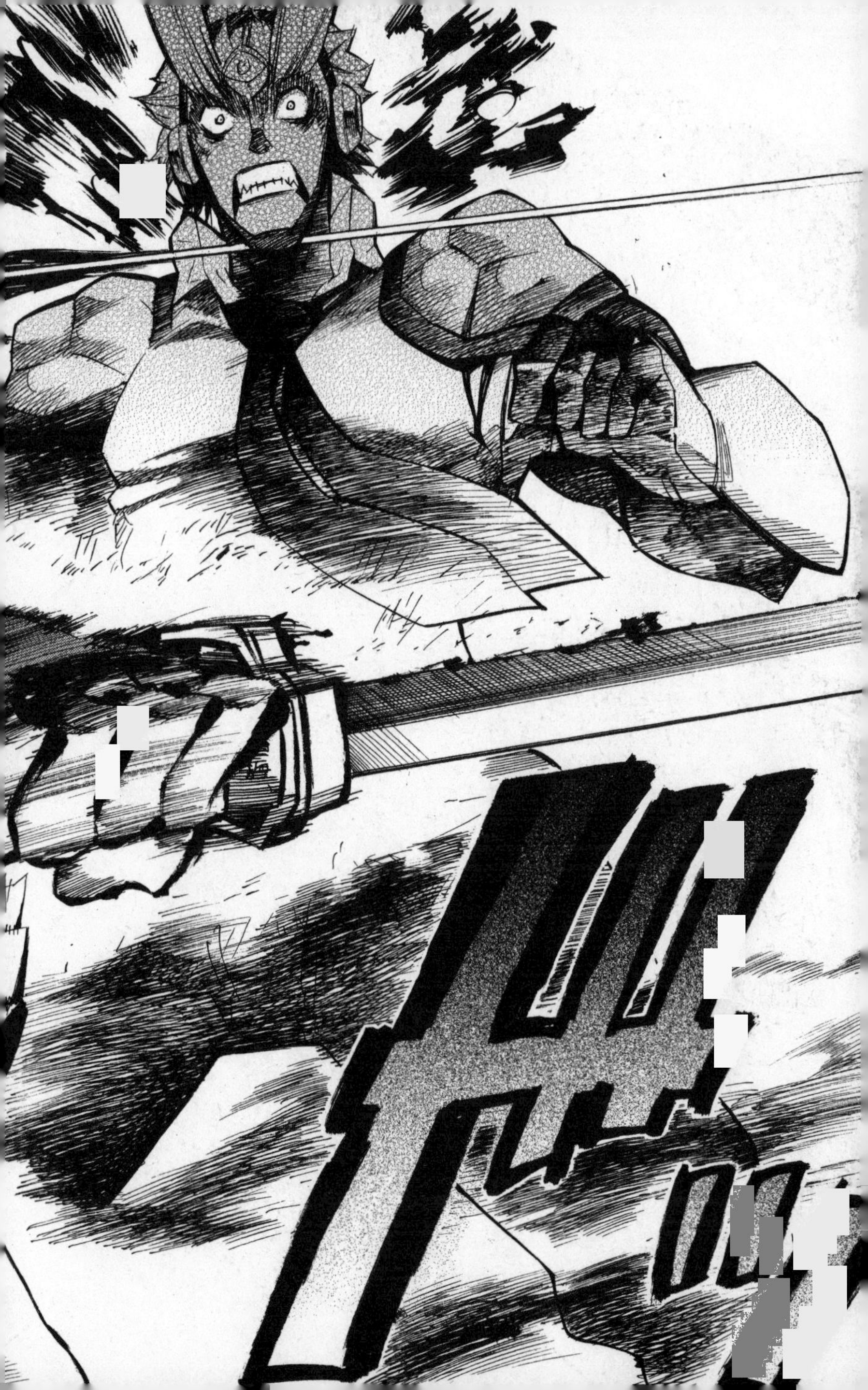

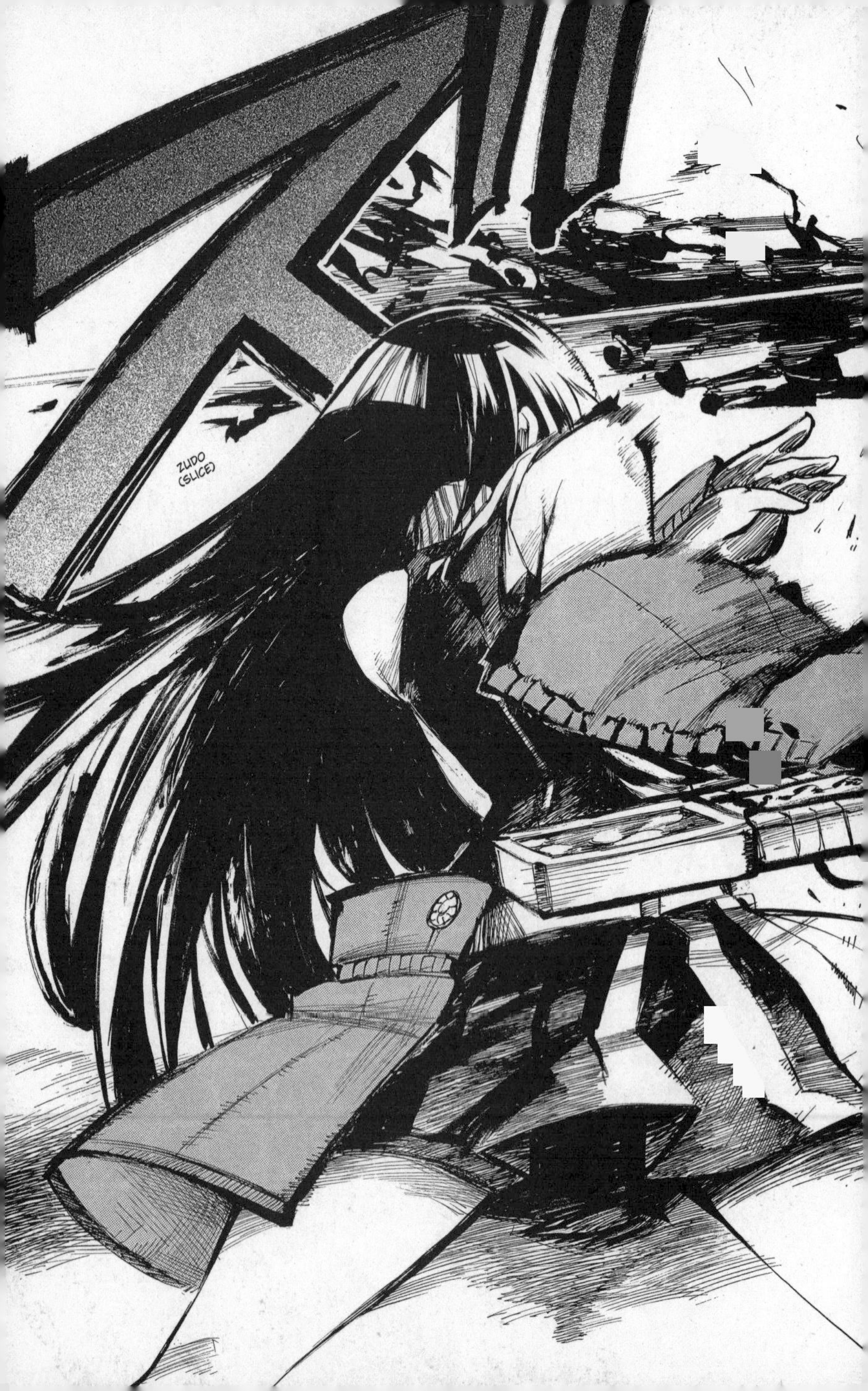
ZUDO
(SLICE)

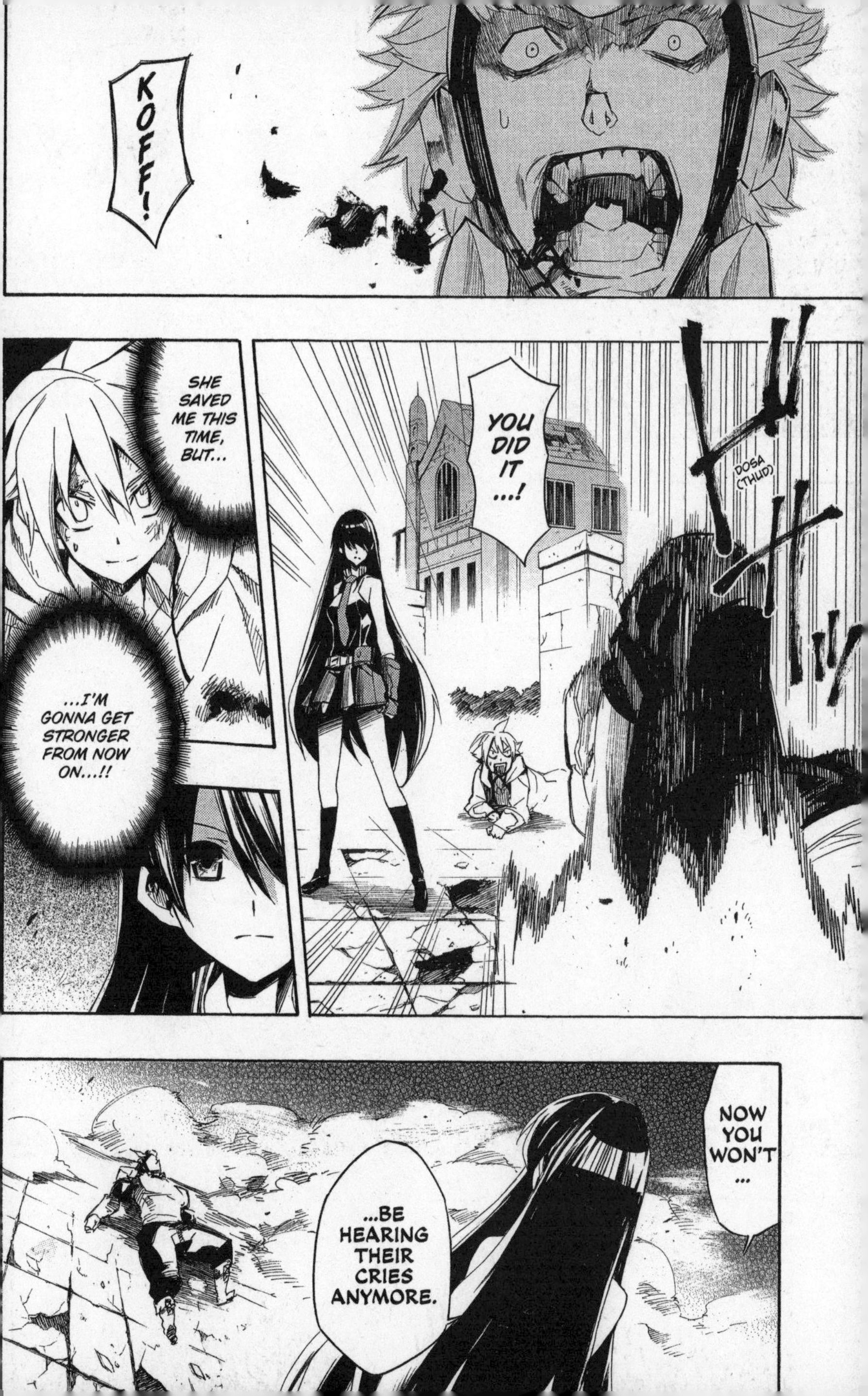
KOFF!
YOU DID IT ...!
DOSA (THUD)
SHE SAVED ME THIS TIME, BUT...
...I'M GONNA GET STRONGER FROM NOW ON...!!
NOW YOU WON'T ...
...BE HEARING THEIR CRIES ANYMORE.

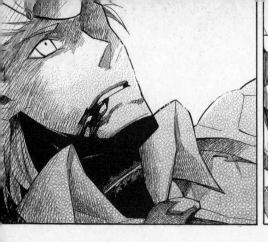

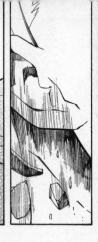

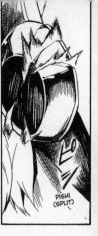

PISHI
(SPLIT)

THE
NOISE...

...STOPPED...

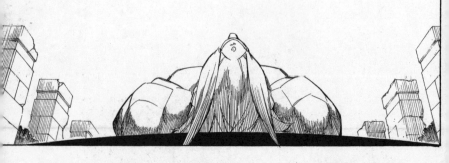

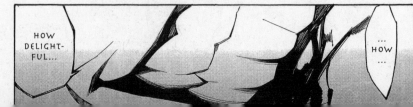

HOW
DELIGHT-
FUL...

...
HOW
...

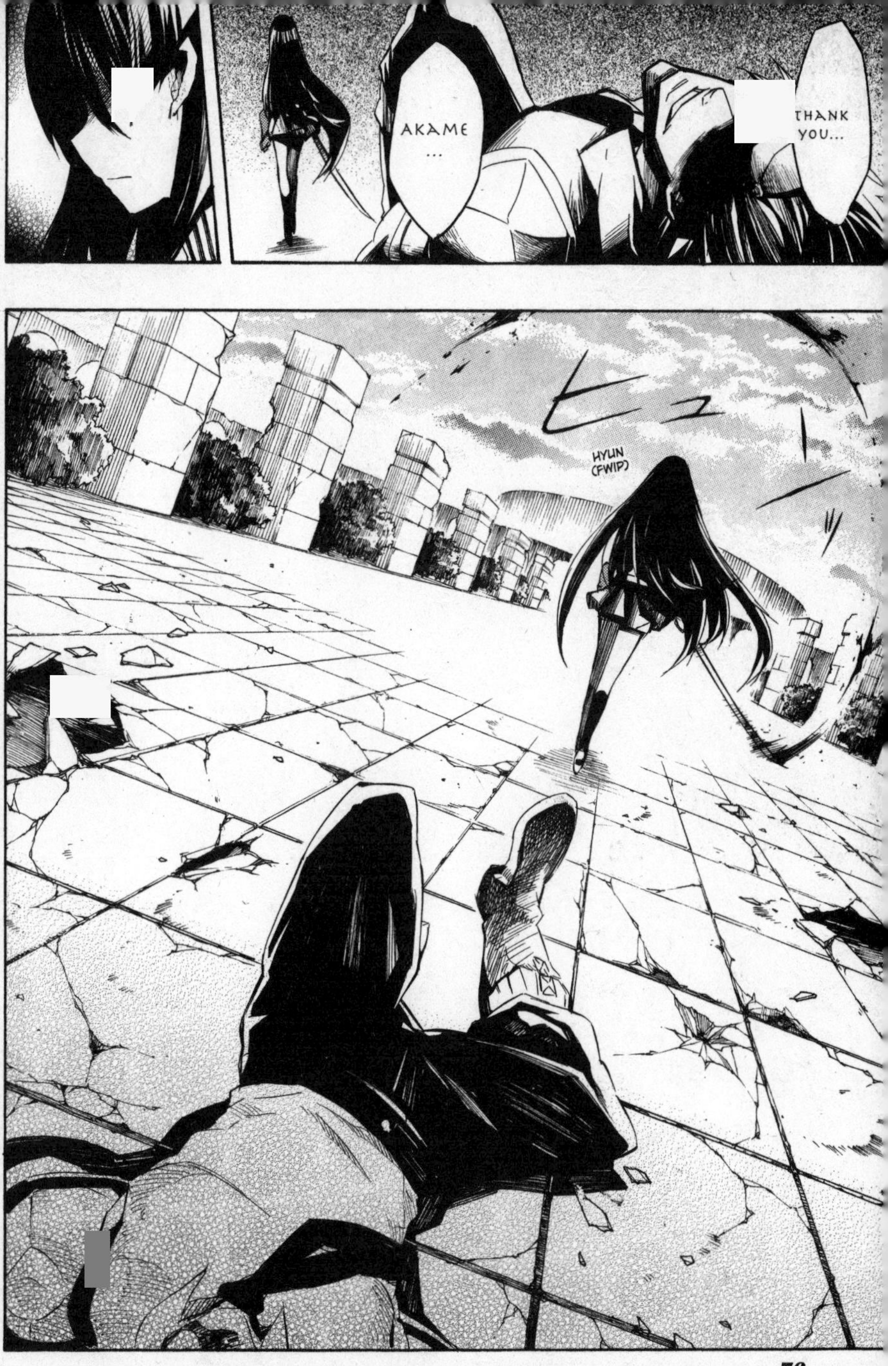
THANK YOU...
AKAME ...
ヒュ
HYUN (FWIP)

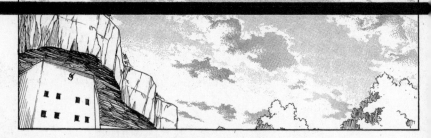

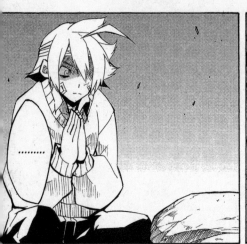

....

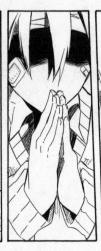

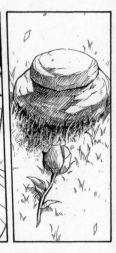

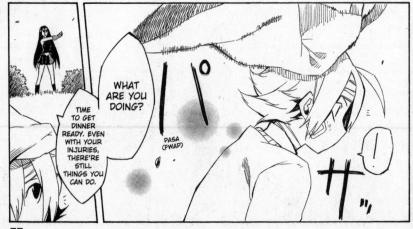

WHAT ARE YOU DOING?

TIME TO GET DINNER READY. EVEN WITH YOUR INJURIES, THERE'RE STILL THINGS YOU CAN DO.

PASA (FWAP)

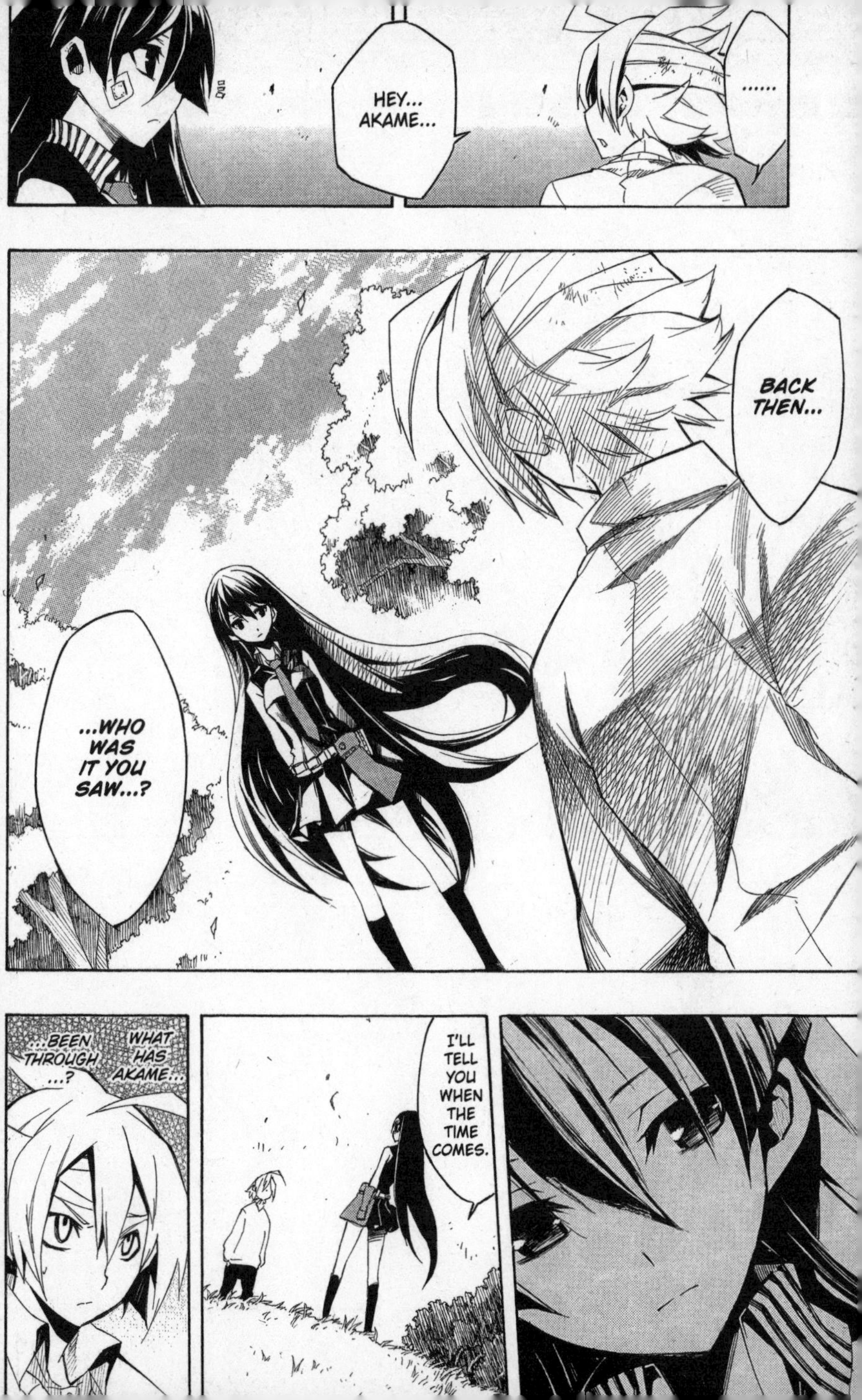
HEY... AKAME...
......
BACK THEN...
...WHO WAS IT YOU SAW...?
I'LL TELL YOU WHEN THE TIME COMES.
WHAT HAS AKAME... ...BEEN THROUGH ...?

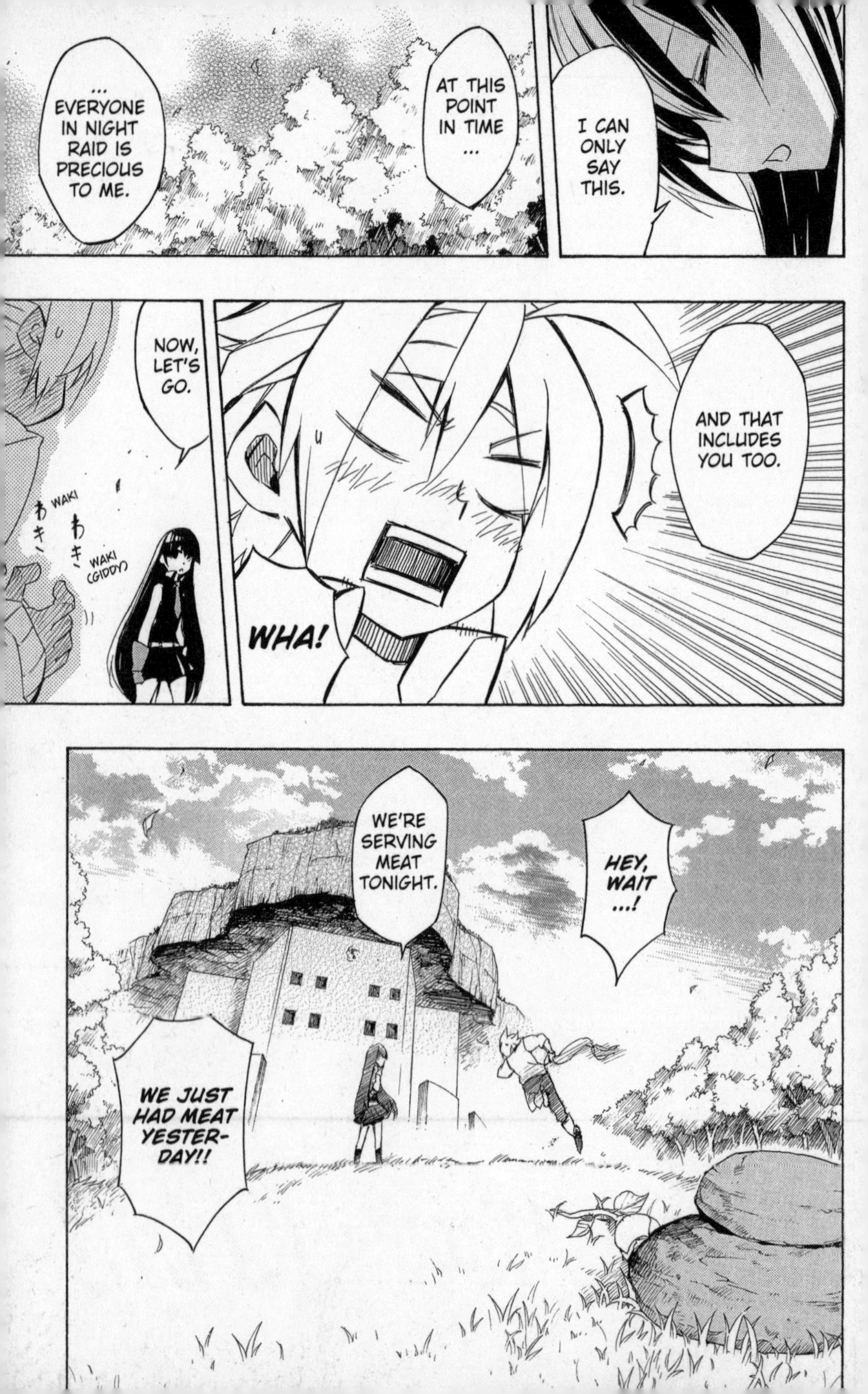
I CAN ONLY SAY THIS.
AT THIS POINT IN TIME ...
... EVERYONE IN NIGHT RAID IS PRECIOUS TO ME.
AND THAT INCLUDES YOU TOO.
WHA!
NOW, LET'S GO.
わき WAKI
わき WAKI (GIDDY)
WE'RE SERVING MEAT TONIGHT.
HEY, WAIT ...!
WE JUST HAD MEAT YESTER-DAY!!

Akame ga KILL!

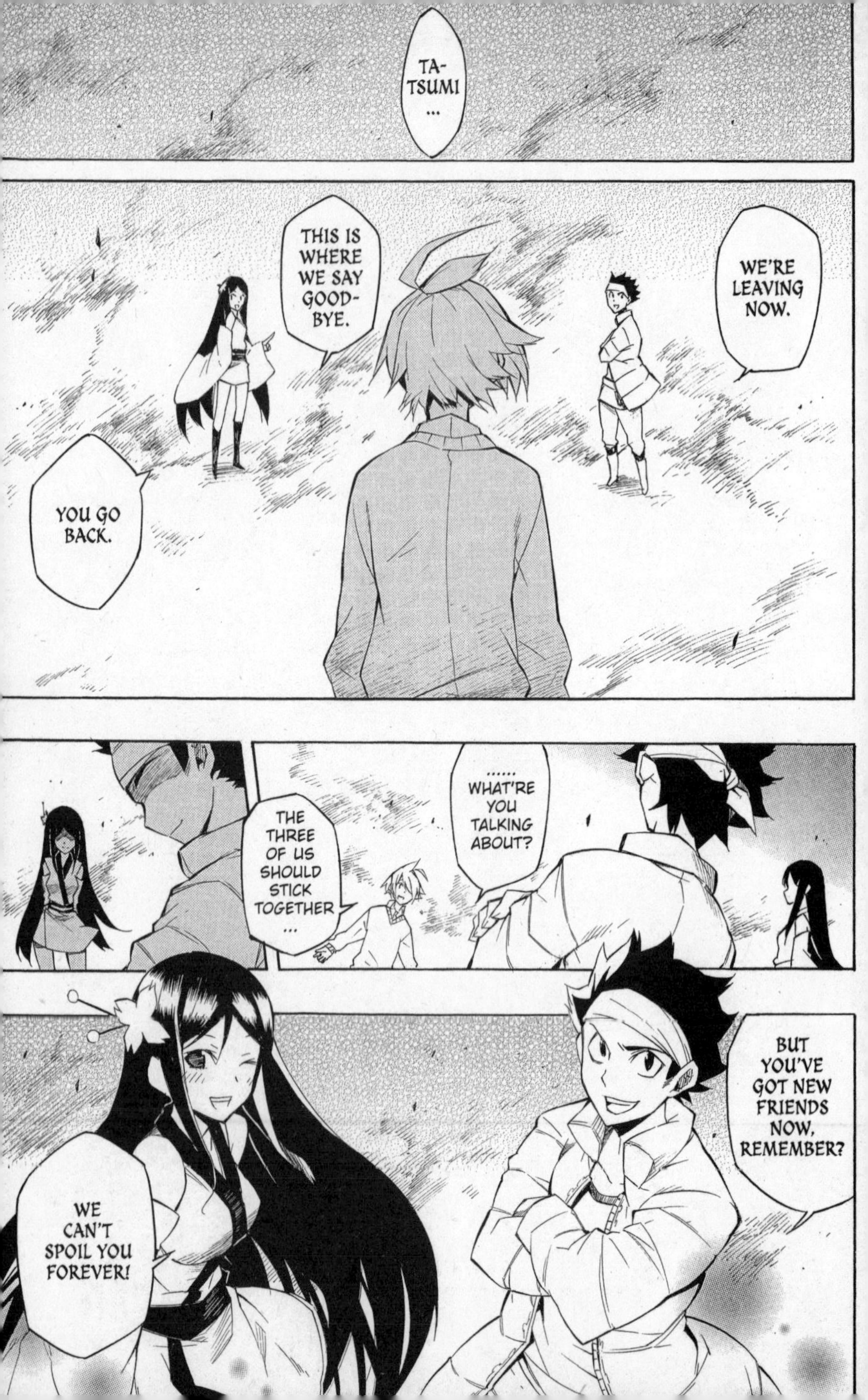
TA-TSUMI ...
WE'RE LEAVING NOW.
THIS IS WHERE WE SAY GOOD-BYE.
YOU GO BACK.
...... WHAT'RE YOU TALKING ABOUT?
THE THREE OF US SHOULD STICK TOGETHER ...
BUT YOU'VE GOT NEW FRIENDS NOW, REMEMBER?
WE CAN'T SPOIL YOU FOREVER!

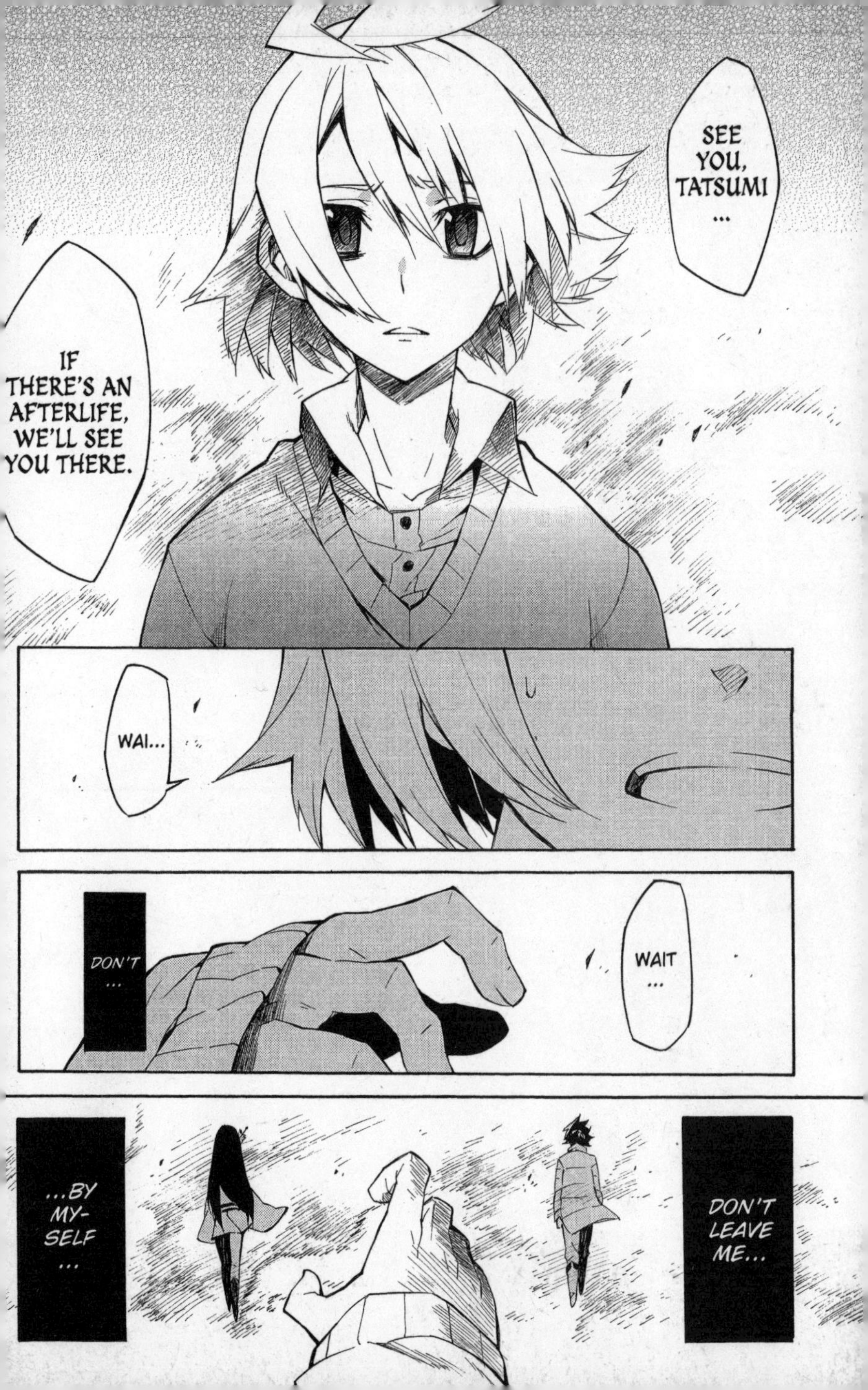
SEE YOU, TATSUMI ...
IF THERE'S AN AFTERLIFE, WE'LL SEE YOU THERE.
WAI...
WAIT ...
DON'T ...
DON'T LEAVE ME...
...BY MY-SELF ...

Chapter 7 Kill the Fantasy

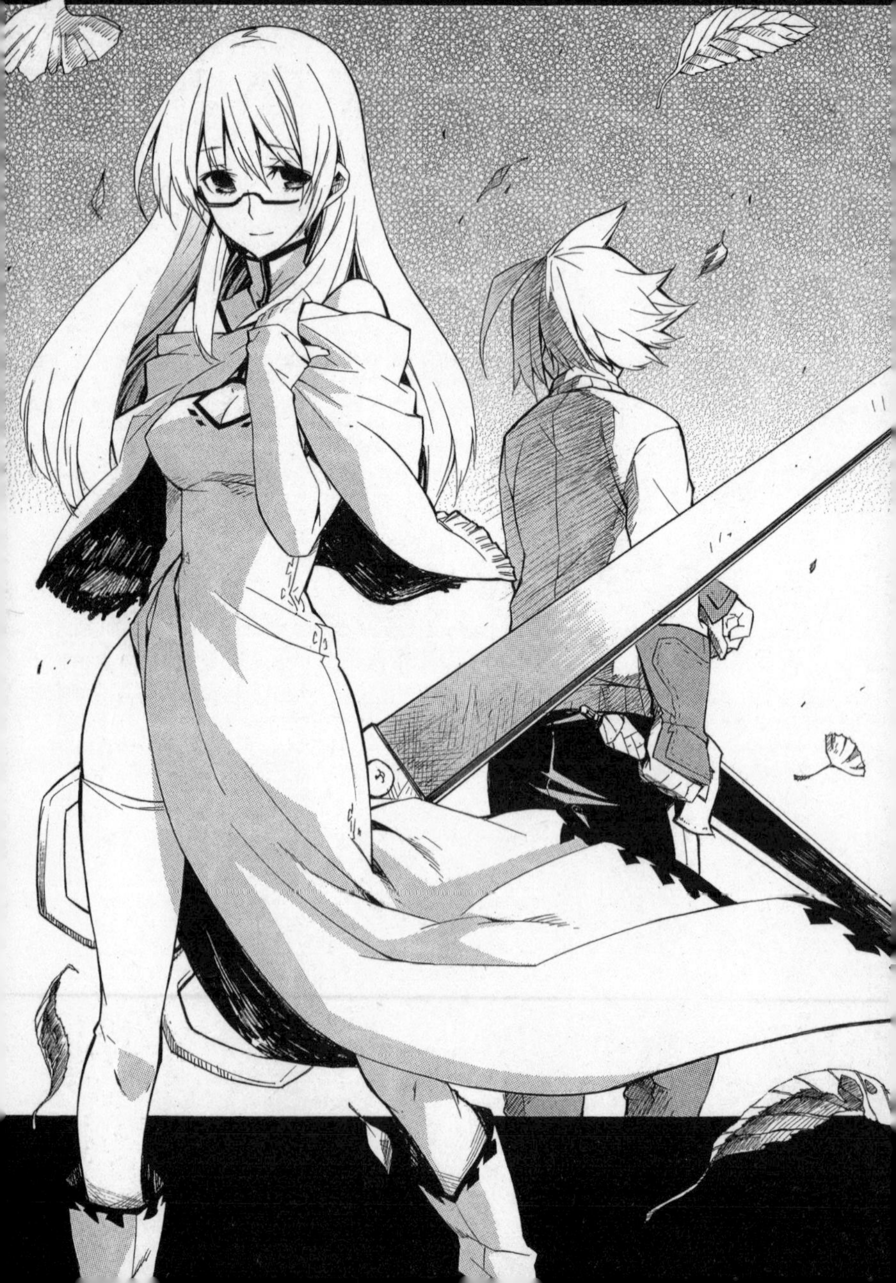

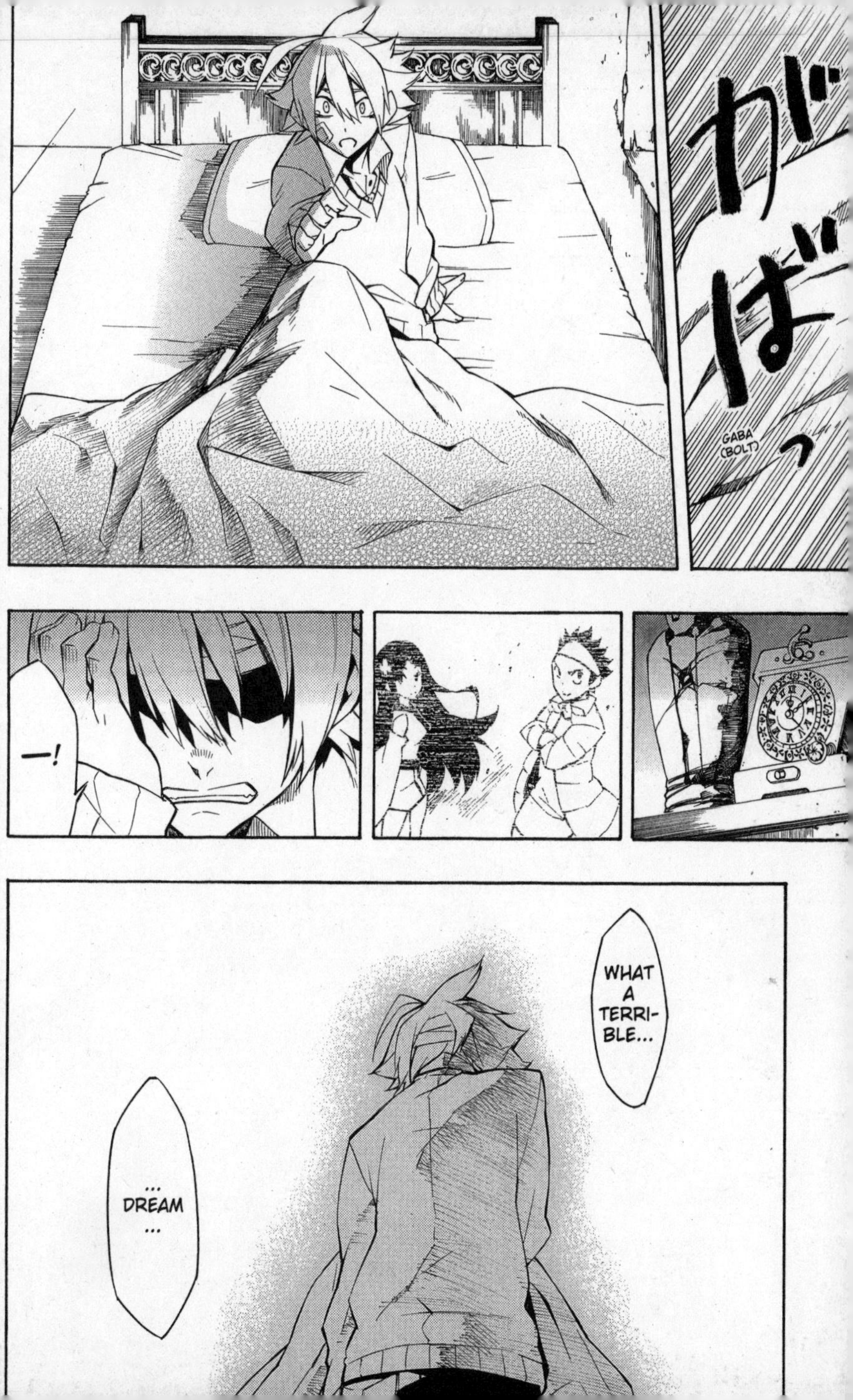
がばっ
GABA (BOLT)
—!
WHAT A TERRI-BLE...
...DREAM...

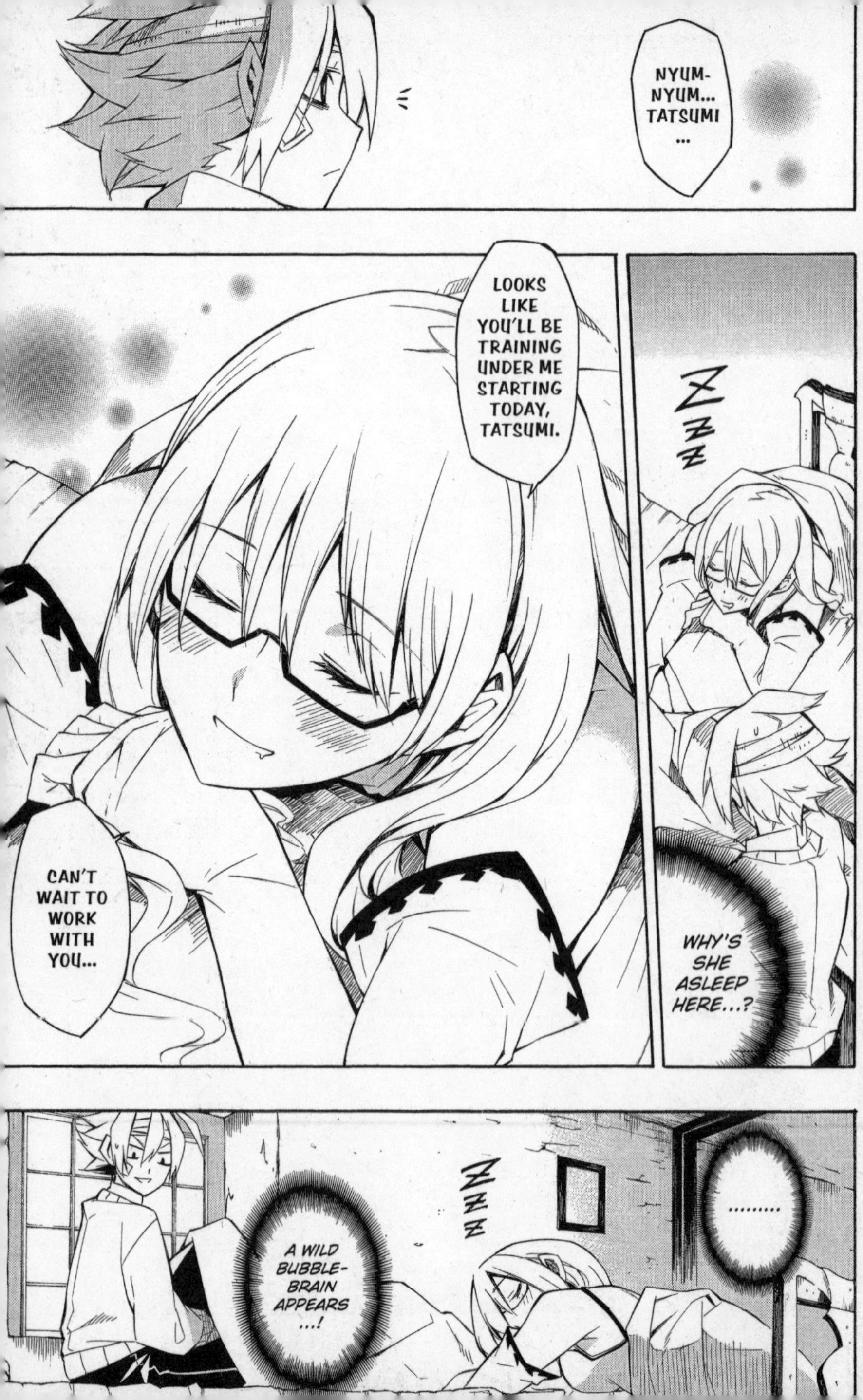
NYUM-NYUM... TATSUMI ...
ZZZ
WHY'S SHE ASLEEP HERE...?
LOOKS LIKE YOU'LL BE TRAINING UNDER ME STARTING TODAY, TATSUMI.
CAN'T WAIT TO WORK WITH YOU...
....
ZZZ
A WILD BUBBLE-BRAIN APPEARS ...!

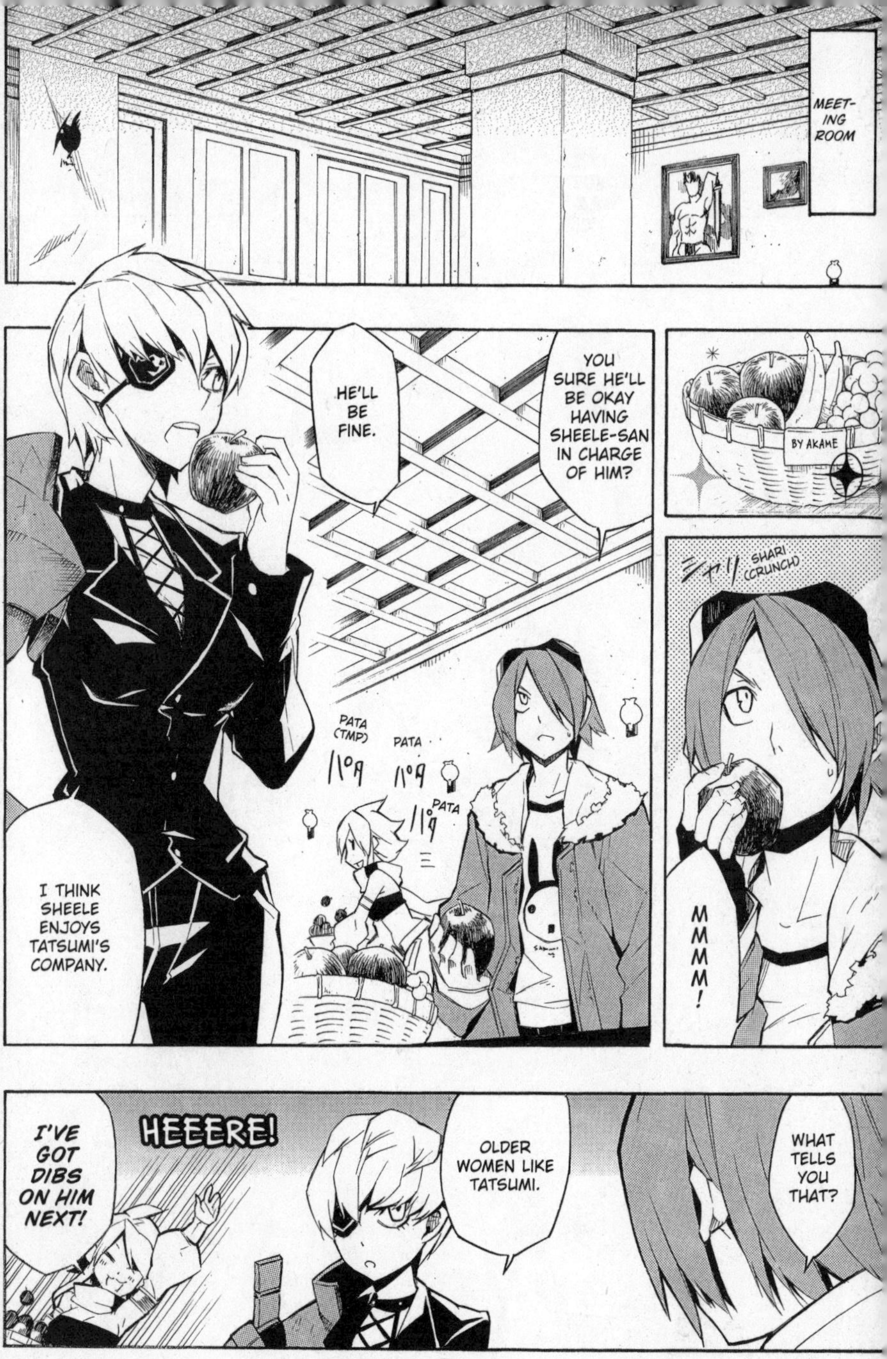
MEETING ROOM
BY AKAME
SHARI (CRUNCH)
MMMM!
YOU SURE HE'LL BE OKAY HAVING SHEELE-SAN IN CHARGE OF HIM?
HE'LL BE FINE.
PATA (TMP)
PATA
PATA
I THINK SHEELE ENJOYS TATSUMI'S COMPANY.
WHAT TELLS YOU THAT?
OLDER WOMEN LIKE TATSUMI.
HEEEERE!
I'VE GOT DIBS ON HIM NEXT!

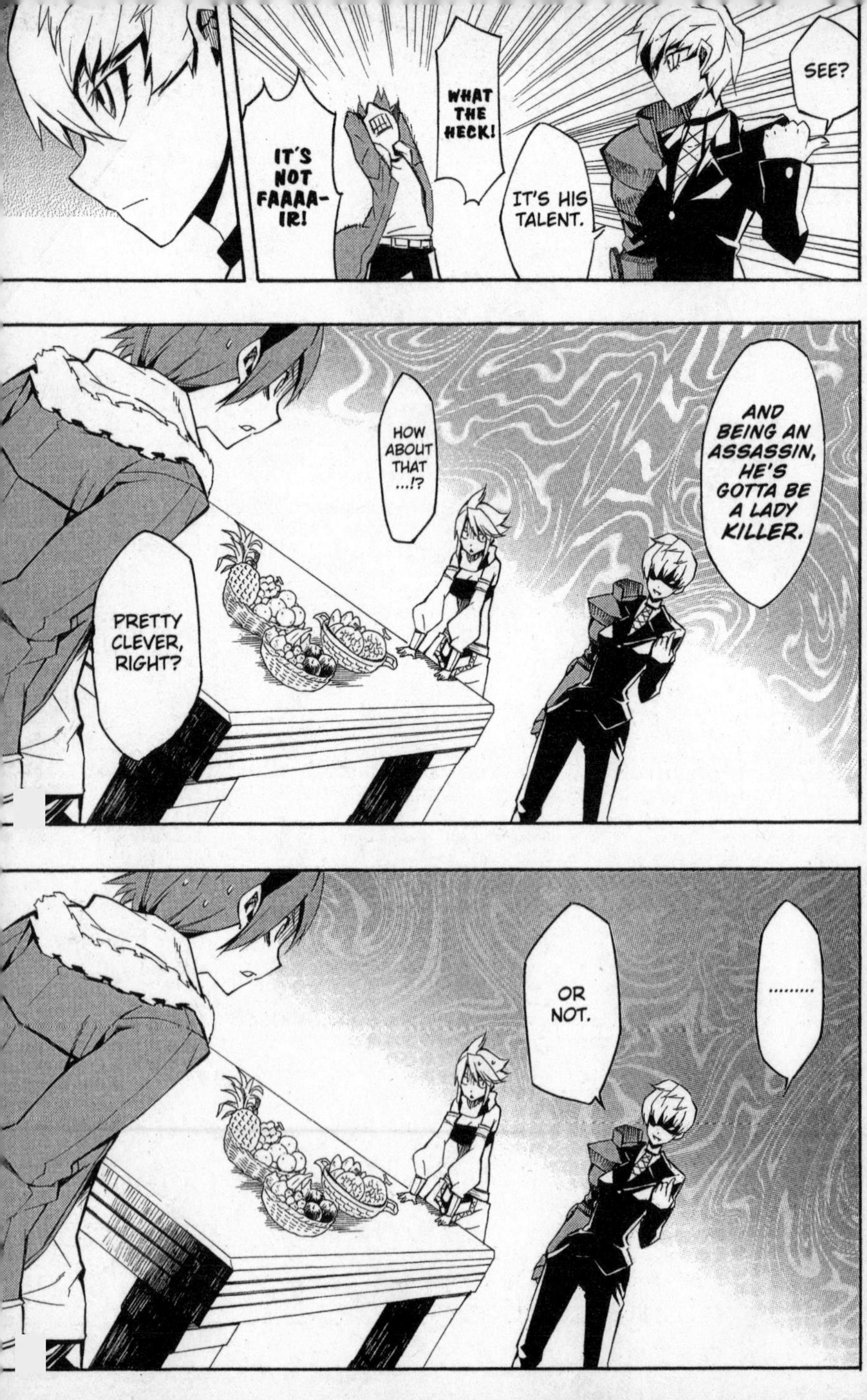
SEE?
IT'S HIS TALENT.
WHAT THE HECK!
IT'S NOT FAAAA-IR!
AND BEING AN ASSASSIN, HE'S GOTTA BE A LADY KILLER.
HOW ABOUT THAT ...!?
PRETTY CLEVER, RIGHT?
....
OR NOT.

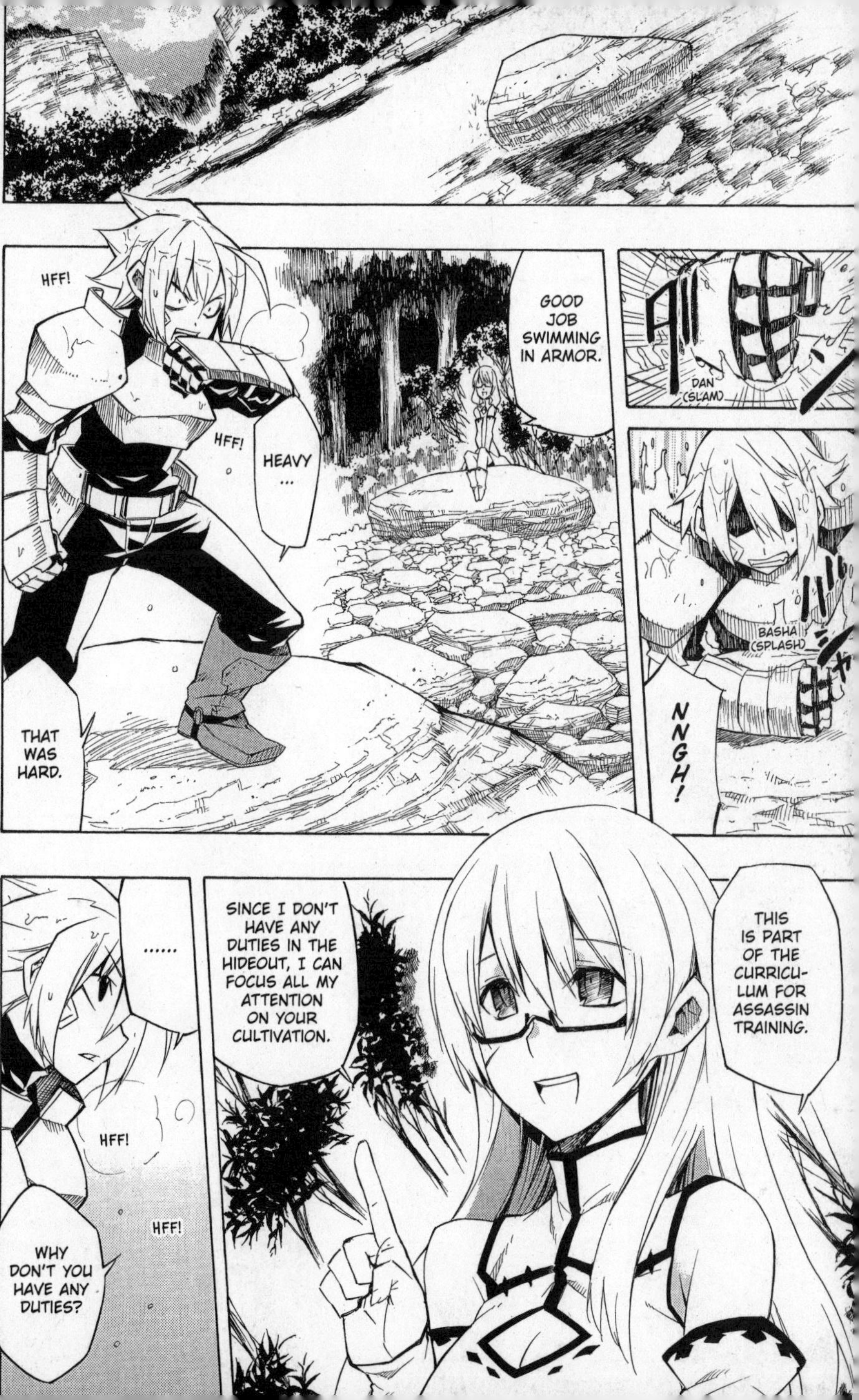
DAN (SLAM)
BASHA (SPLASH)
NNGH!
GOOD JOB SWIMMING IN ARMOR.
HEAVY ...
HFF!
HFF!
THAT WAS HARD.
THIS IS PART OF THE CURRICU-LUM FOR ASSASSIN TRAINING.
SINCE I DON'T HAVE ANY DUTIES IN THE HIDEOUT, I CAN FOCUS ALL MY ATTENTION ON YOUR CULTIVATION.
......
HFF!
HFF!
WHY DON'T YOU HAVE ANY DUTIES?

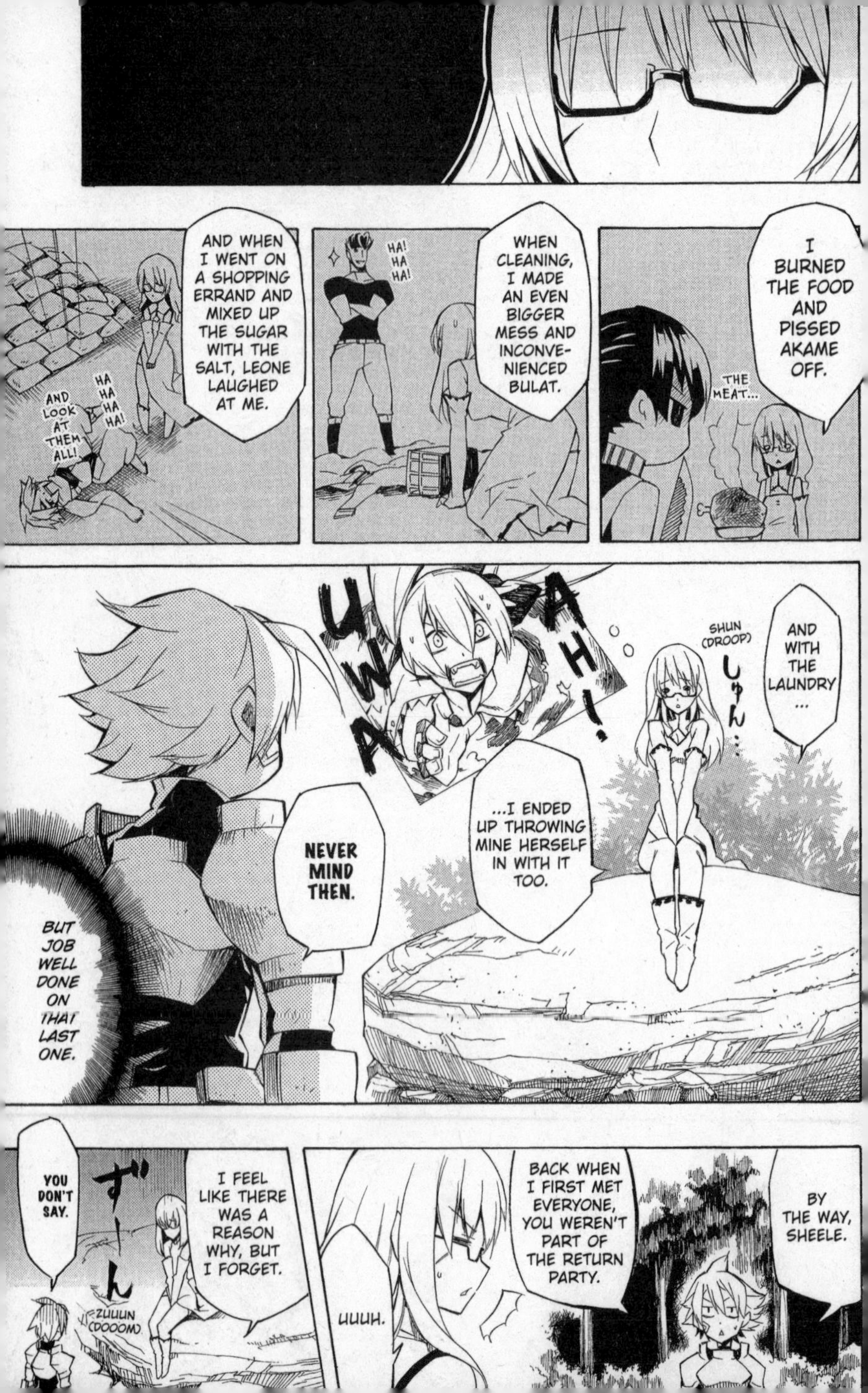
I BURNED THE FOOD AND PISSED AKAME OFF.
THE MEAT...
WHEN CLEANING, I MADE AN EVEN BIGGER MESS AND INCONVENIENCED BULAT.
HA! HA HA!
AND WHEN I WENT ON A SHOPPING ERRAND AND MIXED UP THE SUGAR WITH THE SALT, LEONE LAUGHED AT ME.
HA HA HA HA!
AND LOOK AT THEM ALL!
AND WITH THE LAUNDRY...
SHUN (DROOP)
しゅん…
...I ENDED UP THROWING MINE HERSELF IN WITH IT TOO.
UWAAH!
NEVER MIND THEN.
BUT JOB WELL DONE ON THAT LAST ONE.
BY THE WAY, SHEELE.
BACK WHEN I FIRST MET EVERYONE, YOU WEREN'T PART OF THE RETURN PARTY.
UUUH.
I FEEL LIKE THERE WAS A REASON WHY, BUT I FORGET.
ずーん
ZUUUN (DOOOM)
YOU DON'T SAY.

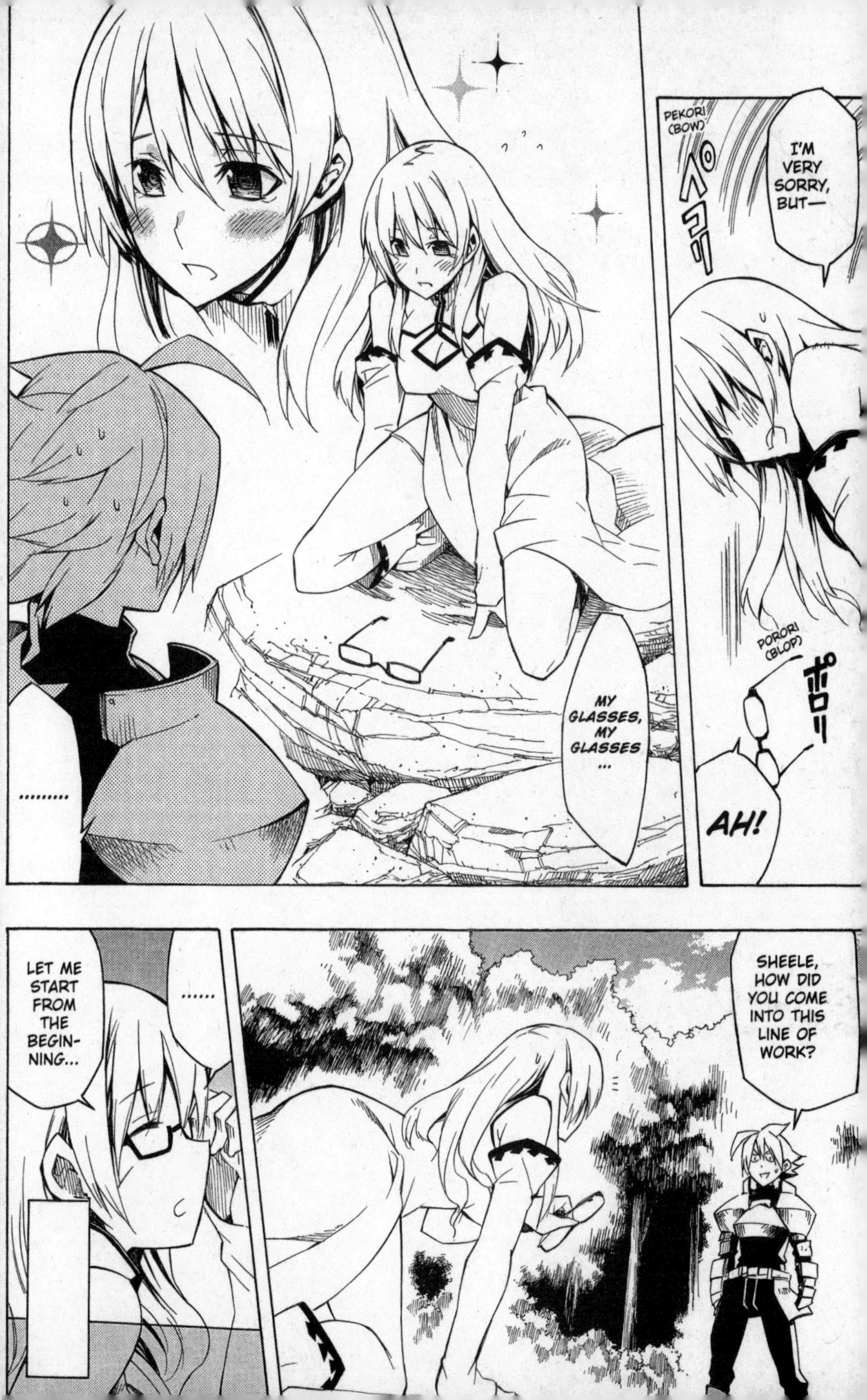

I'M VERY SORRY, BUT—
PEKORI (BOW)
POROR (BLOP)
AH!
MY GLASSES, MY GLASSES...
....
SHEELE, HOW DID YOU COME INTO THIS LINE OF WORK?
......
LET ME START FROM THE BEGIN-NING...

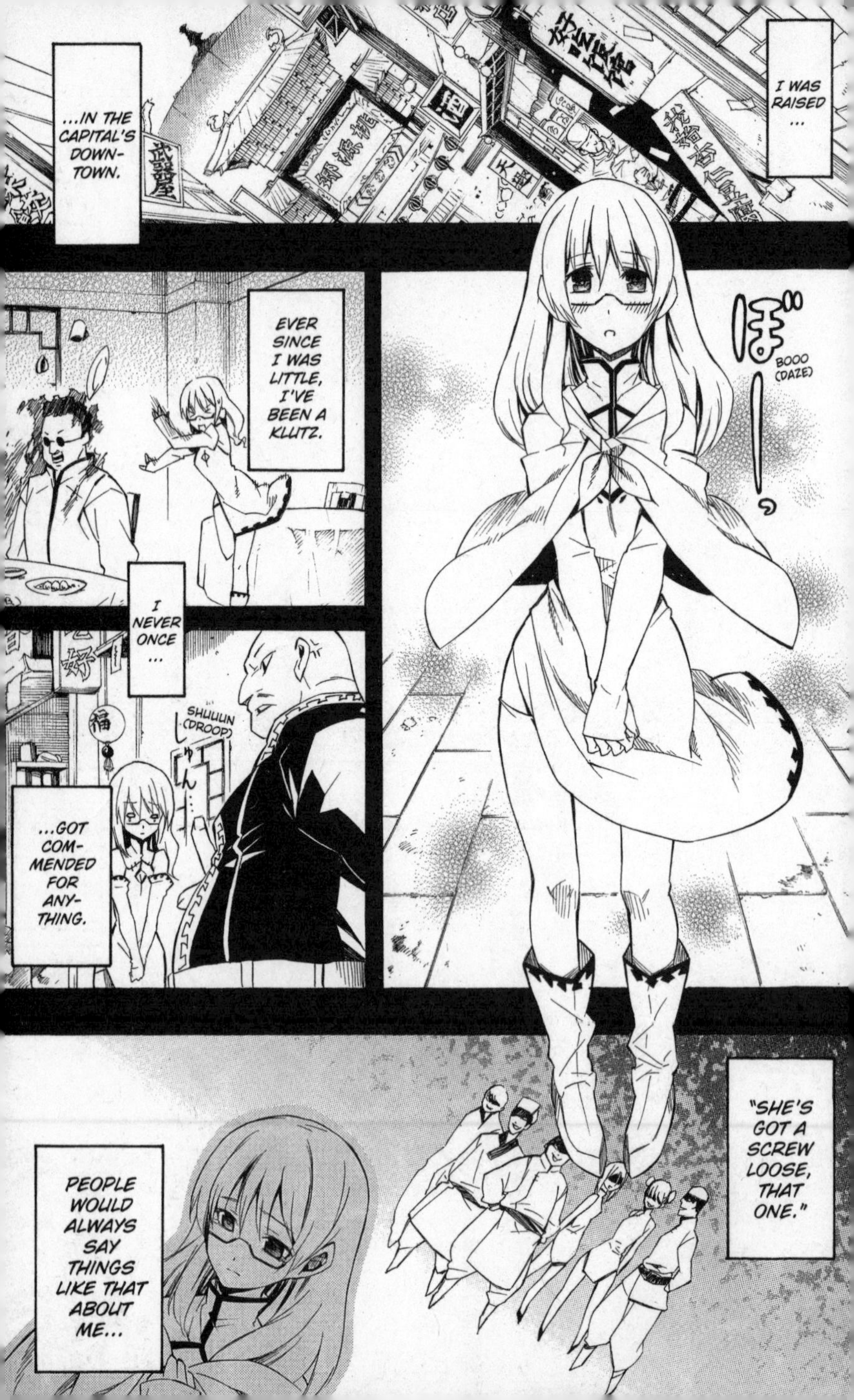

I WAS RAISED...
...IN THE CAPITAL'S DOWN-TOWN.
ぼーっ
BOOO (DAZE)
EVER SINCE I WAS LITTLE, I'VE BEEN A KLUTZ.
I NEVER ONCE...
しゅん…
SHUUUN (DROOP)
...GOT COM-MENDED FOR ANY-THING.
"SHE'S GOT A SCREW LOOSE, THAT ONE."
PEOPLE WOULD ALWAYS SAY THINGS LIKE THAT ABOUT ME...

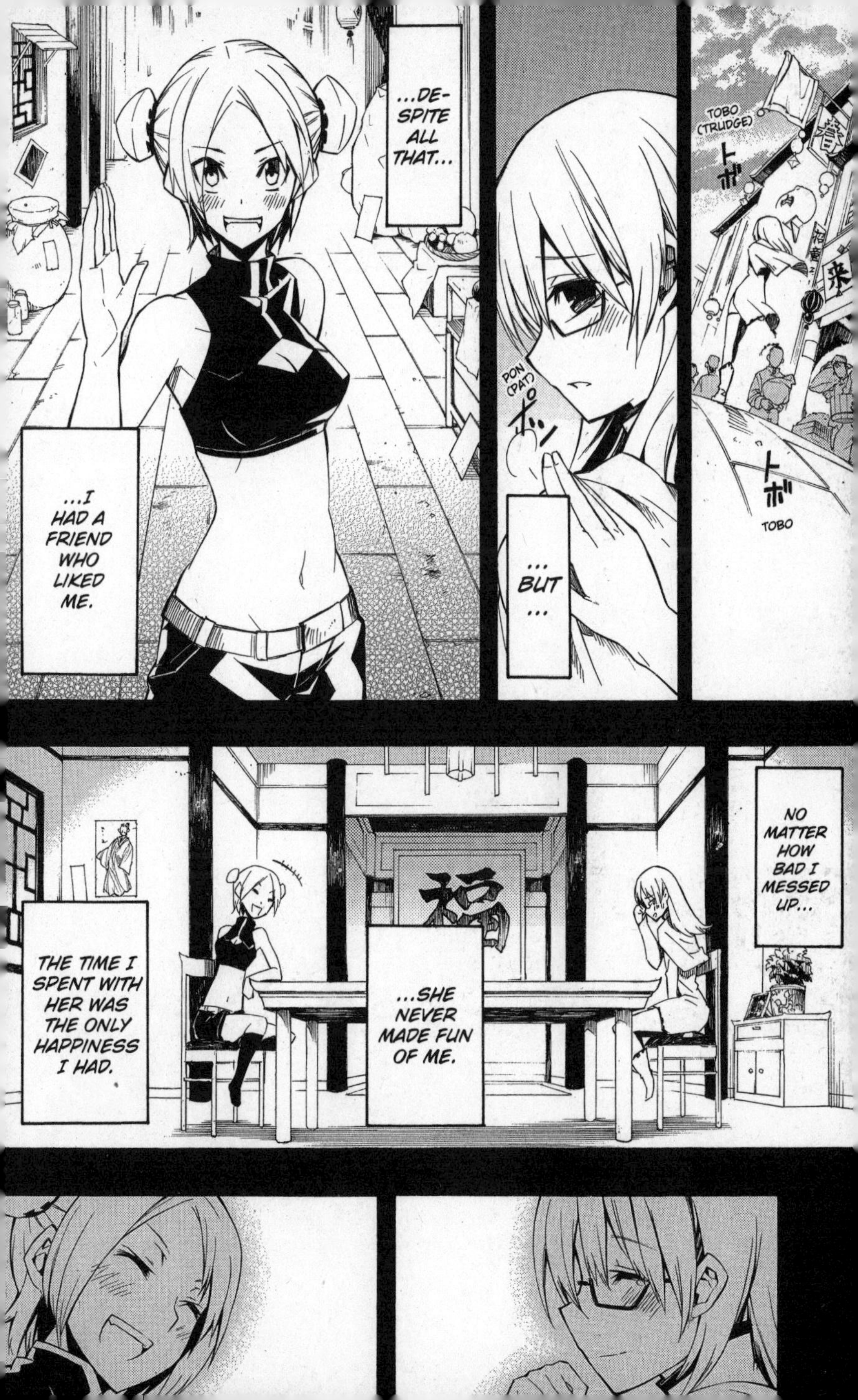

TOBO (TRUDGE)
トボ
トボ
TOBO
PON (PAT)
ポン
...BUT...
...DE-SPITE ALL THAT...
...I HAD A FRIEND WHO LIKED ME.
NO MATTER HOW BAD I MESSED UP...
...SHE NEVER MADE FUN OF ME.
THE TIME I SPENT WITH HER WAS THE ONLY HAPPINESS I HAD.

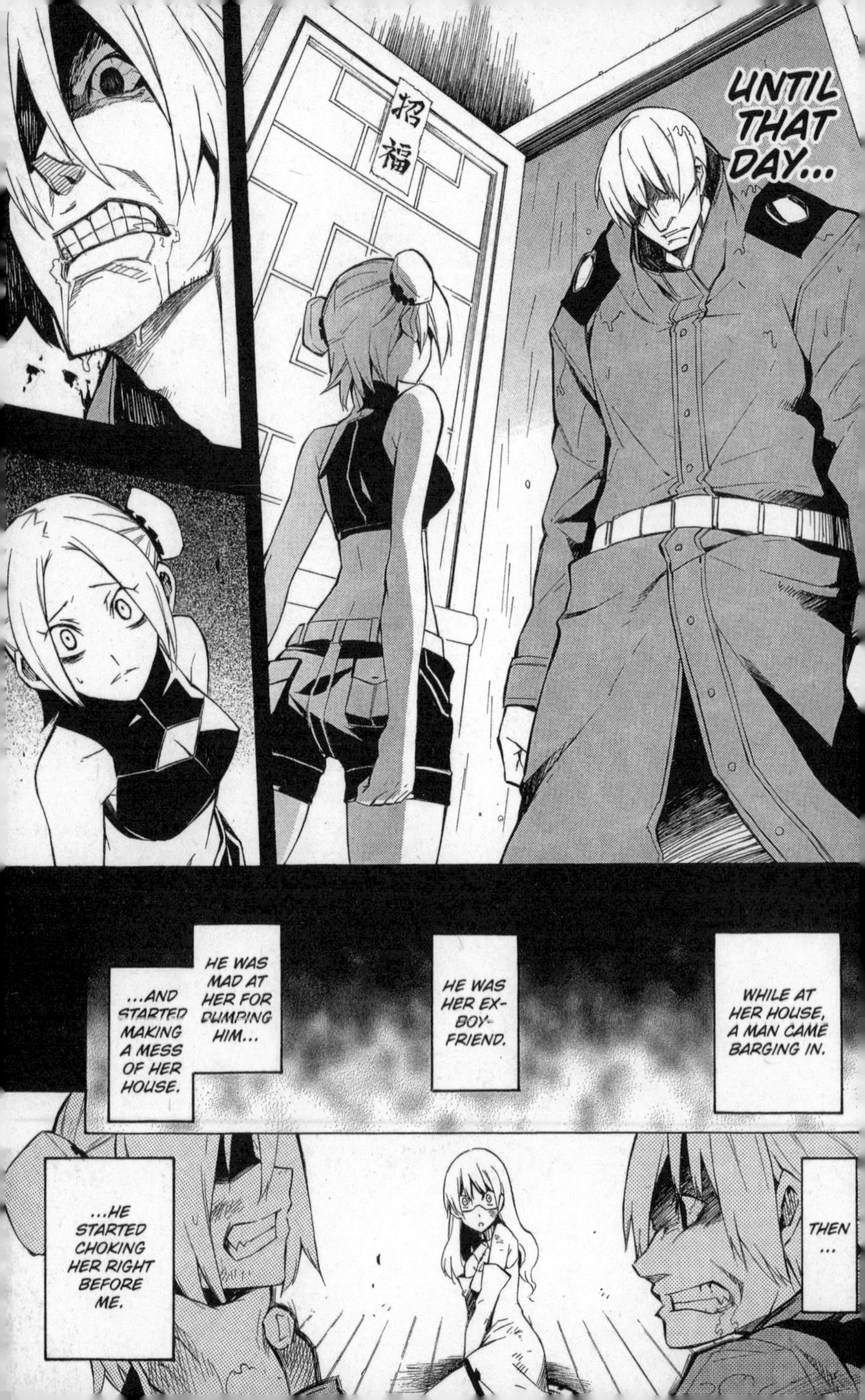
UNTIL THAT DAY...
招福
WHILE AT HER HOUSE, A MAN CAME BARGING IN.
HE WAS HER EX-BOY-FRIEND.
HE WAS MAD AT HER FOR DUMPING HIM...
...AND STARTED MAKING A MESS OF HER HOUSE.
THEN...
...HE STARTED CHOKING HER RIGHT BEFORE ME.

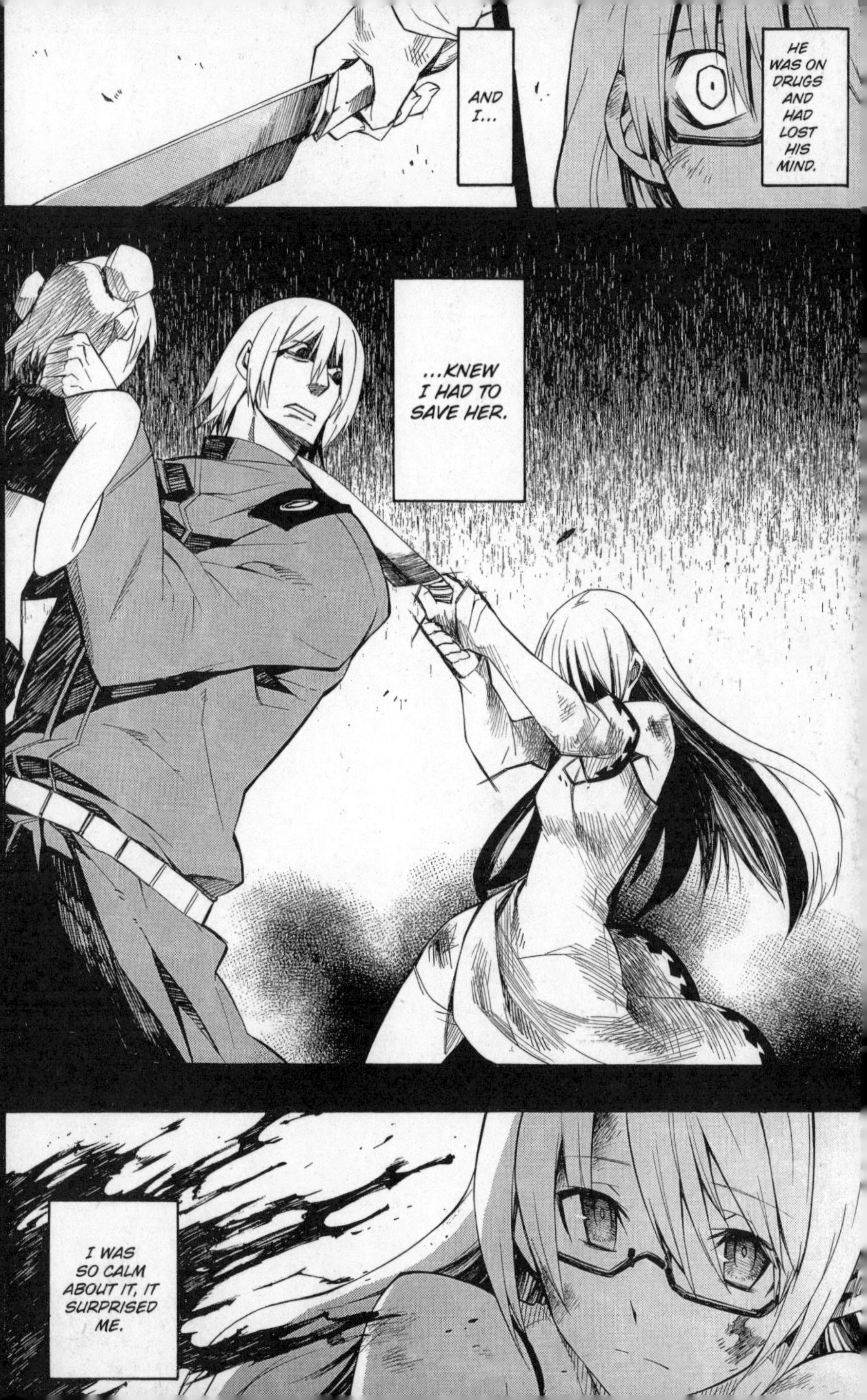
HE WAS ON DRUGS AND HAD LOST HIS MIND.
AND I...
...KNEW I HAD TO SAVE HER.
I WAS SO CALM ABOUT IT, IT SURPRISED ME.

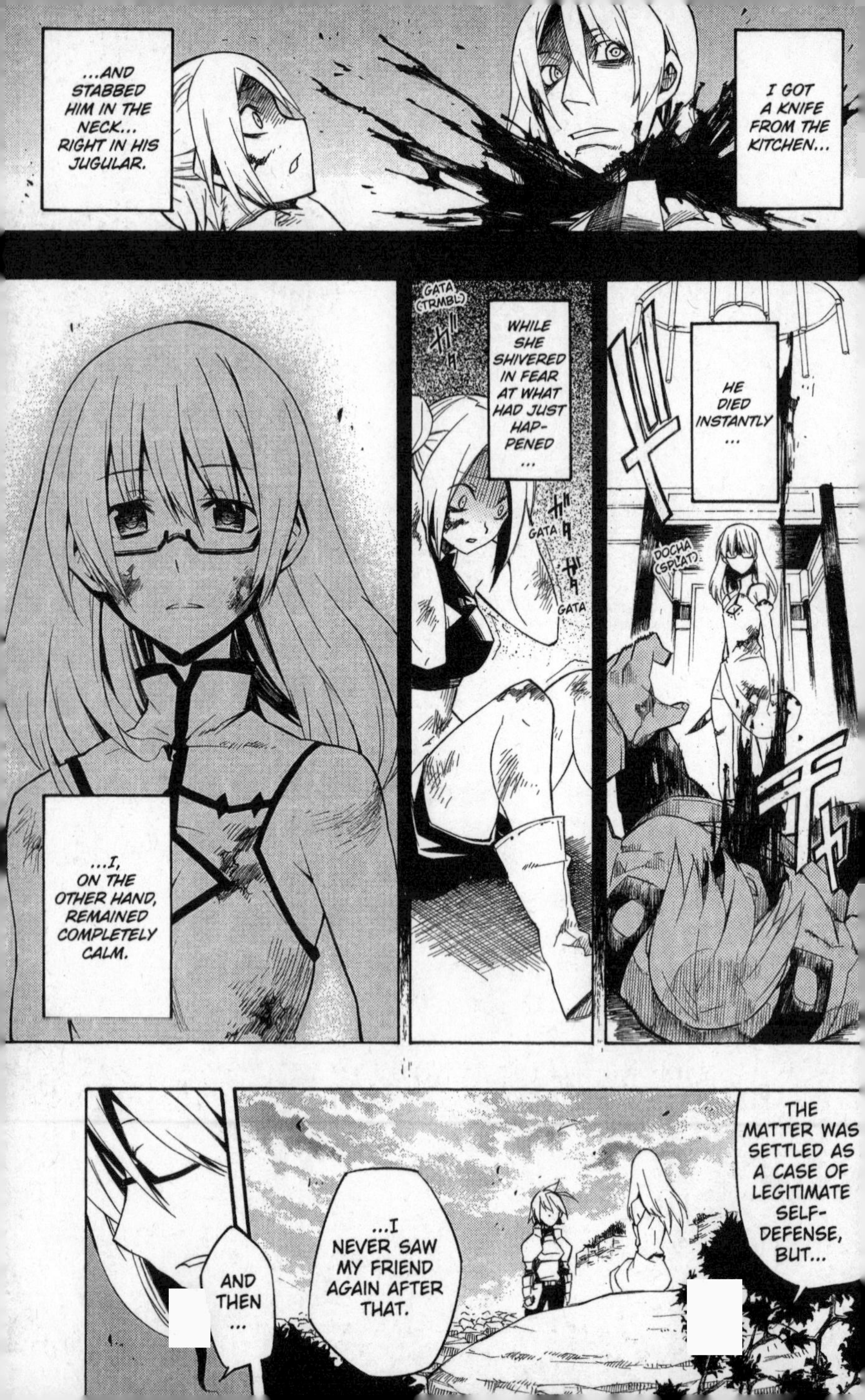
I GOT A KNIFE FROM THE KITCHEN...
...AND STABBED HIM IN THE NECK... RIGHT IN HIS JUGULAR.
HE DIED INSTANTLY ...
DOCHA (SPLAT)
GATA (TRMBL)
WHILE SHE SHIVERED IN FEAR AT WHAT HAD JUST HAP-PENED ...
GATA
GATA
...I, ON THE OTHER HAND, REMAINED COMPLETELY CALM.
THE MATTER WAS SETTLED AS A CASE OF LEGITIMATE SELF-DEFENSE, BUT...
...I NEVER SAW MY FRIEND AGAIN AFTER THAT.
AND THEN ...

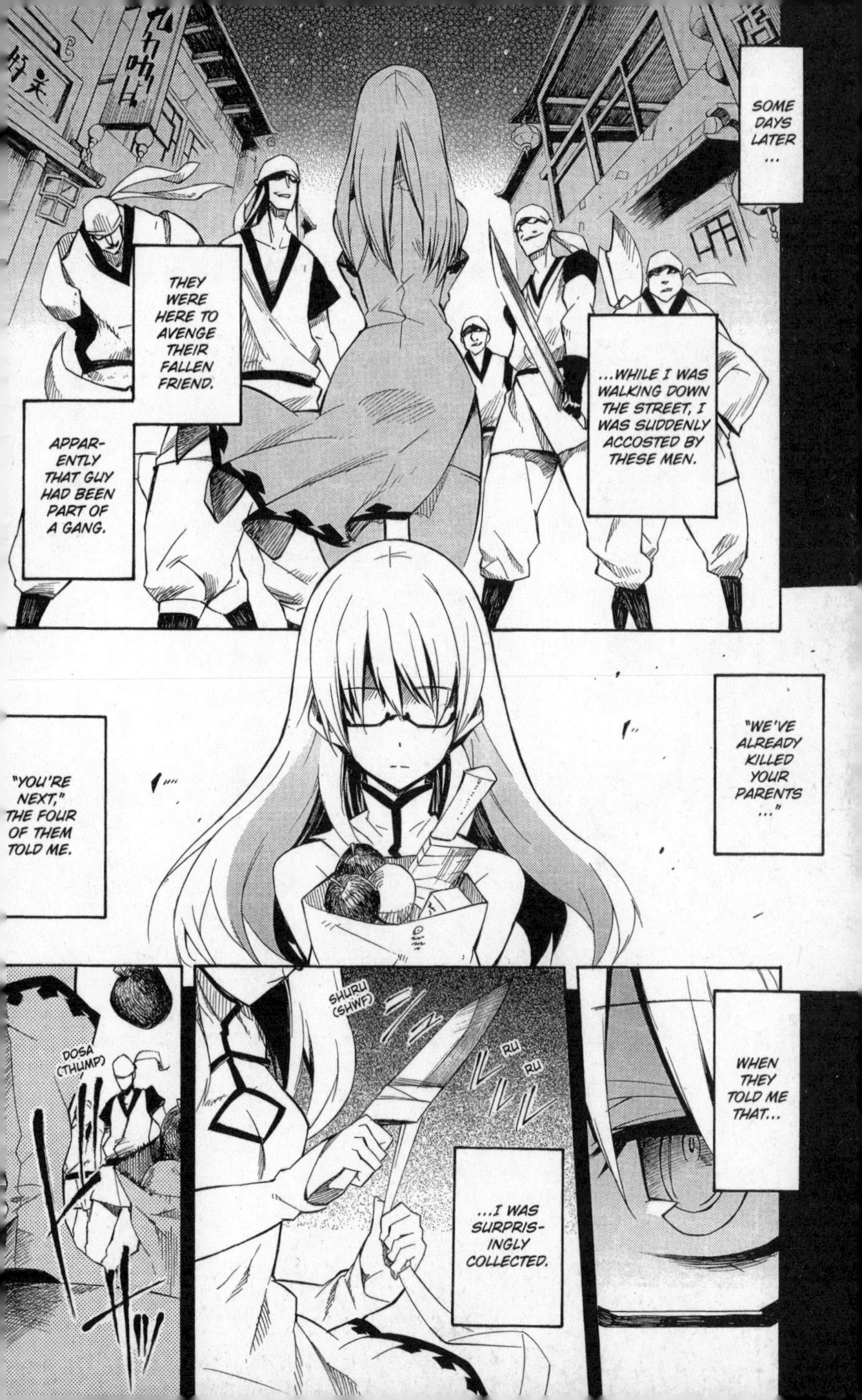
SOME DAYS LATER...
...WHILE I WAS WALKING DOWN THE STREET, I WAS SUDDENLY ACCOSTED BY THESE MEN.
THEY WERE HERE TO AVENGE THEIR FALLEN FRIEND.
APPAR-ENTLY THAT GUY HAD BEEN PART OF A GANG.
"WE'VE ALREADY KILLED YOUR PARENTS..."
"YOU'RE NEXT," THE FOUR OF THEM TOLD ME.
WHEN THEY TOLD ME THAT...
SHURU (SHWF)
RU RU
...I WAS SURPRIS-INGLY COLLECTED.
DOSA (THUMP)

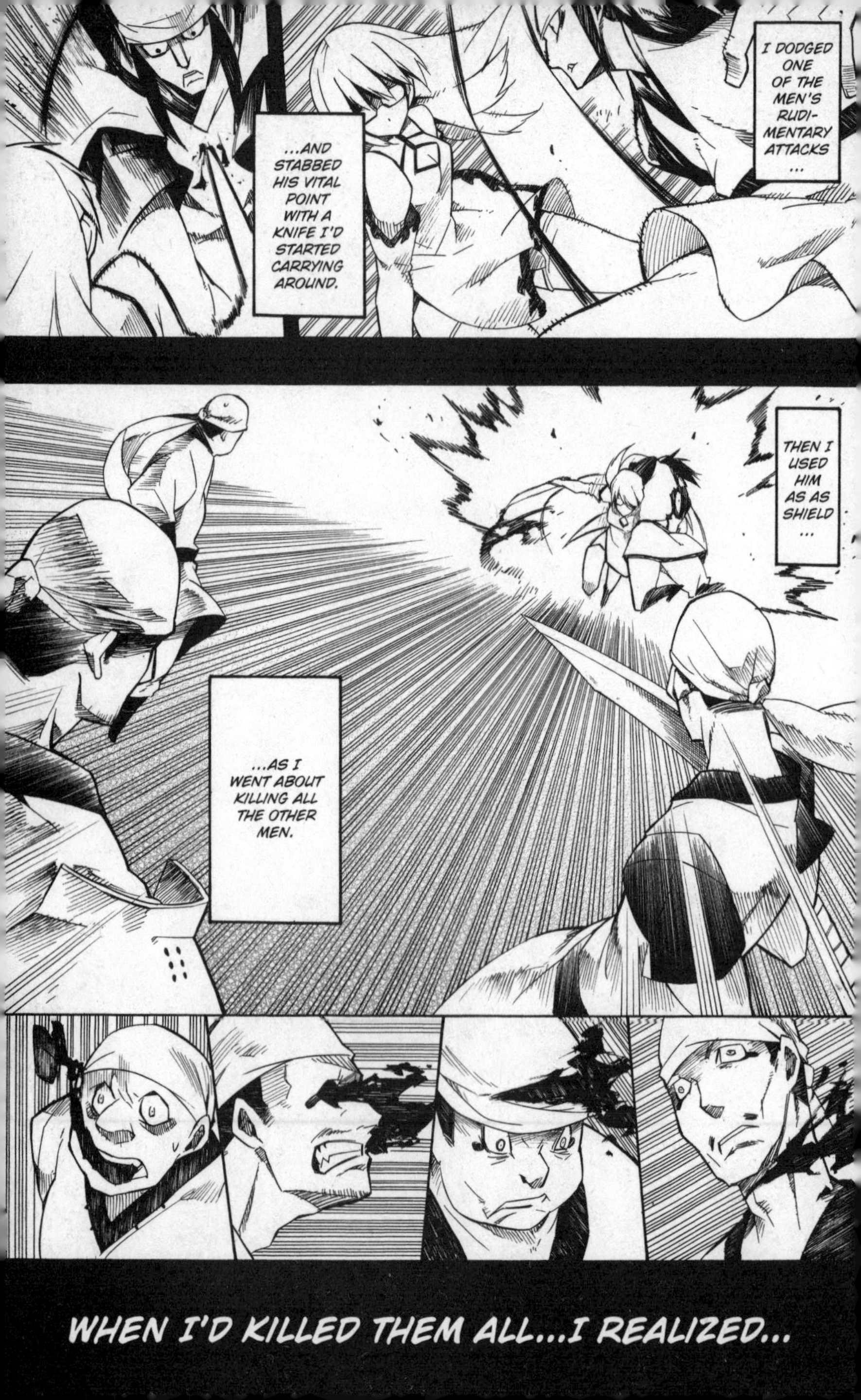
I DODGED ONE OF THE MEN'S RUDIMENTARY ATTACKS...
...AND STABBED HIS VITAL POINT WITH A KNIFE I'D STARTED CARRYING AROUND.
THEN I USED HIM AS AS SHIELD...
...AS I WENT ABOUT KILLING ALL THE OTHER MEN.
WHEN I'D KILLED THEM ALL...I REALIZED...

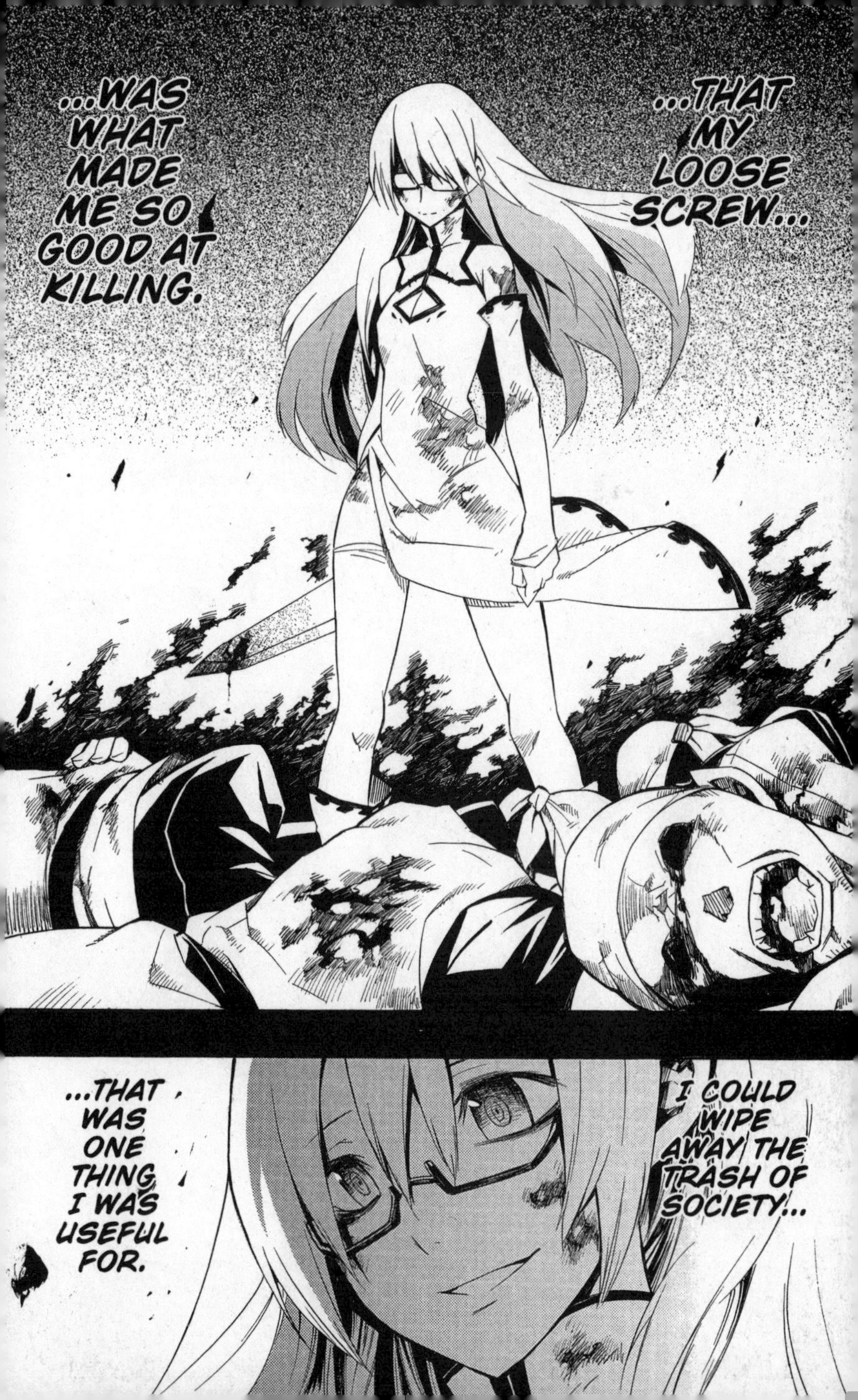
...THAT MY LOOSE SCREW...
...WAS WHAT MADE ME SO GOOD AT KILLING.
I COULD WIPE AWAY THE TRASH OF SOCIETY...
...THAT WAS ONE THING I WAS USEFUL FOR.

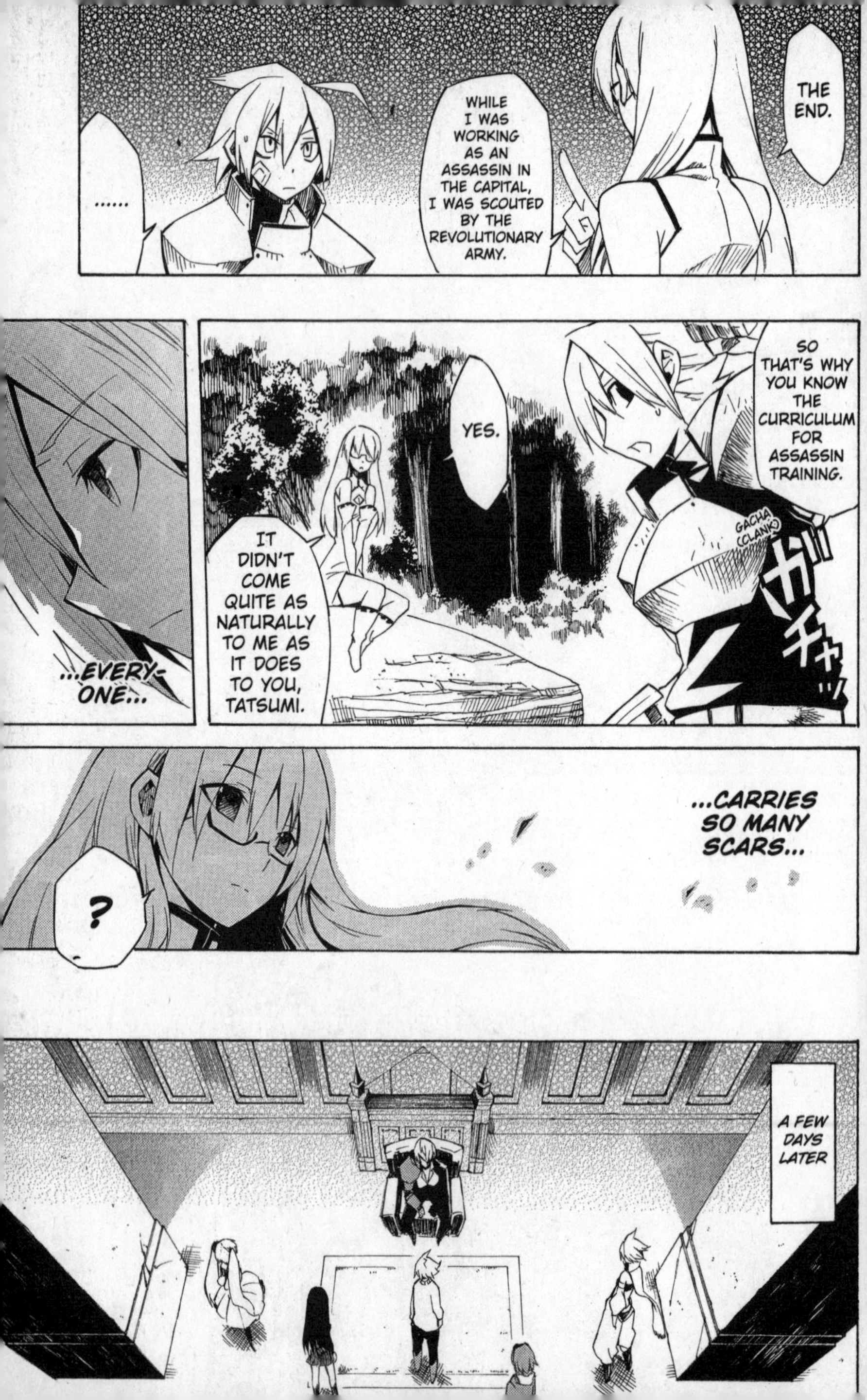
THE END.
WHILE I WAS WORKING AS AN ASSASSIN IN THE CAPITAL, I WAS SCOUTED BY THE REVOLUTIONARY ARMY.
......
SO THAT'S WHY YOU KNOW THE CURRICULUM FOR ASSASSIN TRAINING.
GACHA (CLANK)
ガチャッ
YES.
IT DIDN'T COME QUITE AS NATURALLY TO ME AS IT DOES TO YOU, TATSUMI.
...EVERY-ONE...
...CARRIES SO MANY SCARS...
?
A FEW DAYS LATER

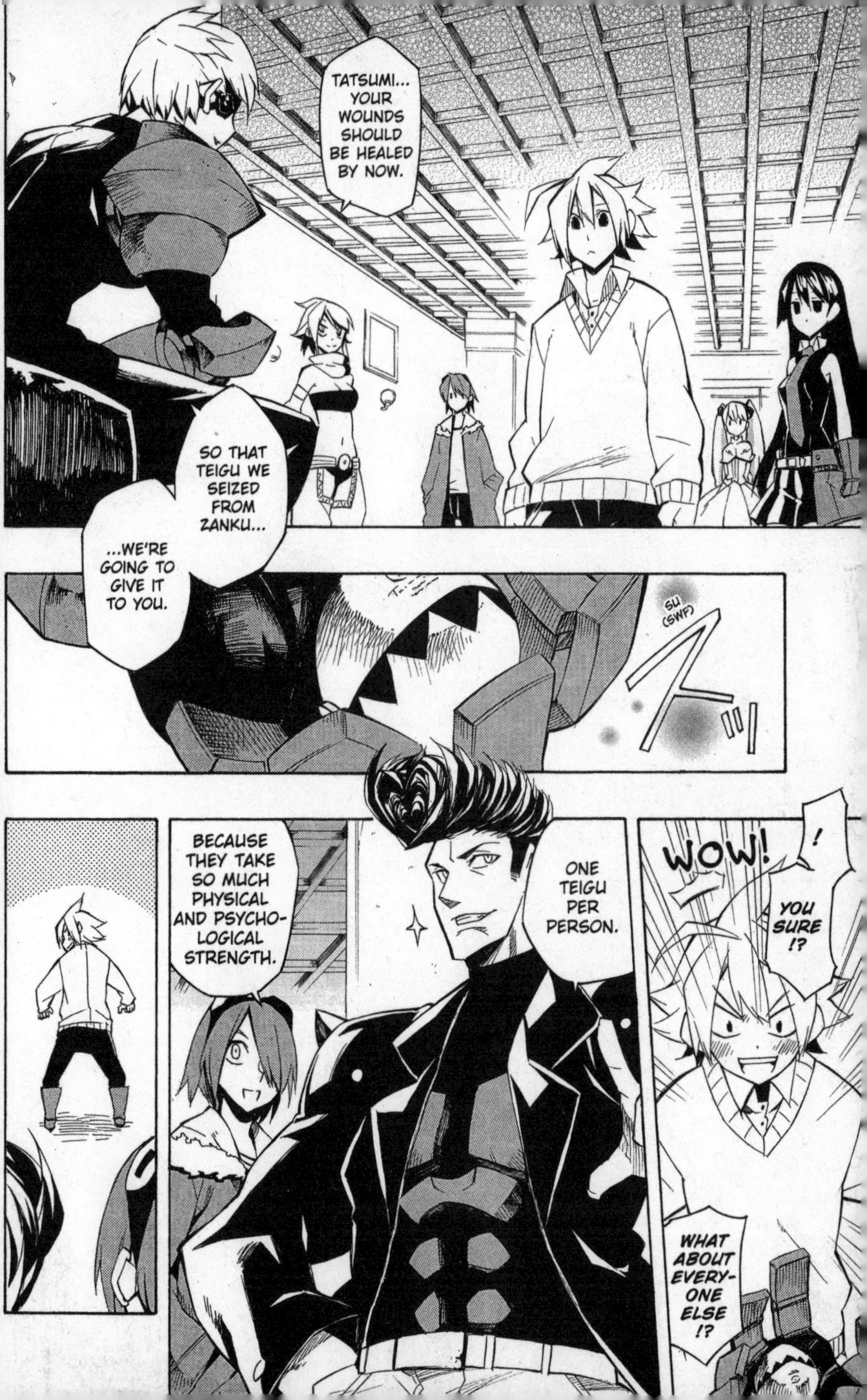
TATSUMI... YOUR WOUNDS SHOULD BE HEALED BY NOW.
SO THAT TEIGU WE SEIZED FROM ZANKU...
...WE'RE GOING TO GIVE IT TO YOU.
SU (SWF)
WOW!
!
YOU SURE!?
WHAT ABOUT EVERY-ONE ELSE!?
ONE TEIGU PER PERSON.
BECAUSE THEY TAKE SO MUCH PHYSICAL AND PSYCHO-LOGICAL STRENGTH.

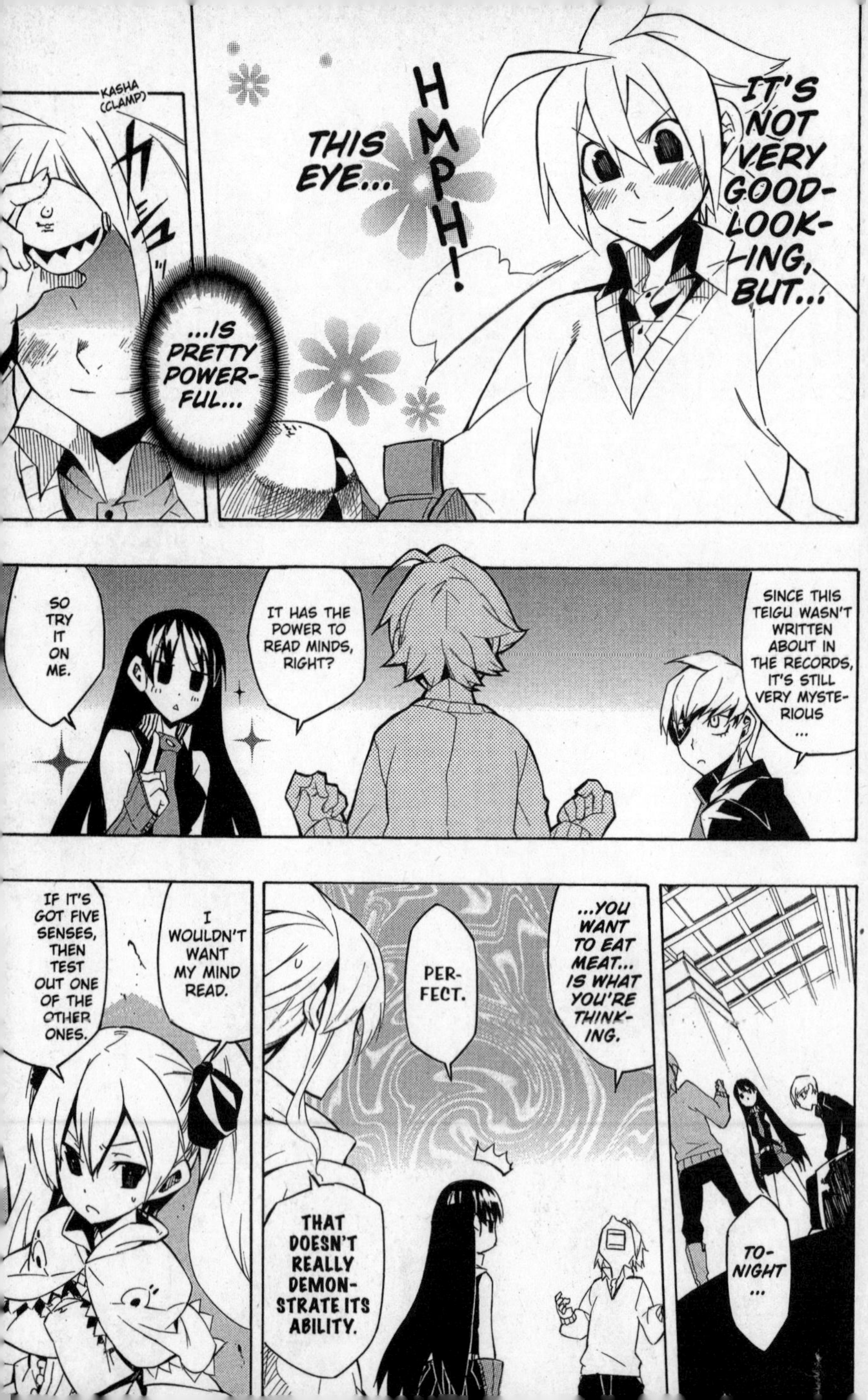
IT'S NOT VERY GOOD-LOOKING, BUT...
HMPH!
THIS EYE...
...IS PRETTY POWERFUL...
KASHA (CLAMP)
SINCE THIS TEIGU WASN'T WRITTEN ABOUT IN THE RECORDS, IT'S STILL VERY MYSTERIOUS...
IT HAS THE POWER TO READ MINDS, RIGHT?
SO TRY IT ON ME.
TONIGHT...
...YOU WANT TO EAT MEAT... IS WHAT YOU'RE THINKING.
PERFECT.
THAT DOESN'T REALLY DEMONSTRATE ITS ABILITY.
I WOULDN'T WANT MY MIND READ.
IF IT'S GOT FIVE SENSES, THEN TEST OUT ONE OF THE OTHER ONES.

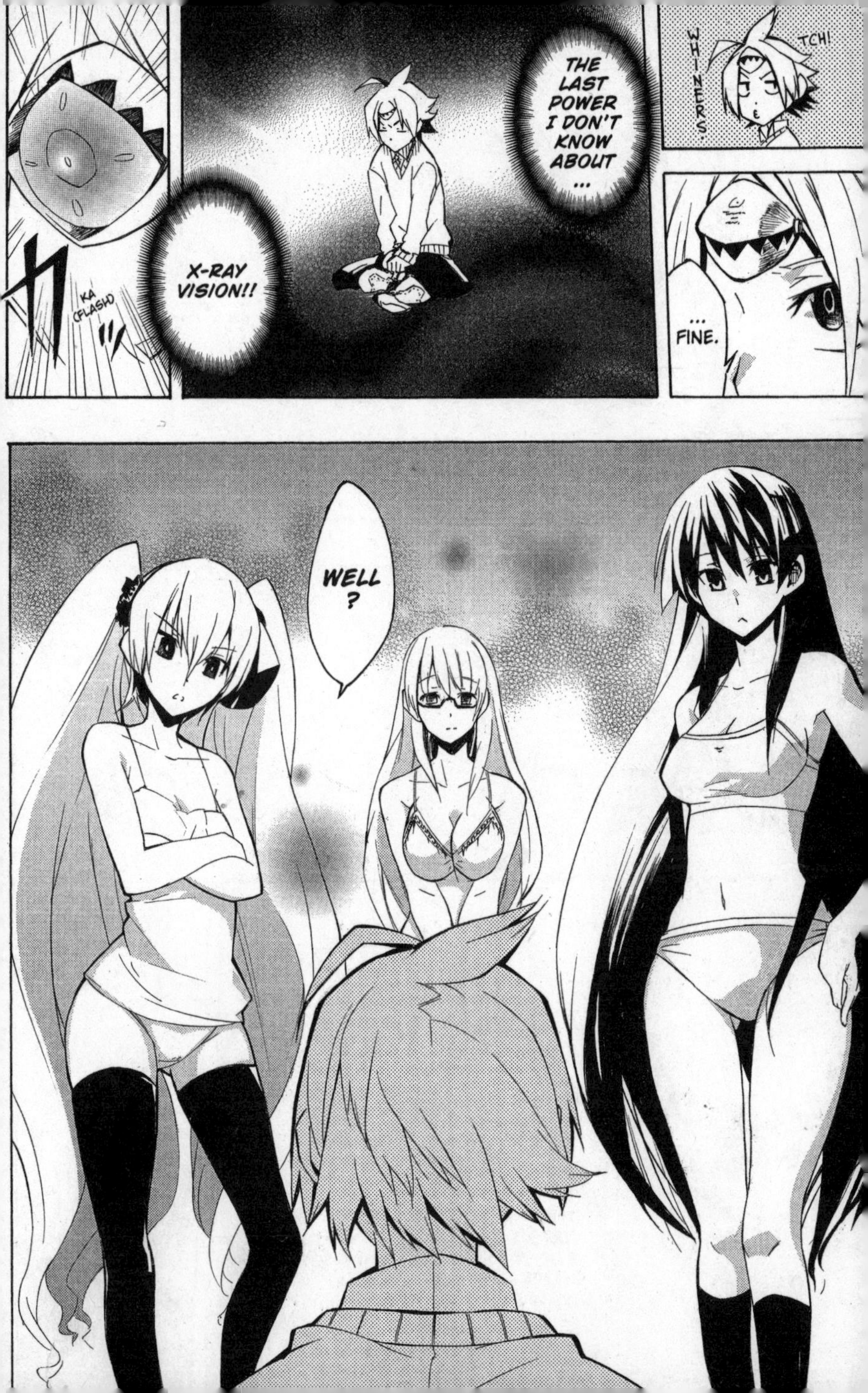
WHINERS.
TCHI!
... FINE.
THE LAST POWER I DON'T KNOW ABOUT ...
X-RAY VISION!!
KA (FLASH)
WELL ?

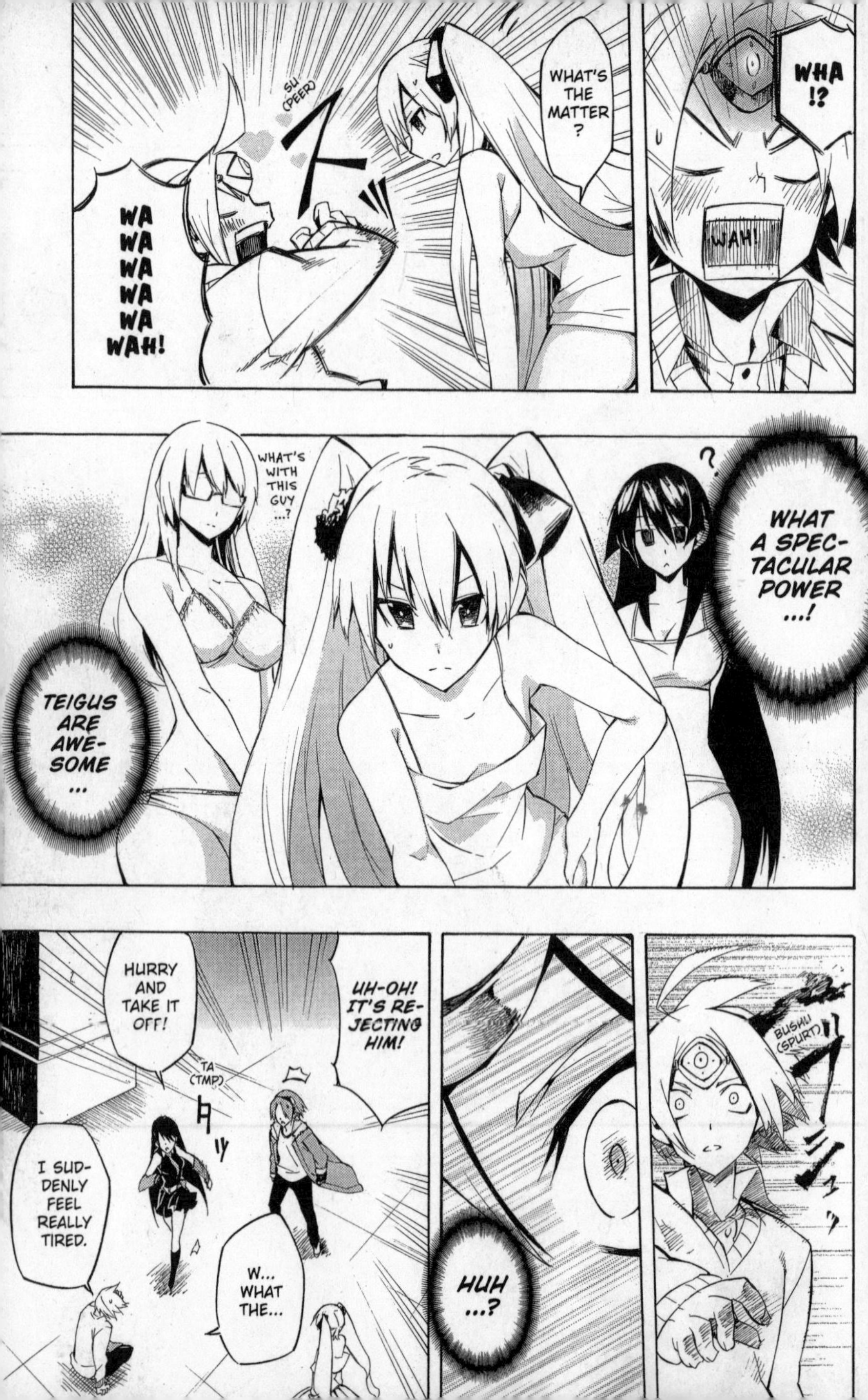
WHA !?
WAH!
WHAT'S THE MATTER ?
SU (PEER)
WA WA WA WA WA WAH!
?
WHAT A SPEC-TACULAR POWER ...!
WHAT'S WITH THIS GUY ...?
TEIGUS ARE AWE-SOME ...
BUSHU (SPURT)
HUH ...?
UH-OH! IT'S RE-JECTING HIM!
HURRY AND TAKE IT OFF!
TA (TMP)
W... WHAT THE...
I SUD-DENLY FEEL REALLY TIRED.

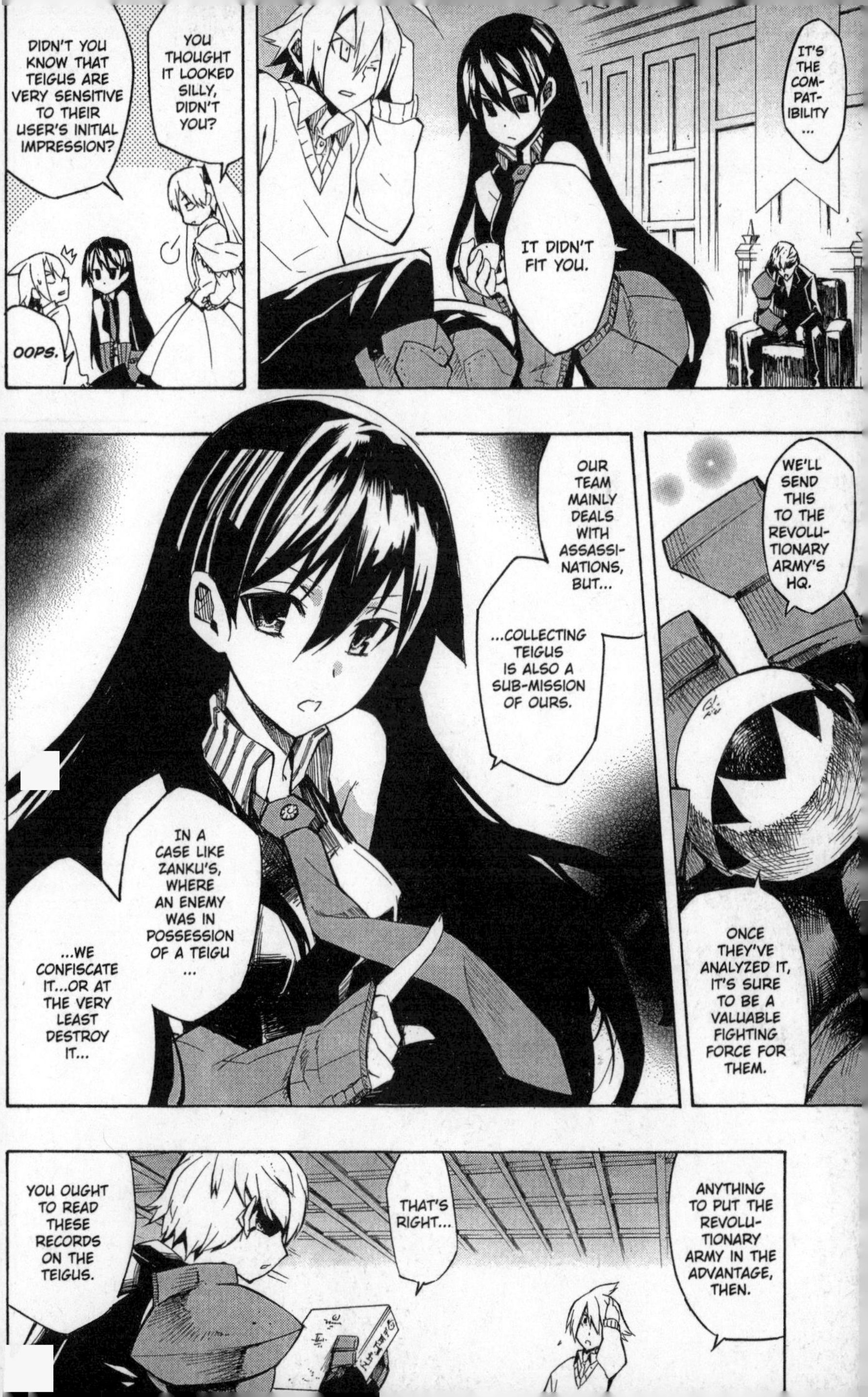
IT'S THE COMPATIBILITY...
IT DIDN'T FIT YOU.
YOU THOUGHT IT LOOKED SILLY, DIDN'T YOU?
DIDN'T YOU KNOW THAT TEIGUS ARE VERY SENSITIVE TO THEIR USER'S INITIAL IMPRESSION?
OOPS.
WE'LL SEND THIS TO THE REVOLUTIONARY ARMY'S HQ.
ONCE THEY'VE ANALYZED IT, IT'S SURE TO BE A VALUABLE FIGHTING FORCE FOR THEM.
OUR TEAM MAINLY DEALS WITH ASSASSINATIONS, BUT...
...COLLECTING TEIGUS IS ALSO A SUB-MISSION OF OURS.
IN A CASE LIKE ZANKU'S, WHERE AN ENEMY WAS IN POSSESSION OF A TEIGU...
...WE CONFISCATE IT...OR AT THE VERY LEAST DESTROY IT...
ANYTHING TO PUT THE REVOLUTIONARY ARMY IN THE ADVANTAGE, THEN.
THAT'S RIGHT...
YOU OUGHT TO READ THESE RECORDS ON THE TEIGUS.

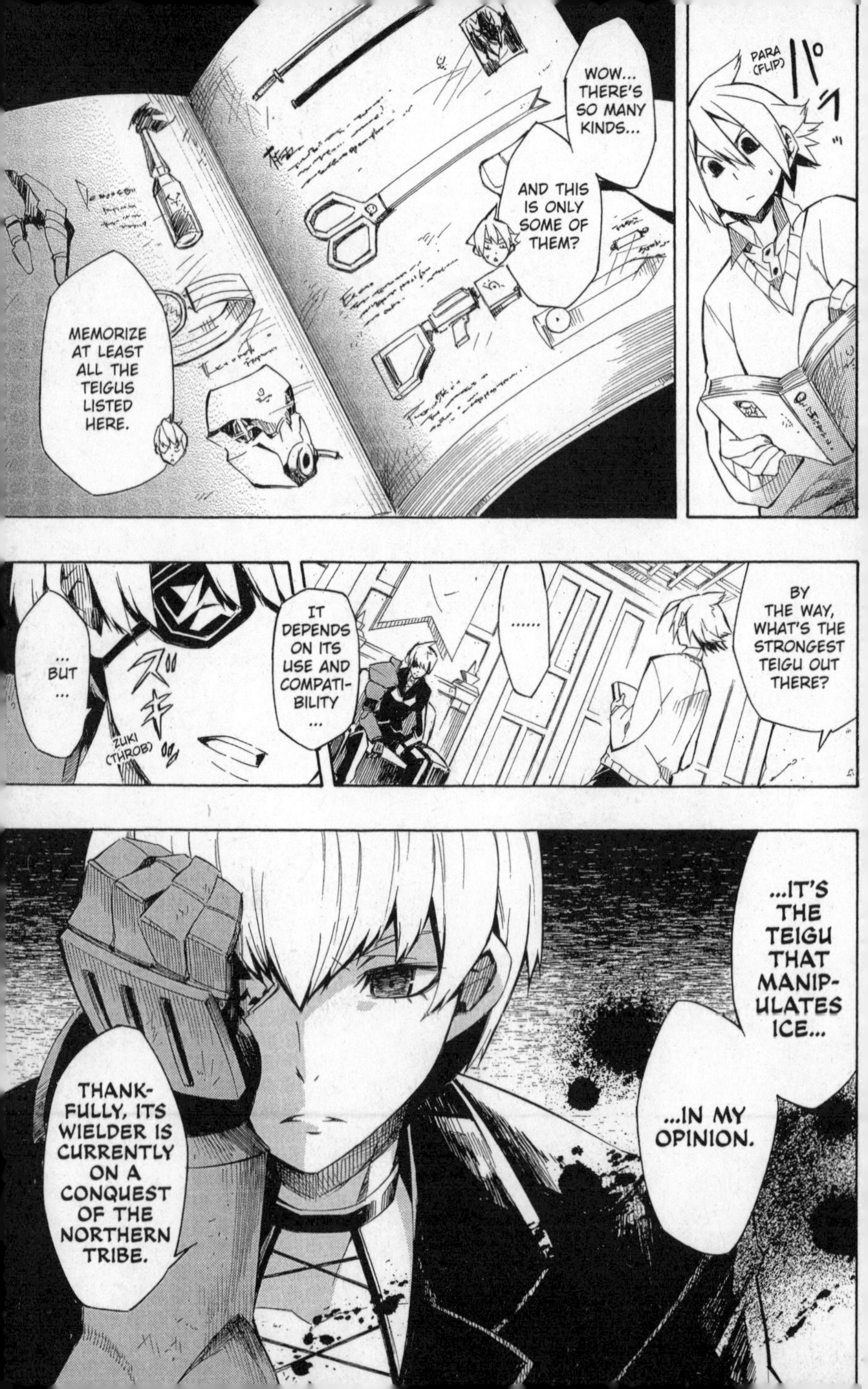
PARA (FLIP)
WOW... THERE'S SO MANY KINDS...
AND THIS IS ONLY SOME OF THEM?
MEMORIZE AT LEAST ALL THE TEIGUS LISTED HERE.
BY THE WAY, WHAT'S THE STRONGEST TEIGU OUT THERE?
......
IT DEPENDS ON ITS USE AND COMPATI-BILITY ...
... BUT ...
ZUKI (THROB)
...IT'S THE TEIGU THAT MANIP-ULATES ICE...
...IN MY OPINION.
THANK-FULLY, ITS WIELDER IS CURRENTLY ON A CONQUEST OF THE NORTHERN TRIBE.

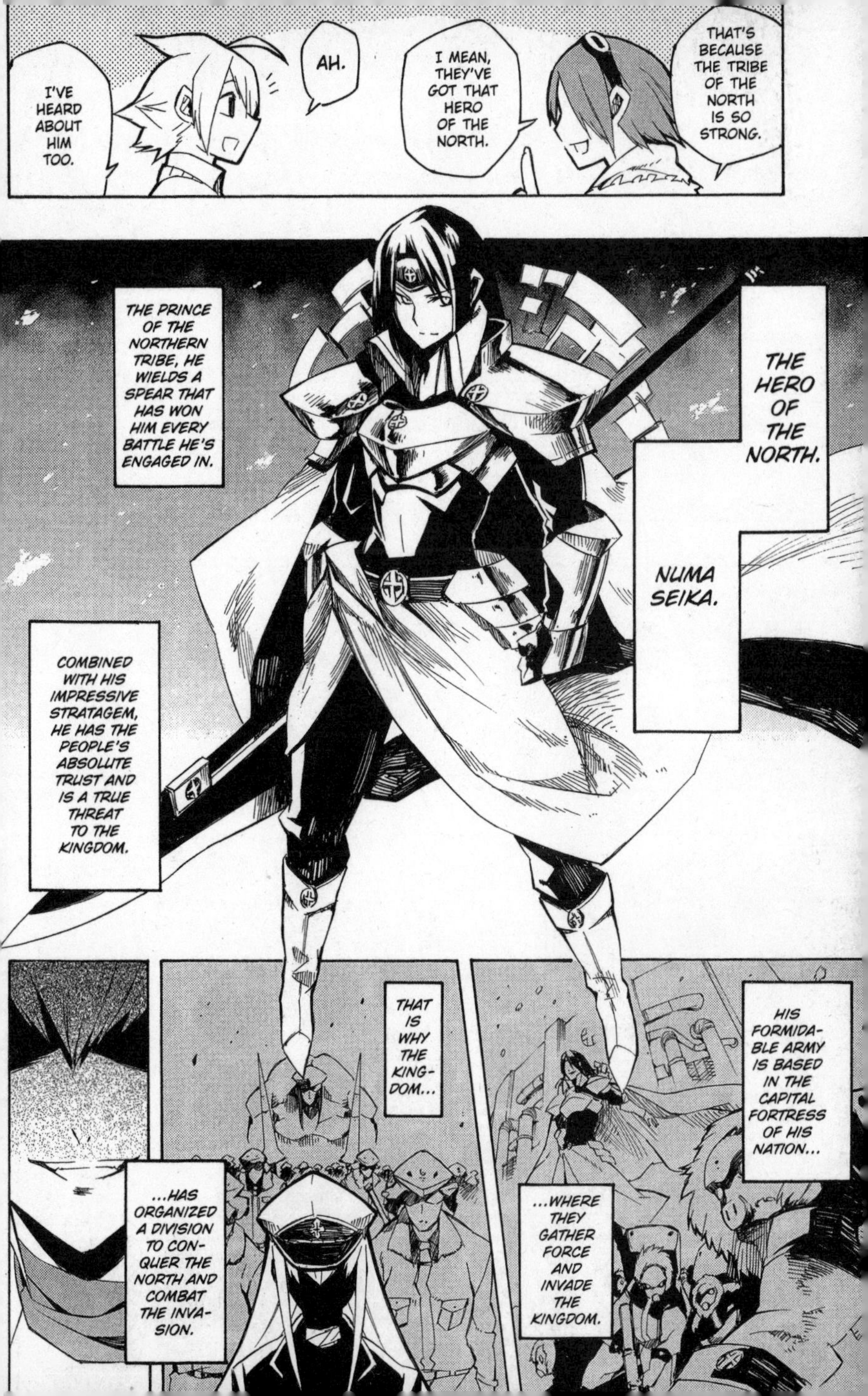
THAT'S BECAUSE THE TRIBE OF THE NORTH IS SO STRONG.
I MEAN, THEY'VE GOT THAT HERO OF THE NORTH.
AH.
I'VE HEARD ABOUT HIM TOO.
THE HERO OF THE NORTH.
NUMA SEIKA.
THE PRINCE OF THE NORTHERN TRIBE, HE WIELDS A SPEAR THAT HAS WON HIM EVERY BATTLE HE'S ENGAGED IN.
COMBINED WITH HIS IMPRESSIVE STRATAGEM, HE HAS THE PEOPLE'S ABSOLUTE TRUST AND IS A TRUE THREAT TO THE KINGDOM.
HIS FORMIDA-BLE ARMY IS BASED IN THE CAPITAL FORTRESS OF HIS NATION...
...WHERE THEY GATHER FORCE AND INVADE THE KINGDOM.
THAT IS WHY THE KING-DOM...
...HAS ORGANIZED A DIVISION TO CON-QUER THE NORTH AND COMBAT THE INVA-SION.

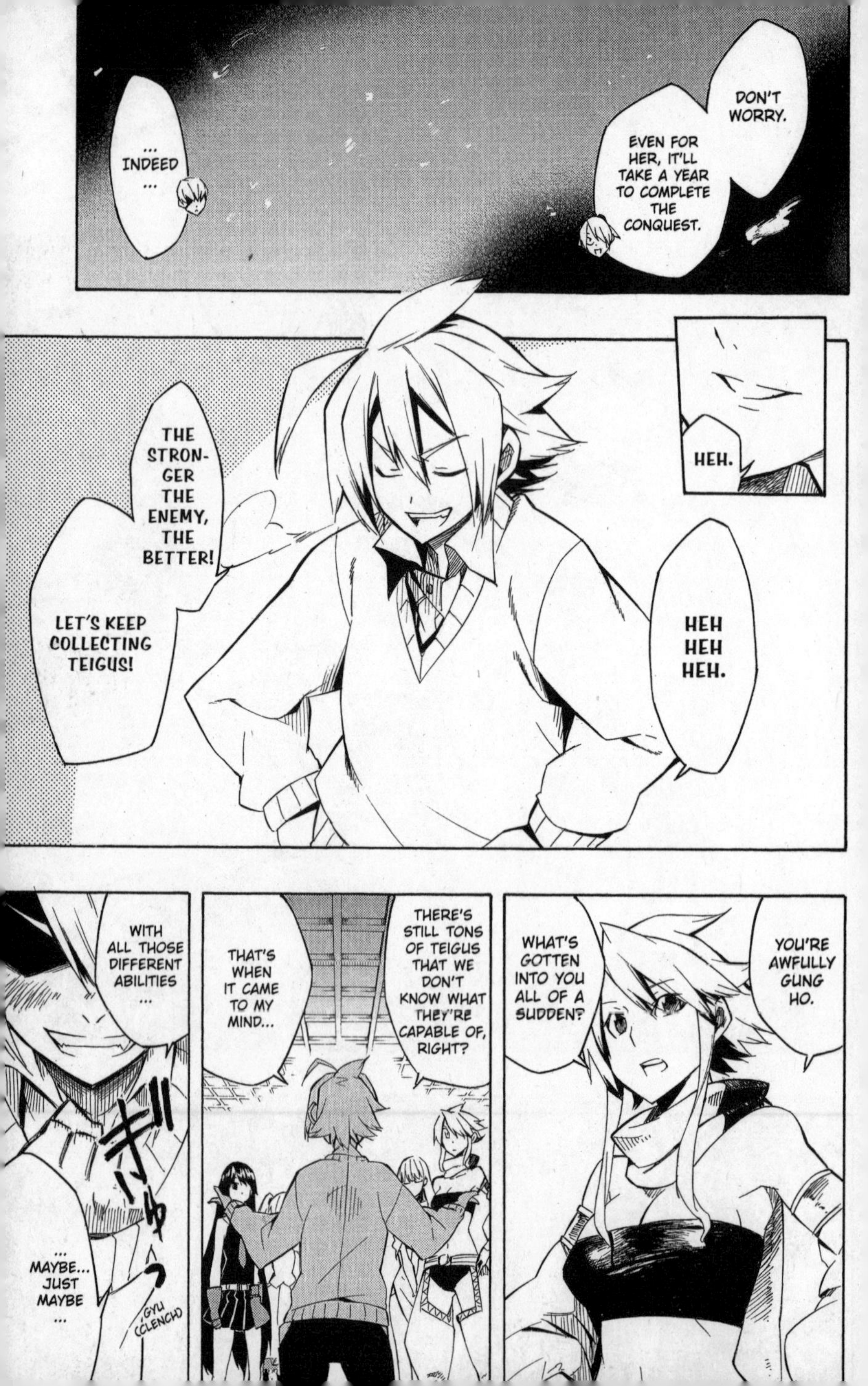
DON'T WORRY.
EVEN FOR HER, IT'LL TAKE A YEAR TO COMPLETE THE CONQUEST.
... INDEED ...
HEH.
HEH HEH HEH.
THE STRONGER THE ENEMY, THE BETTER!
LET'S KEEP COLLECTING TEIGUS!
YOU'RE AWFULLY GUNG HO.
WHAT'S GOTTEN INTO YOU ALL OF A SUDDEN?
THERE'S STILL TONS OF TEIGUS THAT WE DON'T KNOW WHAT THEY'RE CAPABLE OF, RIGHT?
THAT'S WHEN IT CAME TO MY MIND...
WITH ALL THOSE DIFFERENT ABILITIES ...
GYU (CLENCH)
... MAYBE... JUST MAYBE ...

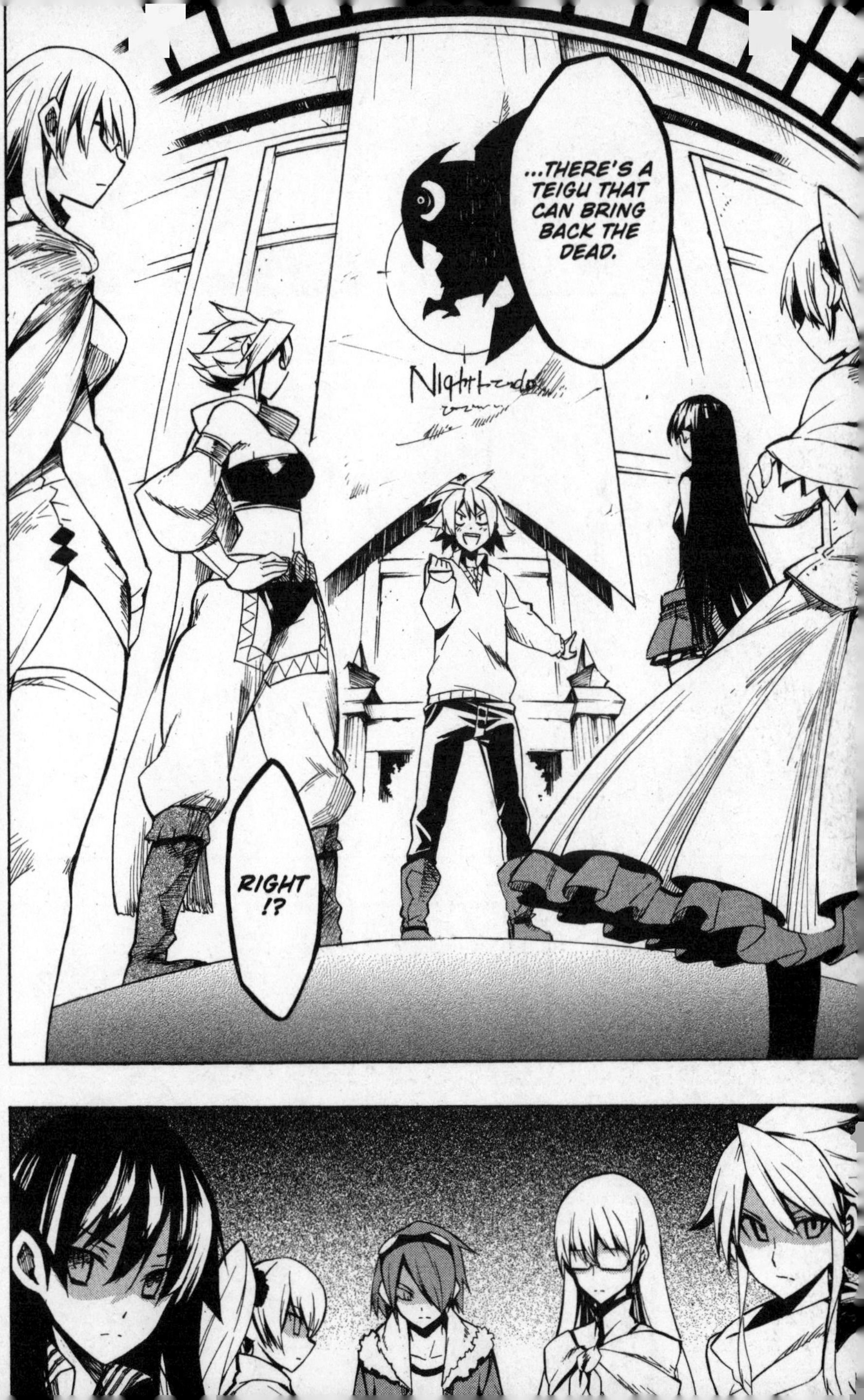
...THERE'S A TEIGU THAT CAN BRING BACK THE DEAD.
RIGHT !?

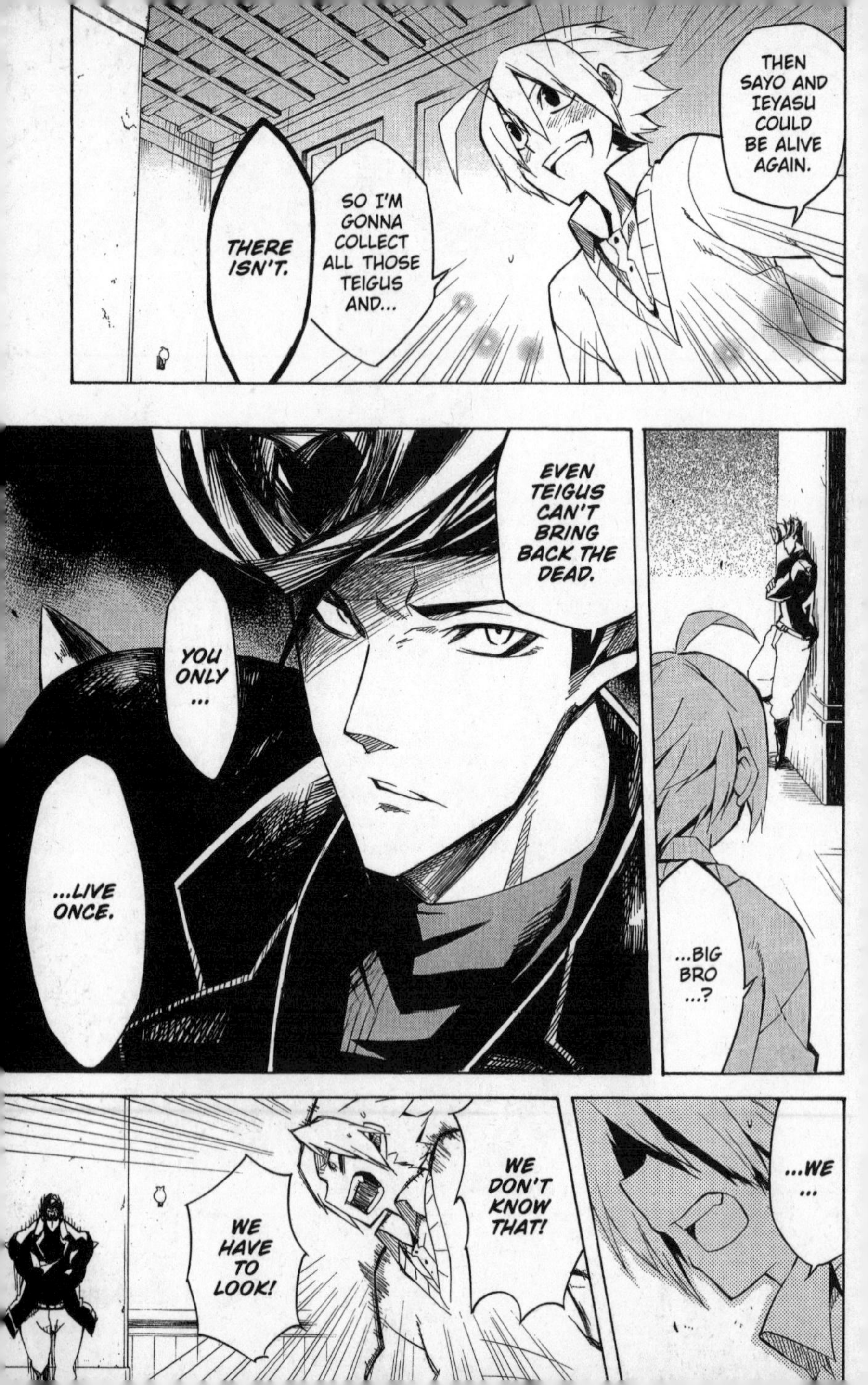
THEN SAYO AND IEYASU COULD BE ALIVE AGAIN.
SO I'M GONNA COLLECT ALL THOSE TEIGUS AND...
THERE ISN'T.
...BIG BRO ...?
EVEN TEIGUS CAN'T BRING BACK THE DEAD.
YOU ONLY ...
...LIVE ONCE.
...WE ...
WE DON'T KNOW THAT!
WE HAVE TO LOOK!

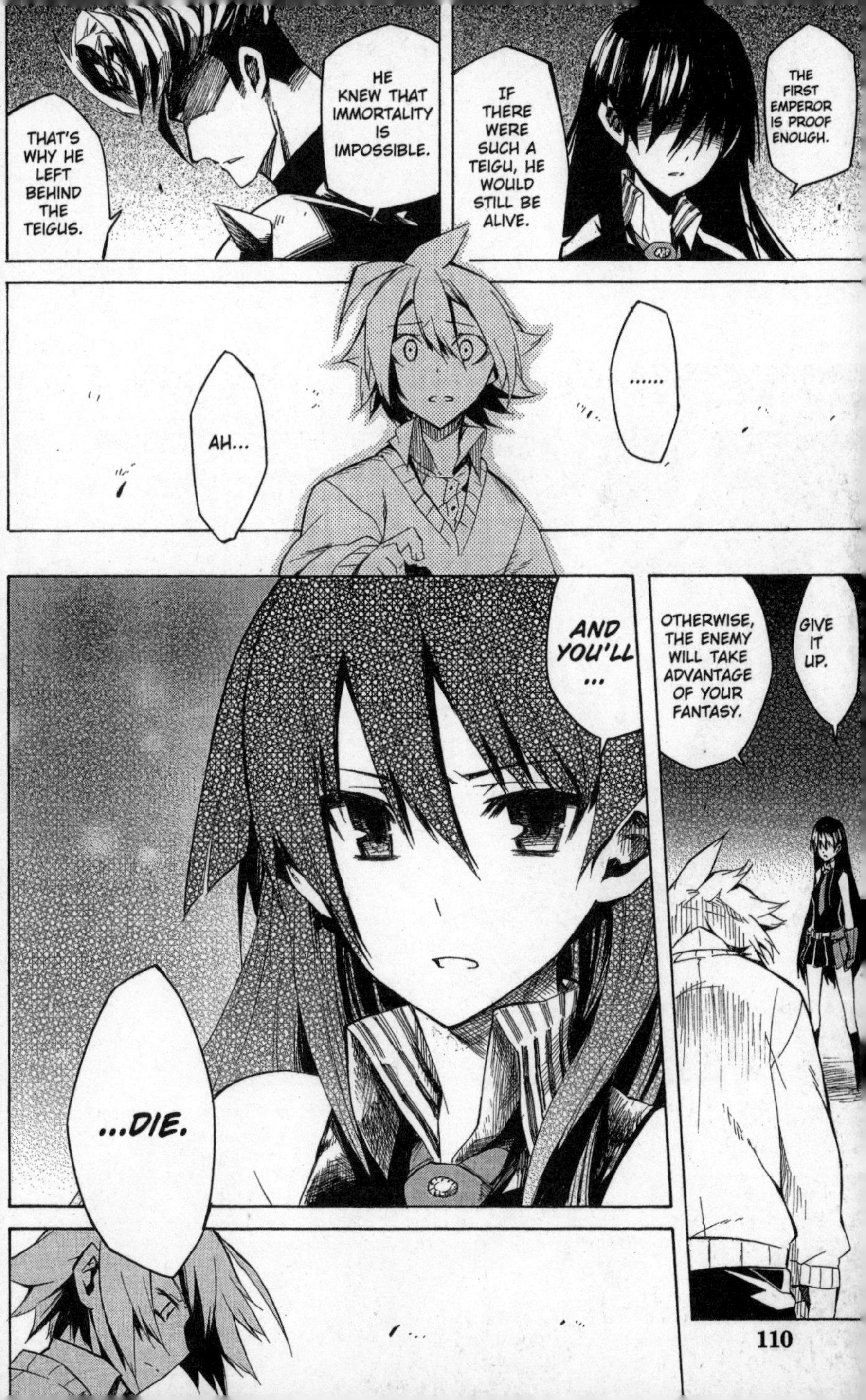
THE FIRST EMPEROR IS PROOF ENOUGH.
IF THERE WERE SUCH A TEIGU, HE WOULD STILL BE ALIVE.
HE KNEW THAT IMMORTALITY IS IMPOSSIBLE.
THAT'S WHY HE LEFT BEHIND THE TEIGUS.
......
AH...
GIVE IT UP.
OTHERWISE, THE ENEMY WILL TAKE ADVANTAGE OF YOUR FANTASY.
AND YOU'LL...
...DIE.

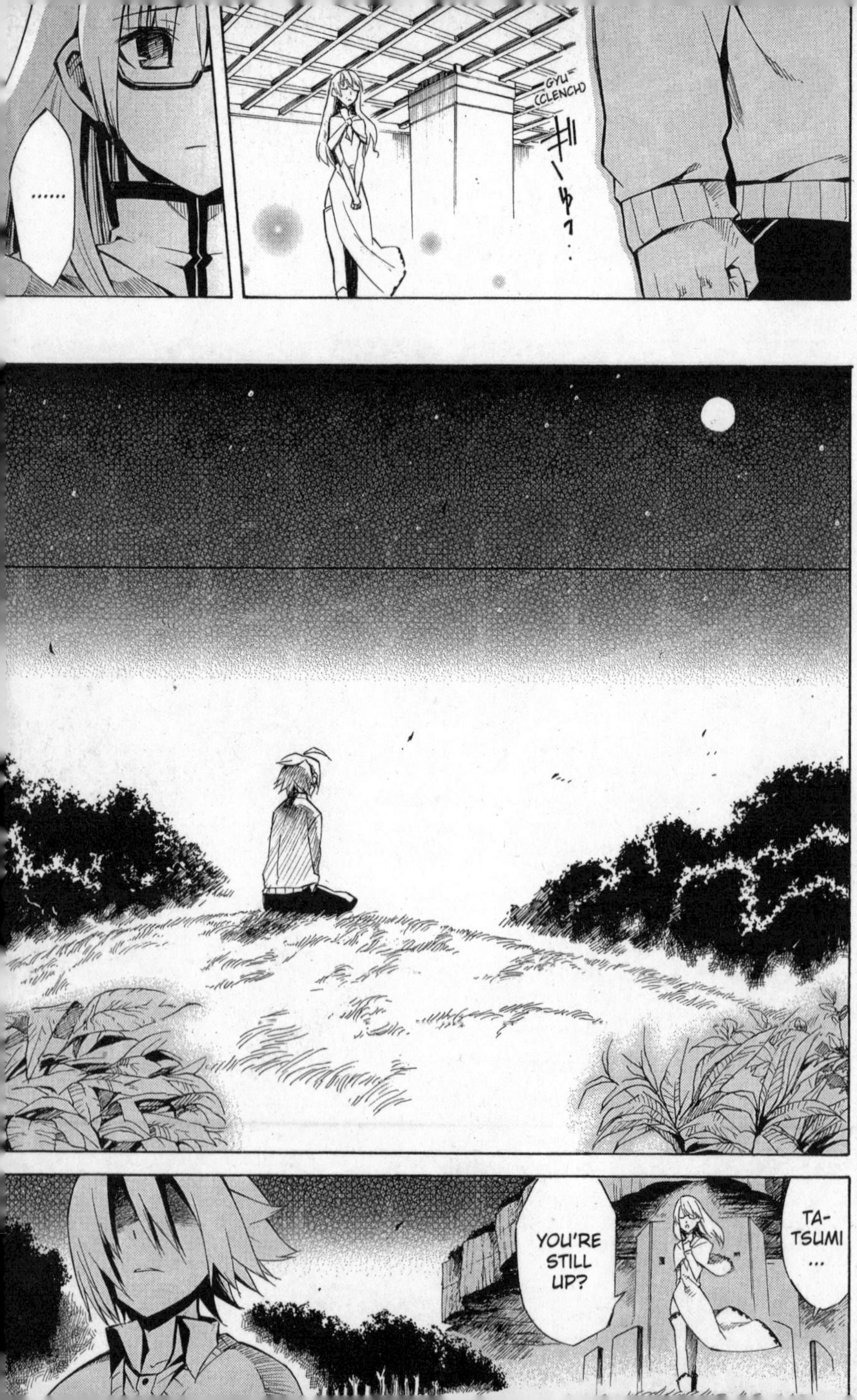
GYU (CLENCH)
......
TA-TSUMI ...
YOU'RE STILL UP?

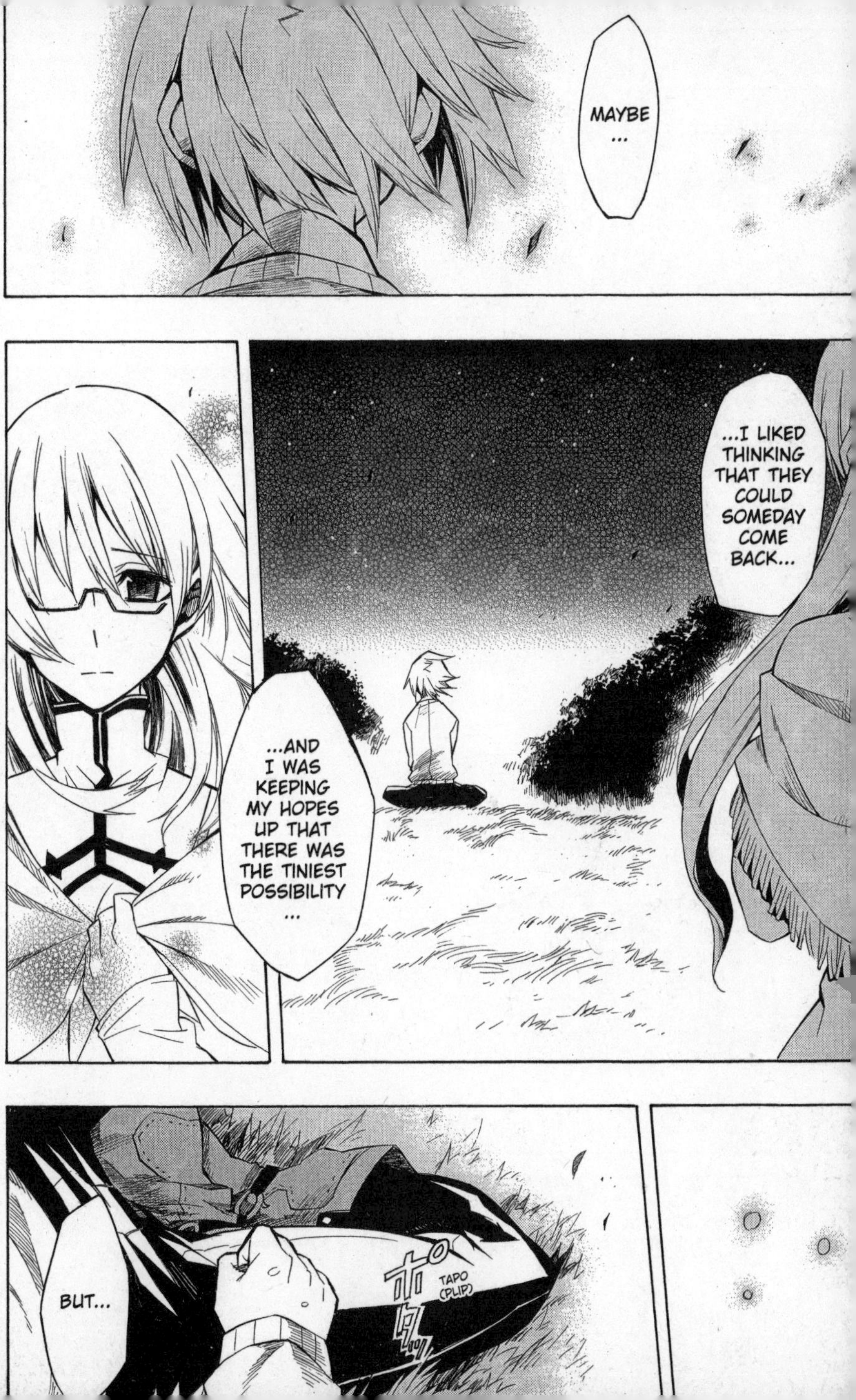
MAYBE ...
...I LIKED THINKING THAT THEY COULD SOMEDAY COME BACK...
...AND I WAS KEEPING MY HOPES UP THAT THERE WAS THE TINIEST POSSIBILITY ...
TAPO (PLIP)
BUT...

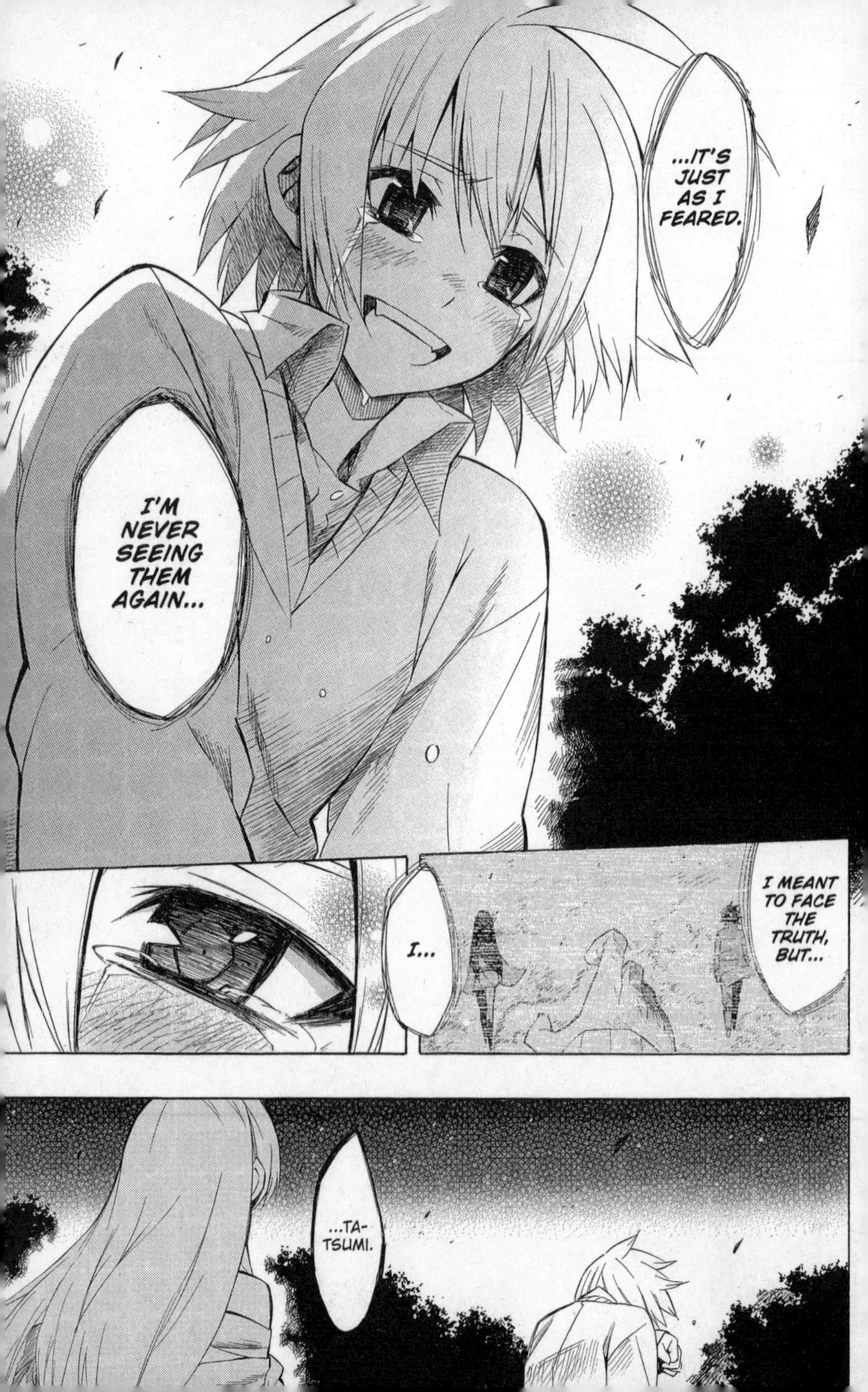
...IT'S JUST AS I FEARED.
I'M NEVER SEEING THEM AGAIN...
I MEANT TO FACE THE TRUTH, BUT...
I...
...TA-TSUMI.

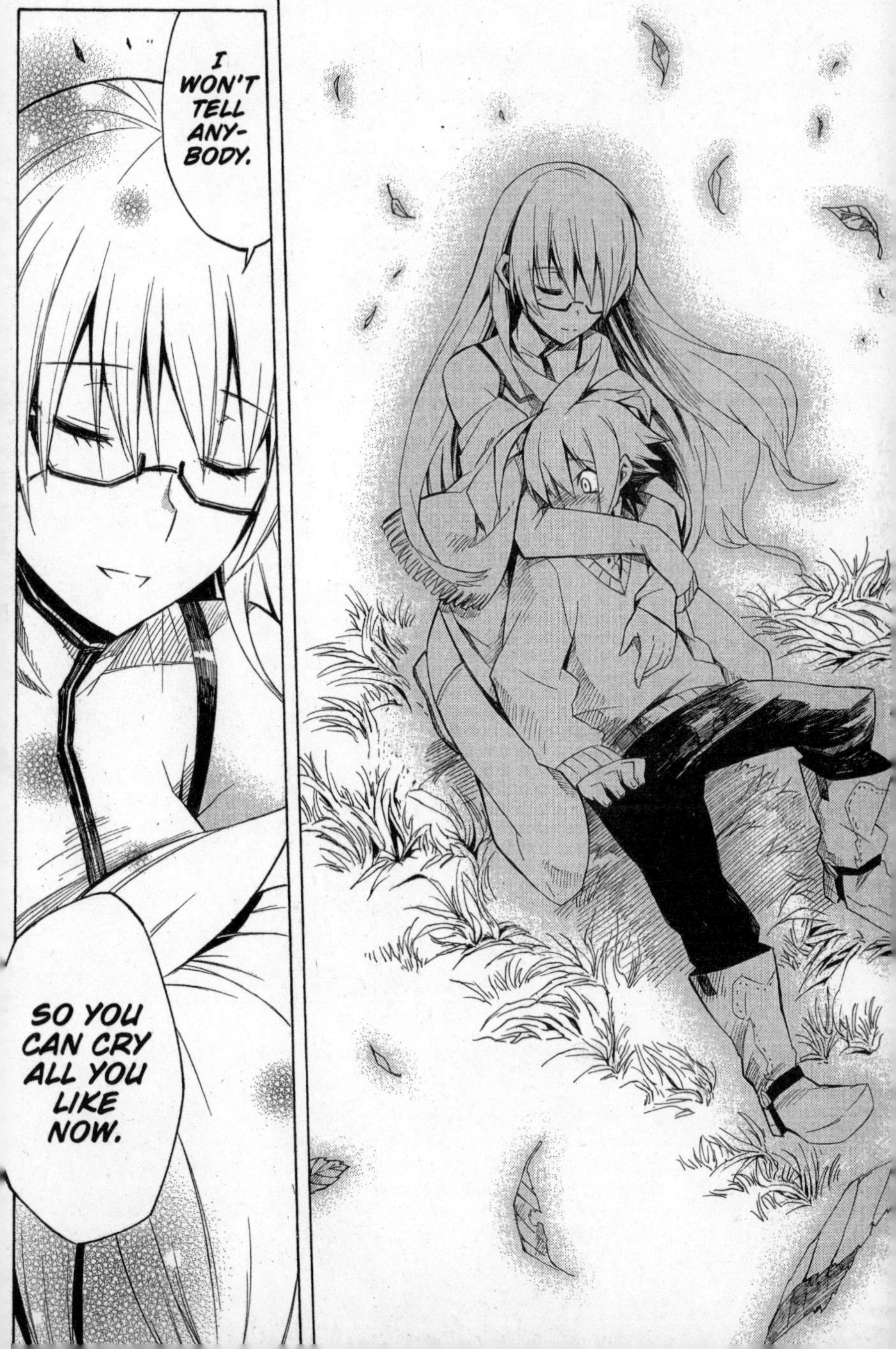
...
I WON'T TELL ANYBODY.
SO YOU CAN CRY ALL YOU LIKE NOW.

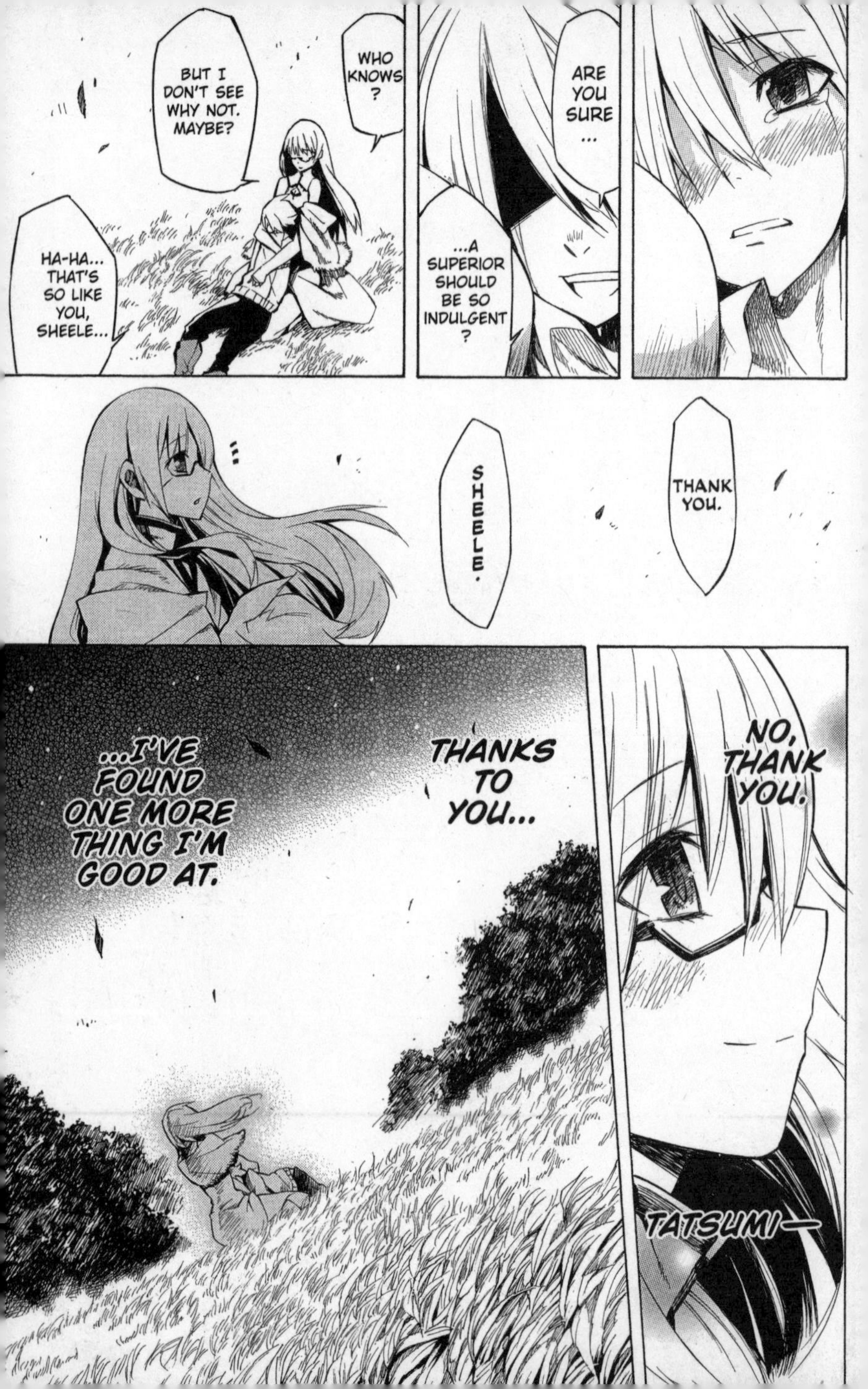
ARE YOU SURE...
...A SUPERIOR SHOULD BE SO INDULGENT?
WHO KNOWS?
BUT I DON'T SEE WHY NOT. MAYBE?
HA-HA... THAT'S SO LIKE YOU, SHEELE...
THANK YOU.
SHEELE.
NO, THANK YOU.
TATSUMI—
THANKS TO YOU...
...I'VE FOUND ONE MORE THING I'M GOOD AT.

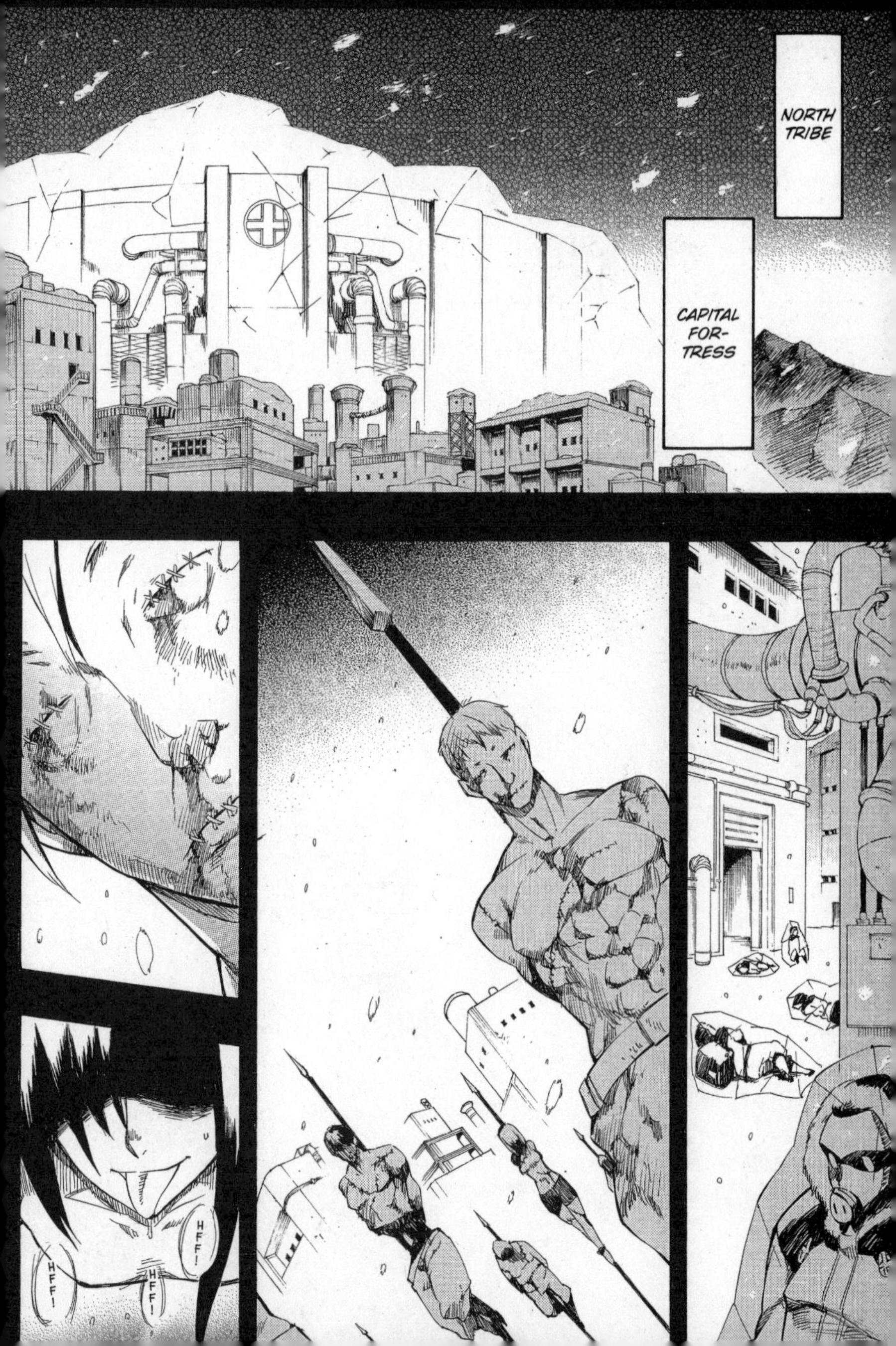
NORTH TRIBE
CAPITAL FOR-TRESS
HFF!
HFF!
HFF!

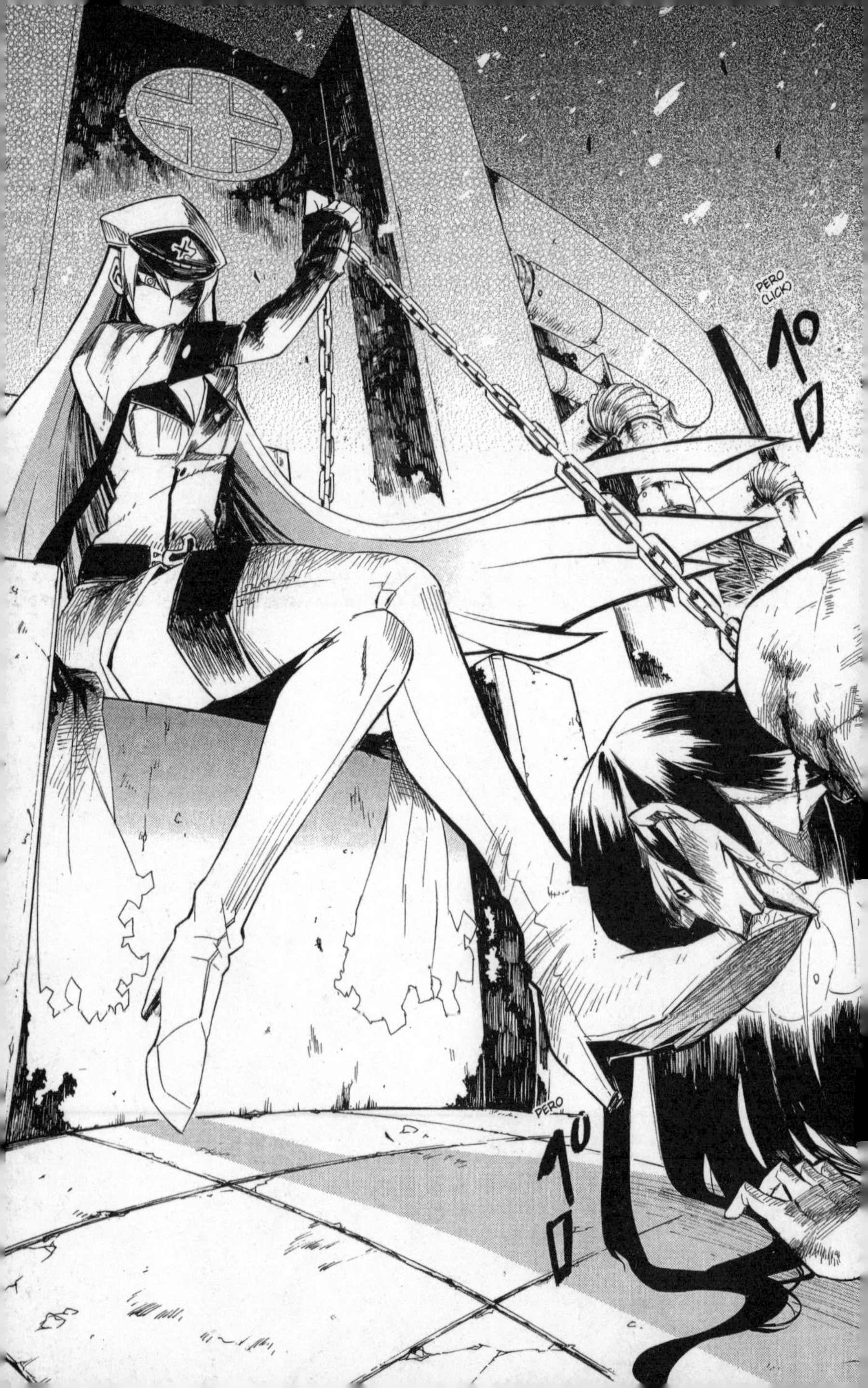
PERO (LICK)
PERO

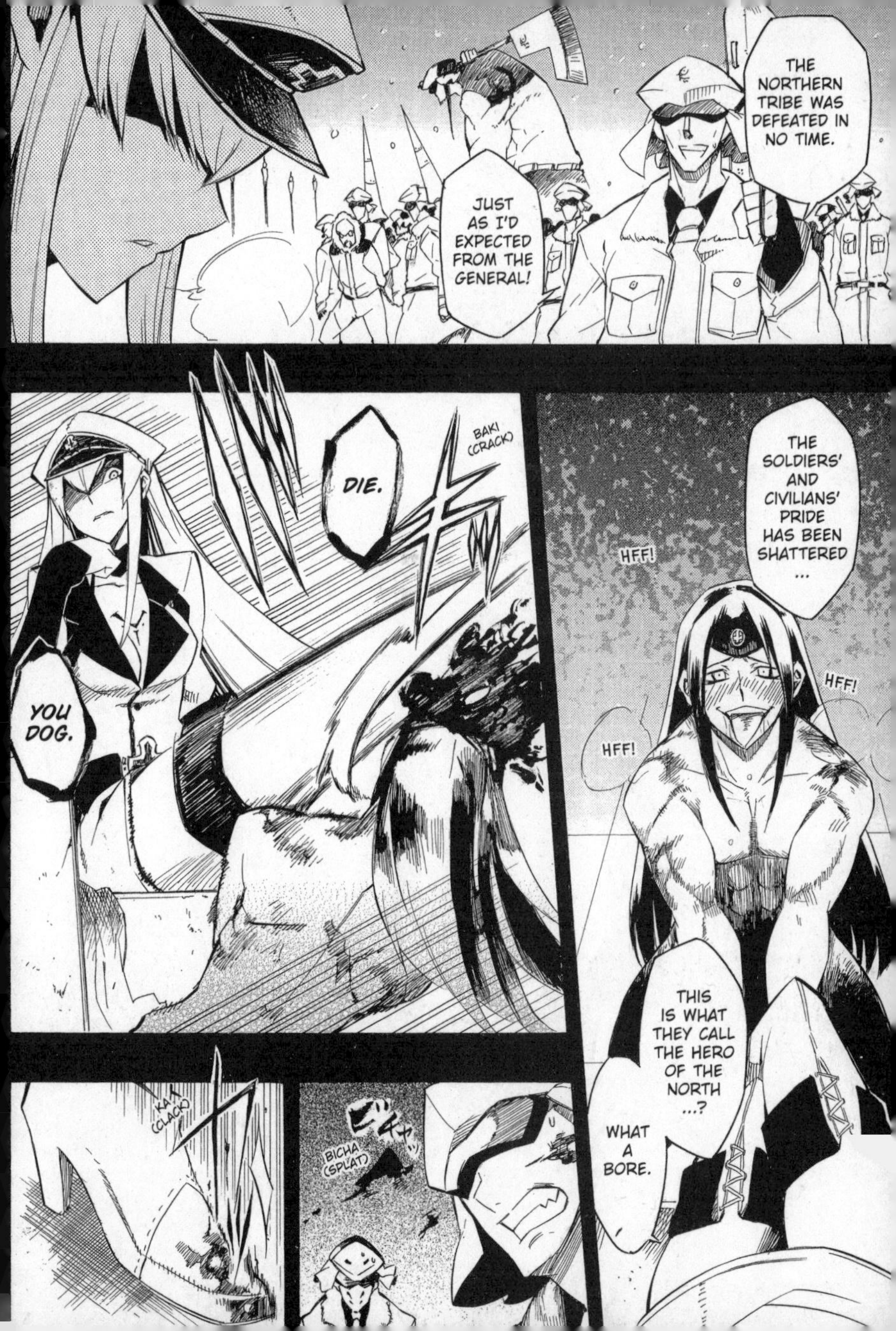
THE NORTHERN TRIBE WAS DEFEATED IN NO TIME.
JUST AS I'D EXPECTED FROM THE GENERAL!
THE SOLDIERS' AND CIVILIANS' PRIDE HAS BEEN SHATTERED ...
HFF!
HFF!
HFF!
THIS IS WHAT THEY CALL THE HERO OF THE NORTH ...?
WHAT A BORE.
BAKI (CRACK)
DIE.
YOU DOG.
BICHA (SPLAT)
KA (CLACK)

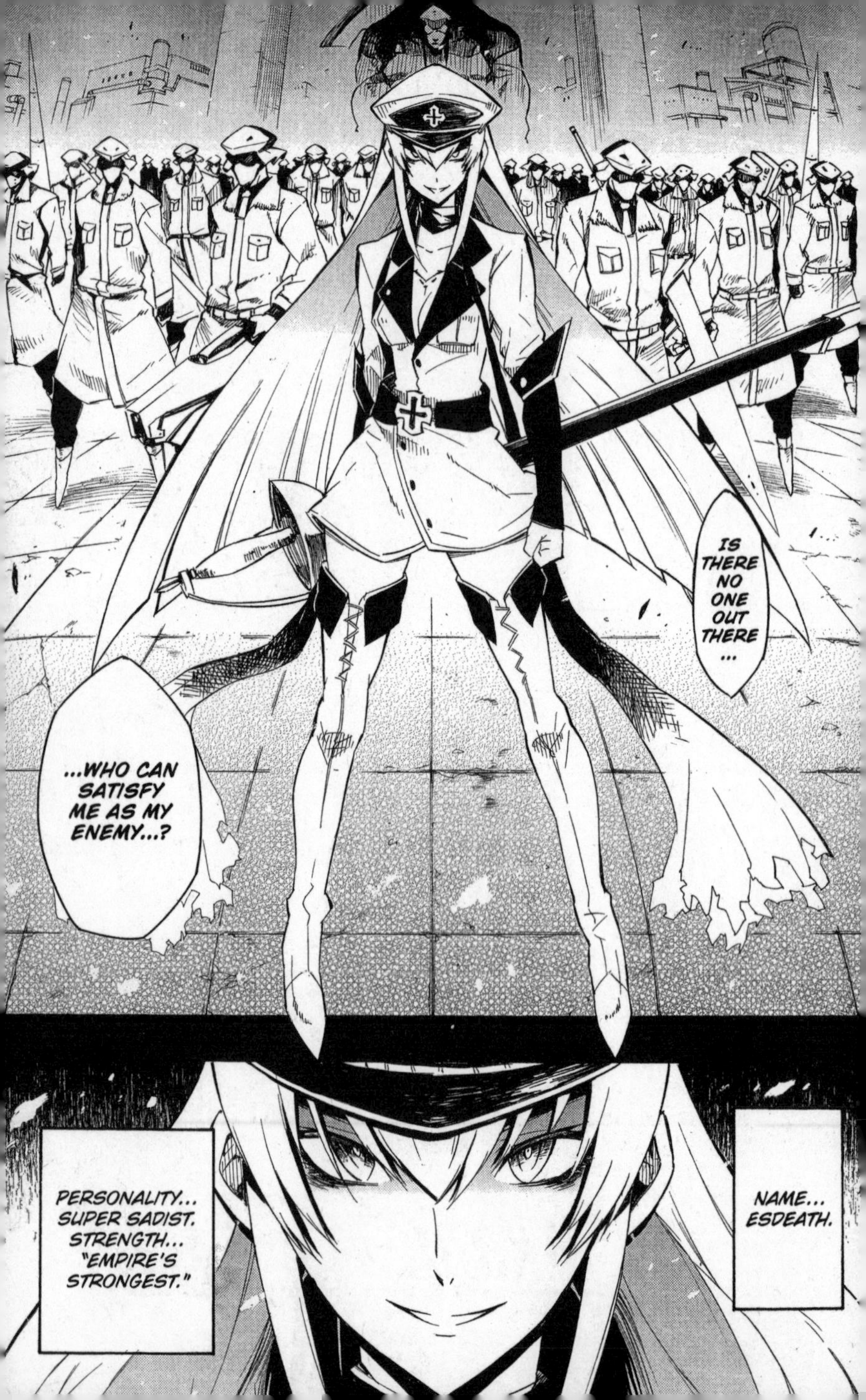
IS THERE NO ONE OUT THERE...
...WHO CAN SATISFY ME AS MY ENEMY...?
NAME... ESDEATH.
PERSONALITY... SUPER SADIST. STRENGTH... "EMPIRE'S STRONGEST."

Akame ga KILL!

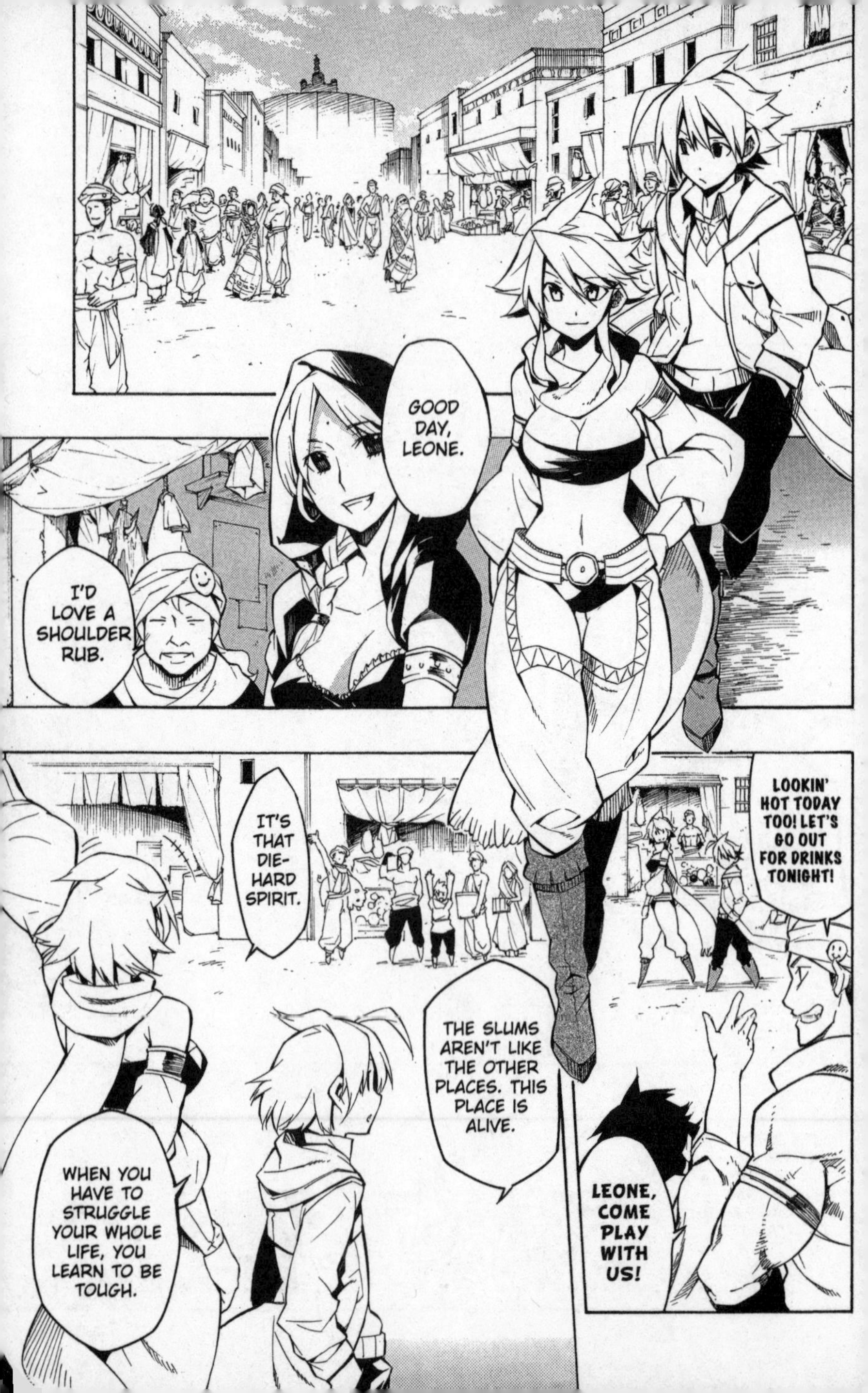
GOOD DAY, LEONE.
I'D LOVE A SHOULDER RUB.
LOOKIN' HOT TODAY TOO! LET'S GO OUT FOR DRINKS TONIGHT!
IT'S THAT DIE-HARD SPIRIT.
LEONE, COME PLAY WITH US!
THE SLUMS AREN'T LIKE THE OTHER PLACES. THIS PLACE IS ALIVE.
WHEN YOU HAVE TO STRUGGLE YOUR WHOLE LIFE, YOU LEARN TO BE TOUGH.

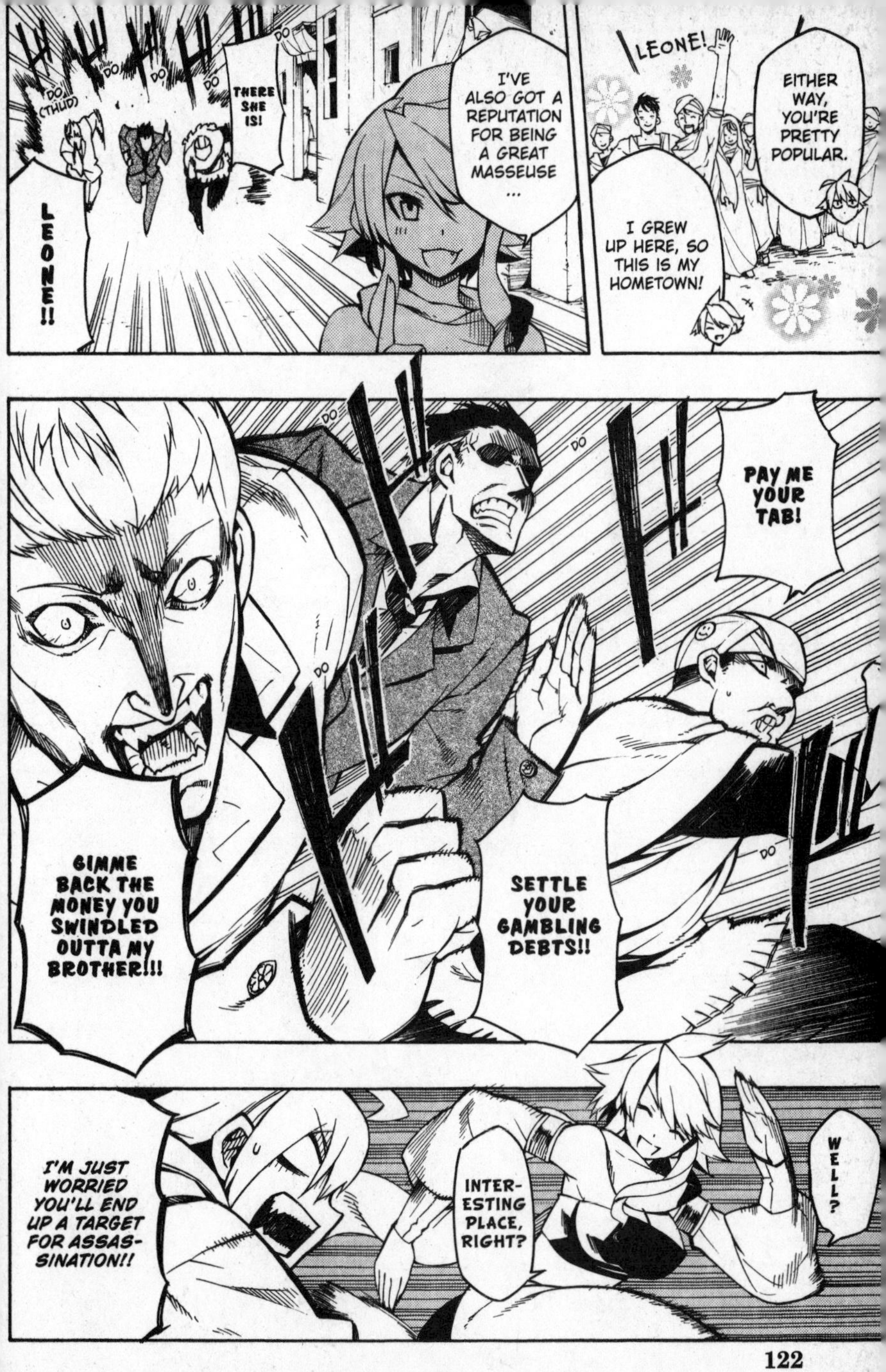
EITHER WAY, YOU'RE PRETTY POPULAR.
LEONE!
I GREW UP HERE, SO THIS IS MY HOMETOWN!
I'VE ALSO GOT A REPUTATION FOR BEING A GREAT MASSEUSE ...
THERE SHE IS!
DO DO DO DO (THUD)
LEONE!!
PAY ME YOUR TAB!
DO DO DO DO
SETTLE YOUR GAMBLING DEBTS!!
GIMME BACK THE MONEY YOU SWINDLED OUTTA MY BROTHER!!!
WELL?
INTER-ESTING PLACE, RIGHT?
I'M JUST WORRIED YOU'LL END UP A TARGET FOR ASSAS-SINATION!!

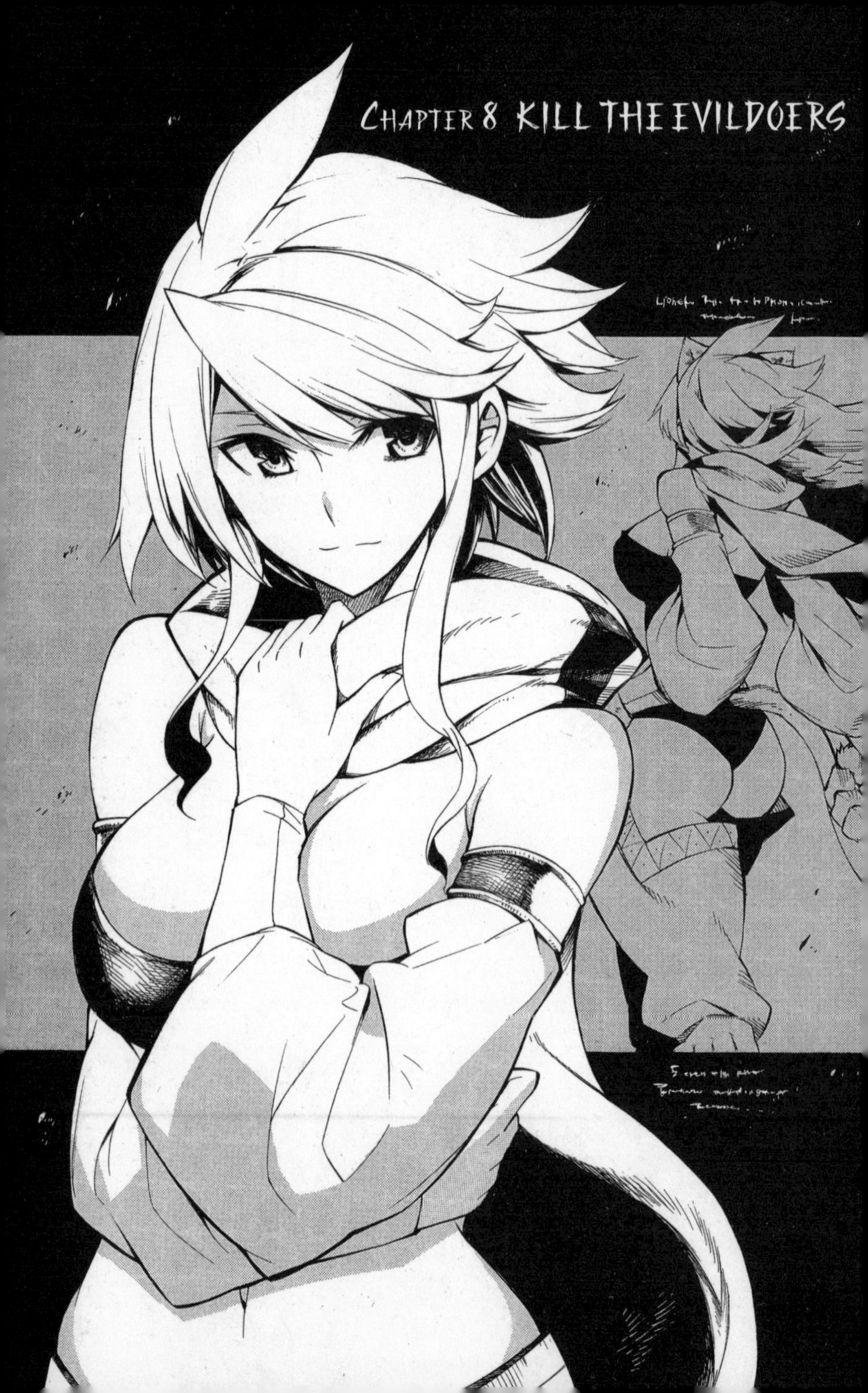
CHAPTER 8 KILL THE EVILDOERS

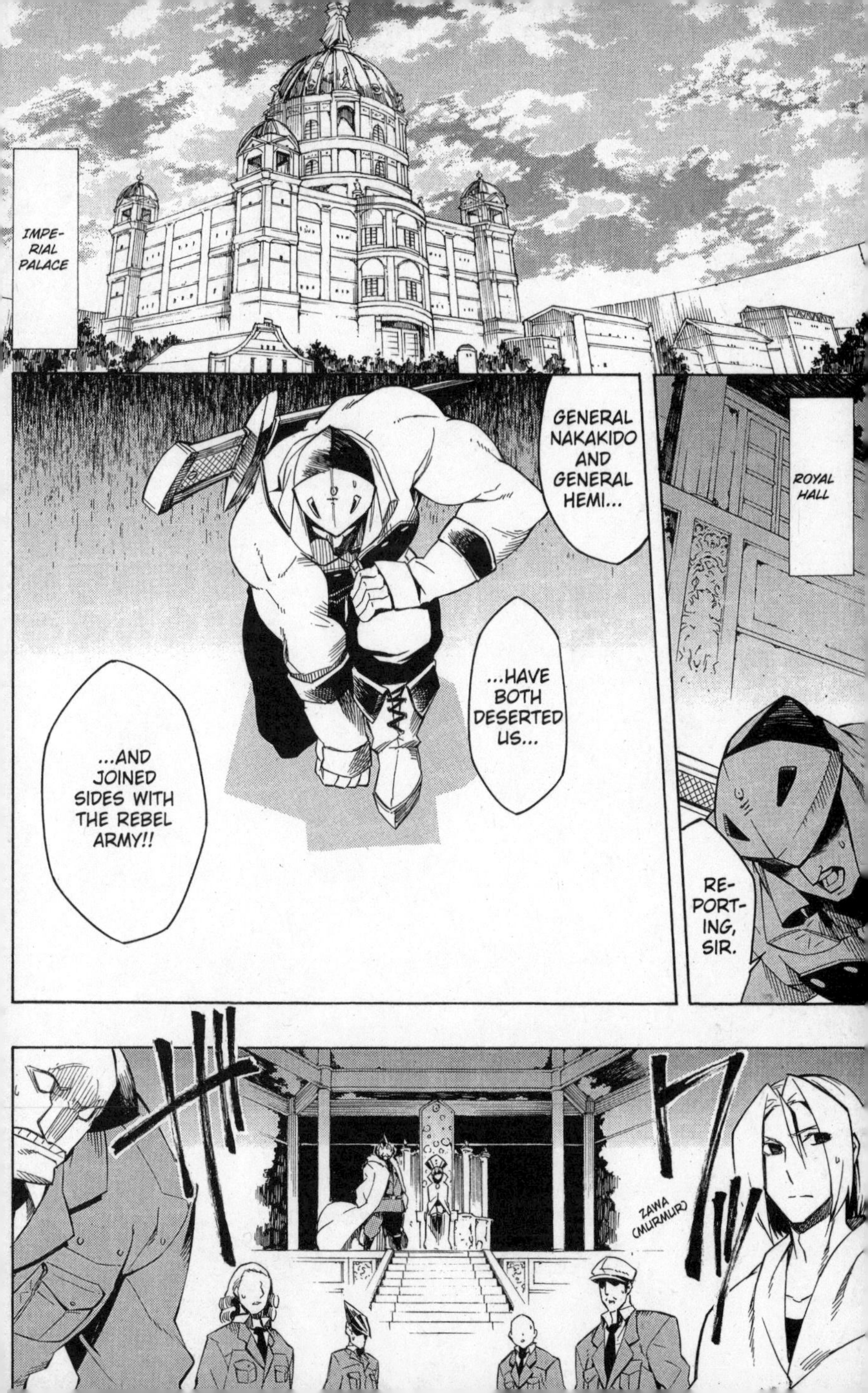
IMPERIAL PALACE
ROYAL HALL
REPORTING, SIR.
GENERAL NAKAKIDO AND GENERAL HEMI...
...HAVE BOTH DESERTED US...
...AND JOINED SIDES WITH THE REBEL ARMY!!
ZAWA (MURMUR)

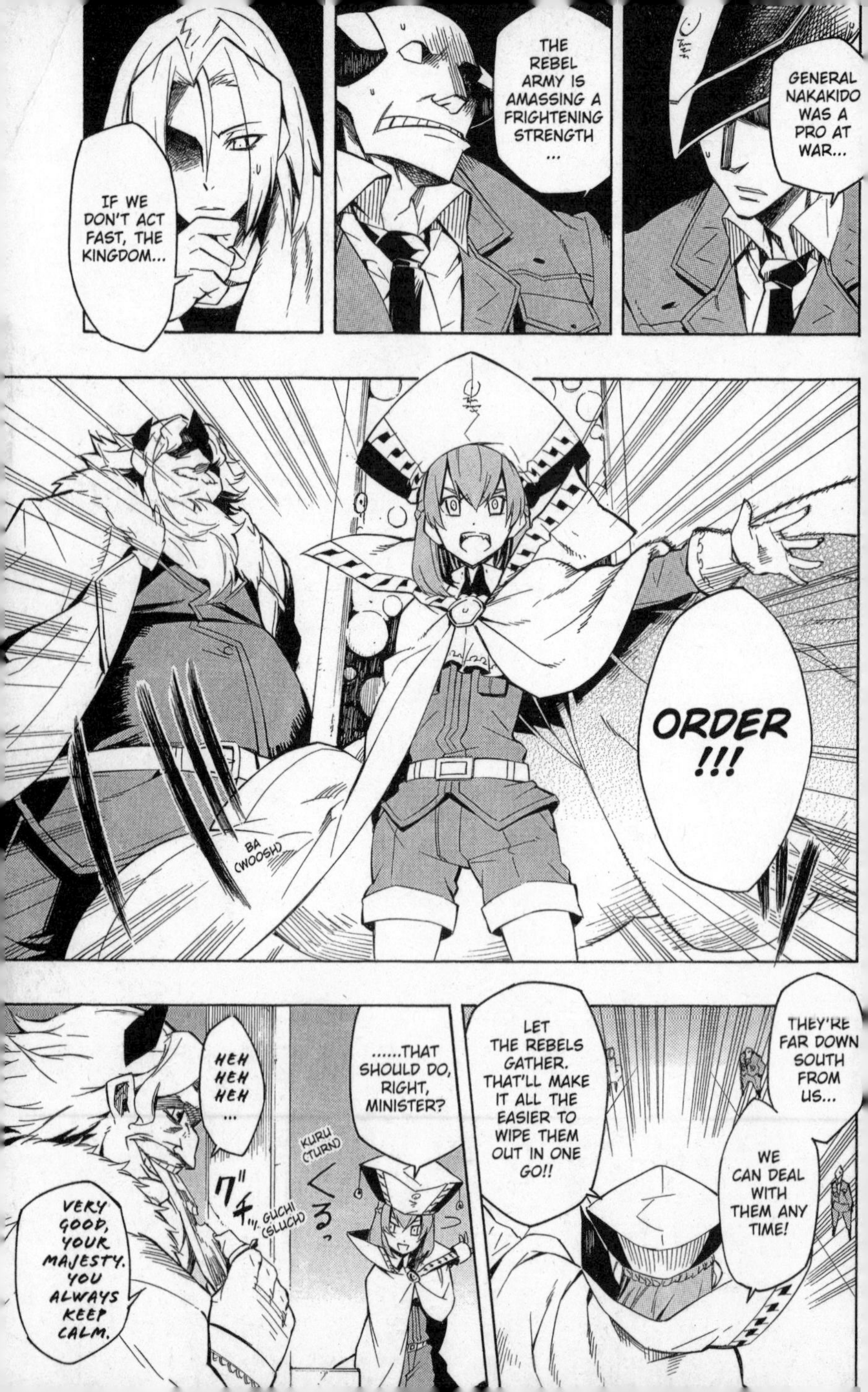
GENERAL NAKAKIDO WAS A PRO AT WAR...
THE REBEL ARMY IS AMASSING A FRIGHTENING STRENGTH ...
IF WE DON'T ACT FAST, THE KINGDOM...
ORDER !!!
BA (WOOSH)
THEY'RE FAR DOWN SOUTH FROM US...
WE CAN DEAL WITH THEM ANY TIME!
LET THE REBELS GATHER. THAT'LL MAKE IT ALL THE EASIER TO WIPE THEM OUT IN ONE GO!!
......THAT SHOULD DO, RIGHT, MINISTER?
くる
KURU (TURN)
HEH HEH HEH ...
グチ
GUCHI (SLUCH)
VERY GOOD, YOUR MAJESTY. YOU ALWAYS KEEP CALM.

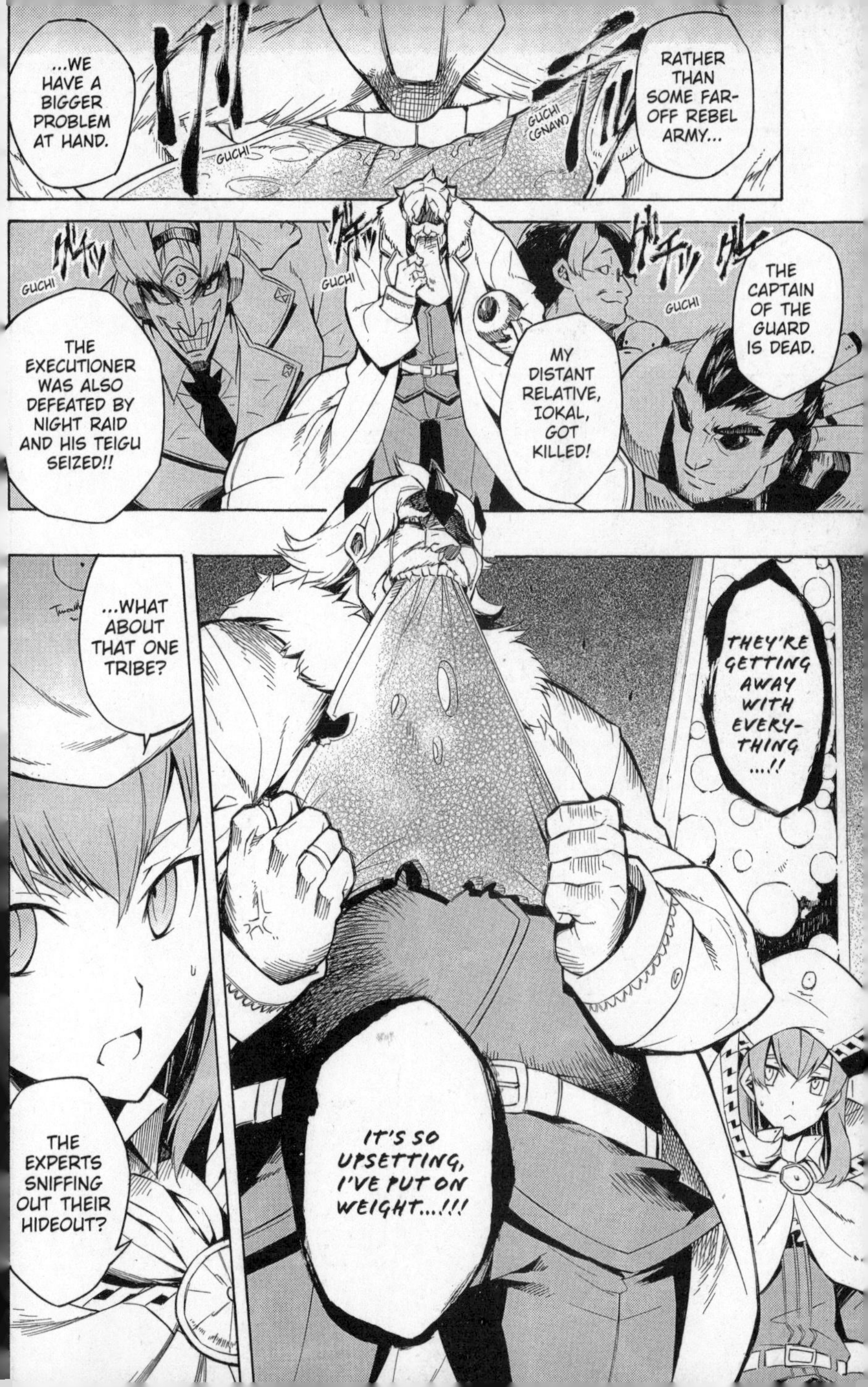
RATHER THAN SOME FAR-OFF REBEL ARMY...
GUCHI (GNAW)
GUCHI
...WE HAVE A BIGGER PROBLEM AT HAND.
THE CAPTAIN OF THE GUARD IS DEAD.
GUCHI
MY DISTANT RELATIVE, IOKAL, GOT KILLED!
GUCHI
GUCHI
THE EXECUTIONER WAS ALSO DEFEATED BY NIGHT RAID AND HIS TEIGU SEIZED!!
THEY'RE GETTING AWAY WITH EVERYTHING...!!
IT'S SO UPSETTING, I'VE PUT ON WEIGHT...!!!
...WHAT ABOUT THAT ONE TRIBE?
THE EXPERTS SNIFFING OUT THEIR HIDEOUT?

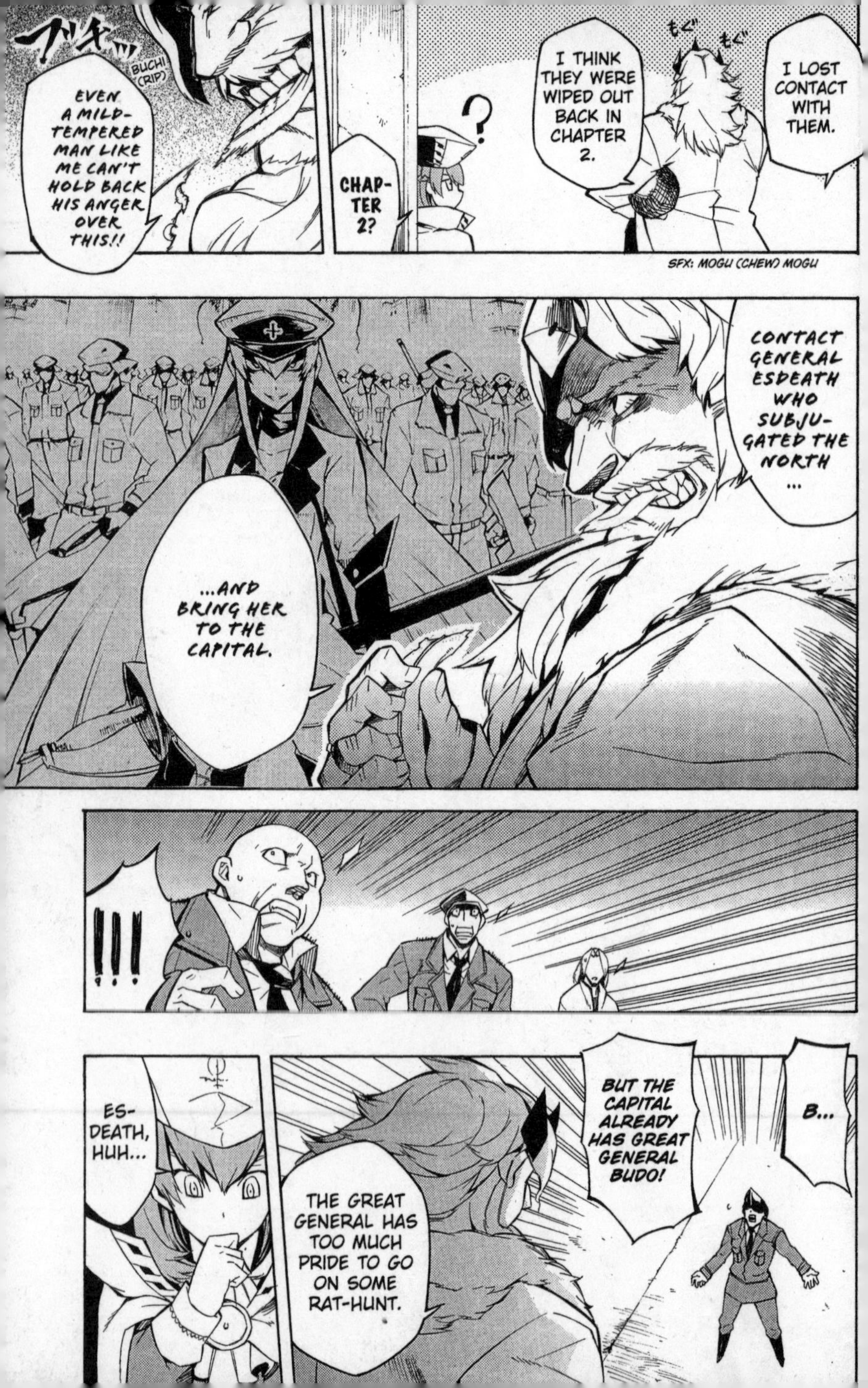

もぐ もぐ
I LOST CONTACT WITH THEM.
I THINK THEY WERE WIPED OUT BACK IN CHAPTER 2.
SFX: MOGU (CHEW) MOGU
?
CHAPTER 2?
BUCHI (RIP)
EVEN A MILD-TEMPERED MAN LIKE ME CAN'T HOLD BACK HIS ANGER OVER THIS!!
CONTACT GENERAL ESDEATH WHO SUBJUGATED THE NORTH...
...AND BRING HER TO THE CAPITAL.
!!!
B...
BUT THE CAPITAL ALREADY HAS GREAT GENERAL BUDO!
THE GREAT GENERAL HAS TOO MUCH PRIDE TO GO ON SOME RAT-HUNT.
ES-DEATH, HUH...

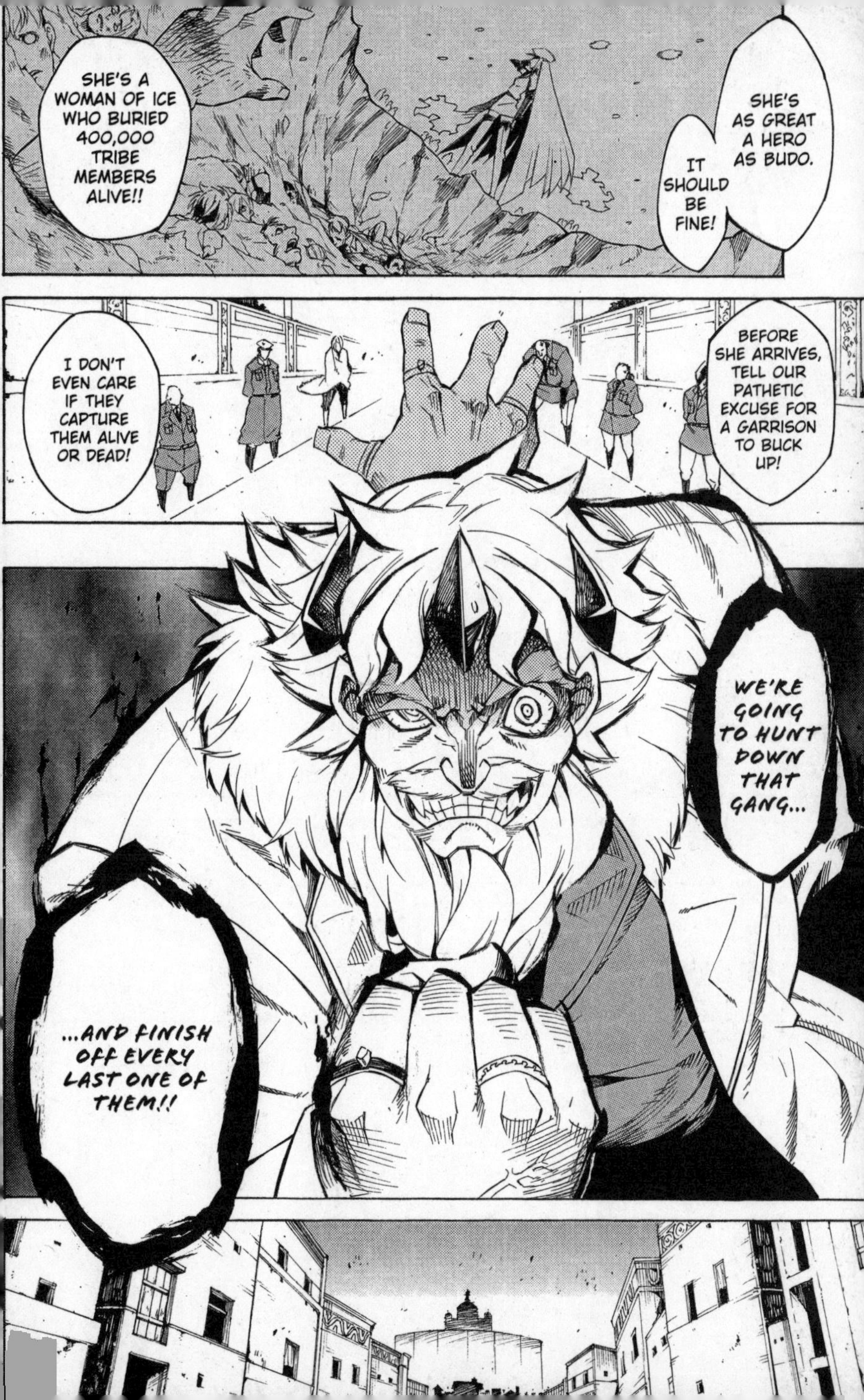
SHE'S AS GREAT A HERO AS BUDO.
IT SHOULD BE FINE!
SHE'S A WOMAN OF ICE WHO BURIED 400,000 TRIBE MEMBERS ALIVE!!
BEFORE SHE ARRIVES, TELL OUR PATHETIC EXCUSE FOR A GARRISON TO BUCK UP!
I DON'T EVEN CARE IF THEY CAPTURE THEM ALIVE OR DEAD!
WE'RE GOING TO HUNT DOWN THAT GANG...
...AND FINISH OFF EVERY LAST ONE OF THEM!!

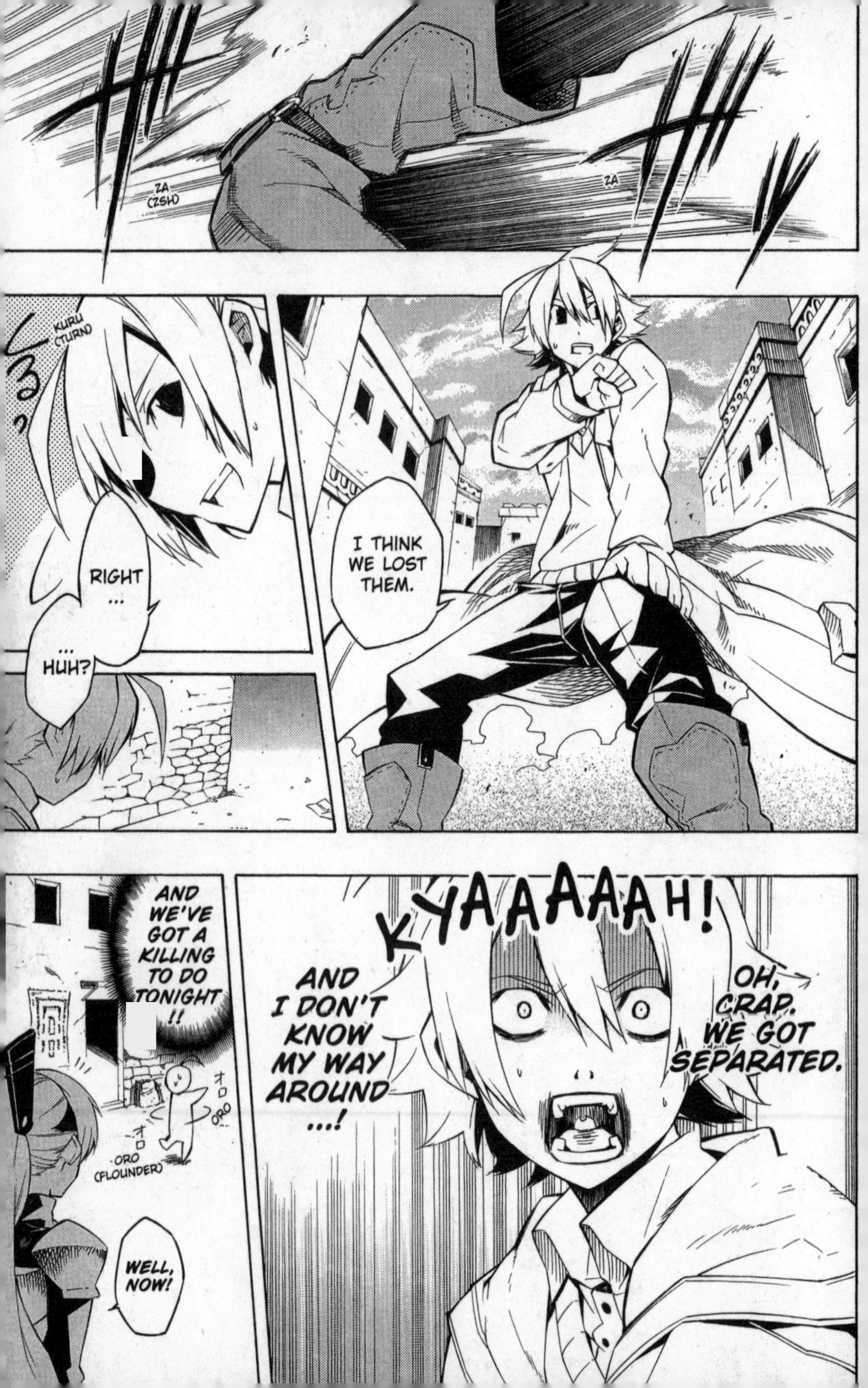
ZA
ZA
(ZSH)
I THINK WE LOST THEM.
KURU
(TURN)
RIGHT ...
... HUH?
KYAAAAAH!
OH, CRAP. WE GOT SEPARATED.
AND I DON'T KNOW MY WAY AROUND ...!
AND WE'VE GOT A KILLING TO DO TONIGHT!!
ORO
ORO
(FLOUNDER)
WELL, NOW!

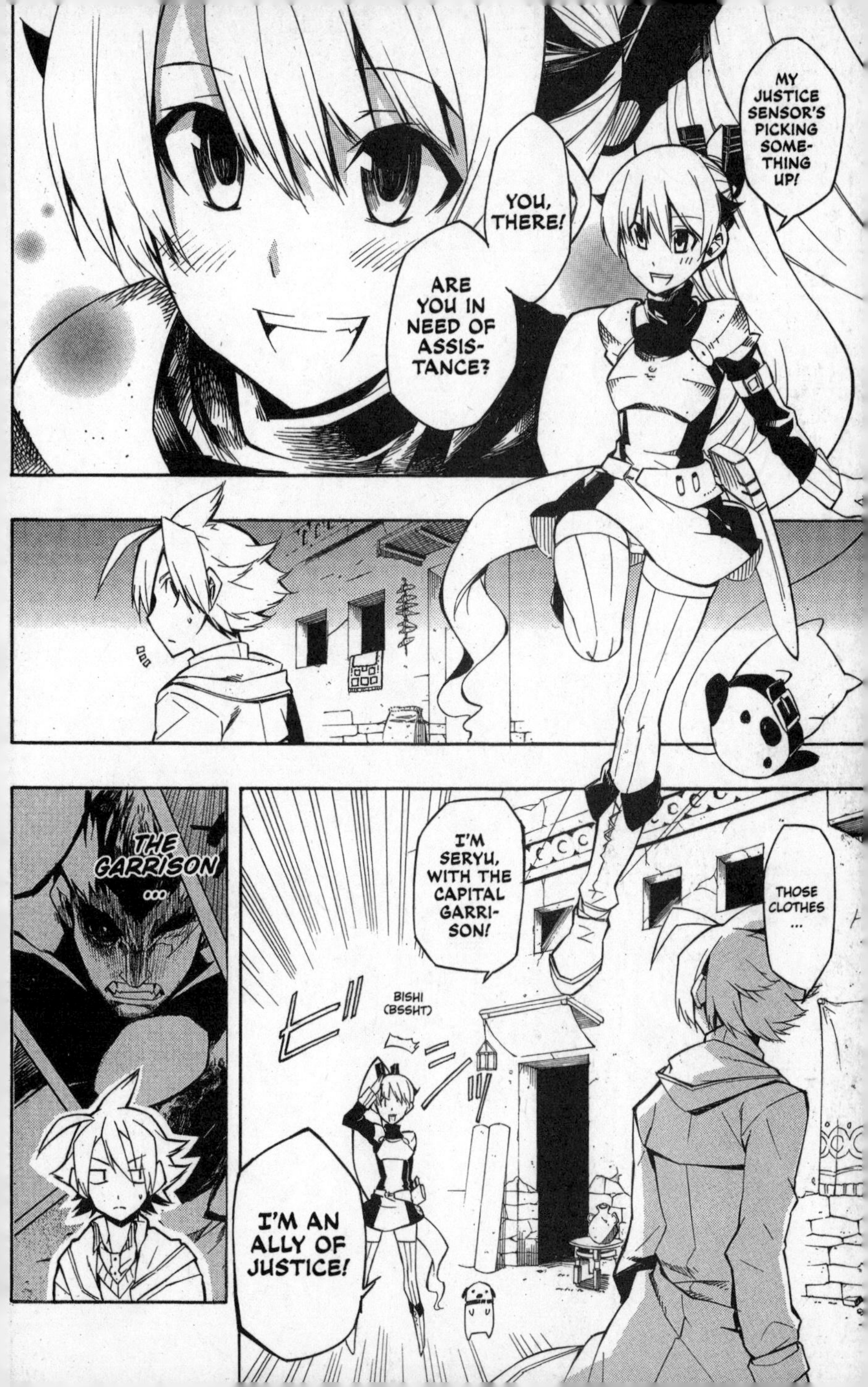
MY JUSTICE SENSOR'S PICKING SOME-THING UP!
YOU, THERE!
ARE YOU IN NEED OF ASSIS-TANCE?
THOSE CLOTHES ...
I'M SERYU, WITH THE CAPITAL GARRI-SON!
BISHI (BSSHT)
I'M AN ALLY OF JUSTICE!
THE GARRISON ...

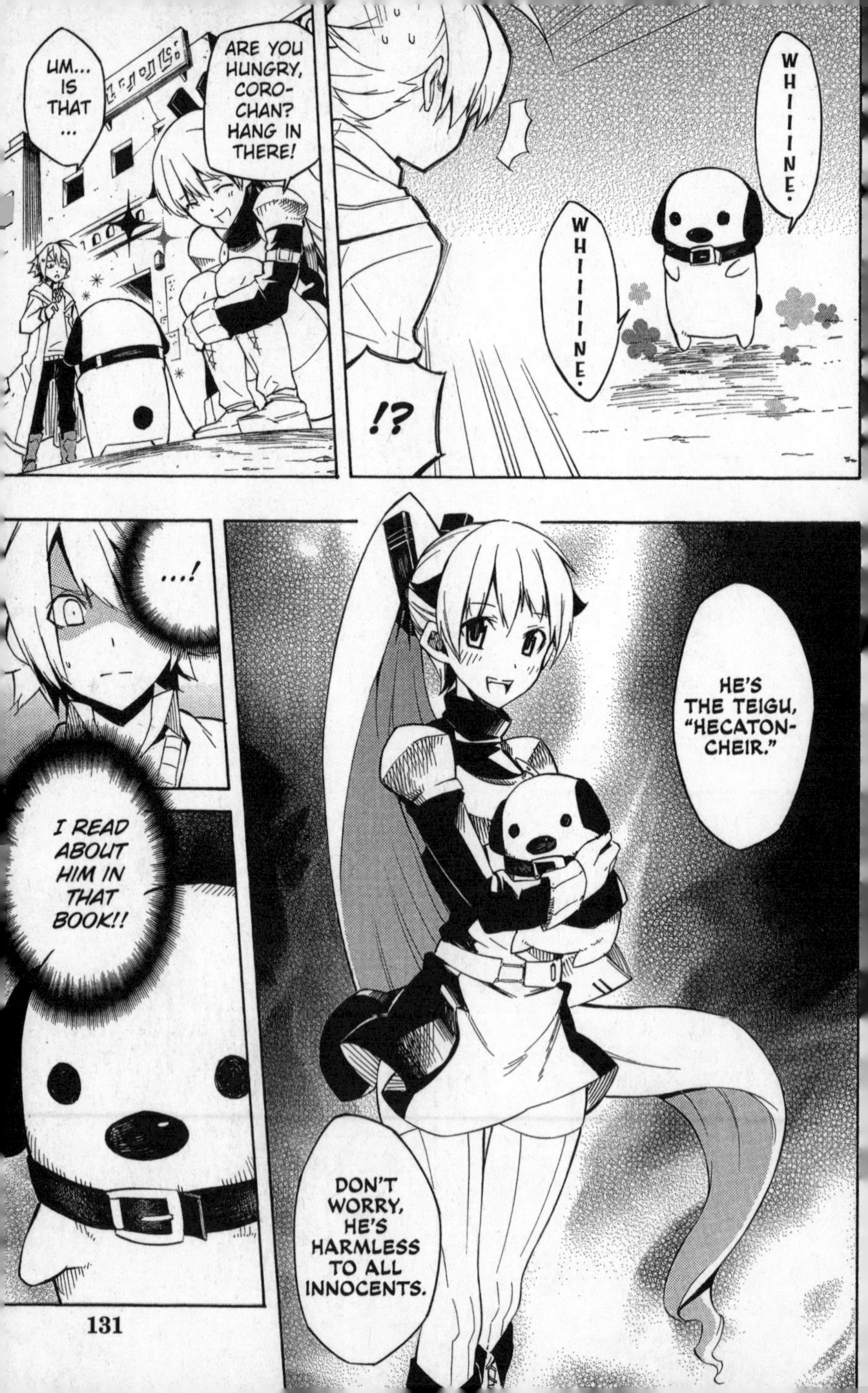
WHIIINE.
WHIIIINE.
!?
ARE YOU HUNGRY, CORO-CHAN? HANG IN THERE!
UM... IS THAT ...
HE'S THE TEIGU, "HECATON-CHEIR."
DON'T WORRY, HE'S HARMLESS TO ALL INNOCENTS.
...!
I READ ABOUT HIM IN THAT BOOK!!

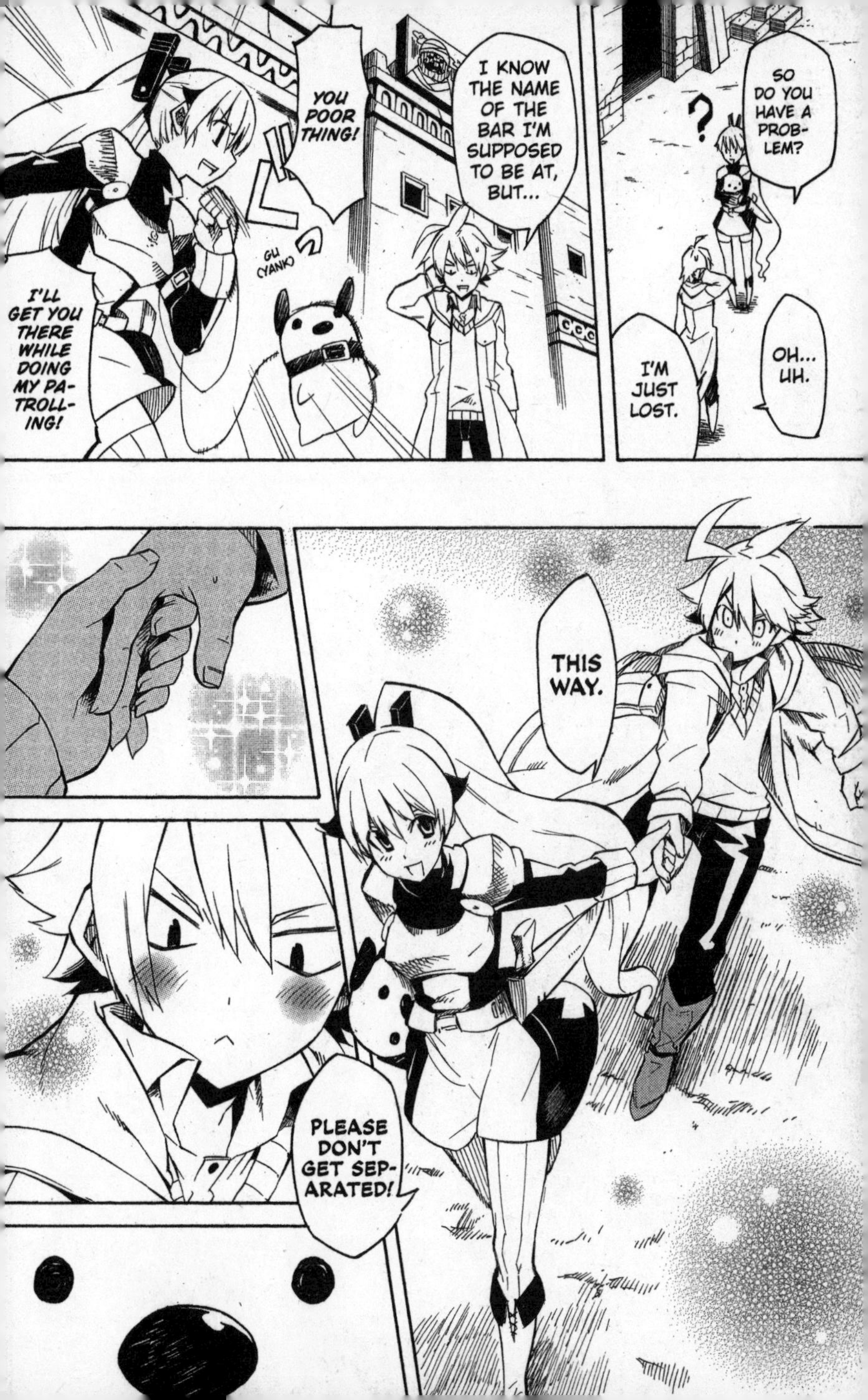
SO DO YOU HAVE A PROB-LEM?
OH... UH.
I'M JUST LOST.
I KNOW THE NAME OF THE BAR I'M SUPPOSED TO BE AT, BUT...
YOU POOR THING!
GU (YANK)
I'LL GET YOU THERE WHILE DOING MY PA-TROLL-ING!
THIS WAY.
PLEASE DON'T GET SEP-ARATED!

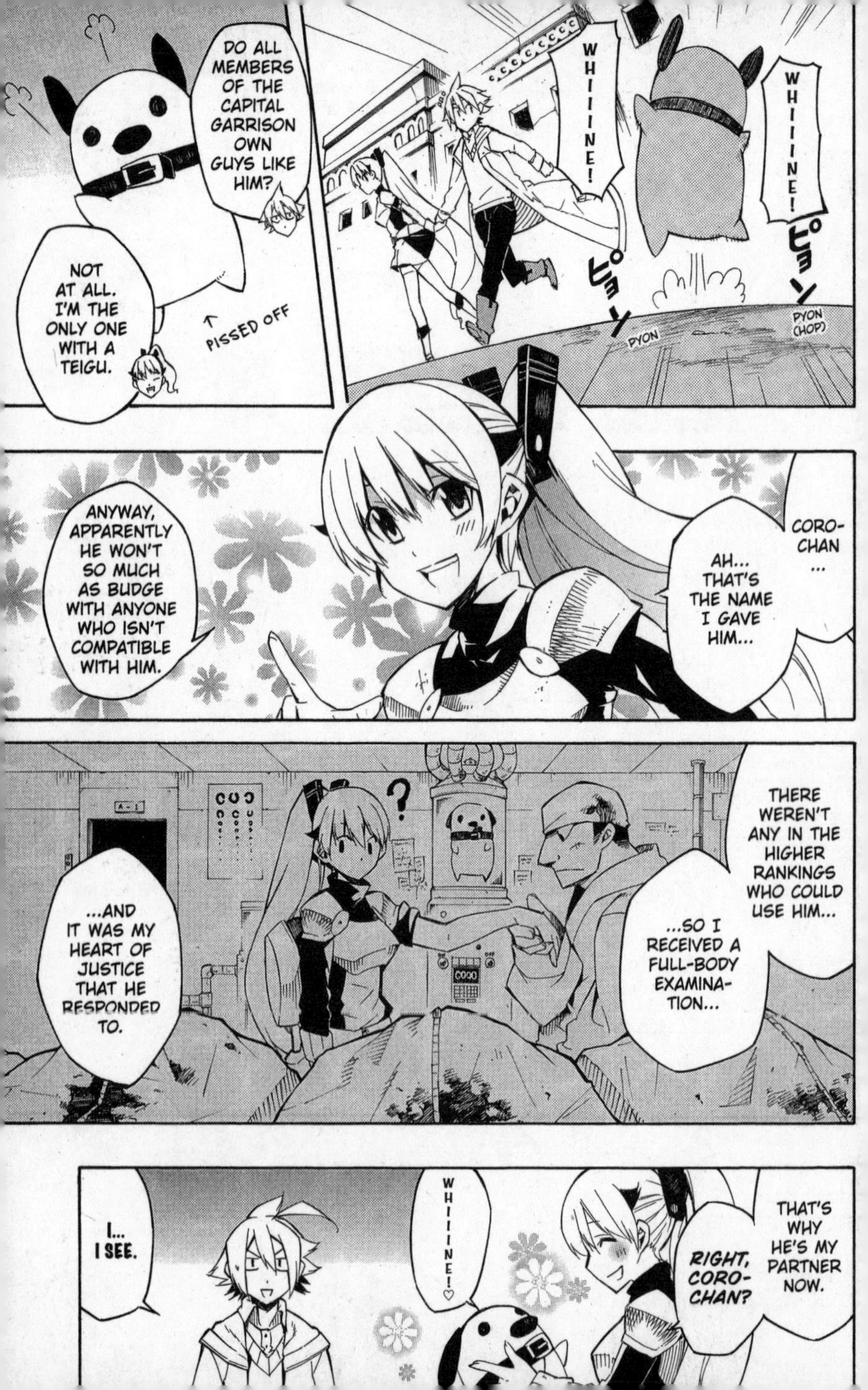
WHIIINE!
WHIIINE!
ピョン
PYON (HOP)
ピョン
PYON
DO ALL MEMBERS OF THE CAPITAL GARRISON OWN GUYS LIKE HIM?
NOT AT ALL. I'M THE ONLY ONE WITH A TEIGU.
↑ PISSED OFF
CORO-CHAN...
AH... THAT'S THE NAME I GAVE HIM...
ANYWAY, APPARENTLY HE WON'T SO MUCH AS BUDGE WITH ANYONE WHO ISN'T COMPATIBLE WITH HIM.
THERE WEREN'T ANY IN THE HIGHER RANKINGS WHO COULD USE HIM...
...SO I RECEIVED A FULL-BODY EXAMINA-TION...
...AND IT WAS MY HEART OF JUSTICE THAT HE RESPONDED TO.
THAT'S WHY HE'S MY PARTNER NOW.
RIGHT, CORO-CHAN?
WHIIINE!♡
I... I SEE.

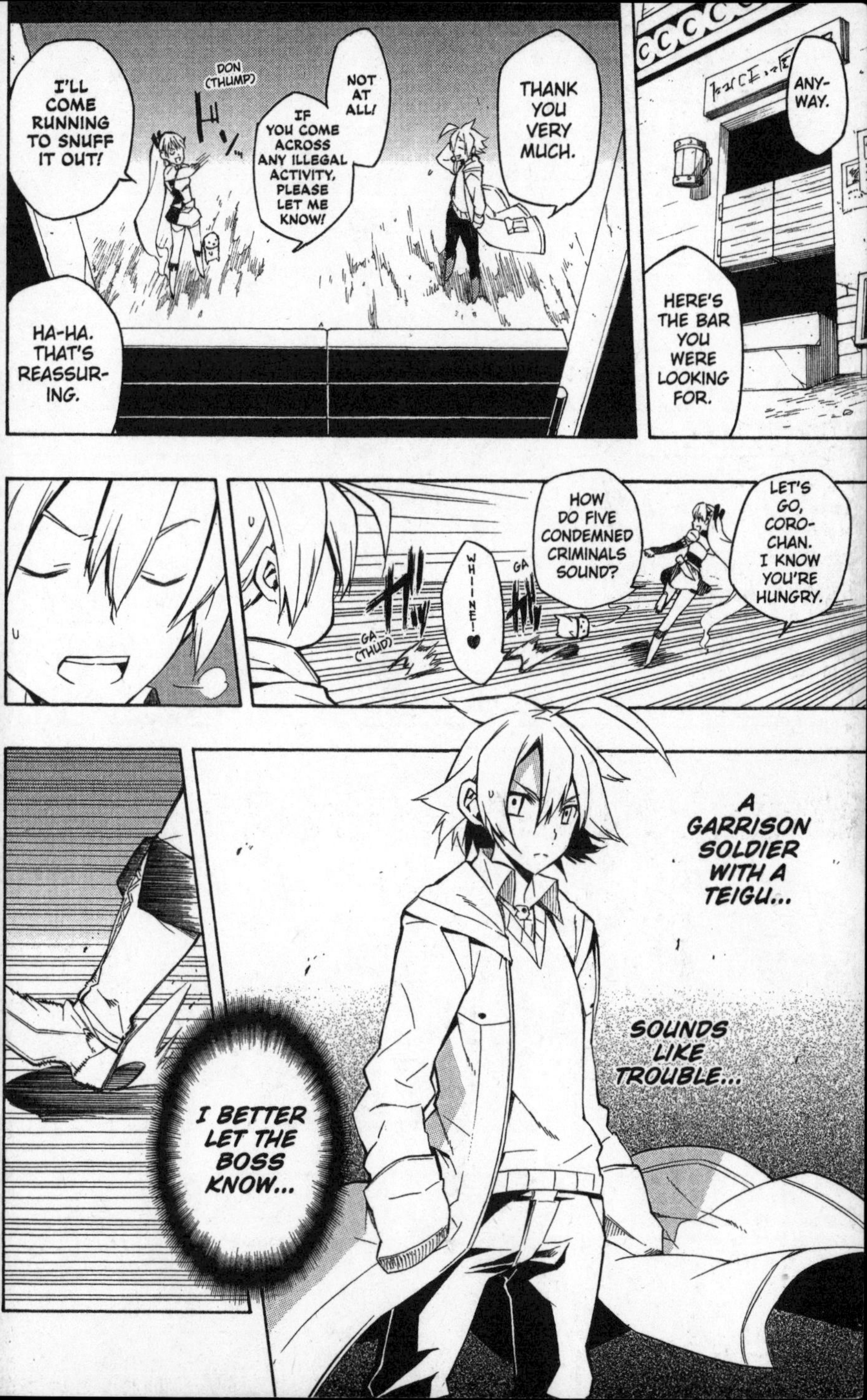
ANYWAY.
HERE'S THE BAR YOU WERE LOOKING FOR.
THANK YOU VERY MUCH.
NOT AT ALL!
IF YOU COME ACROSS ANY ILLEGAL ACTIVITY, PLEASE LET ME KNOW!
DON (THUMP)
I'LL COME RUNNING TO SNUFF IT OUT!
HA-HA. THAT'S REASSURING.
LET'S GO, CORO-CHAN. I KNOW YOU'RE HUNGRY.
HOW DO FIVE CONDEMNED CRIMINALS SOUND?
GA
WHINE!♥
GA (THUD)
A GARRISON SOLDIER WITH A TEIGU...
SOUNDS LIKE TROUBLE...
I BETTER LET THE BOSS KNOW...

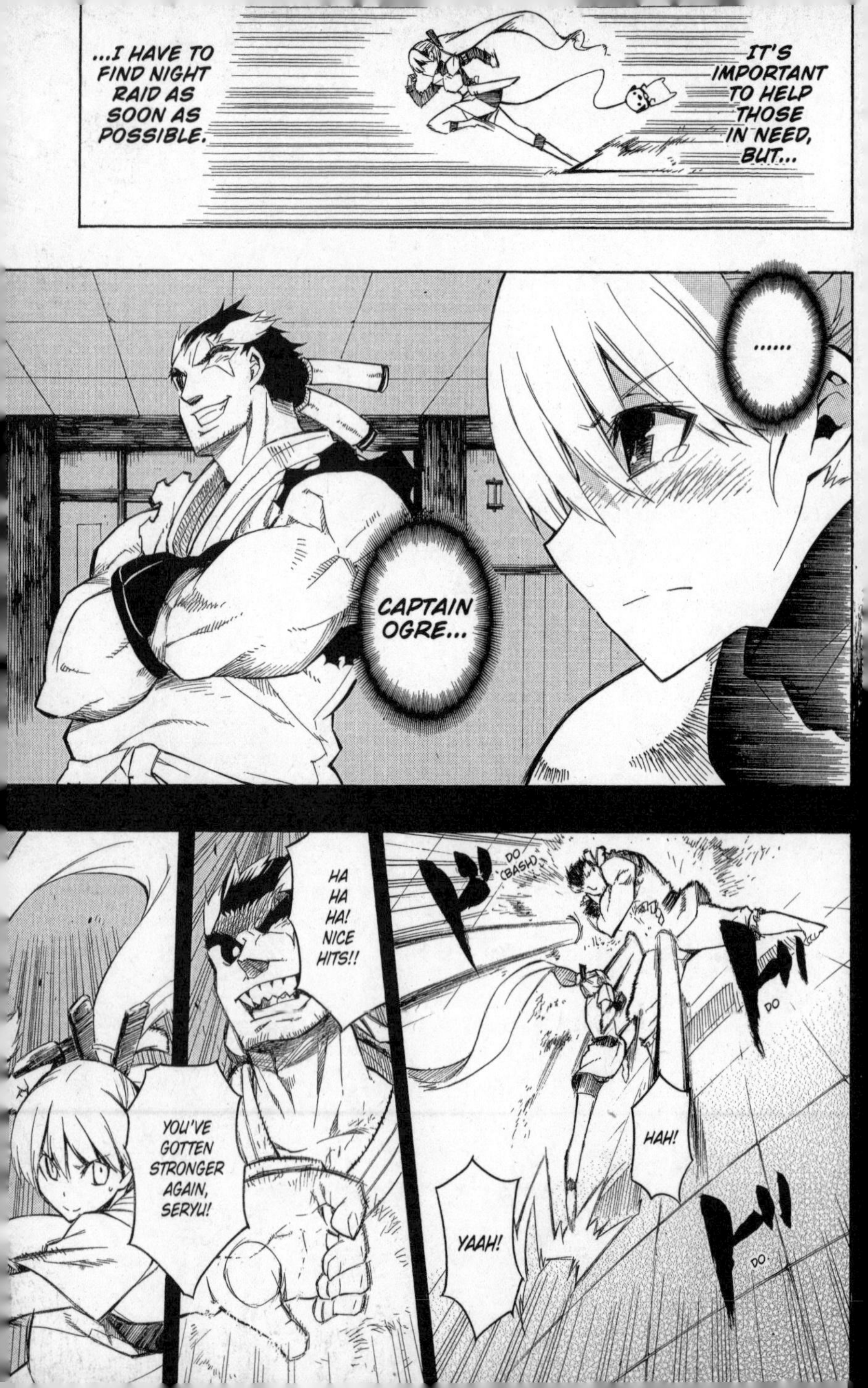
IT'S IMPORTANT TO HELP THOSE IN NEED, BUT...
...I HAVE TO FIND NIGHT RAID AS SOON AS POSSIBLE.
......
CAPTAIN OGRE...
DO (BASH)
DO
HAH!
YAAH!
DO.
HA HA HA! NICE HITS!!
YOU'VE GOTTEN STRONGER AGAIN, SERYU!

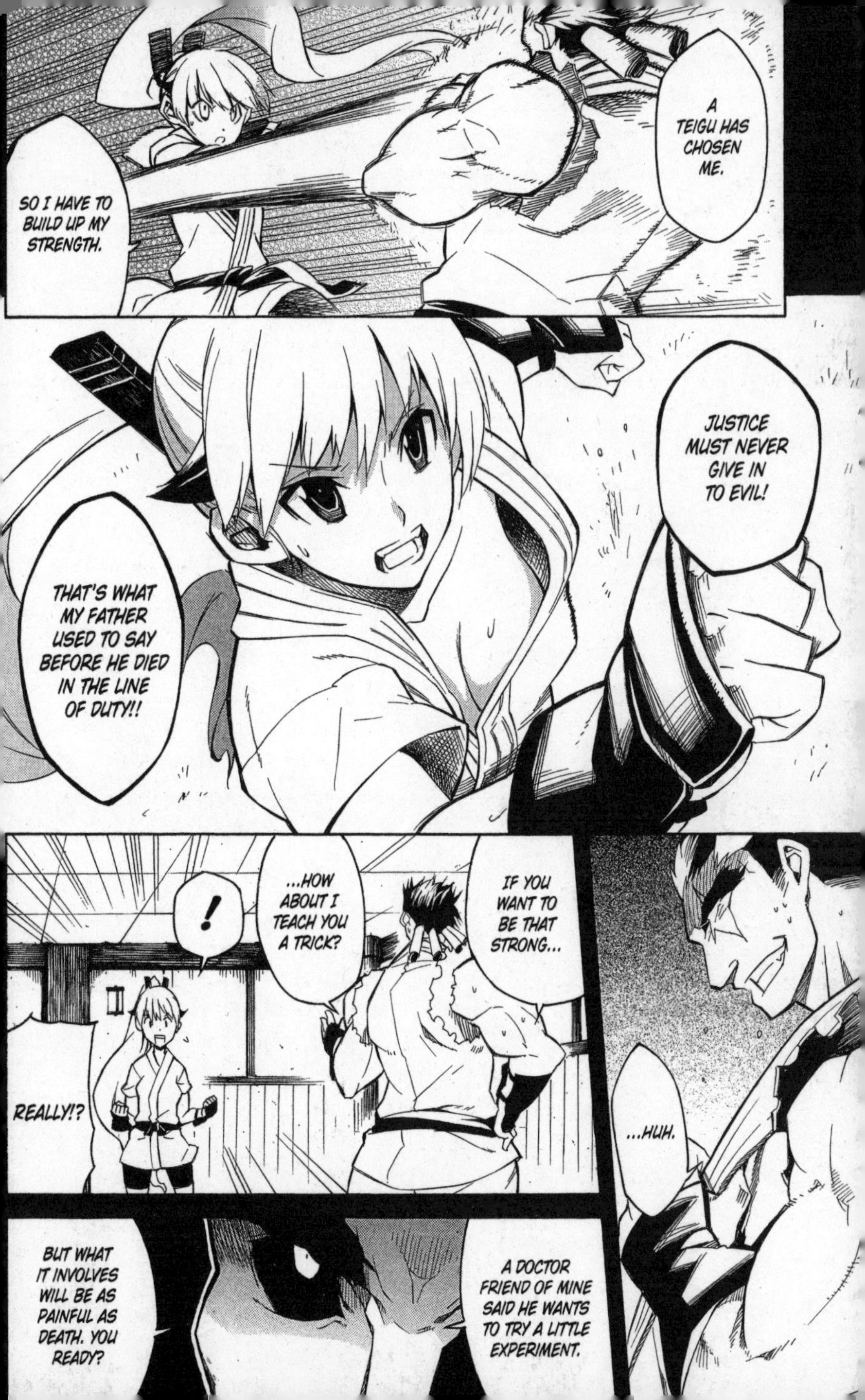
A TEIGU HAS CHOSEN ME.
SO I HAVE TO BUILD UP MY STRENGTH.
JUSTICE MUST NEVER GIVE IN TO EVIL!
THAT'S WHAT MY FATHER USED TO SAY BEFORE HE DIED IN THE LINE OF DUTY!!
...HUH.
IF YOU WANT TO BE THAT STRONG...
...HOW ABOUT I TEACH YOU A TRICK?
!
REALLY!?
A DOCTOR FRIEND OF MINE SAID HE WANTS TO TRY A LITTLE EXPERIMENT.
BUT WHAT IT INVOLVES WILL BE AS PAINFUL AS DEATH. YOU READY?

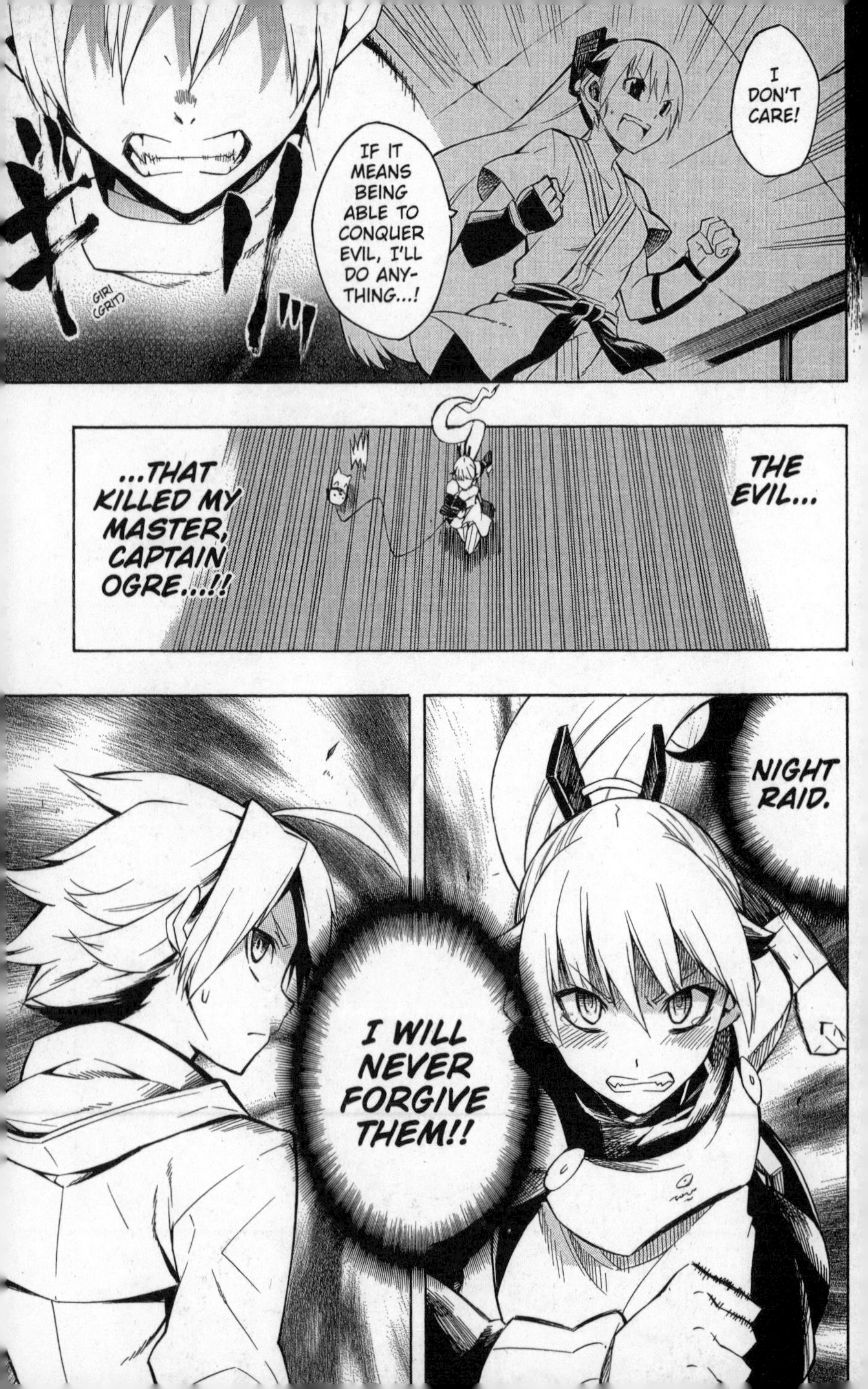

I DON'T CARE!
IF IT MEANS BEING ABLE TO CONQUER EVIL, I'LL DO ANYTHING...!
GIRI (GRIT)
THE EVIL...
...THAT KILLED MY MASTER, CAPTAIN OGRE...!!
NIGHT RAID.
I WILL NEVER FORGIVE THEM!!

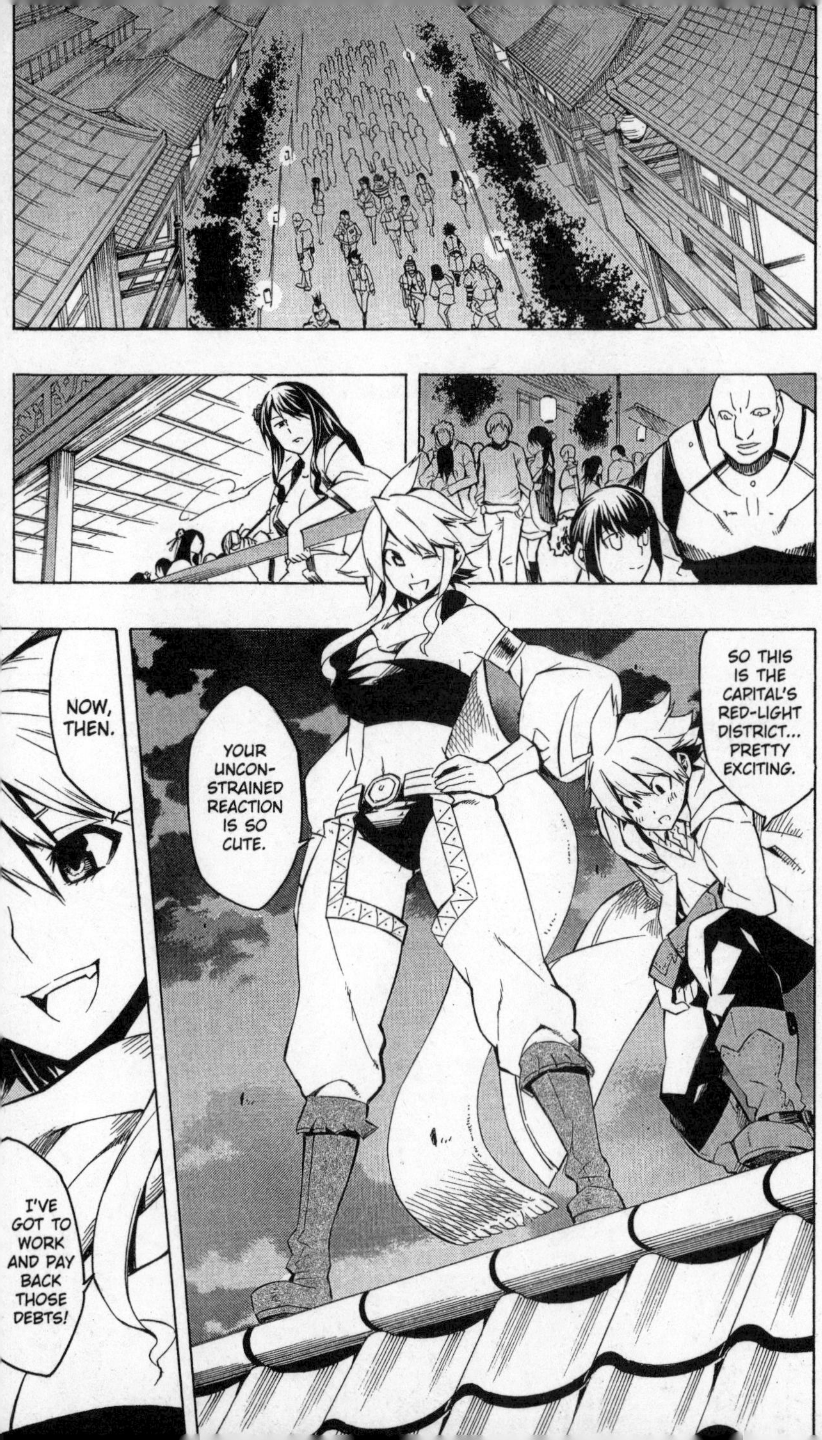
SO THIS IS THE CAPITAL'S RED-LIGHT DISTRICT... PRETTY EXCITING.
YOUR UNCON-STRAINED REACTION IS SO CUTE.
NOW, THEN.
I'VE GOT TO WORK AND PAY BACK THOSE DEBTS!

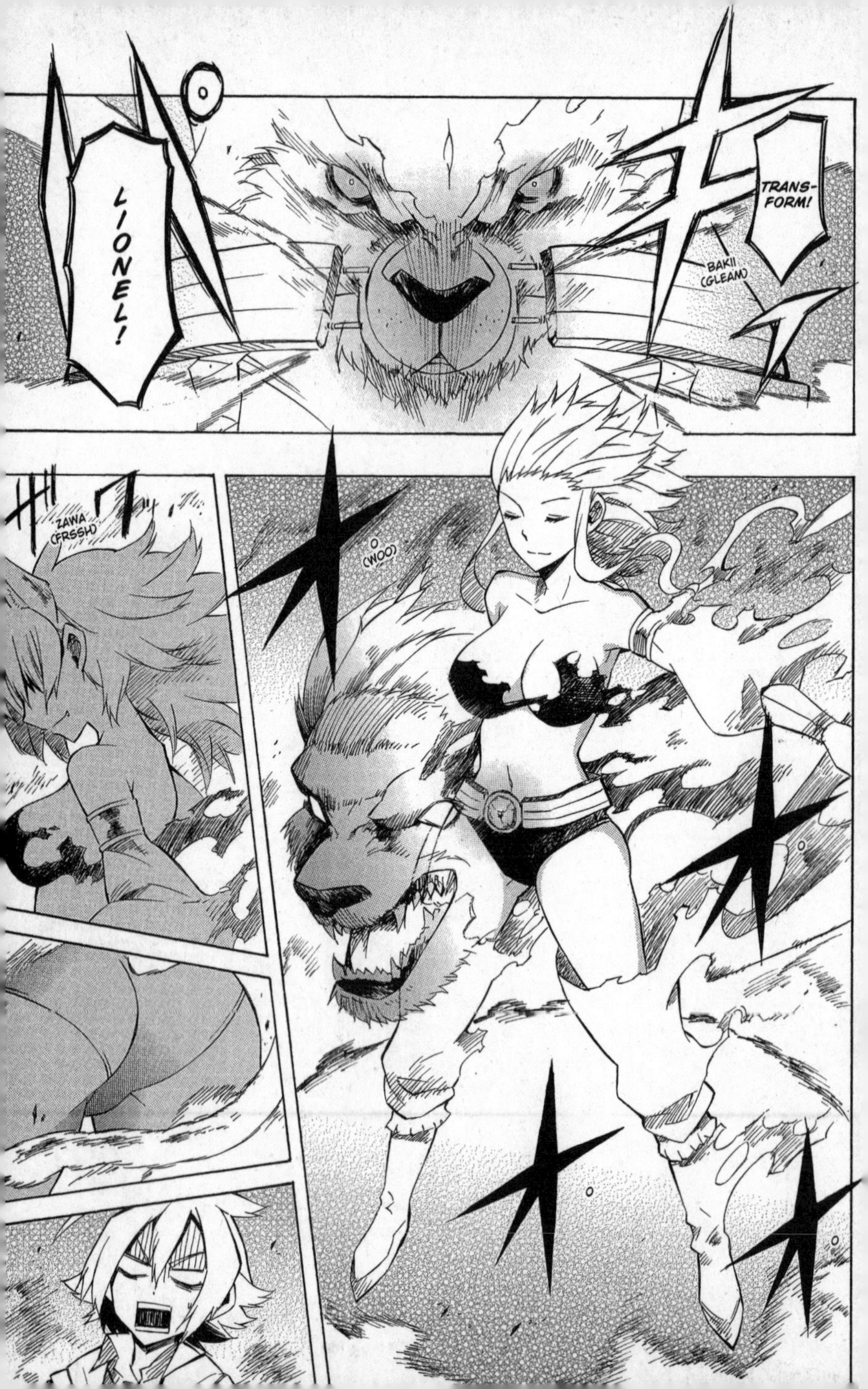
TRANS-FORM!
BAKII (GLEAM)
LIONEL!
O (WOO)
ZAWA (FRSSH)

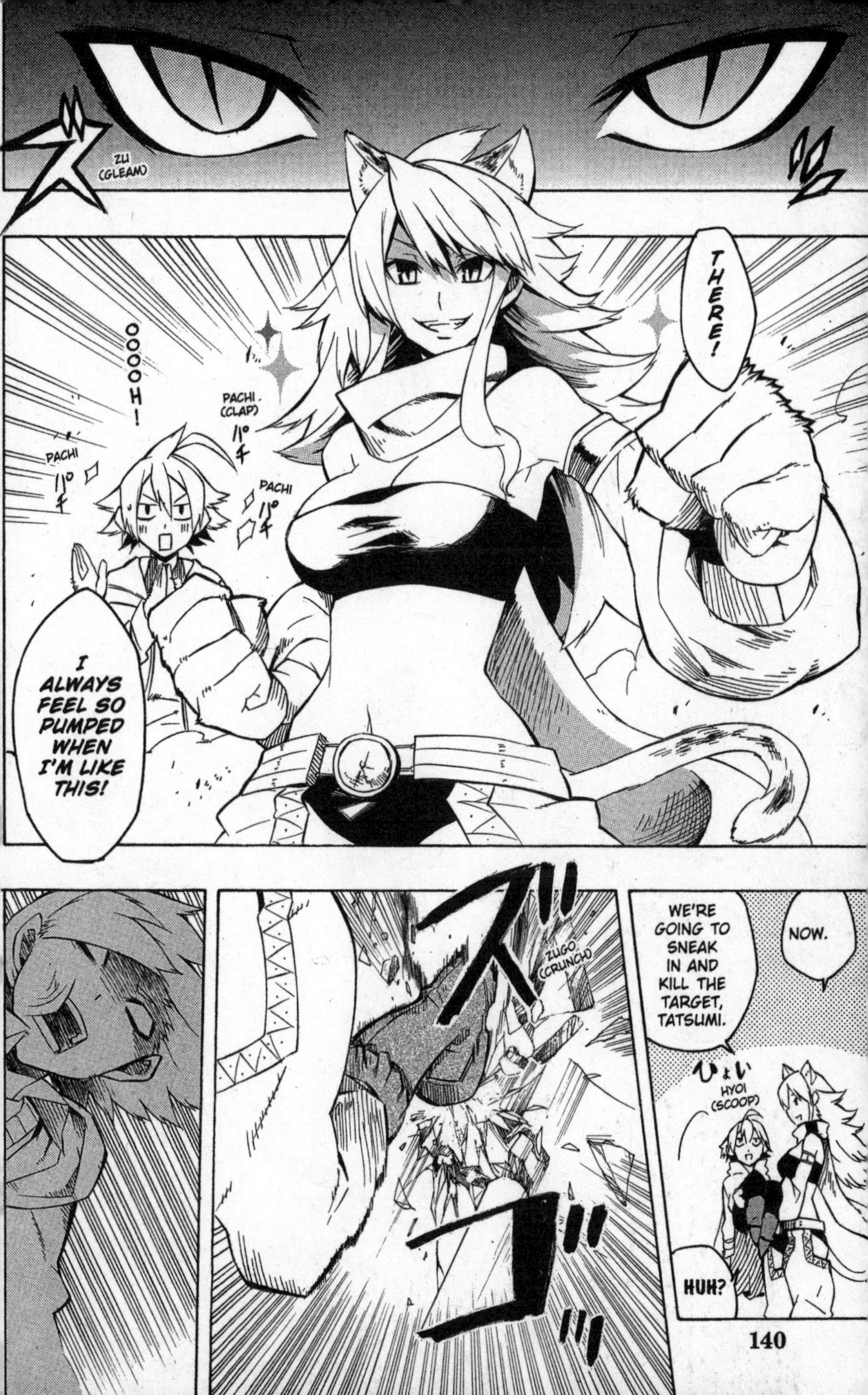
ZU (GLEAM)
THERE!
PACHI (CLAP)
PACHI
PACHI
OOOOH!
I ALWAYS FEEL SO PUMPED WHEN I'M LIKE THIS!
NOW.
WE'RE GOING TO SNEAK IN AND KILL THE TARGET, TATSUMI.
ひょい
HYOI (SCOOP)
HUH?
ZUGO (CRUNCH)

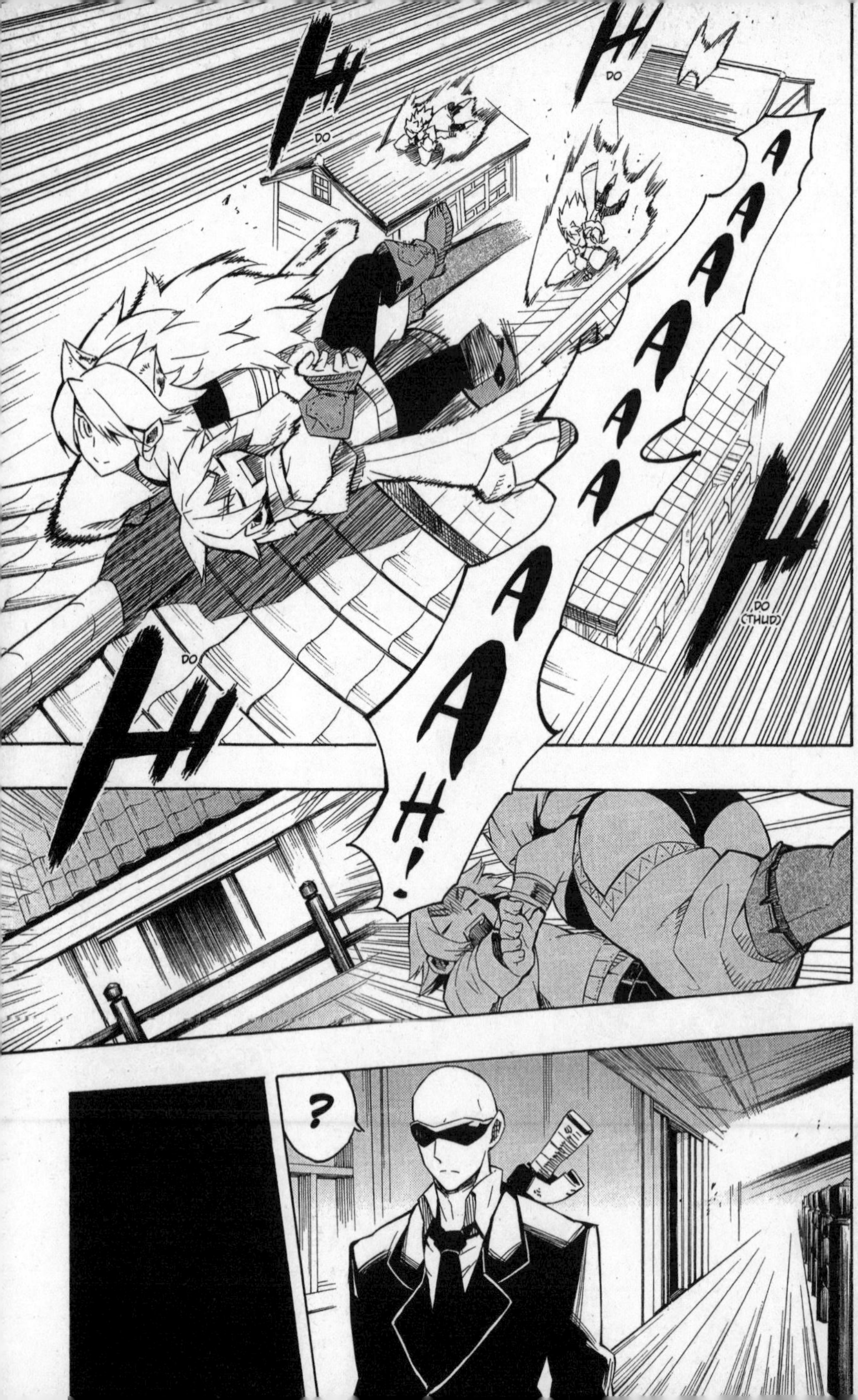
DO
DO
AAAAAAAAAAAH!
DO (THUD)
DO
?

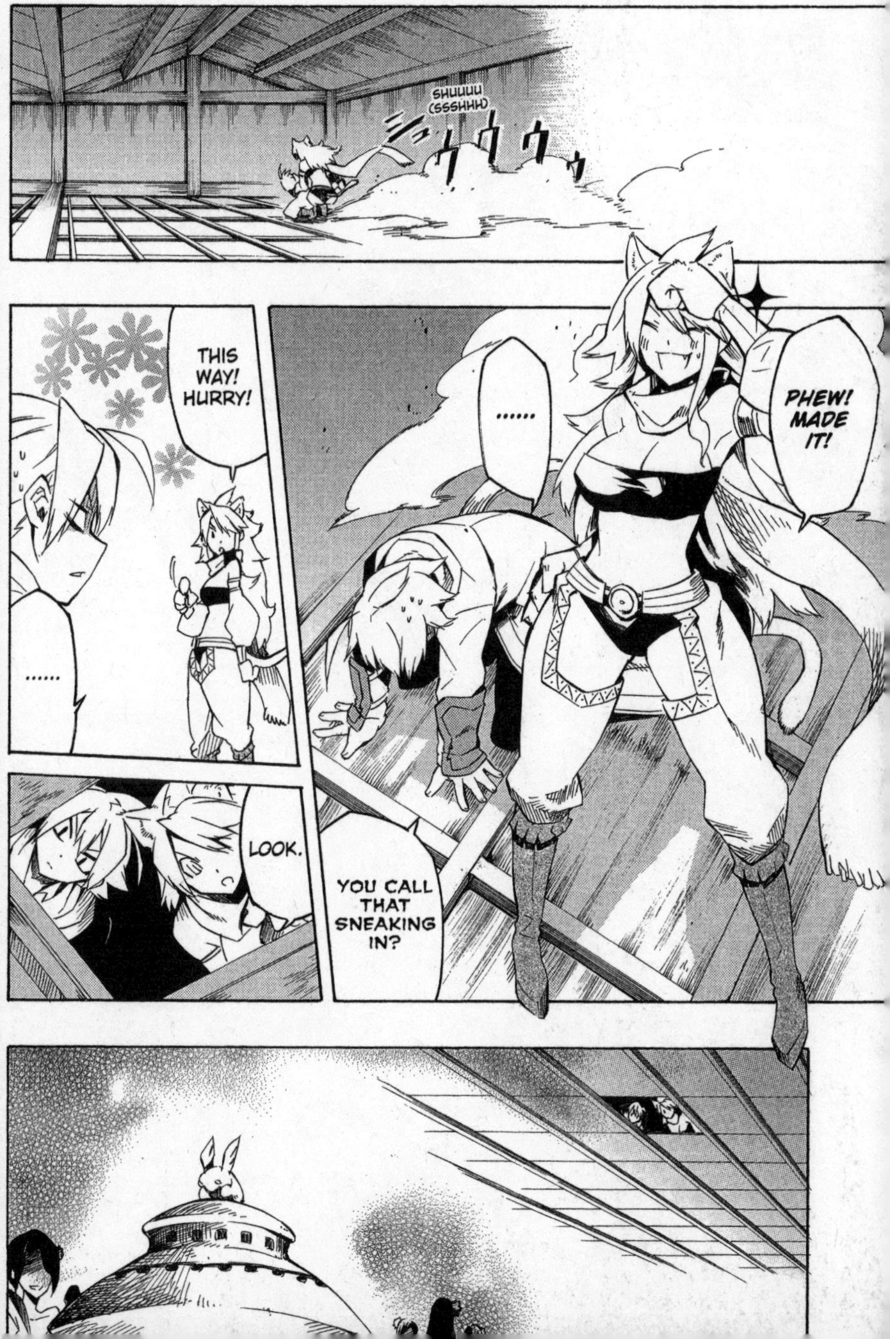
SHUUUU (SSSHHH)
シュウウウゥ
PHEW! MADE IT!
......
YOU CALL THAT SNEAKING IN?
THIS WAY! HURRY!
......
LOOK.

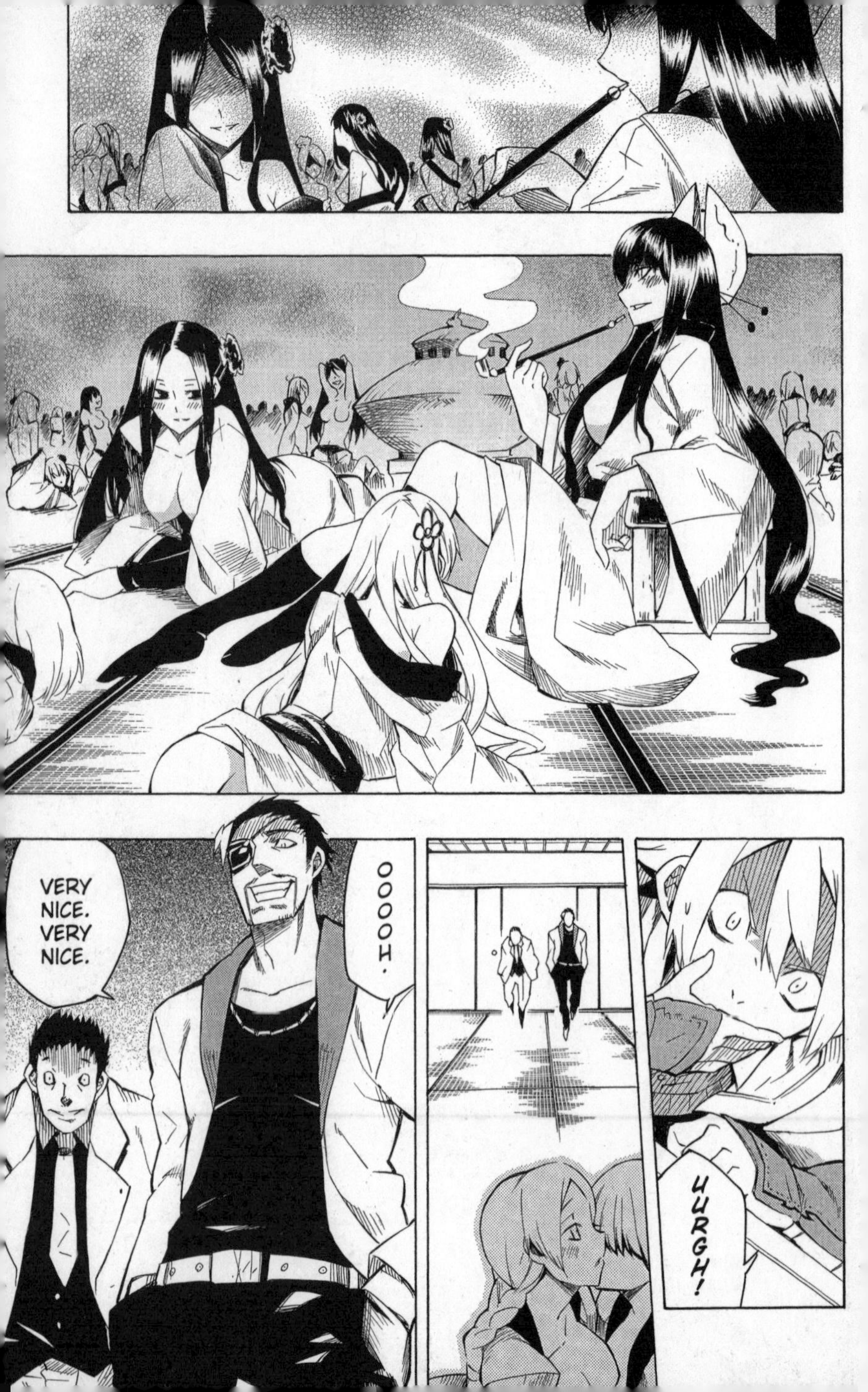
UURGH!
OOOOH.
VERY NICE. VERY NICE.

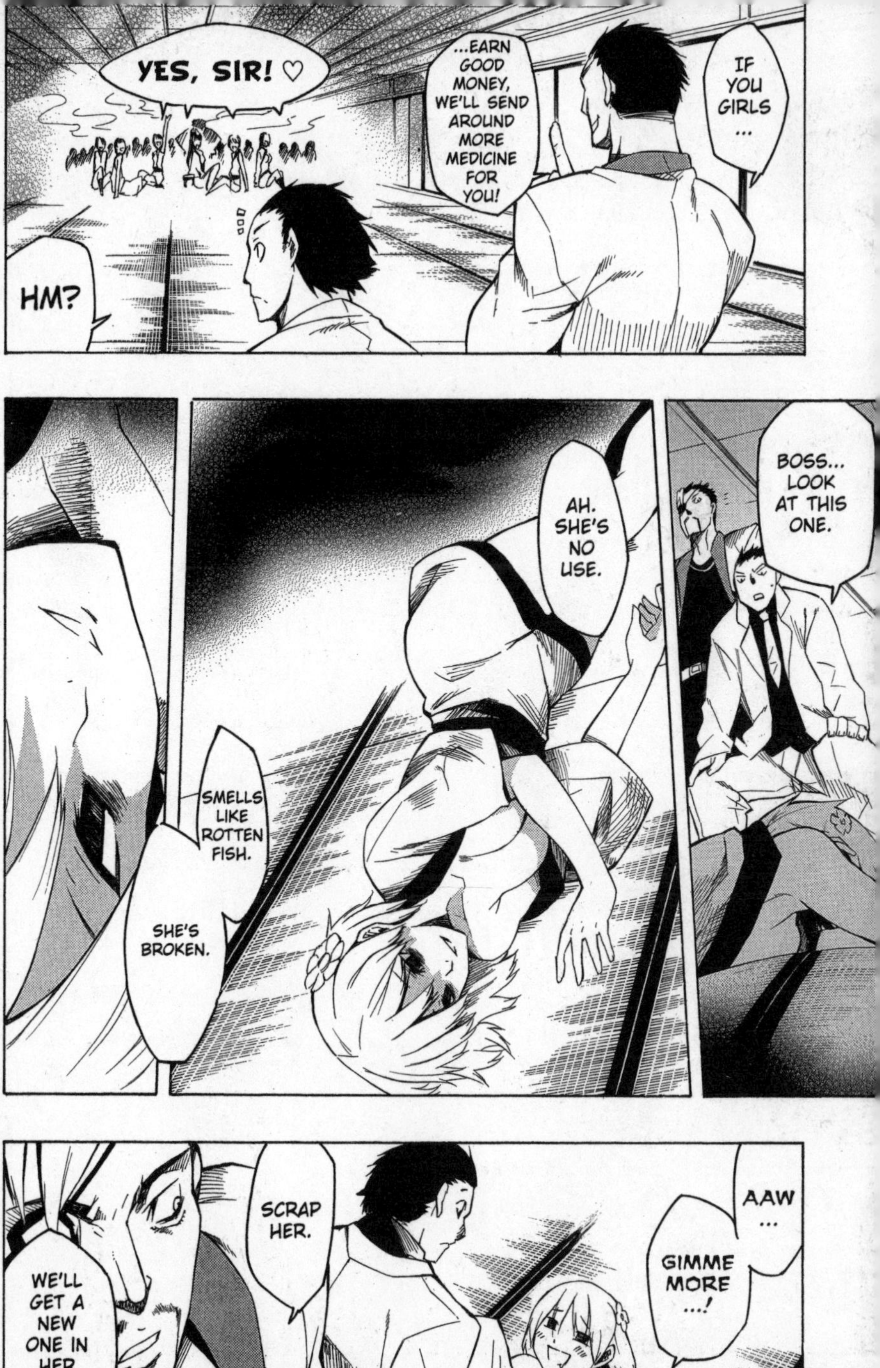
IF YOU GIRLS ...
...EARN GOOD MONEY, WE'LL SEND AROUND MORE MEDICINE FOR YOU!
YES, SIR! ♡
HM?
BOSS... LOOK AT THIS ONE.
AH. SHE'S NO USE.
SMELLS LIKE ROTTEN FISH.
SHE'S BROKEN.
AAW ... GIMME MORE ....!
SCRAP HER.
WE'LL GET A NEW ONE IN HER PLACE.

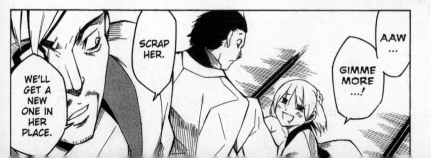

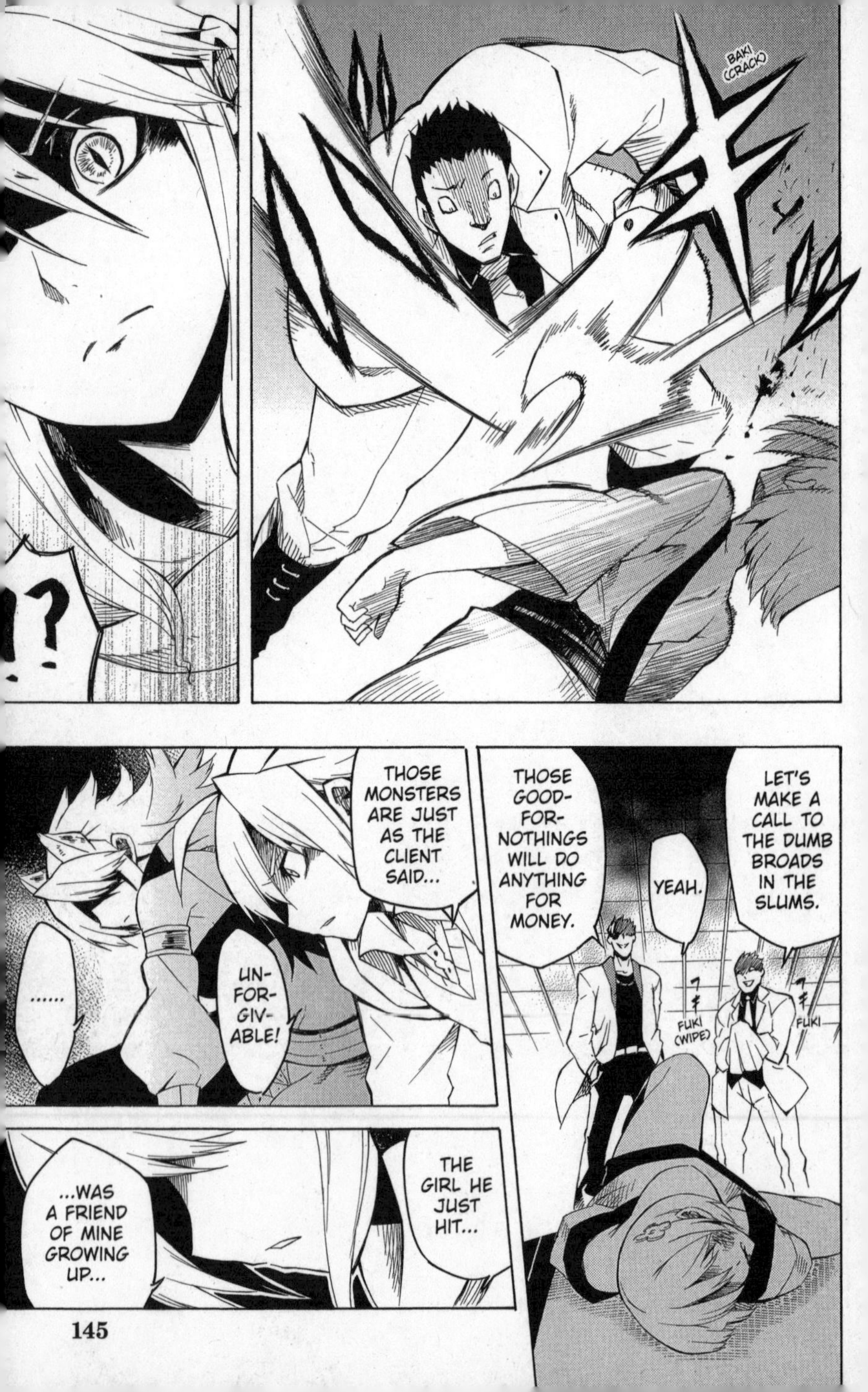
BAKI (CRACK)
?
LET'S MAKE A CALL TO THE DUMB BROADS IN THE SLUMS.
YEAH.
THOSE GOOD-FOR-NOTHINGS WILL DO ANYTHING FOR MONEY.
FUKI
FUKI (WIPE)
THOSE MONSTERS ARE JUST AS THE CLIENT SAID...
UN-FOR-GIV-ABLE!
......
THE GIRL HE JUST HIT...
...WAS A FRIEND OF MINE GROWING UP...

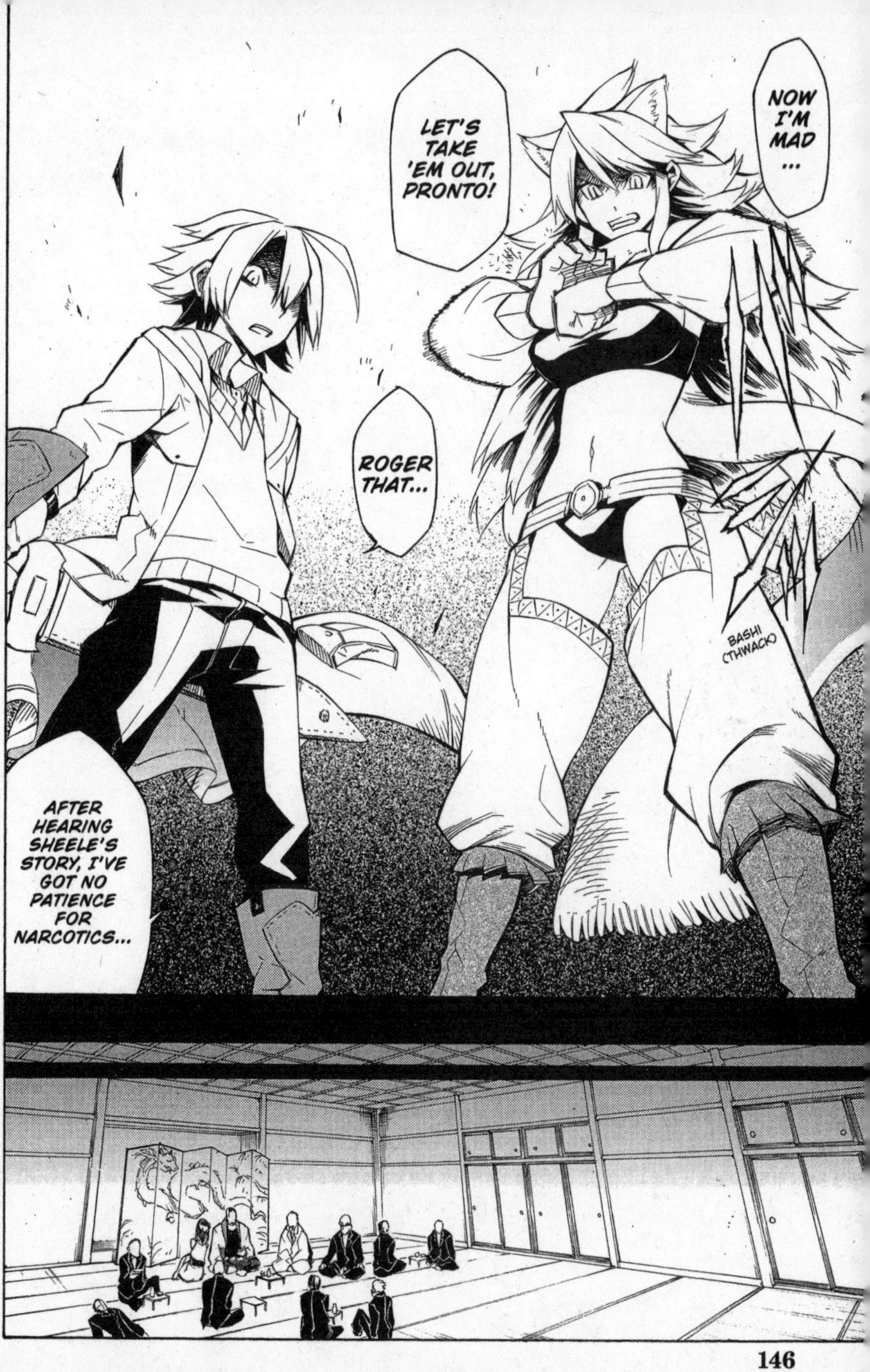
NOW I'M MAD ...
LET'S TAKE 'EM OUT, PRONTO!
ROGER THAT...
BASHI (THWACK)
AFTER HEARING SHEELE'S STORY, I'VE GOT NO PATIENCE FOR NARCOTICS...

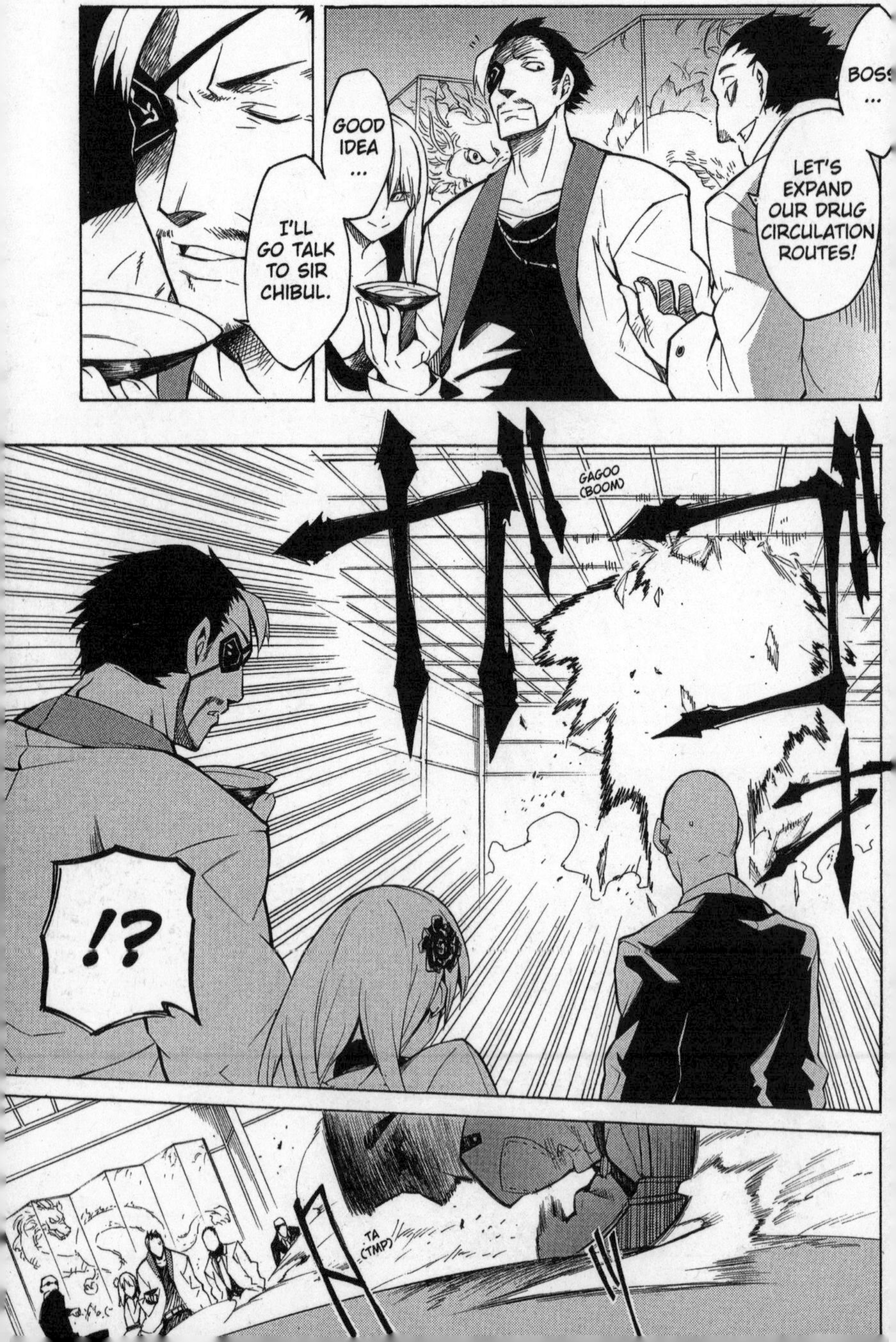
BOSS ...
LET'S EXPAND OUR DRUG CIRCULATION ROUTES!
GOOD IDEA ...
I'LL GO TALK TO SIR CHIBUL.
GAGOO (BOOM)
!?
TA (TMP)

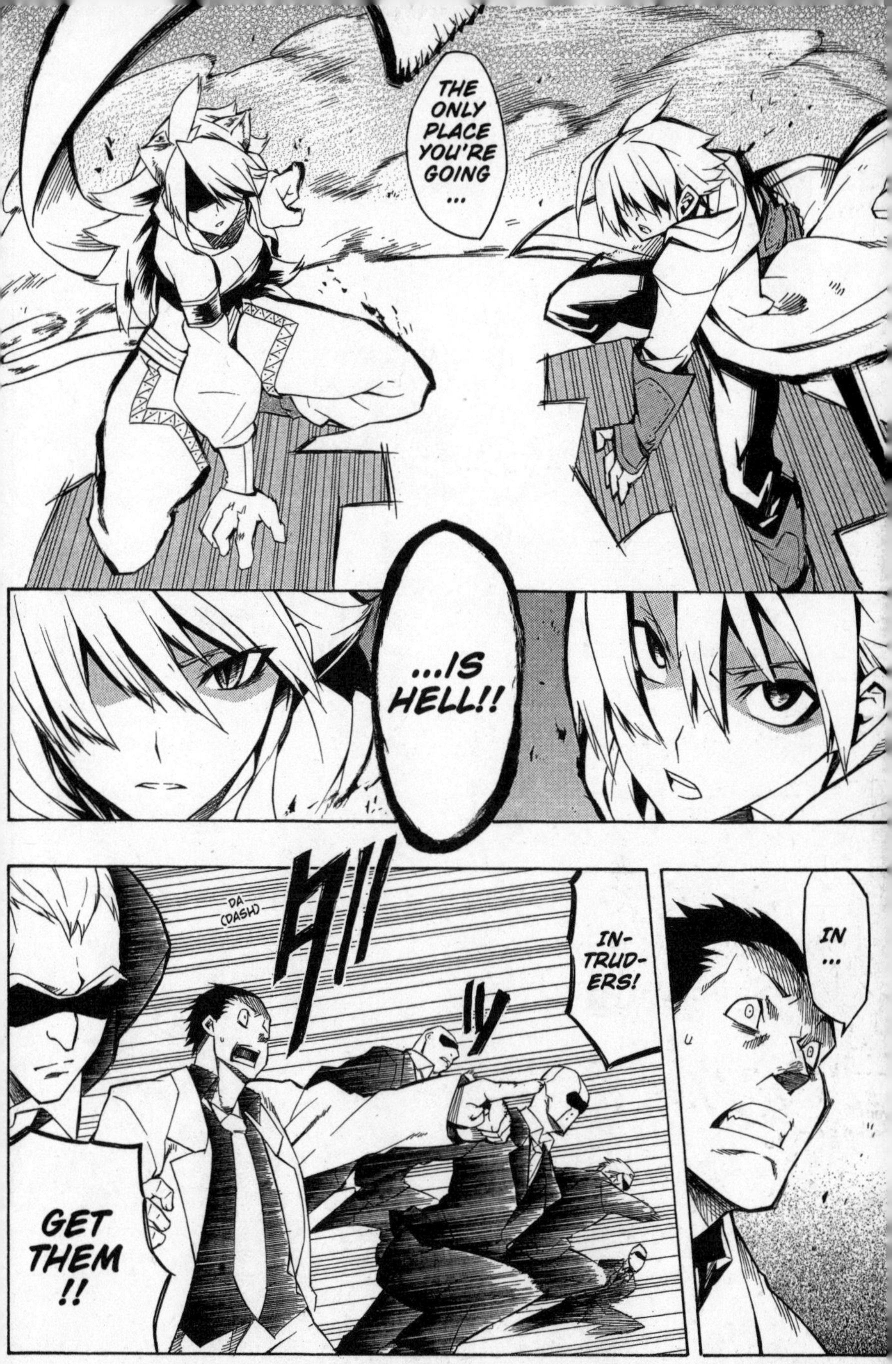
THE ONLY PLACE YOU'RE GOING ...
...IS HELL!!
IN ...
IN-TRUD-ERS!
DA (DASH)
GET THEM !!

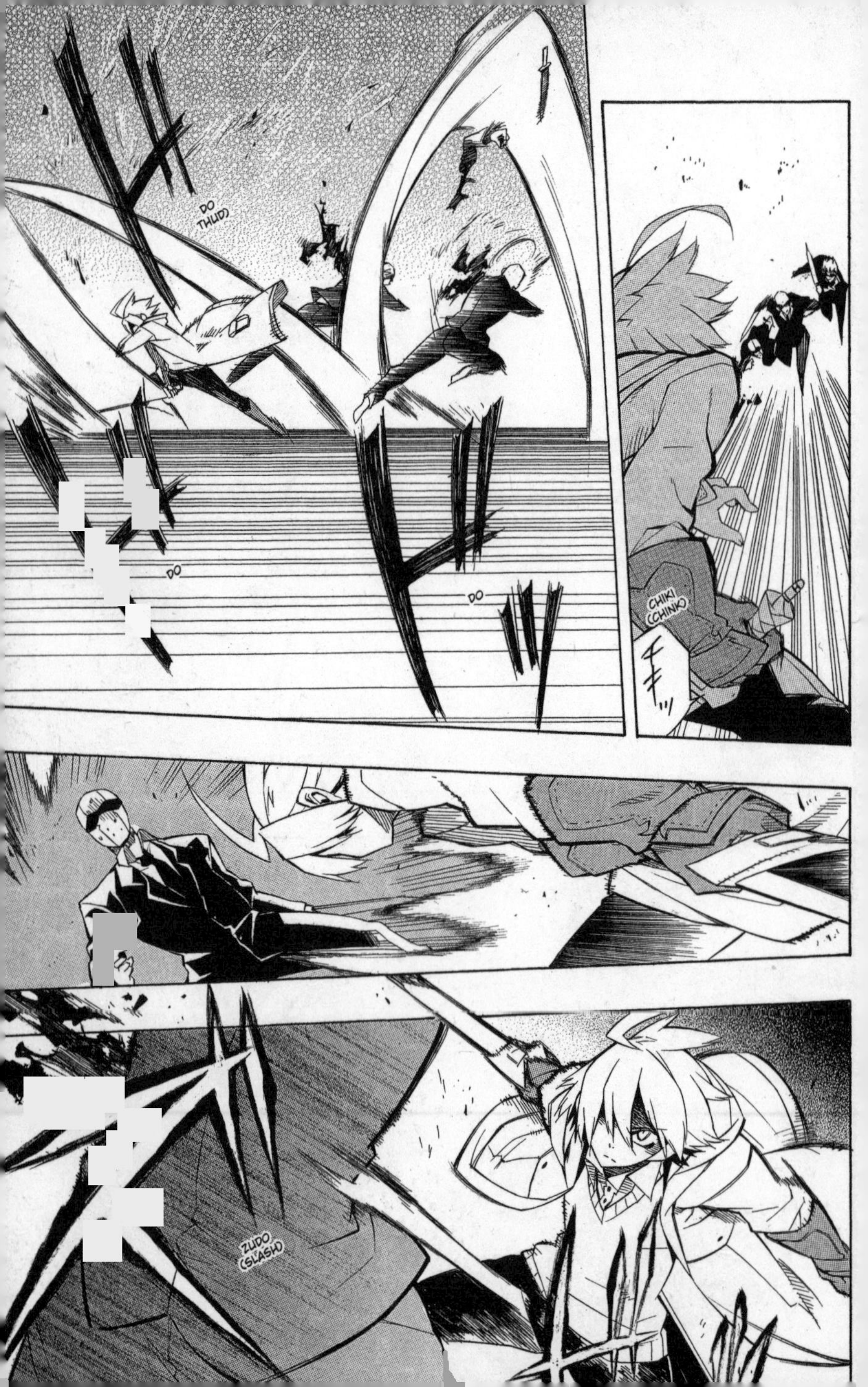

CHIKI (CHINK)
DO THUD)
DO
DO
ZUDO (SLASH)

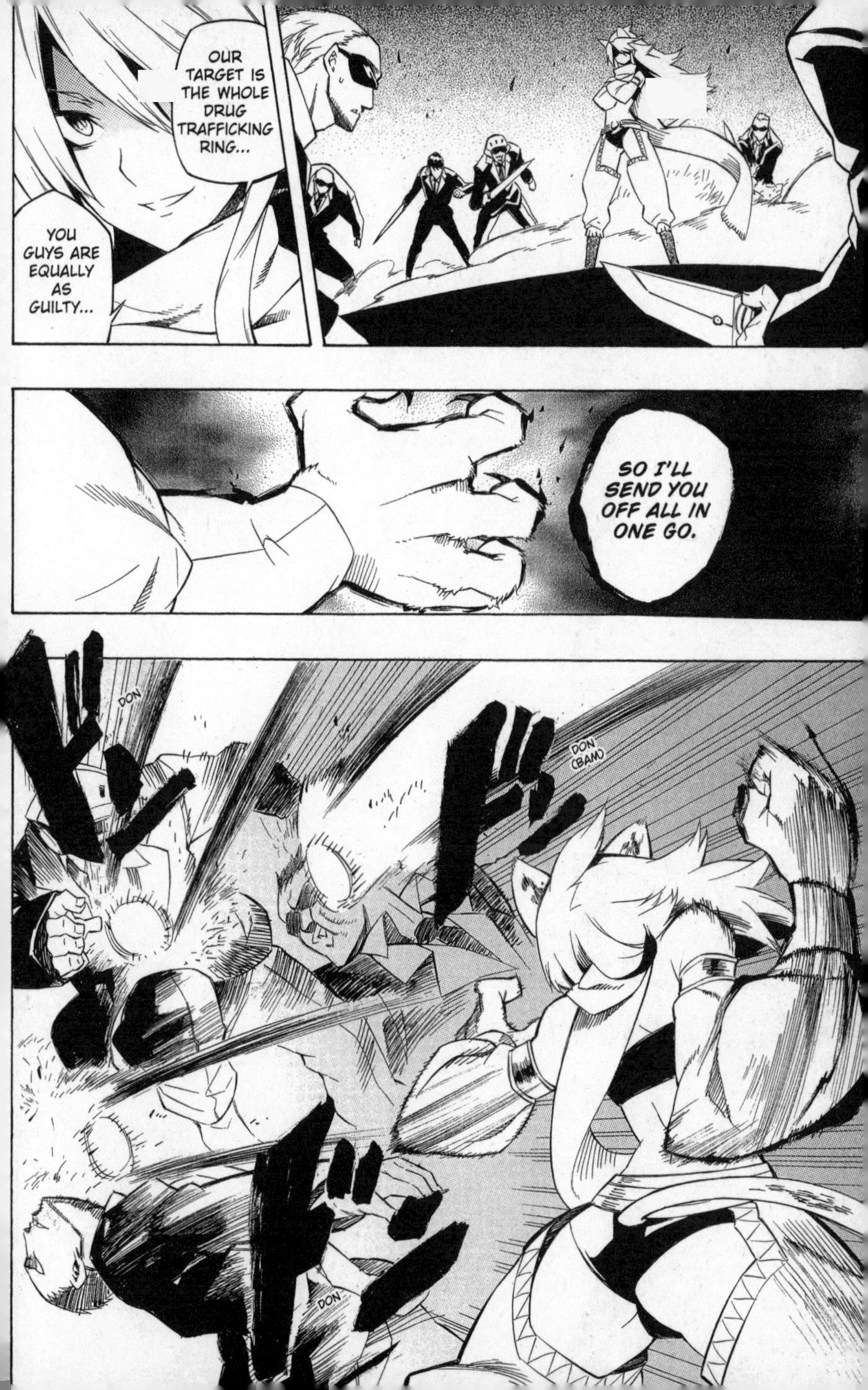
OUR TARGET IS THE WHOLE DRUG TRAFFICKING RING...
YOU GUYS ARE EQUALLY AS GUILTY...
SO I'LL SEND YOU OFF ALL IN ONE GO.
DON (BAM)
DON
DON

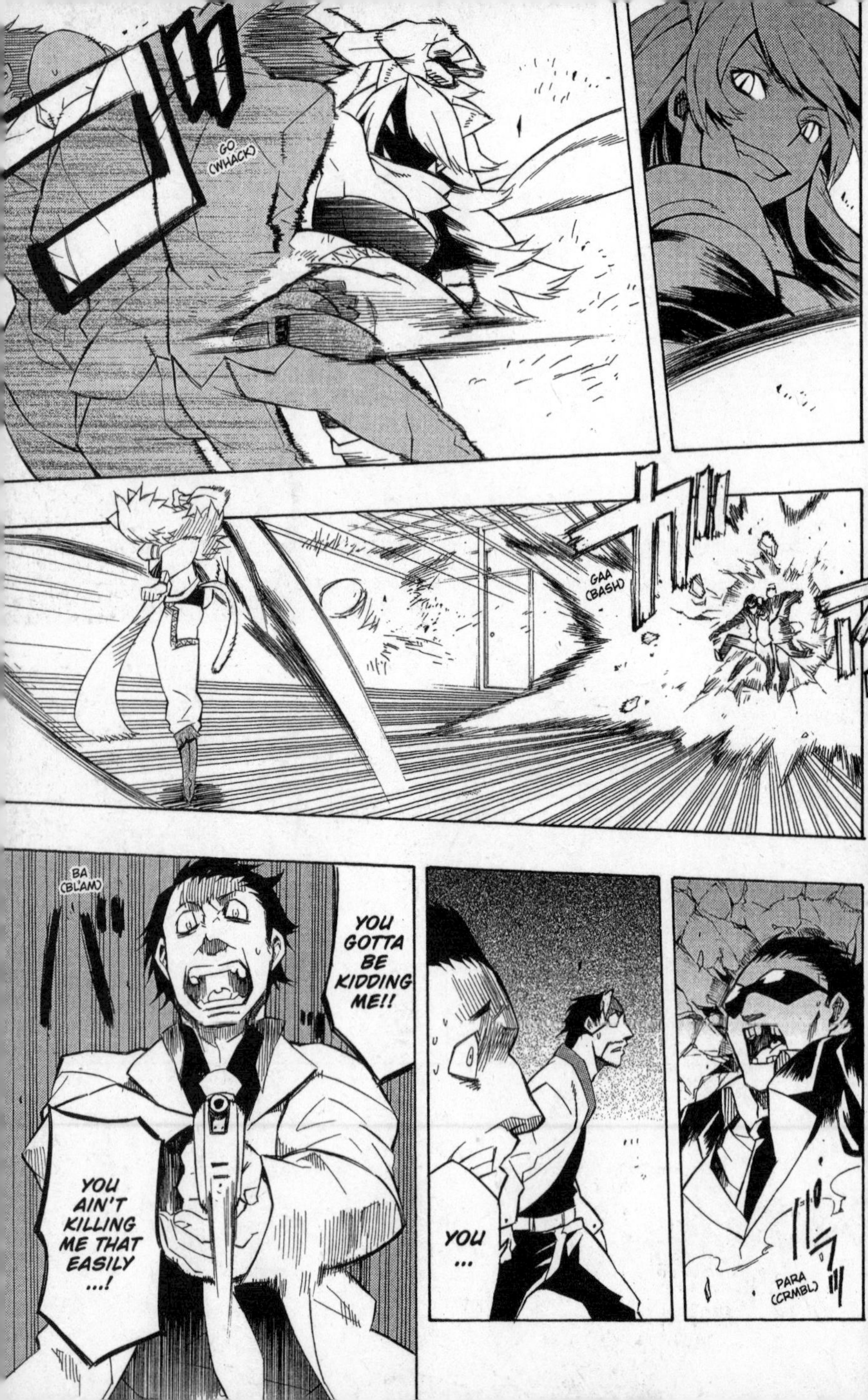
GO (WHACK)
GAA (BASH)
PARA (CRMBL)
YOU ...
YOU GOTTA BE KIDDING ME!!
BA (BL'AM)
YOU AIN'T KILLING ME THAT EASILY ...!

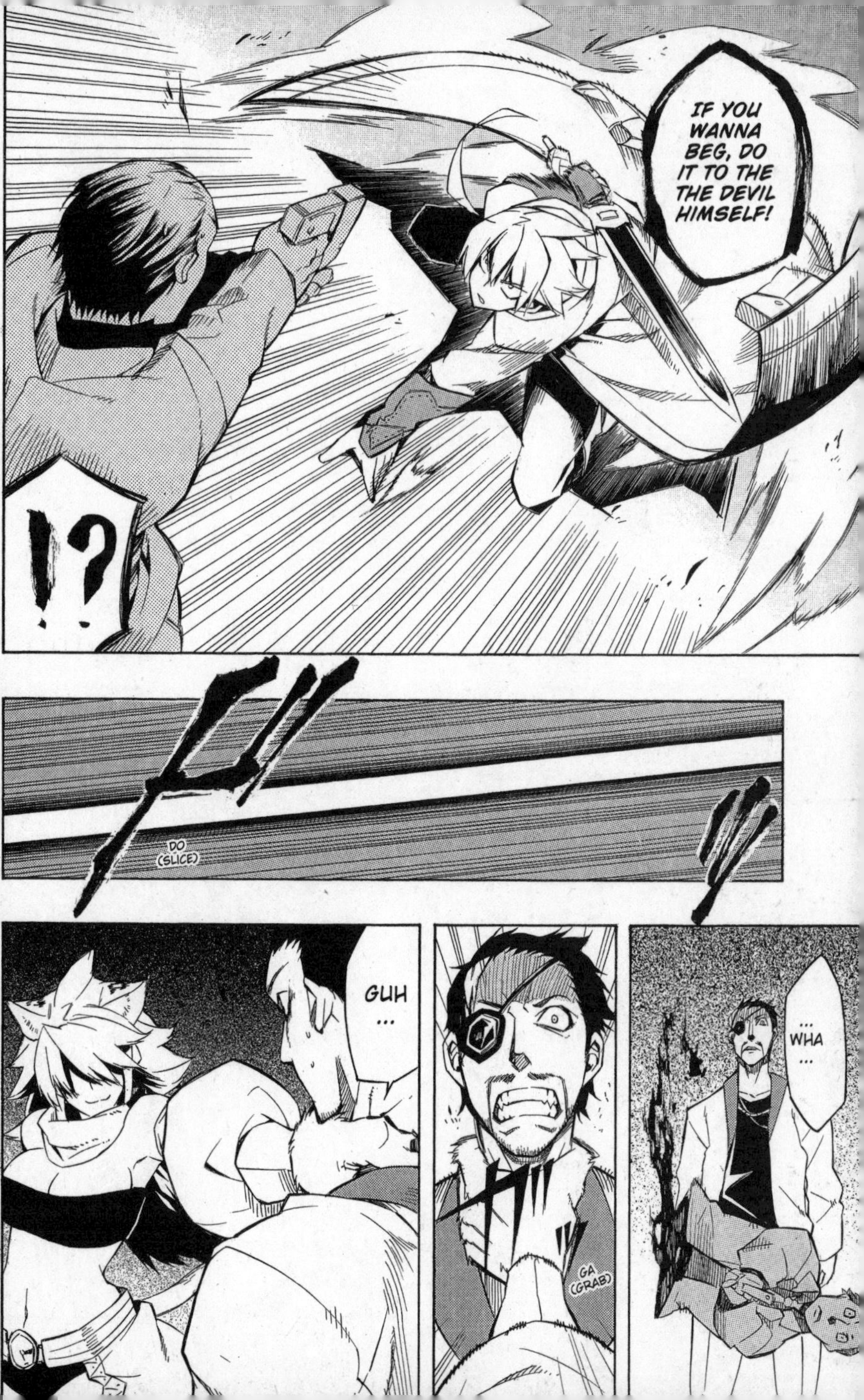
IF YOU WANNA BEG, DO IT TO THE THE DEVIL HIMSELF!
!?
DO (SLICE)
... WHA ...
GA (GRAB)
GUH ...

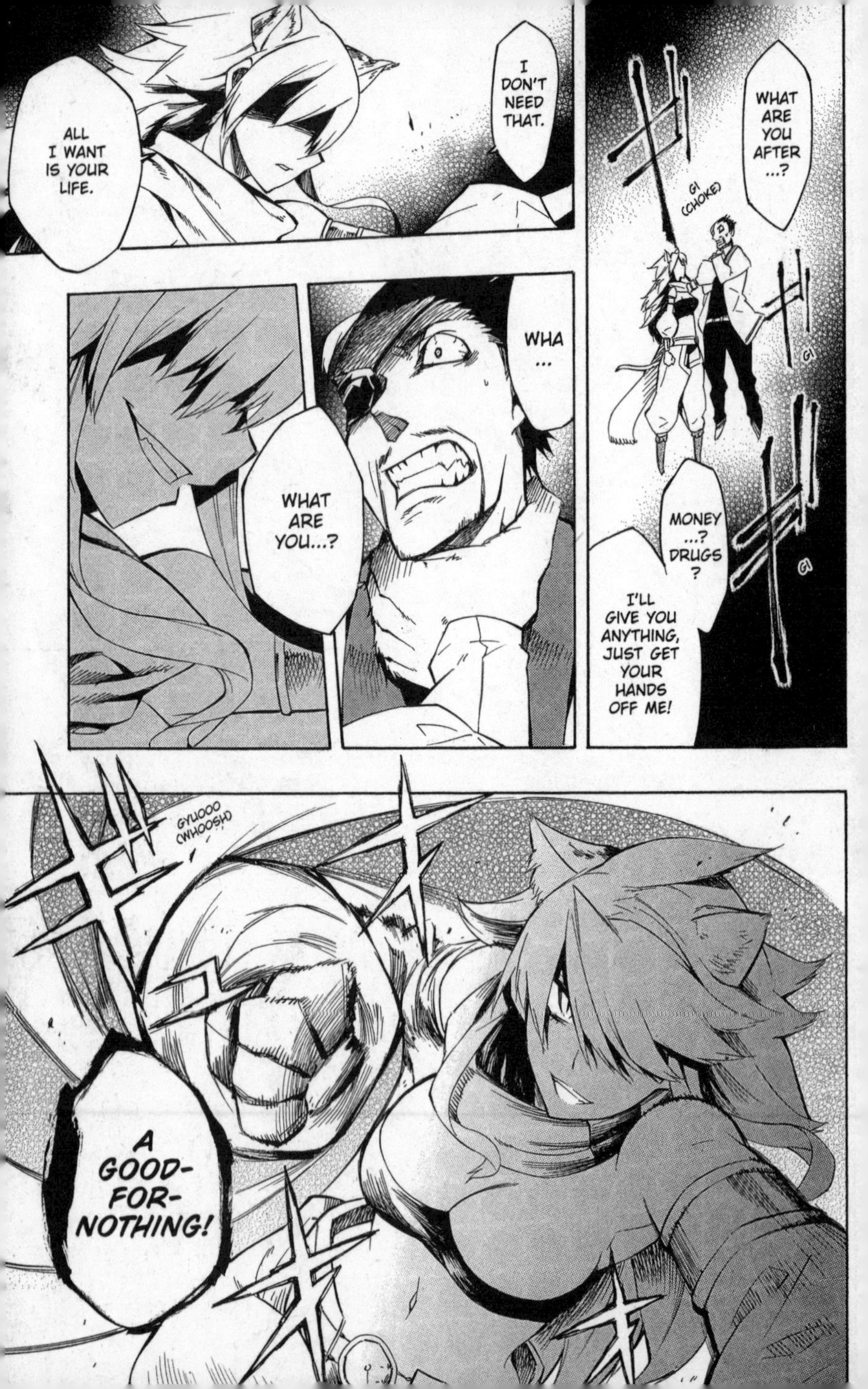
WHAT ARE YOU AFTER ...?
GI (CHOKE)
GI
GI
MONEY ...? DRUGS ?
I'LL GIVE YOU ANYTHING, JUST GET YOUR HANDS OFF ME!
I DON'T NEED THAT.
ALL I WANT IS YOUR LIFE.
WHA ...
WHAT ARE YOU...?
GYUOOO (WHOOSH)
A GOOD-FOR-NOTHING!

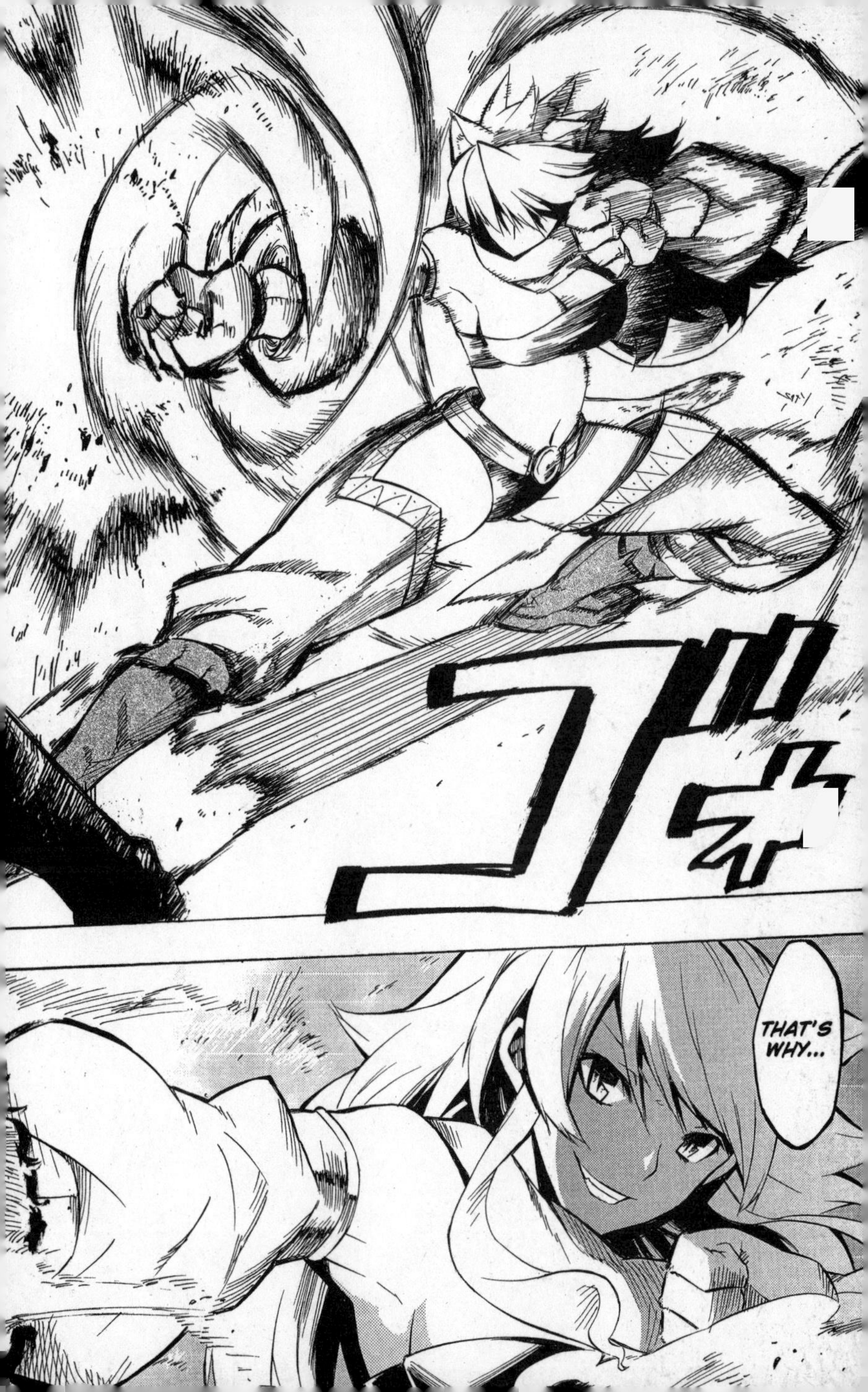
THAT'S WHY...

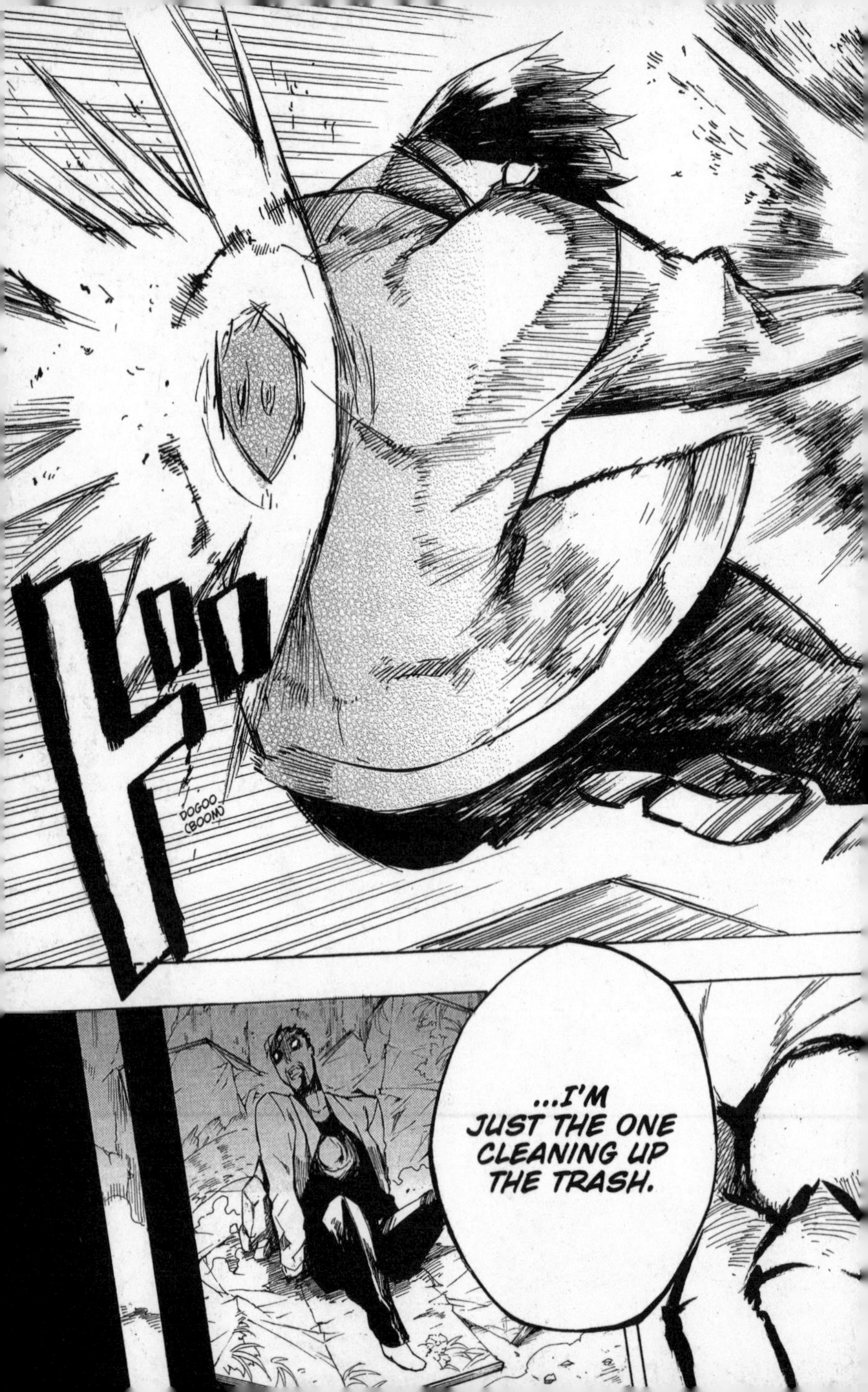
DOGOO (BOOM)
...I'M JUST THE ONE CLEANING UP THE TRASH.

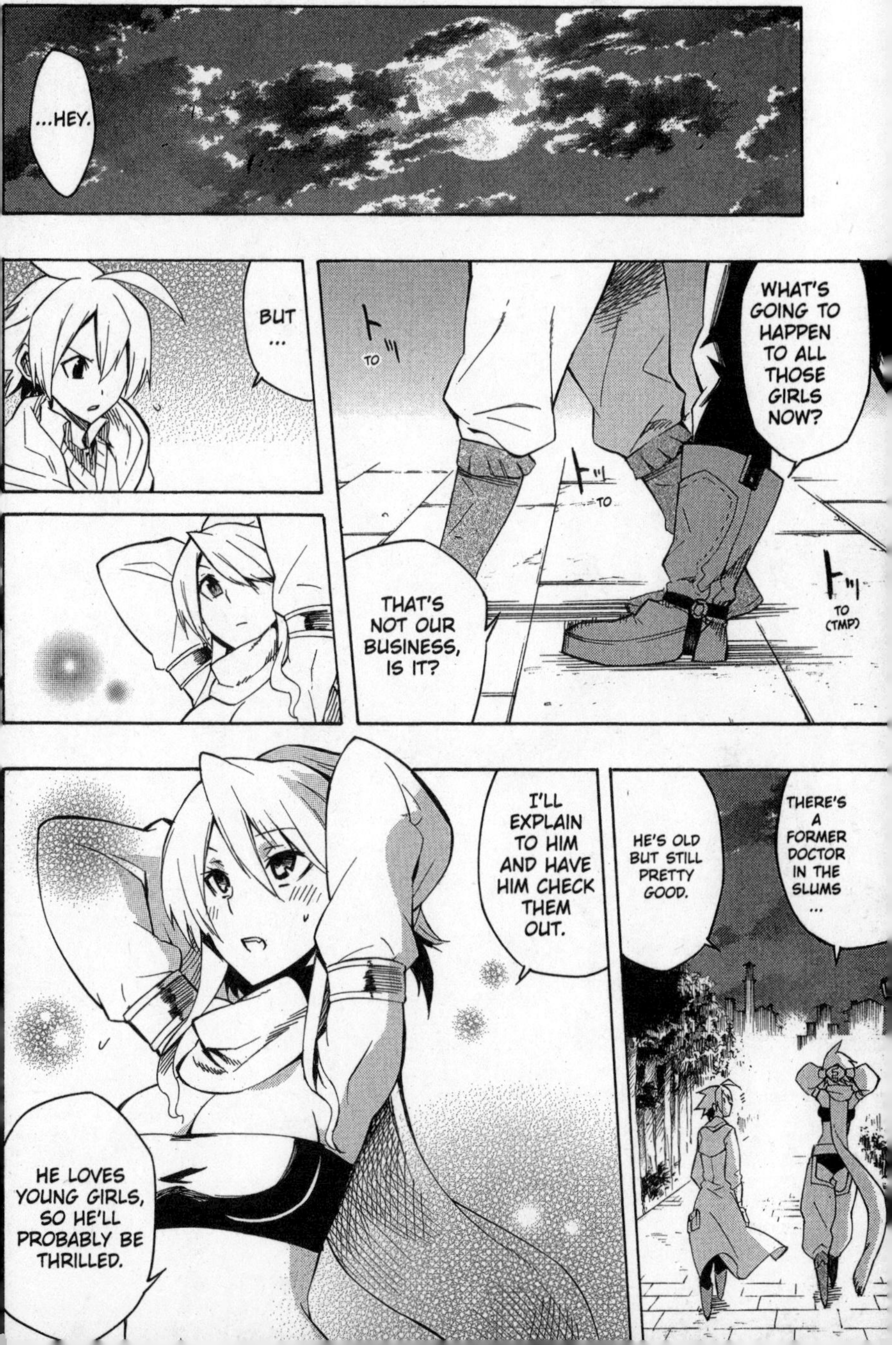
...HEY.
WHAT'S GOING TO HAPPEN TO ALL THOSE GIRLS NOW?
トッ
TO
トッ
TO
トッ
TO (TMP)
BUT ...
THAT'S NOT OUR BUSINESS, IS IT?
THERE'S A FORMER DOCTOR IN THE SLUMS ...
HE'S OLD BUT STILL PRETTY GOOD.
I'LL EXPLAIN TO HIM AND HAVE HIM CHECK THEM OUT.
HE LOVES YOUNG GIRLS, SO HE'LL PROBABLY BE THRILLED.

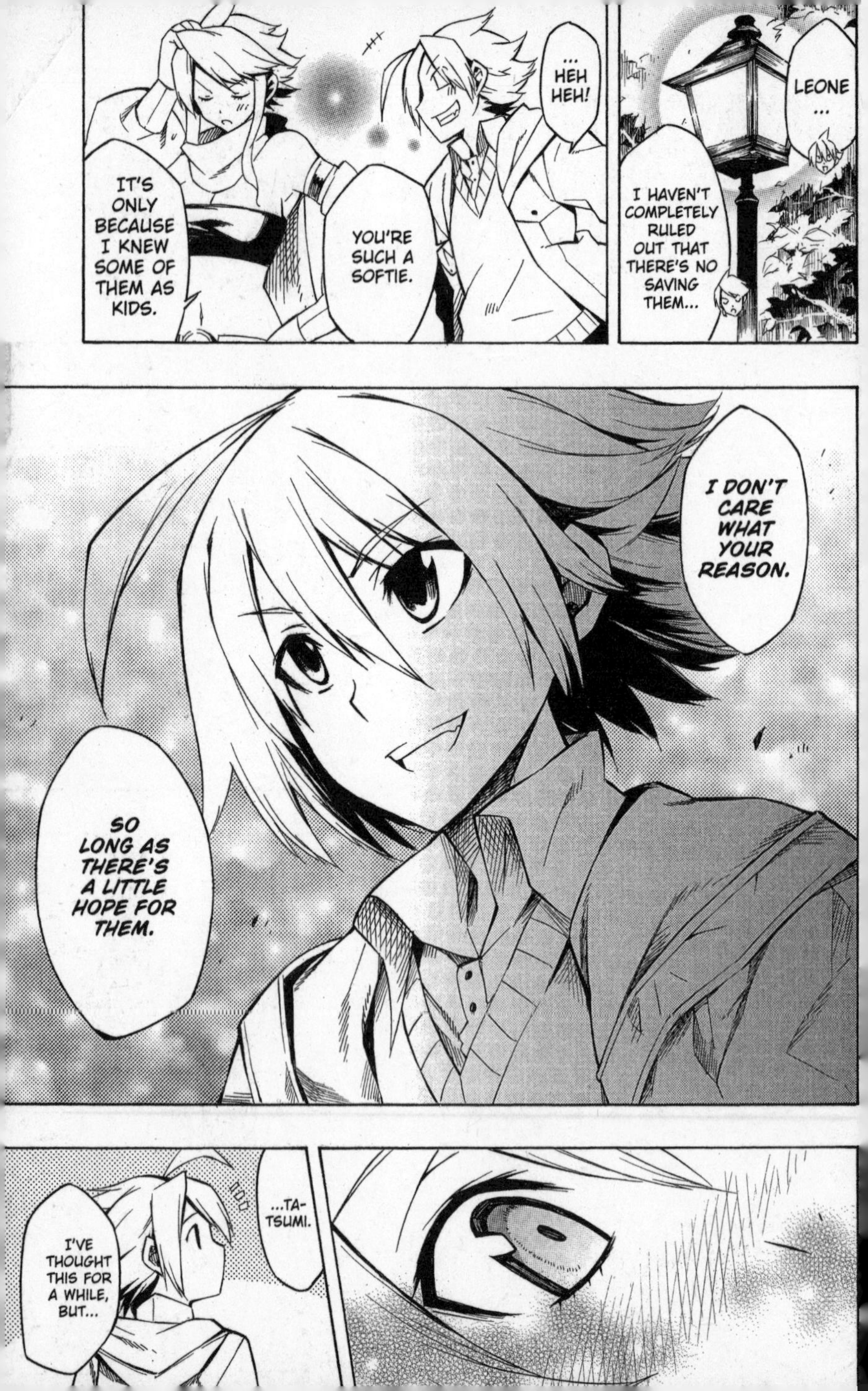
LEONE ...
I HAVEN'T COMPLETELY RULED OUT THAT THERE'S NO SAVING THEM...
... HEH HEH!
YOU'RE SUCH A SOFTIE.
IT'S ONLY BECAUSE I KNEW SOME OF THEM AS KIDS.
I DON'T CARE WHAT YOUR REASON.
SO LONG AS THERE'S A LITTLE HOPE FOR THEM.
...TA-TSUMI.
I'VE THOUGHT THIS FOR A WHILE, BUT...

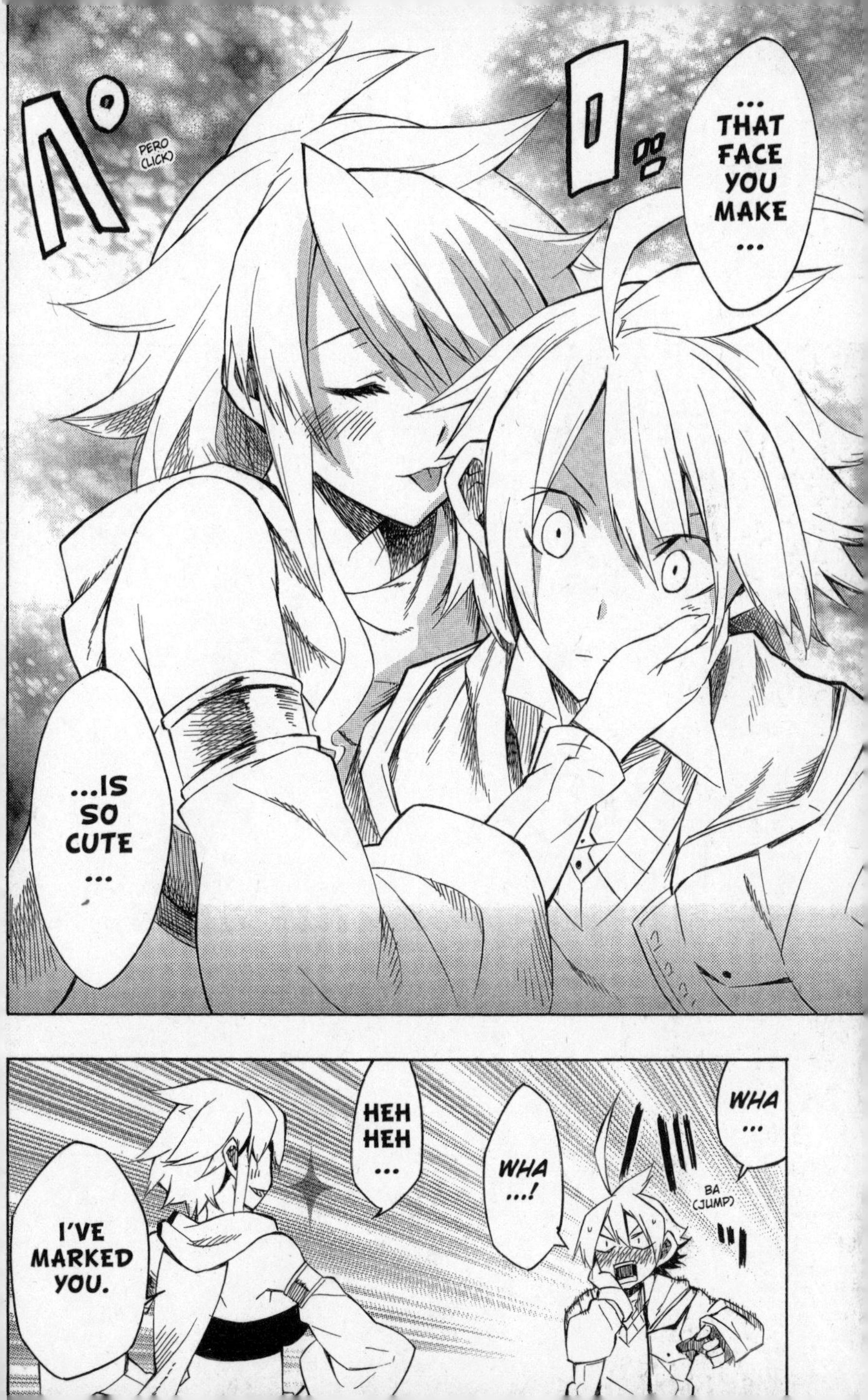
...THAT FACE YOU MAKE...
PERO (LICK)
...IS SO CUTE...
WHA...
BA (JUMP)
WHA...!
HEH HEH...
I'VE MARKED YOU.

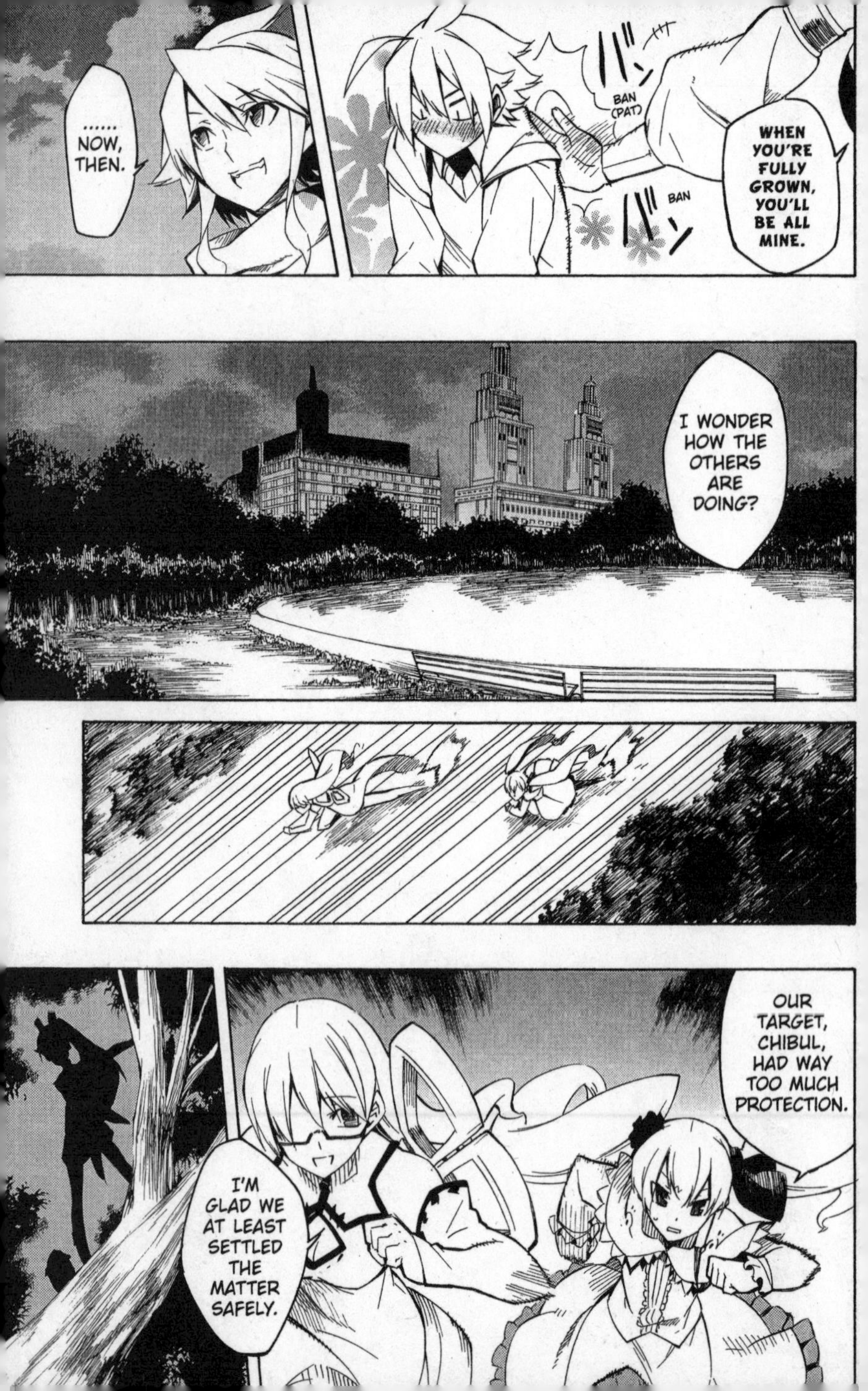
BAN (PAT)
WHEN YOU'RE FULLY GROWN, YOU'LL BE ALL MINE.
BAN
...... NOW, THEN.
I WONDER HOW THE OTHERS ARE DOING?
OUR TARGET, CHIBUL, HAD WAY TOO MUCH PROTECTION.
I'M GLAD WE AT LEAST SETTLED THE MATTER SAFELY.

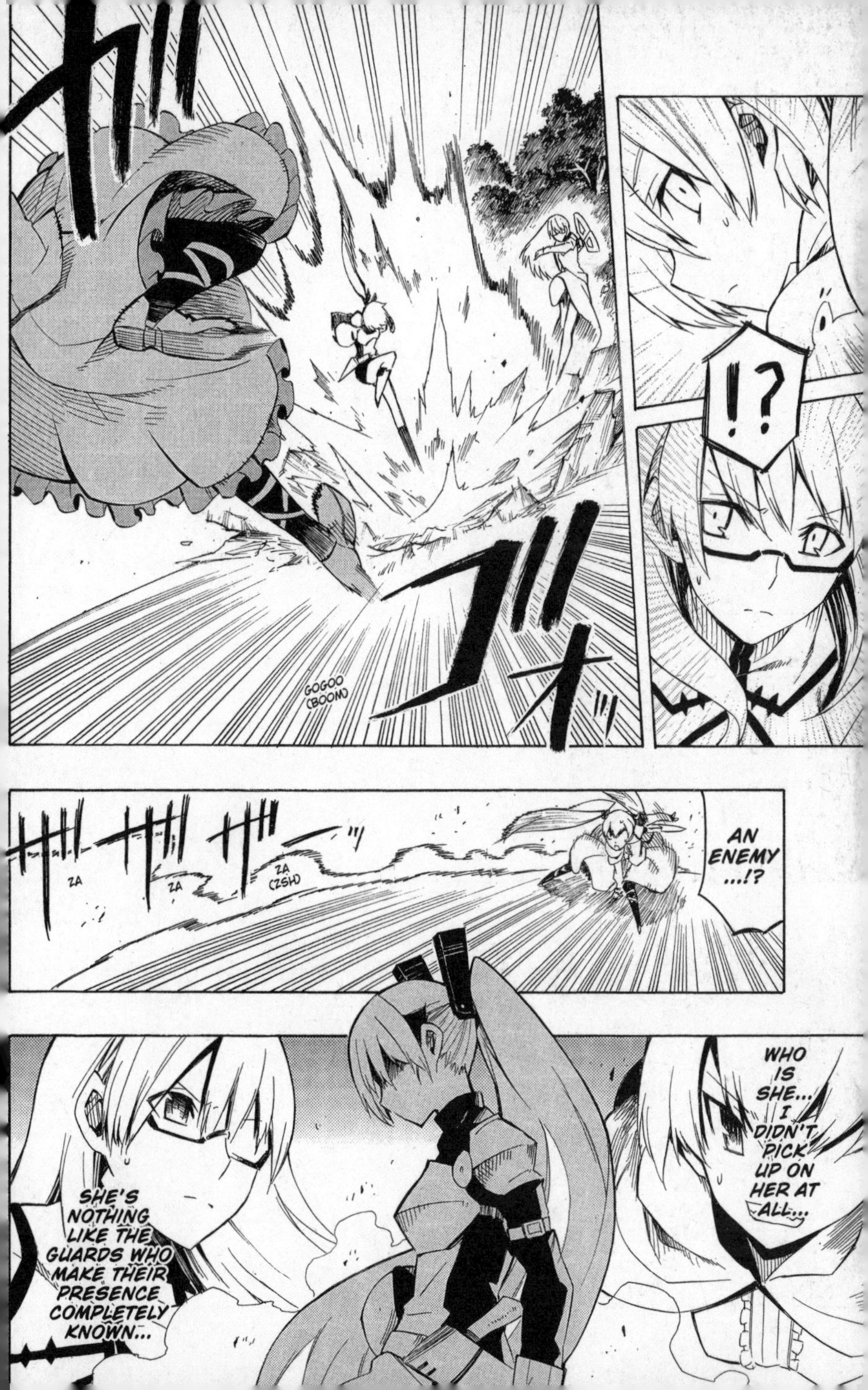
!?
GOGOO (BOOM)
AN ENEMY ...!?
ZA (ZSH)
ZA
ZA
WHO IS SHE... I DIDN'T PICK UP ON HER AT ALL...
SHE'S NOTHING LIKE THE GUARDS WHO MAKE THEIR PRESENCE COMPLETELY KNOWN...

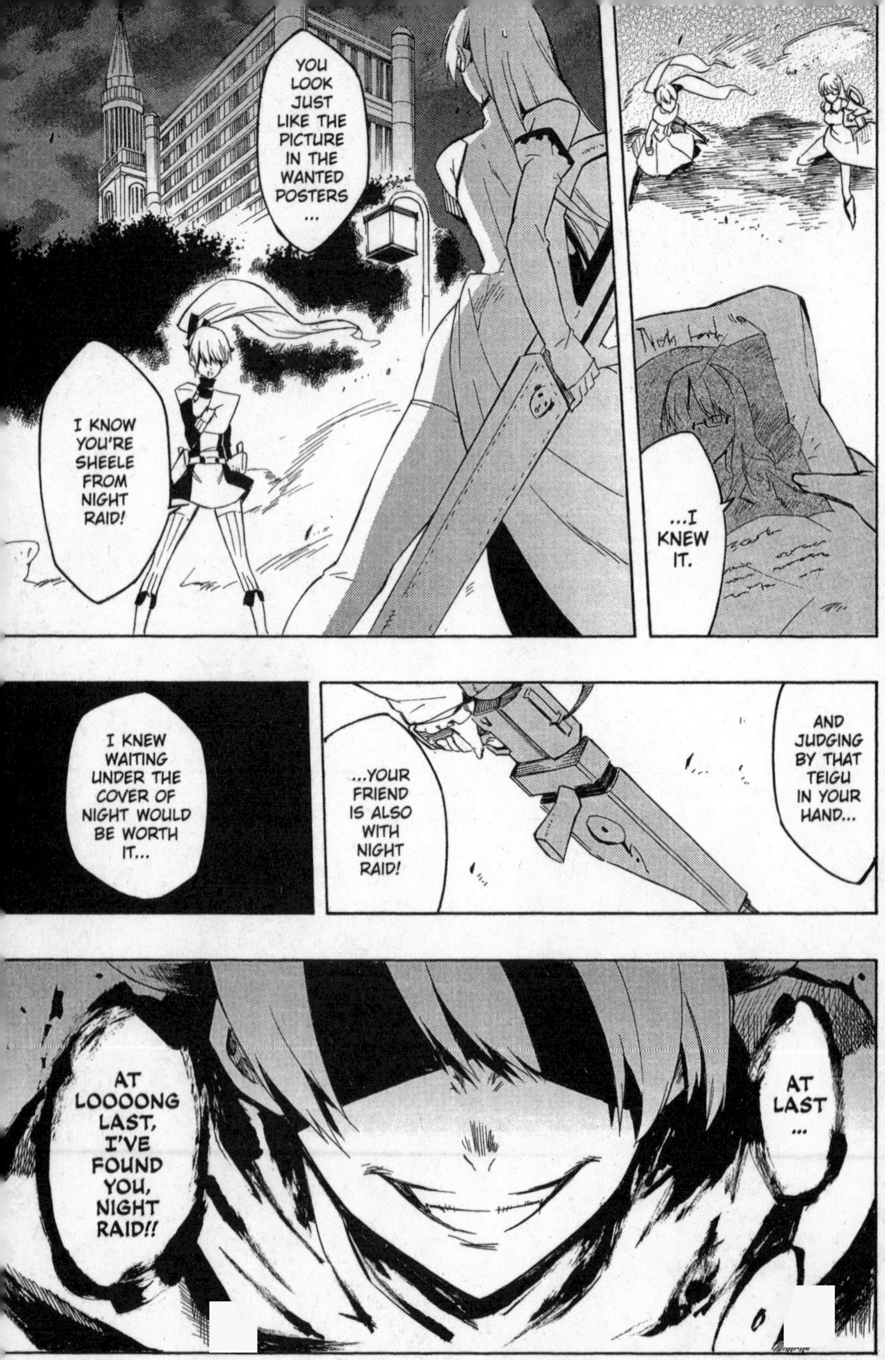
...I KNEW IT.
YOU LOOK JUST LIKE THE PICTURE IN THE WANTED POSTERS ...
I KNOW YOU'RE SHEELE FROM NIGHT RAID!
AND JUDGING BY THAT TEIGU IN YOUR HAND...
...YOUR FRIEND IS ALSO WITH NIGHT RAID!
I KNEW WAITING UNDER THE COVER OF NIGHT WOULD BE WORTH IT...
AT LAST ...
AT LOOOONG LAST, I'VE FOUND YOU, NIGHT RAID!!

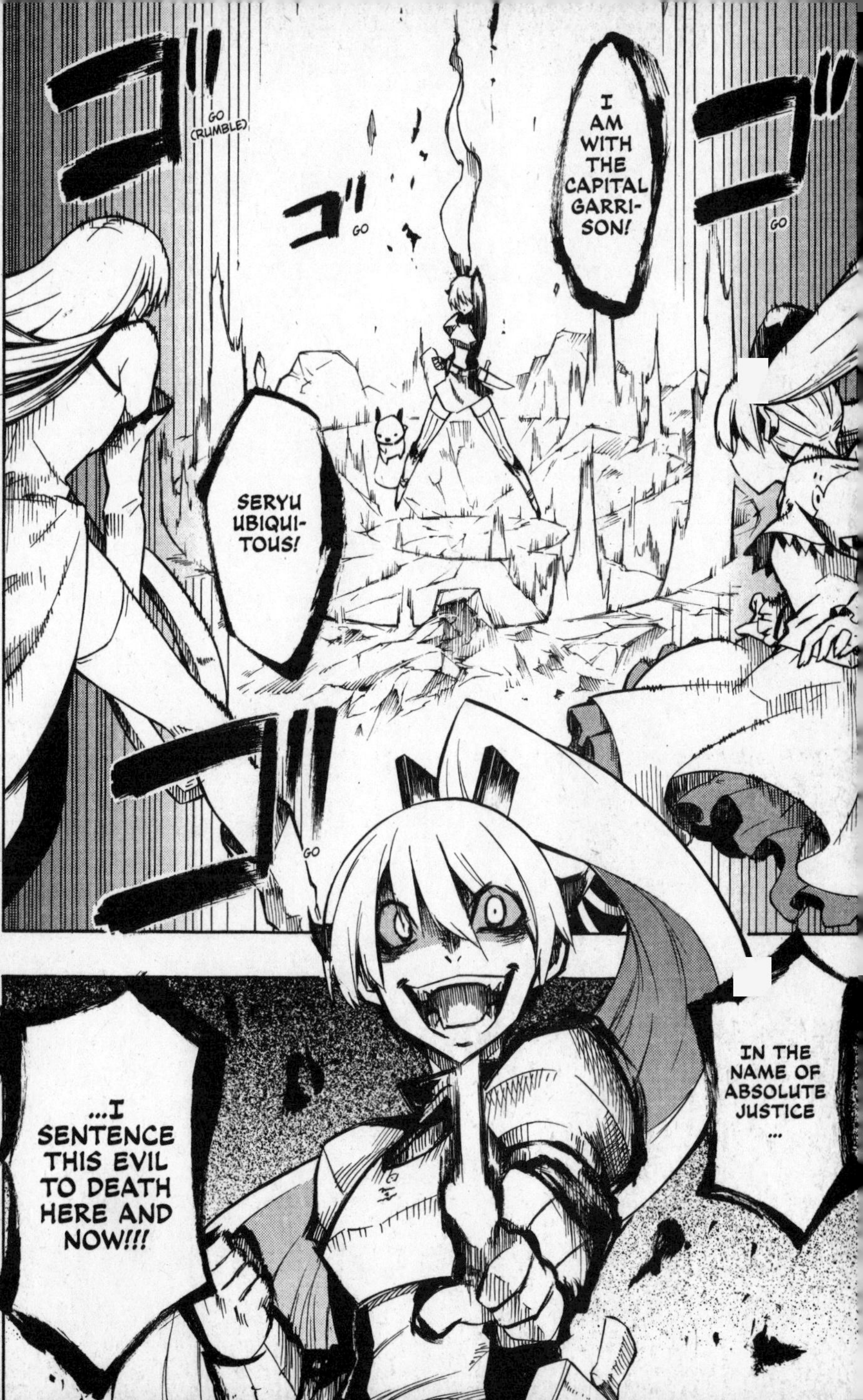
ゴ
GO
I AM WITH THE CAPITAL GARRISON!
ゴ
GO
ゴ
GO (RUMBLE)
SERYU UBIQUITOUS!
ゴ
GO
IN THE NAME OF ABSOLUTE JUSTICE...
...I SENTENCE THIS EVIL TO DEATH HERE AND NOW!!!

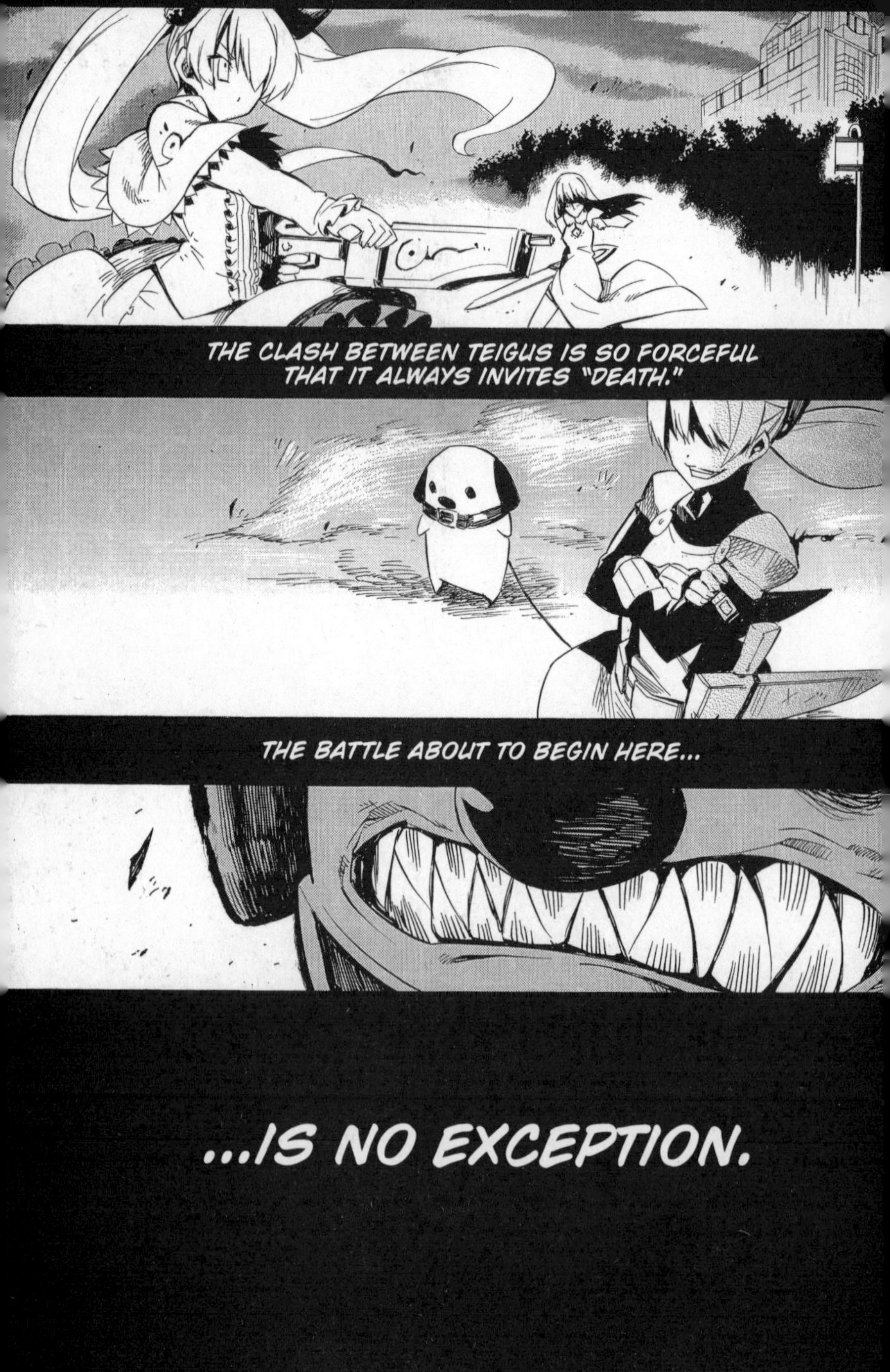
THE CLASH BETWEEN TEIGUS IS SO FORCEFUL THAT IT ALWAYS INVITES "DEATH."
THE BATTLE ABOUT TO BEGIN HERE...
...IS NO EXCEPTION.

Akame ga KILL!

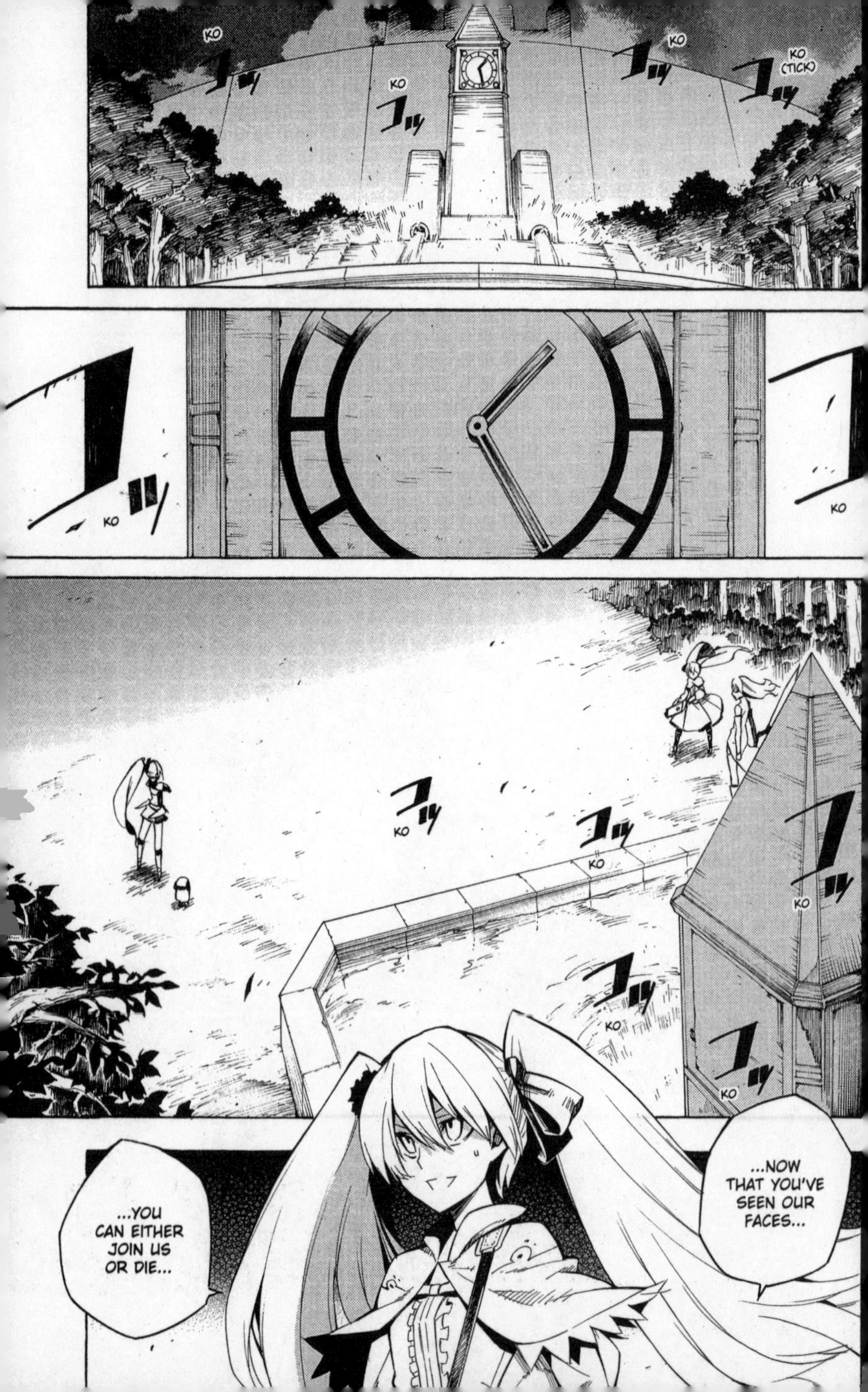
KO (TICK)
KO
KO
KO
KO
KO
KO
KO
KO
KO
KO
...NOW THAT YOU'VE SEEN OUR FACES...
...YOU CAN EITHER JOIN US OR DIE...

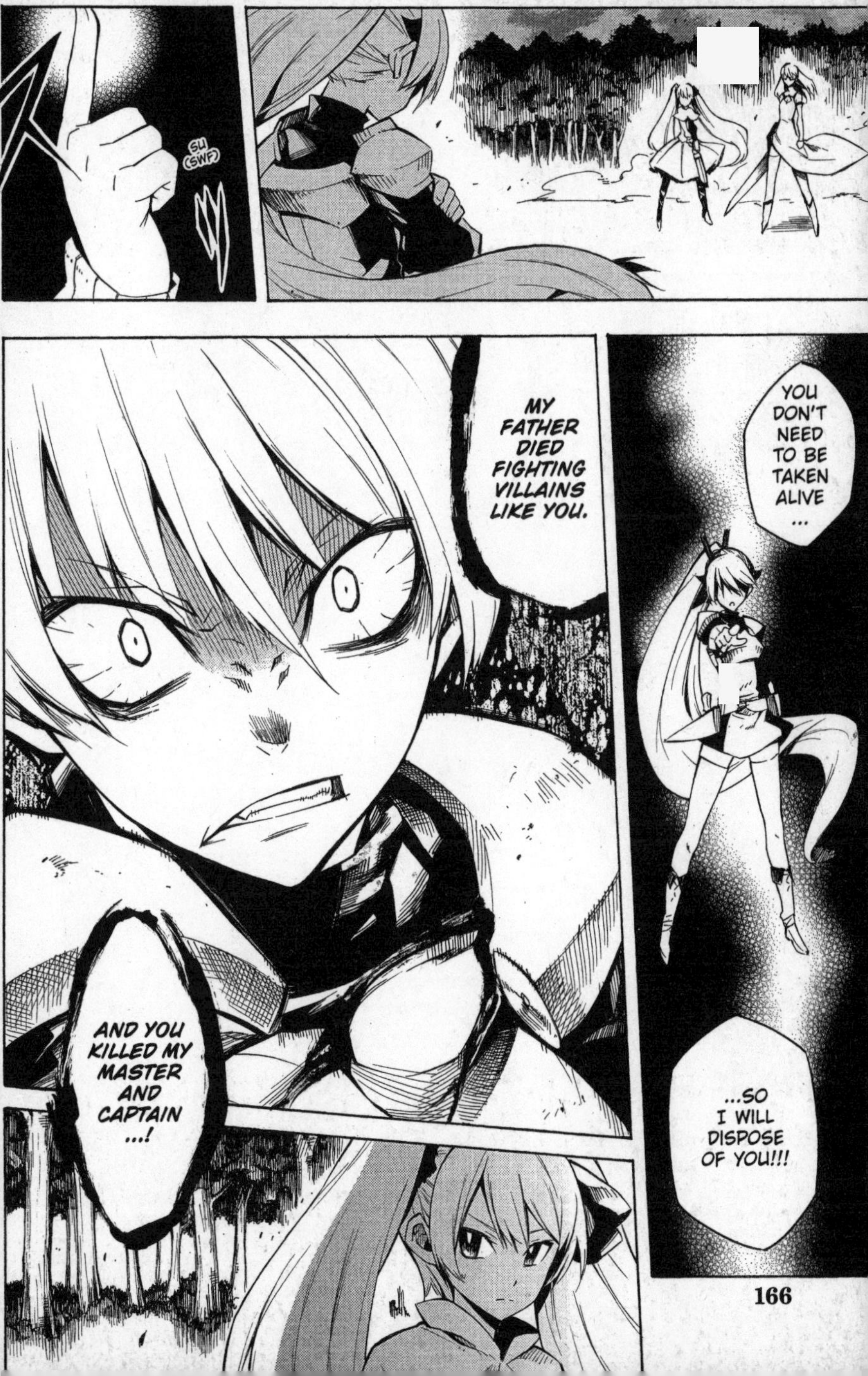
SU (SWF)
YOU DON'T NEED TO BE TAKEN ALIVE ...
...SO I WILL DISPOSE OF YOU!!!
MY FATHER DIED FIGHTING VILLAINS LIKE YOU.
AND YOU KILLED MY MASTER AND CAPTAIN ...!

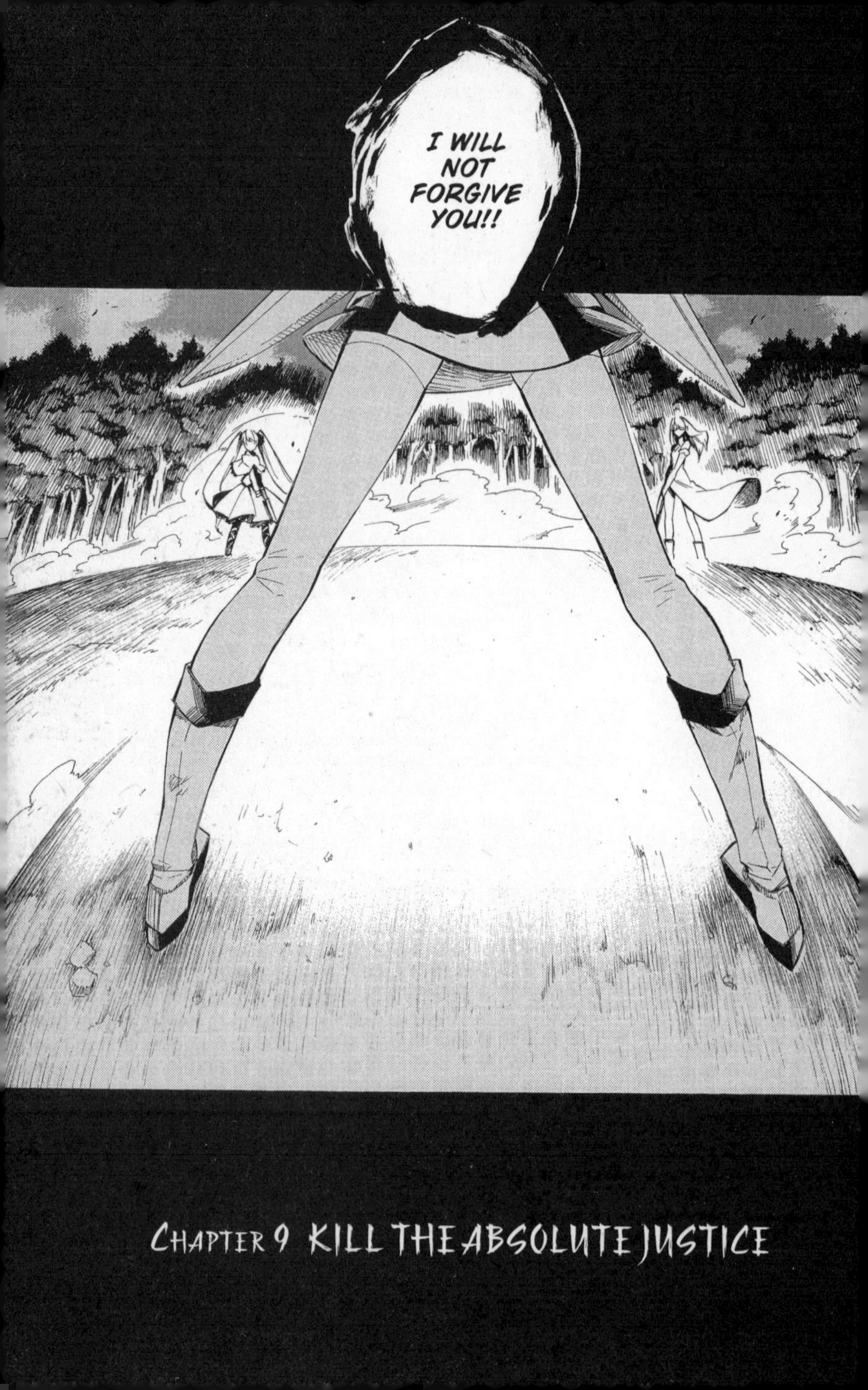
I WILL NOT FORGIVE YOU!!

Chapter 9 KILL THE ABSOLUTE JUSTICE

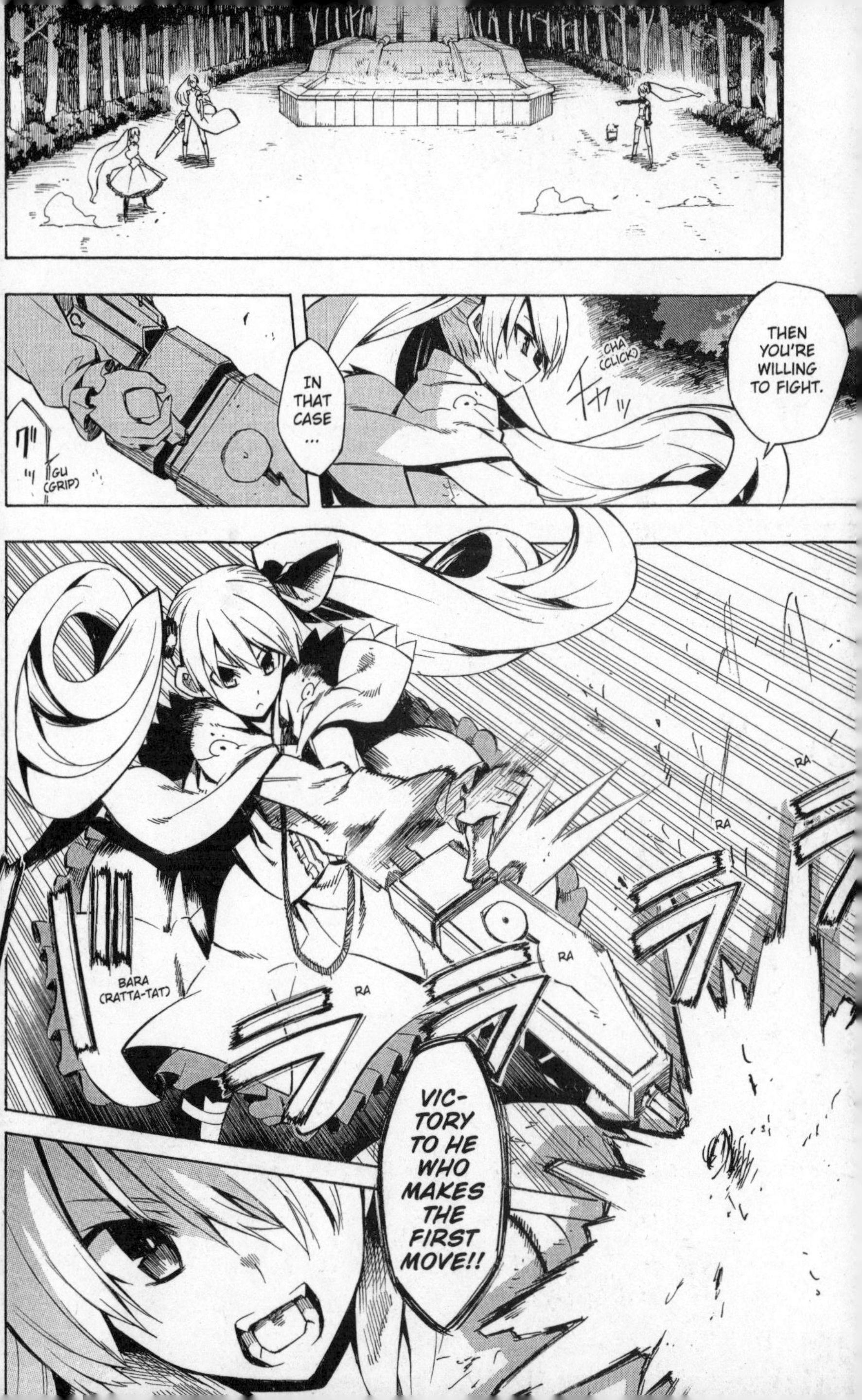
THEN YOU'RE WILLING TO FIGHT.
CHA (CLICK)
IN THAT CASE...
GU (GRIP)
RA
RA
RA
RA
BARA (RATTA-TAT)
VICTORY TO HE WHO MAKES THE FIRST MOVE!!

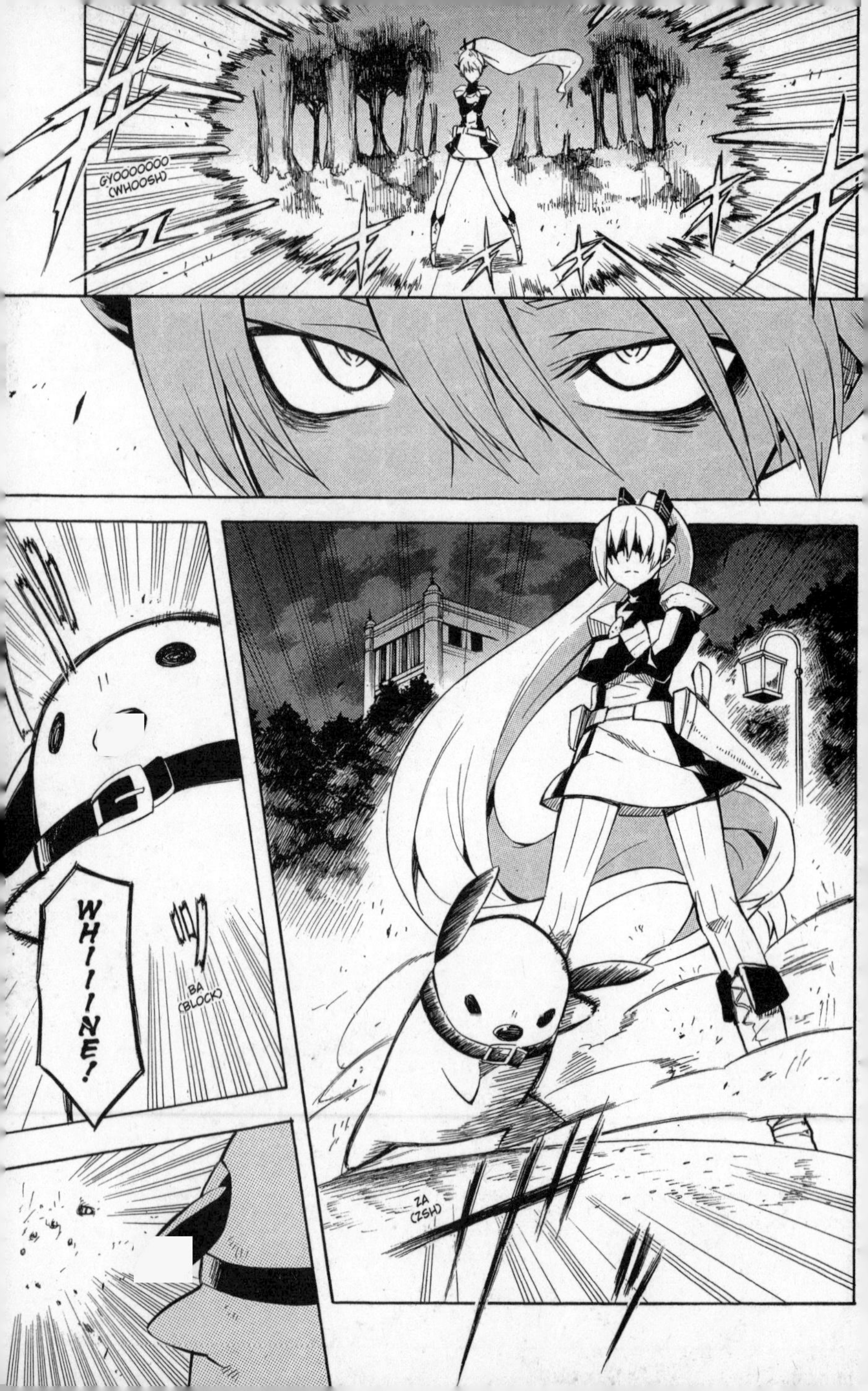
GYOOOOOOO
(WHOOSH)
ZA
(ZSH)
WHIIINE!
BA
(BLOCK)

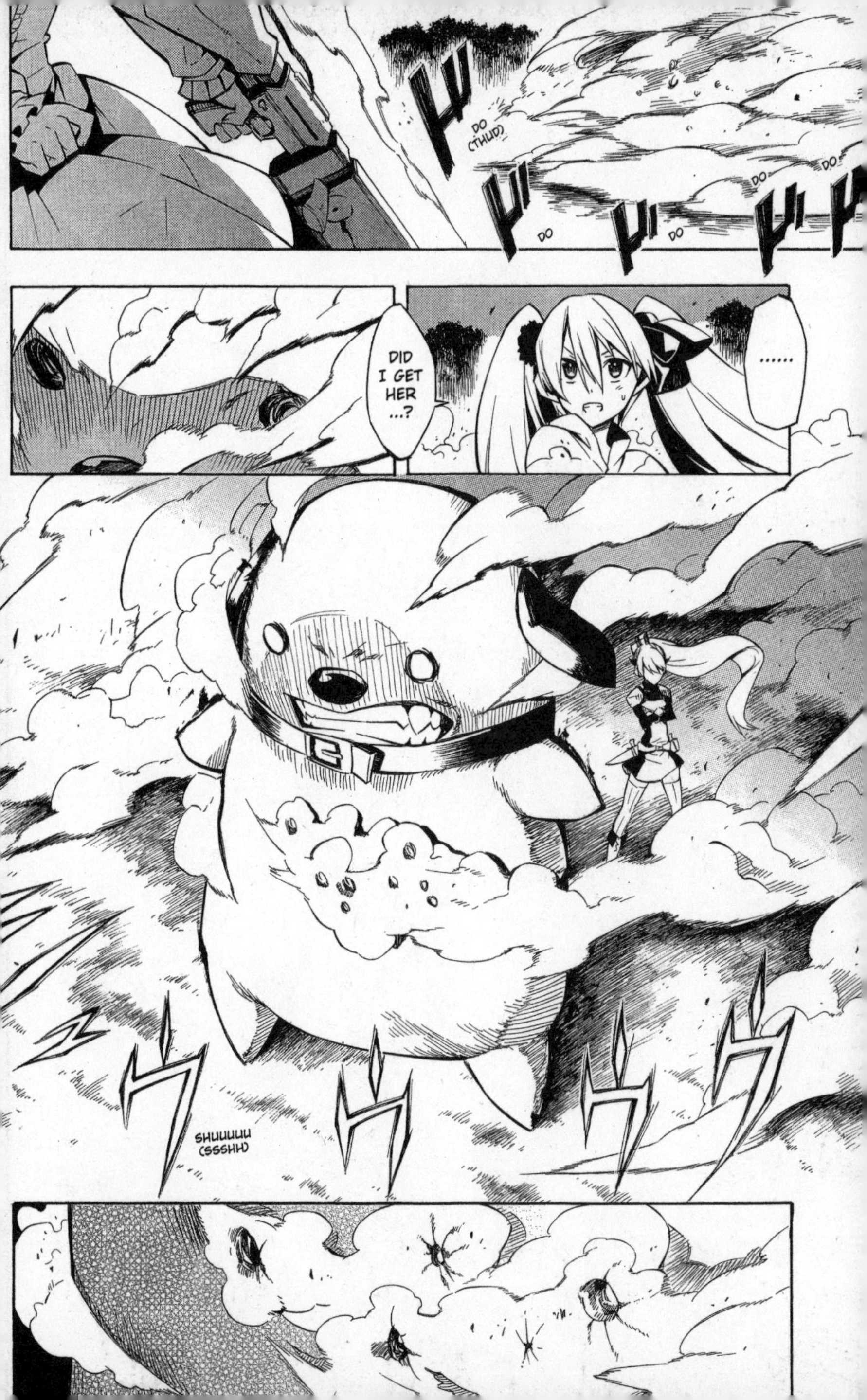
DO
DO
DO (THUD)
DO
DO
......
DID I GET HER ...?
SHUUUUU (SSSHH)

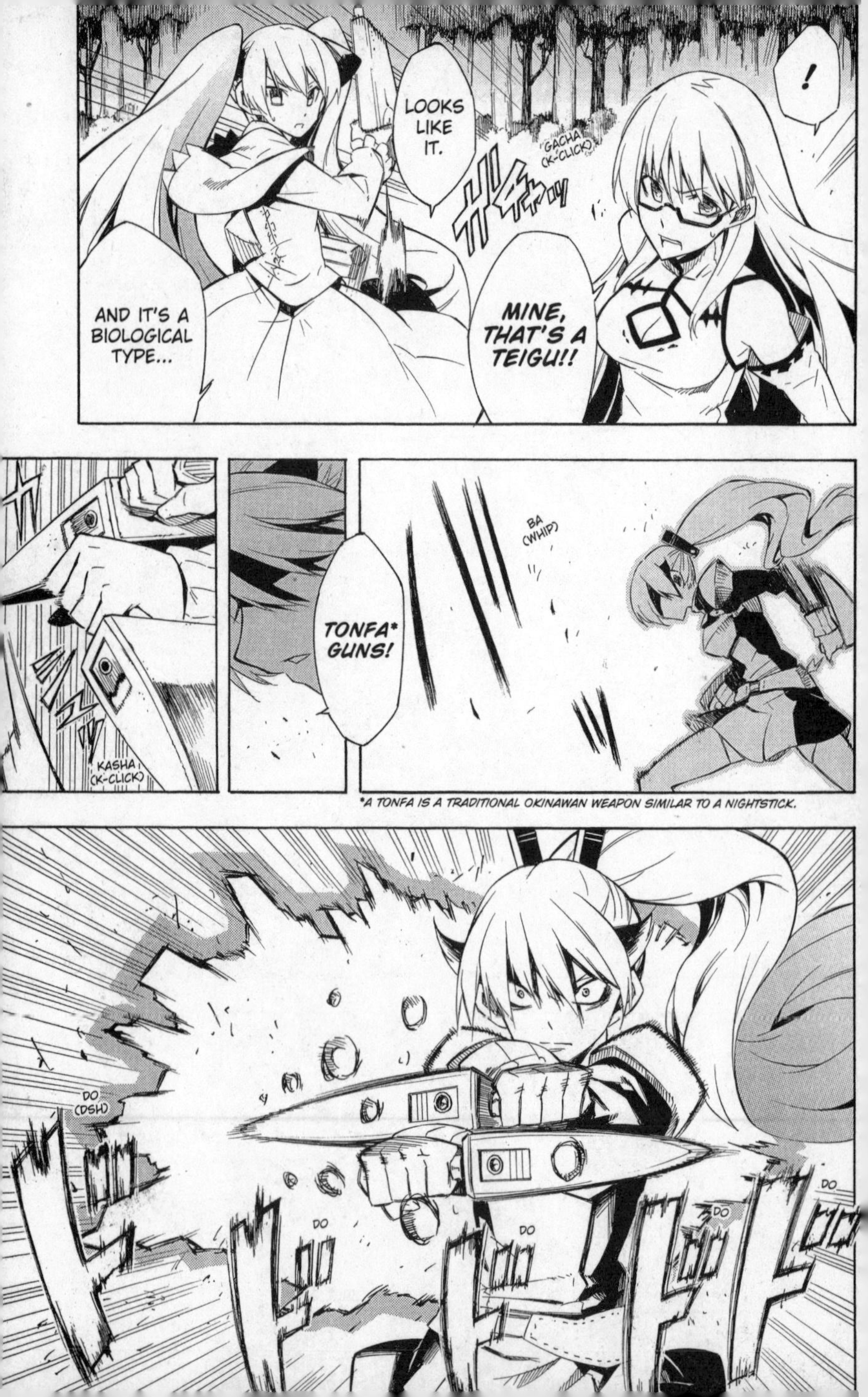
!
MINE, THAT'S A TEIGU!!
GACHA (K-CLICK)
LOOKS LIKE IT.
AND IT'S A BIOLOGICAL TYPE...
BA (WHIP)
TONFA* GUNS!
KASHA (K-CLICK)
DO
DO
DO
DO
DO (DSH)
*A TONFA IS A TRADITIONAL OKINAWAN WEAPON SIMILAR TO A NIGHTSTICK.

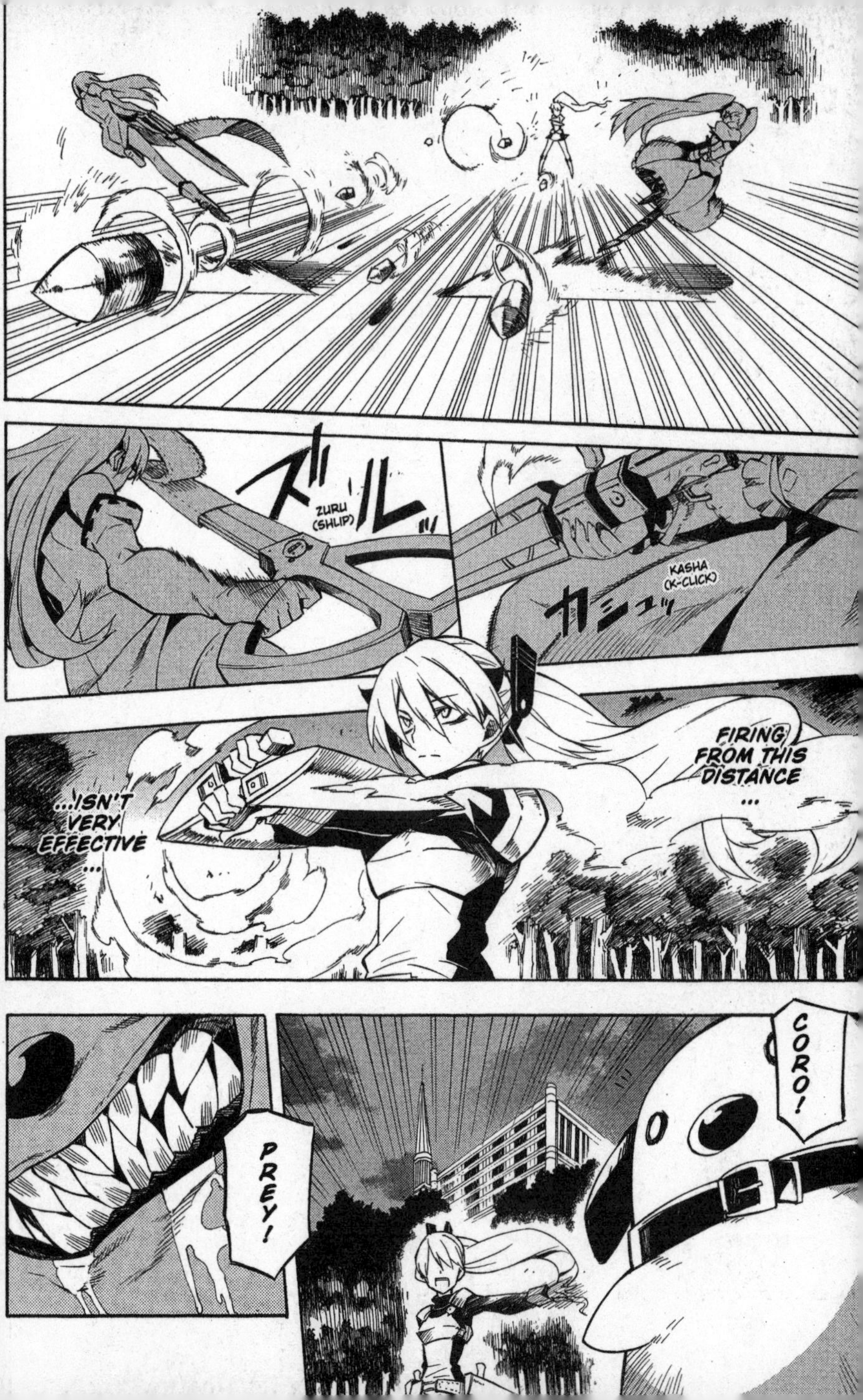
KASHA
(K-CLICK)
ZURU
(SHLIP)
FIRING FROM THIS DISTANCE ...
...ISN'T VERY EFFECTIVE ...
CORO!
PREY!

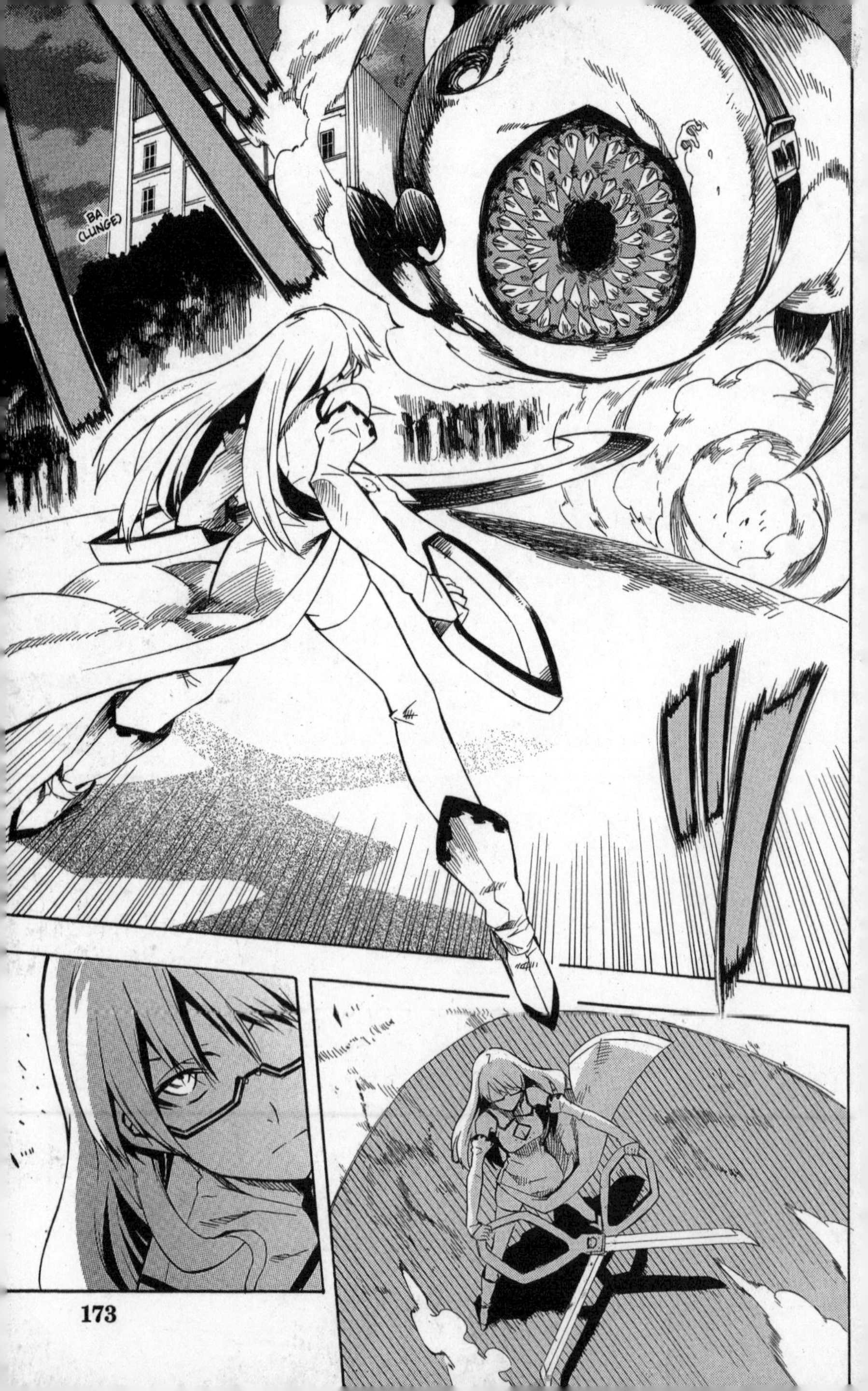
BA
(LUNGE)

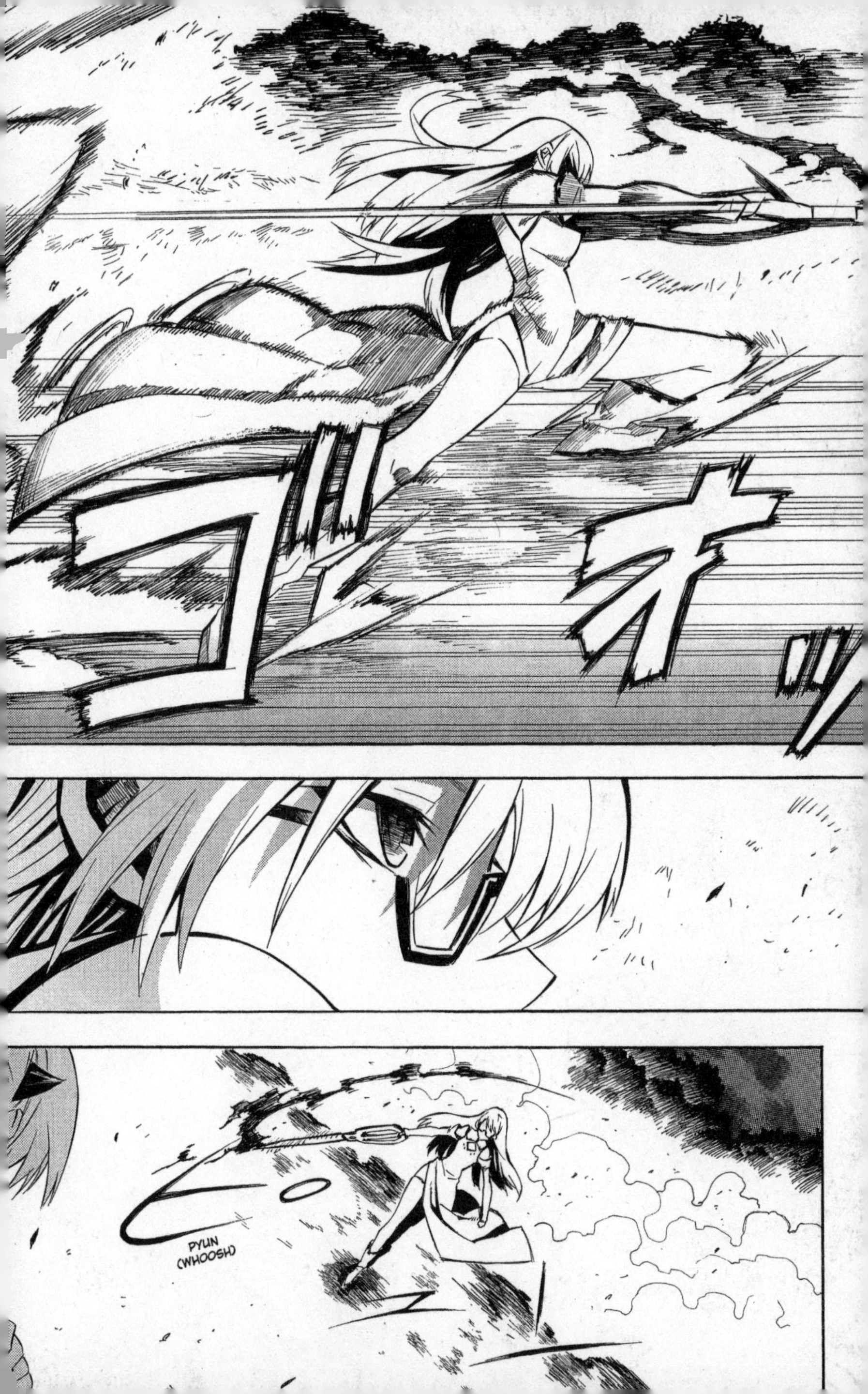
ゴオッ
PYUN
(WHOOSH)

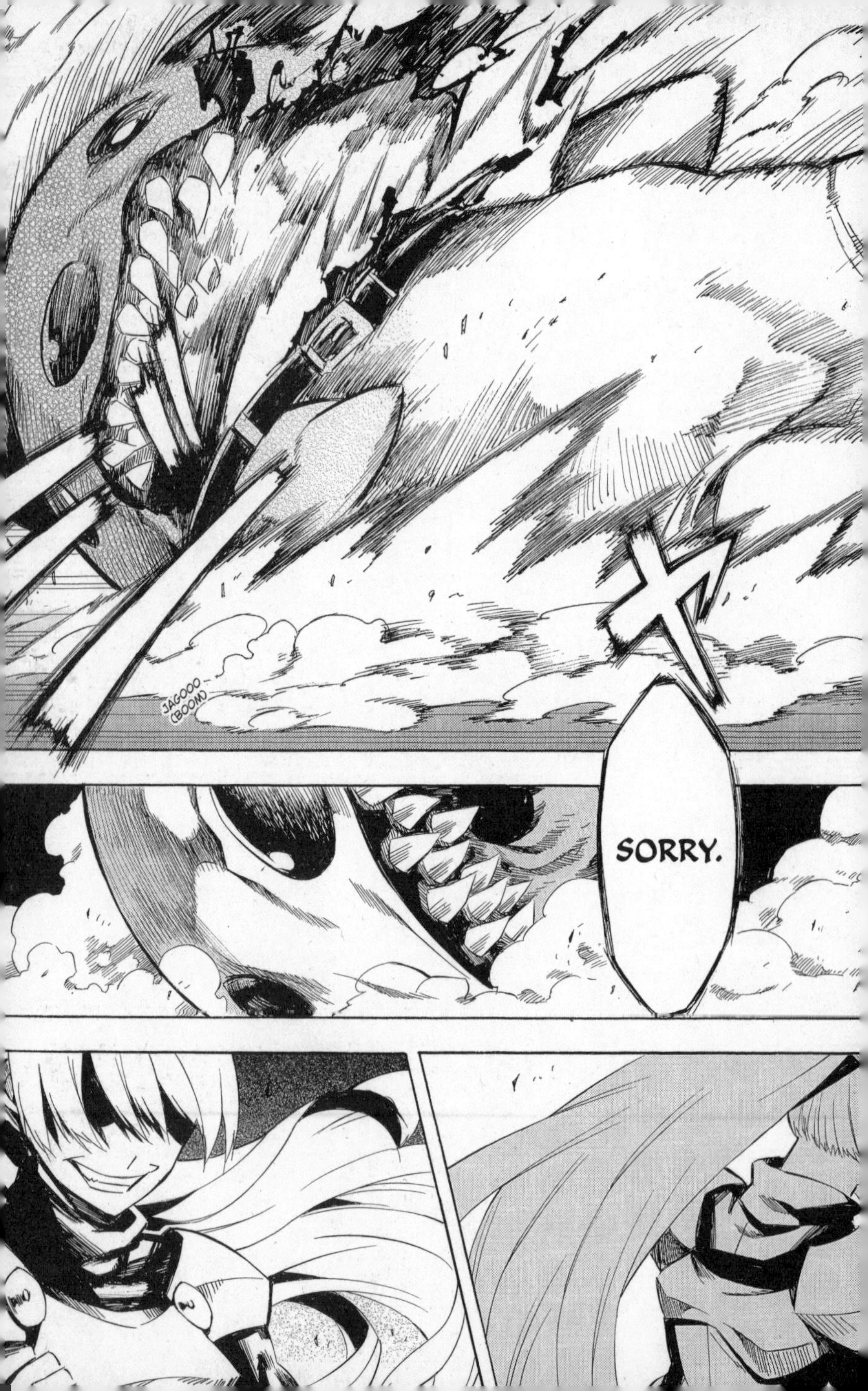

JAGOOO (BOOM)
SORRY.

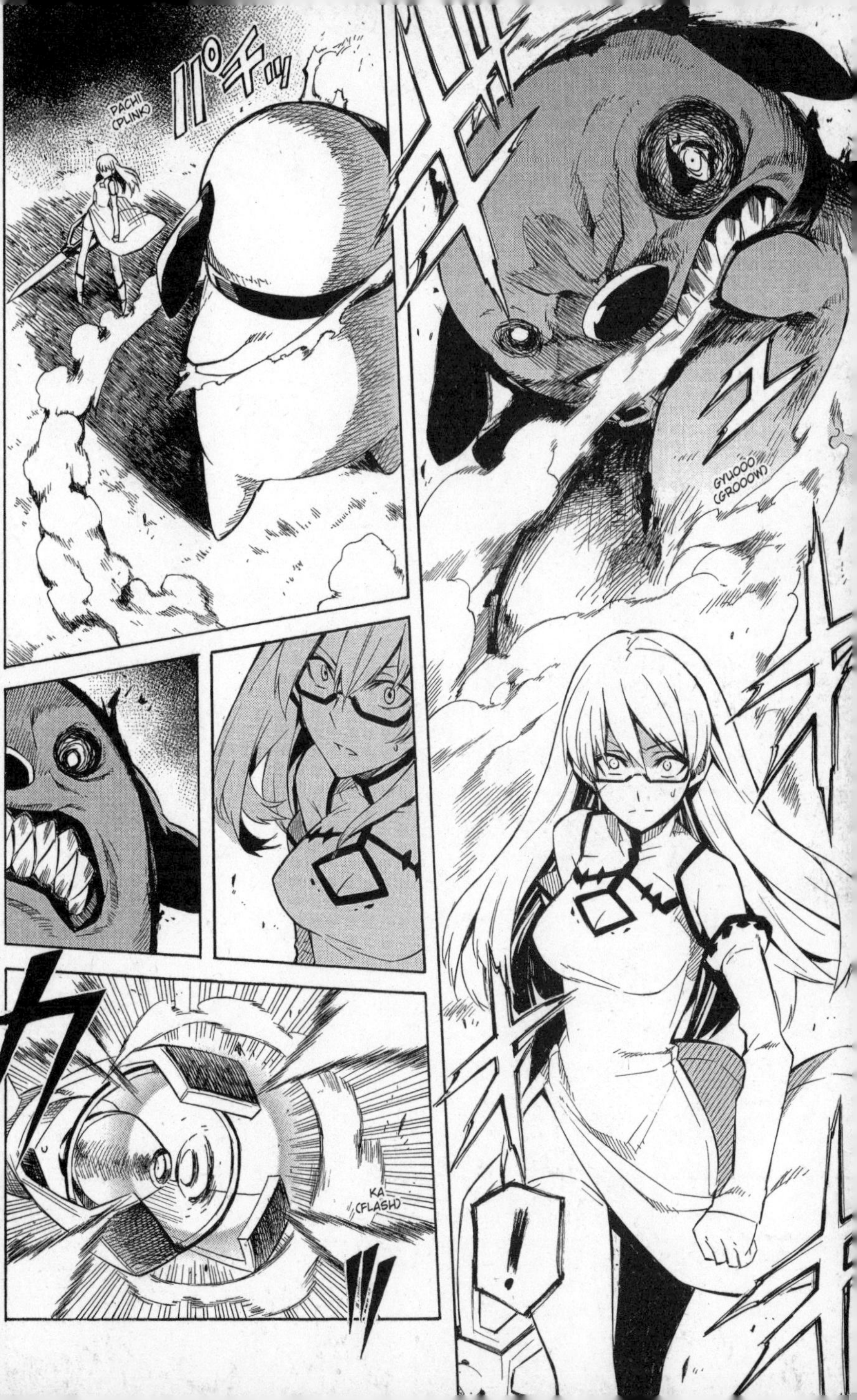
GYUOOO
(GROOOW)
PACHI
(PLINK)
KA
(FLASH)

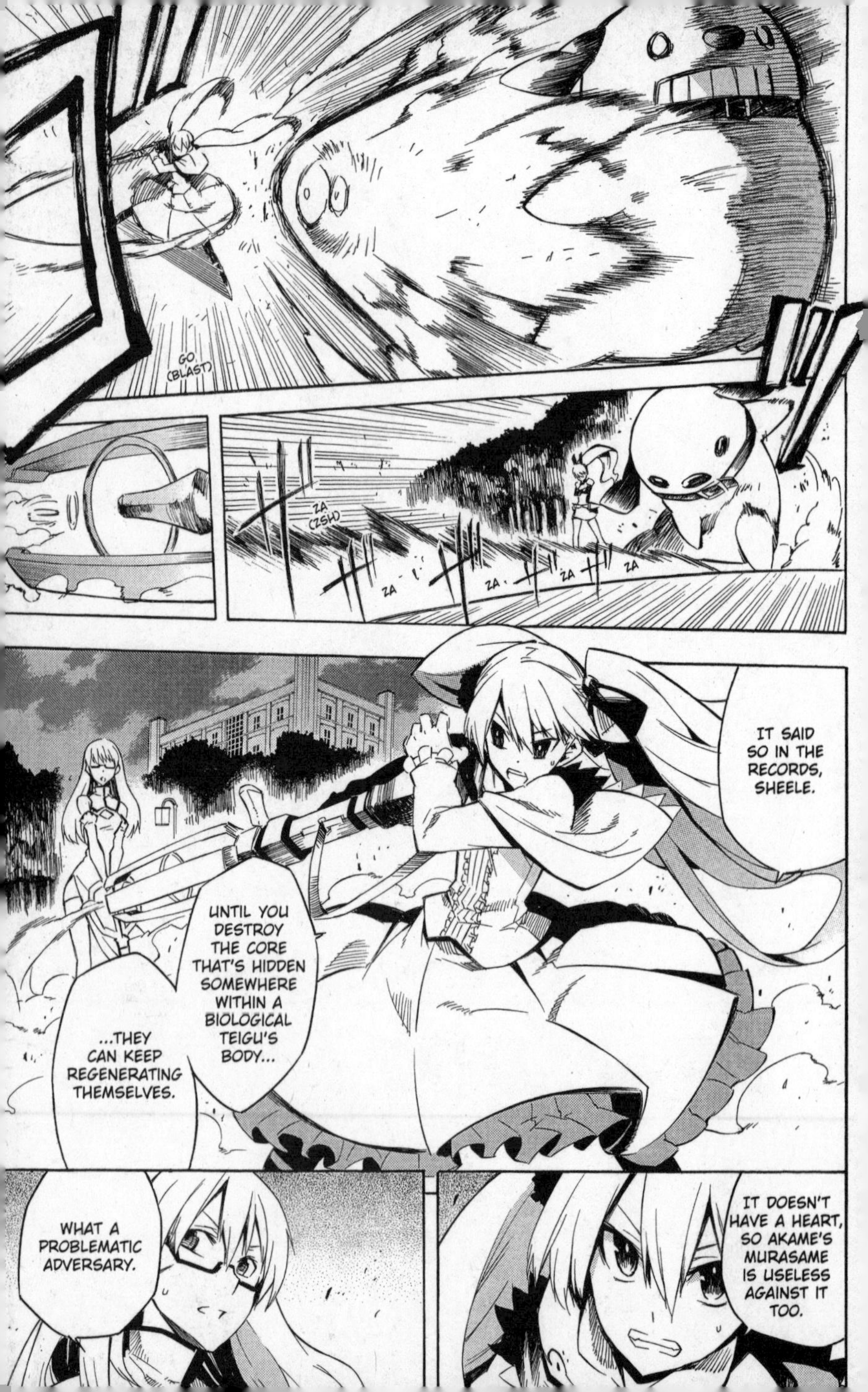
GO (BLAST)
ZA (ZSH)
ZA
ZA
ZA
ZA
IT SAID SO IN THE RECORDS, SHEELE.
UNTIL YOU DESTROY THE CORE THAT'S HIDDEN SOMEWHERE WITHIN A BIOLOGICAL TEIGU'S BODY...
...THEY CAN KEEP REGENERATING THEMSELVES.
IT DOESN'T HAVE A HEART, SO AKAME'S MURASAME IS USELESS AGAINST IT TOO.
WHAT A PROBLEMATIC ADVERSARY.

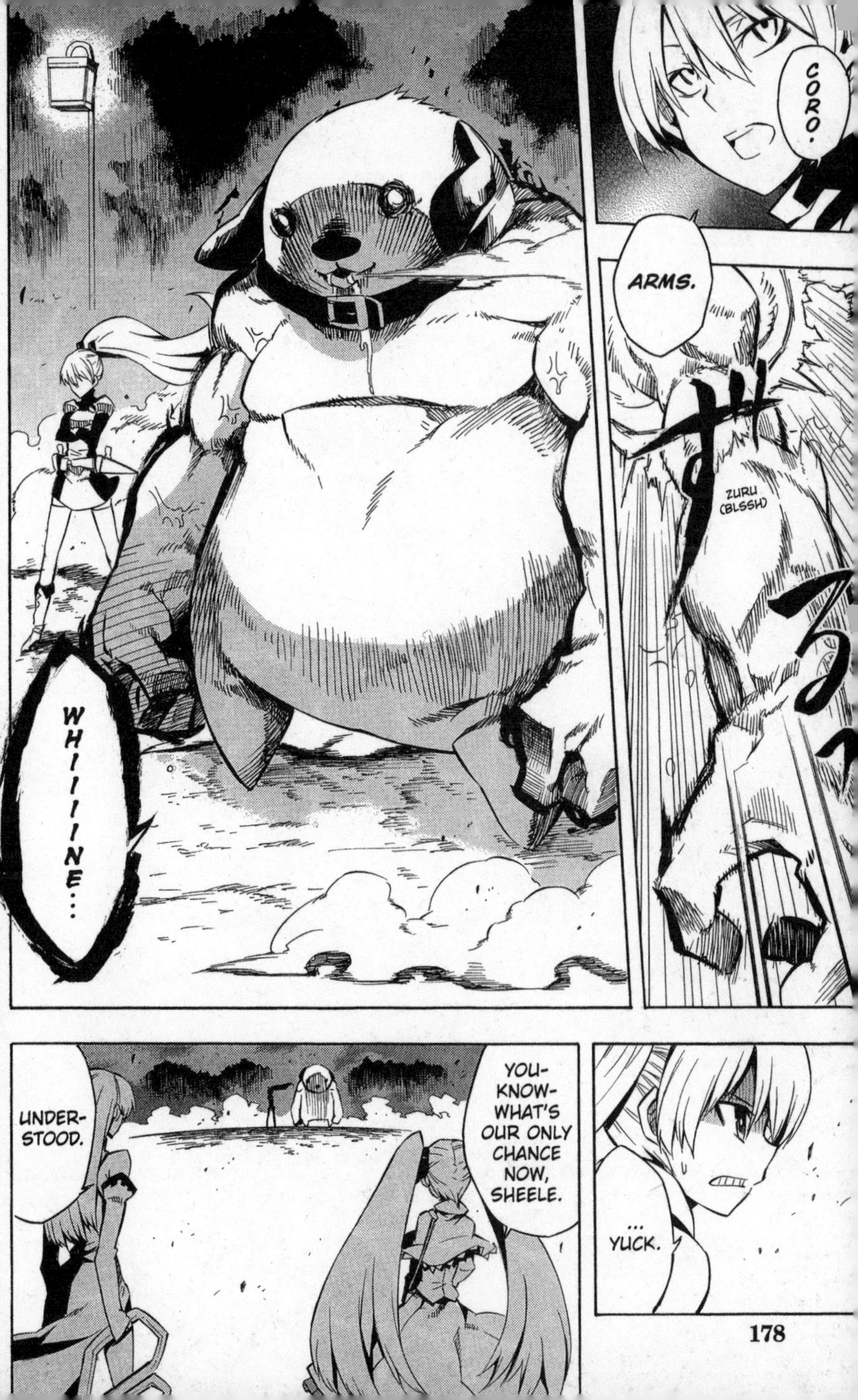
CORO.
ARMS.
ZURU (BLSSH)
WHIIIIINE...
... YUCK.
YOU-KNOW-WHAT'S OUR ONLY CHANCE NOW, SHEELE.
UNDER-STOOD.

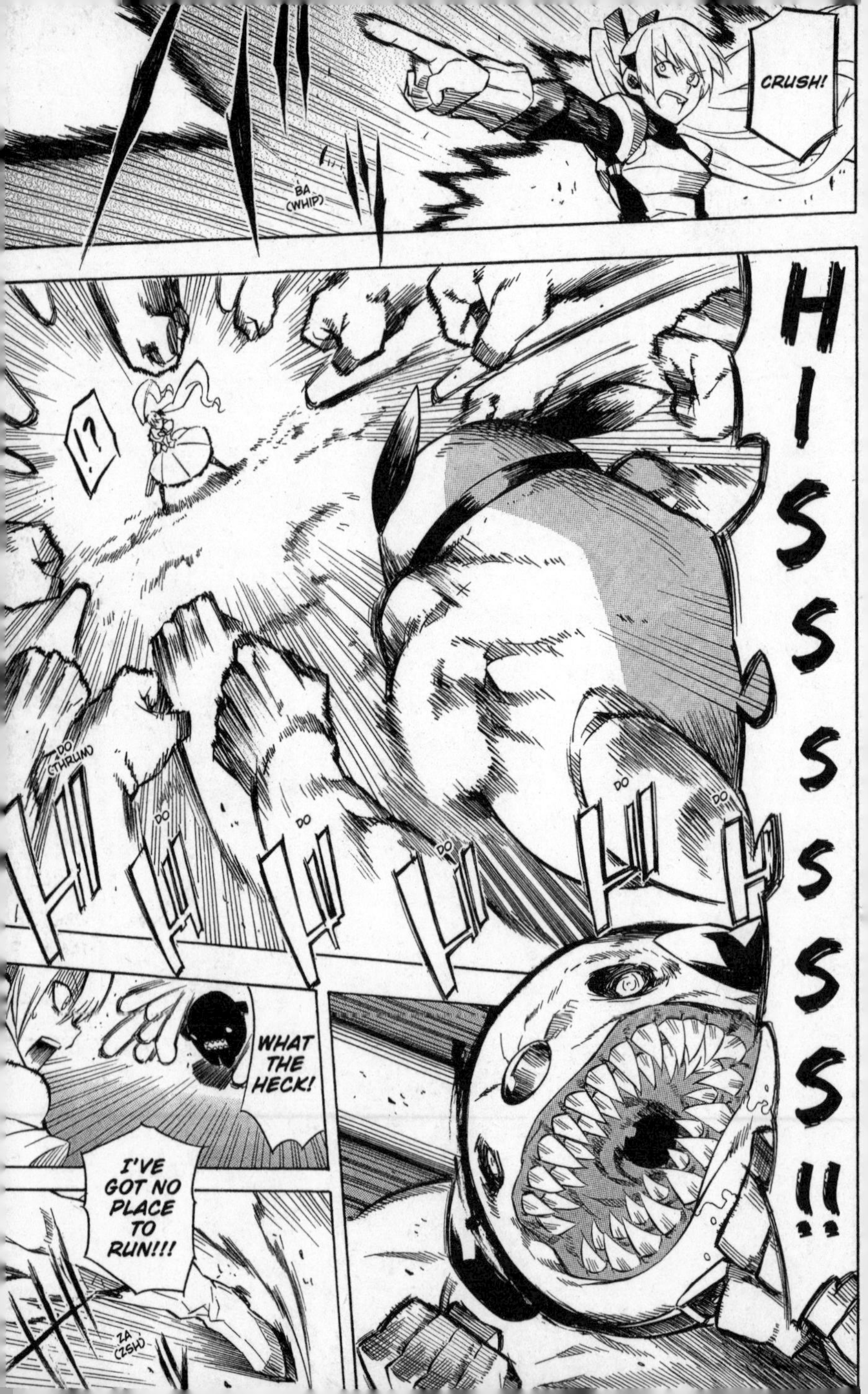
CRUSH!
BA (WHIP)
HISSSSSS!!
!?
DO
DO
DO
DO
DO
DO
DO (THRUM)
WHAT THE HECK!
I'VE GOT NO PLACE TO RUN!!!
ZA (ZSH)

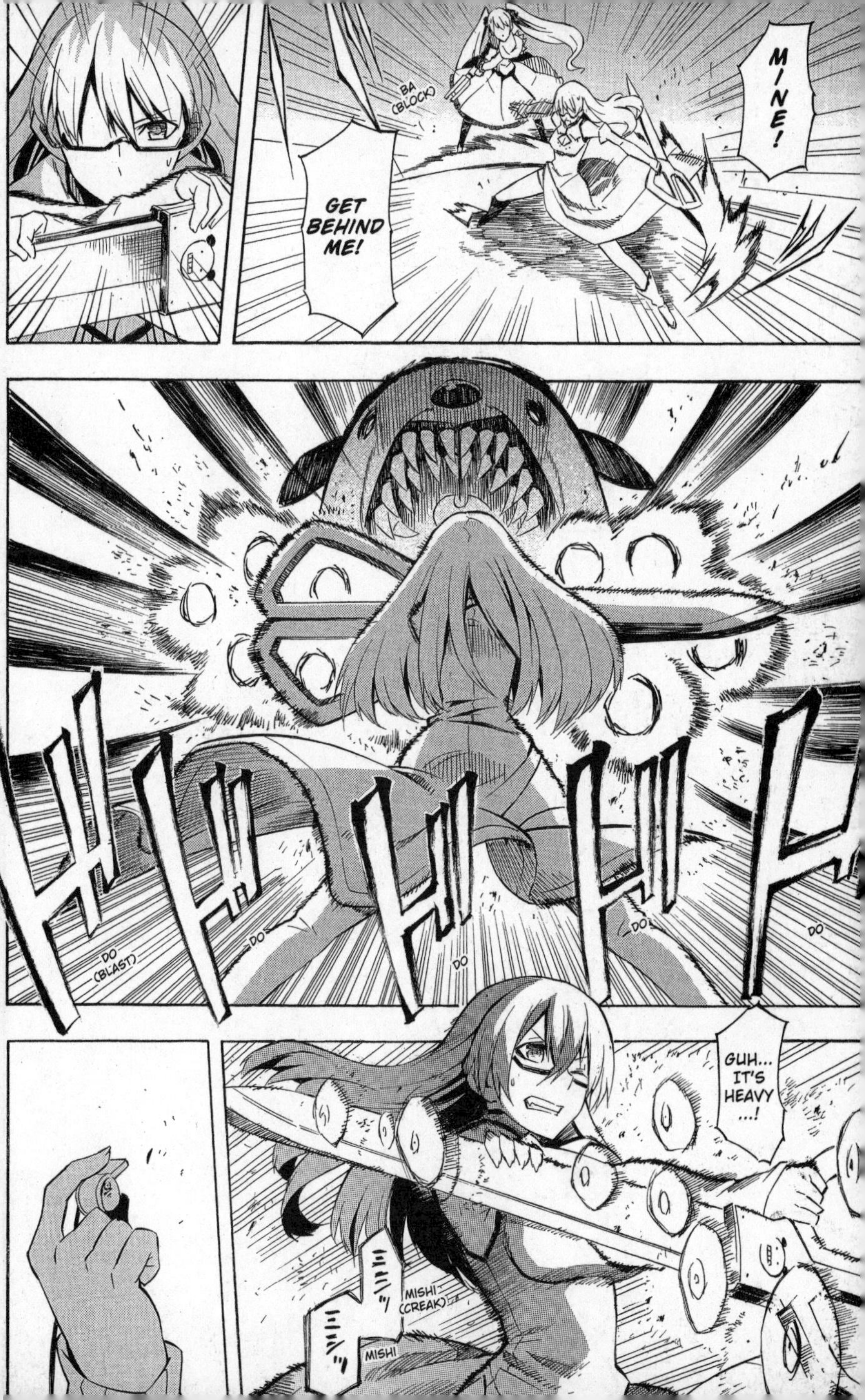
MINE!
BA (BLOCK)
GET BEHIND ME!
DO
DO
DO
DO
DO (BLAST)
GUH... IT'S HEAVY ...!
MISHI (CREAK)
MISHI

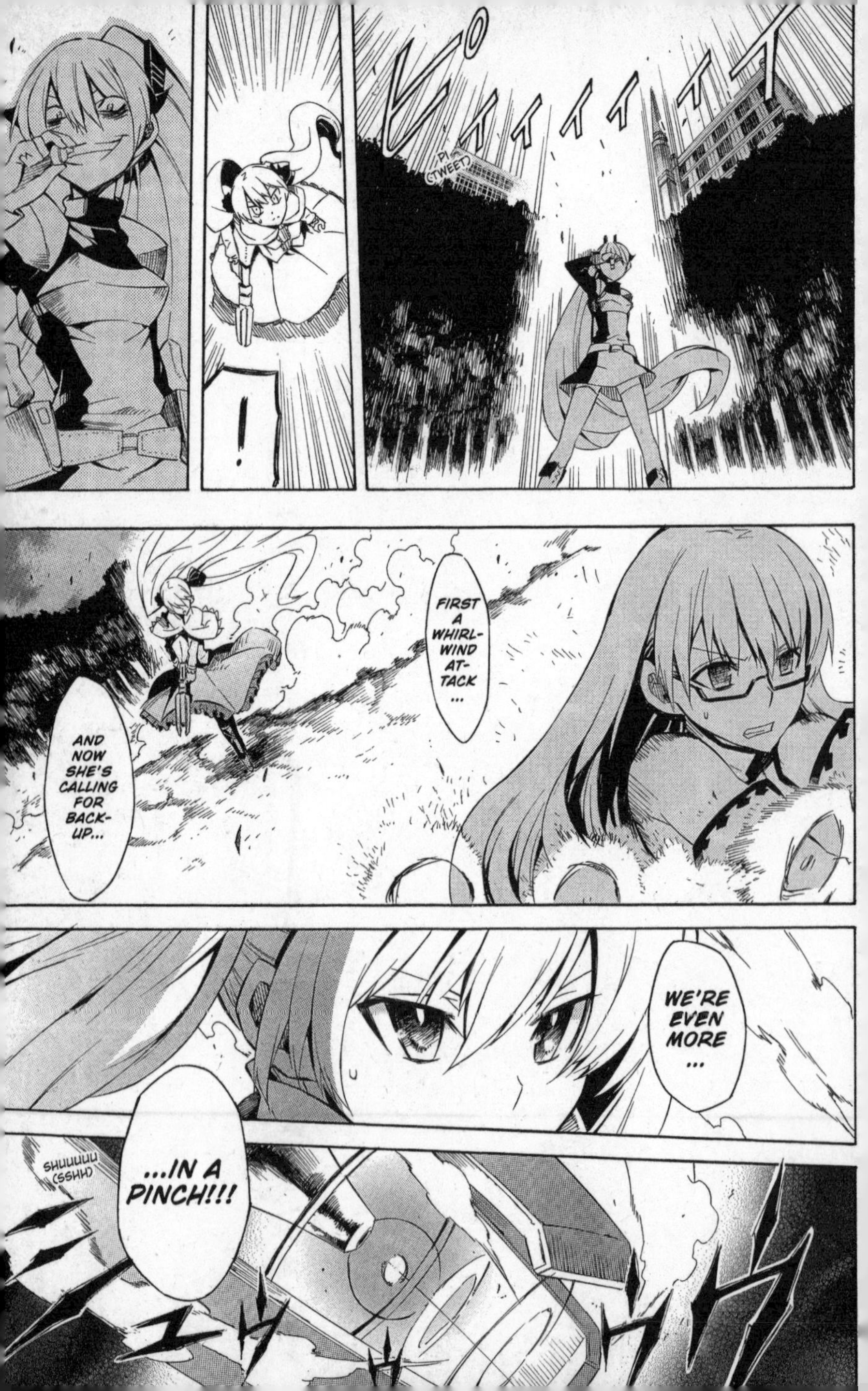
PI
(TWEET)
!
FIRST A WHIRL-WIND AT-TACK...
AND NOW SHE'S CALLING FOR BACK-UP...
WE'RE EVEN MORE...
...IN A PINCH!!!
SHUUUUU
(SSHH)

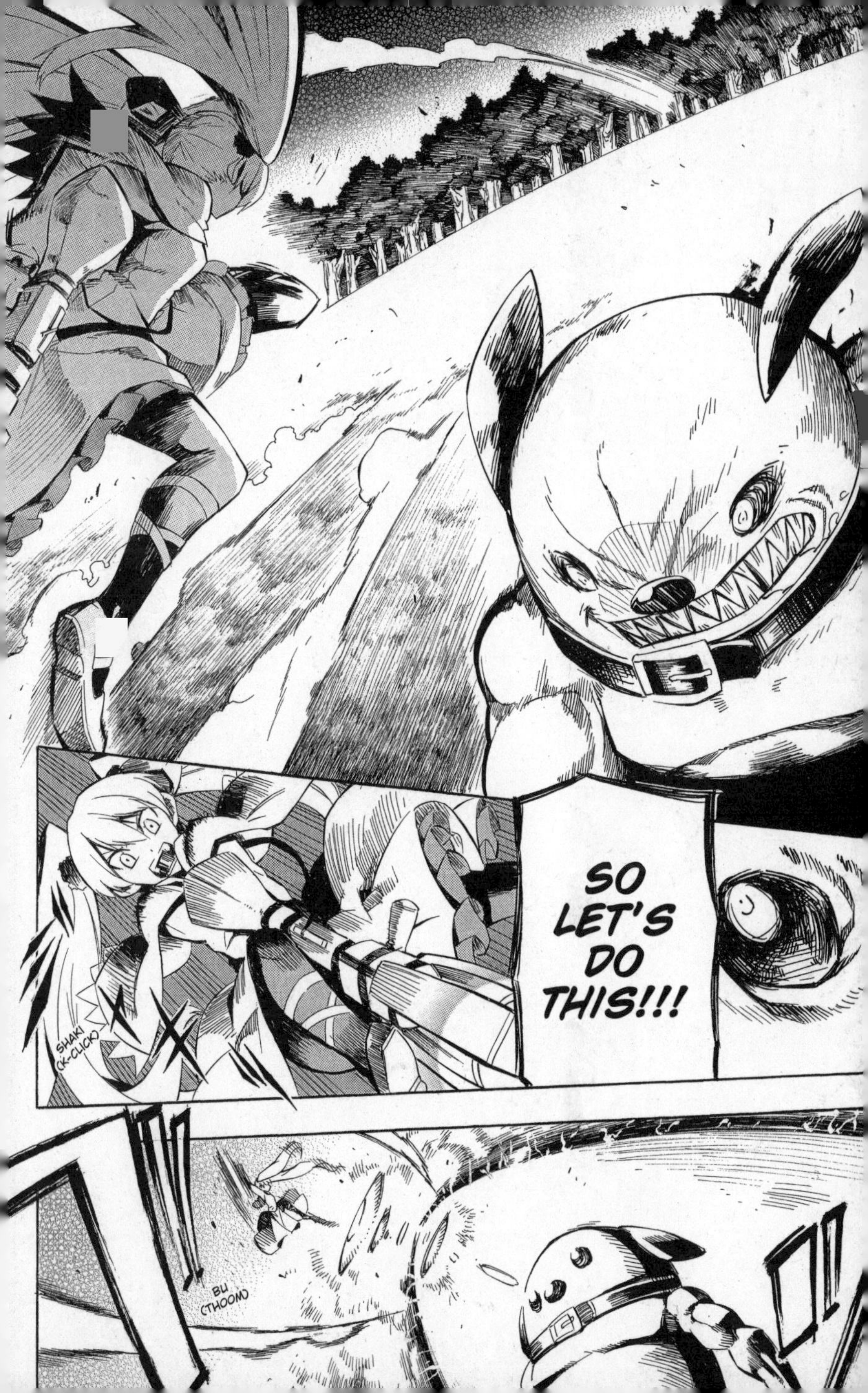
SO LET'S DO THIS!!!
SHAKI (K-CLICK)
BU (THOOM)

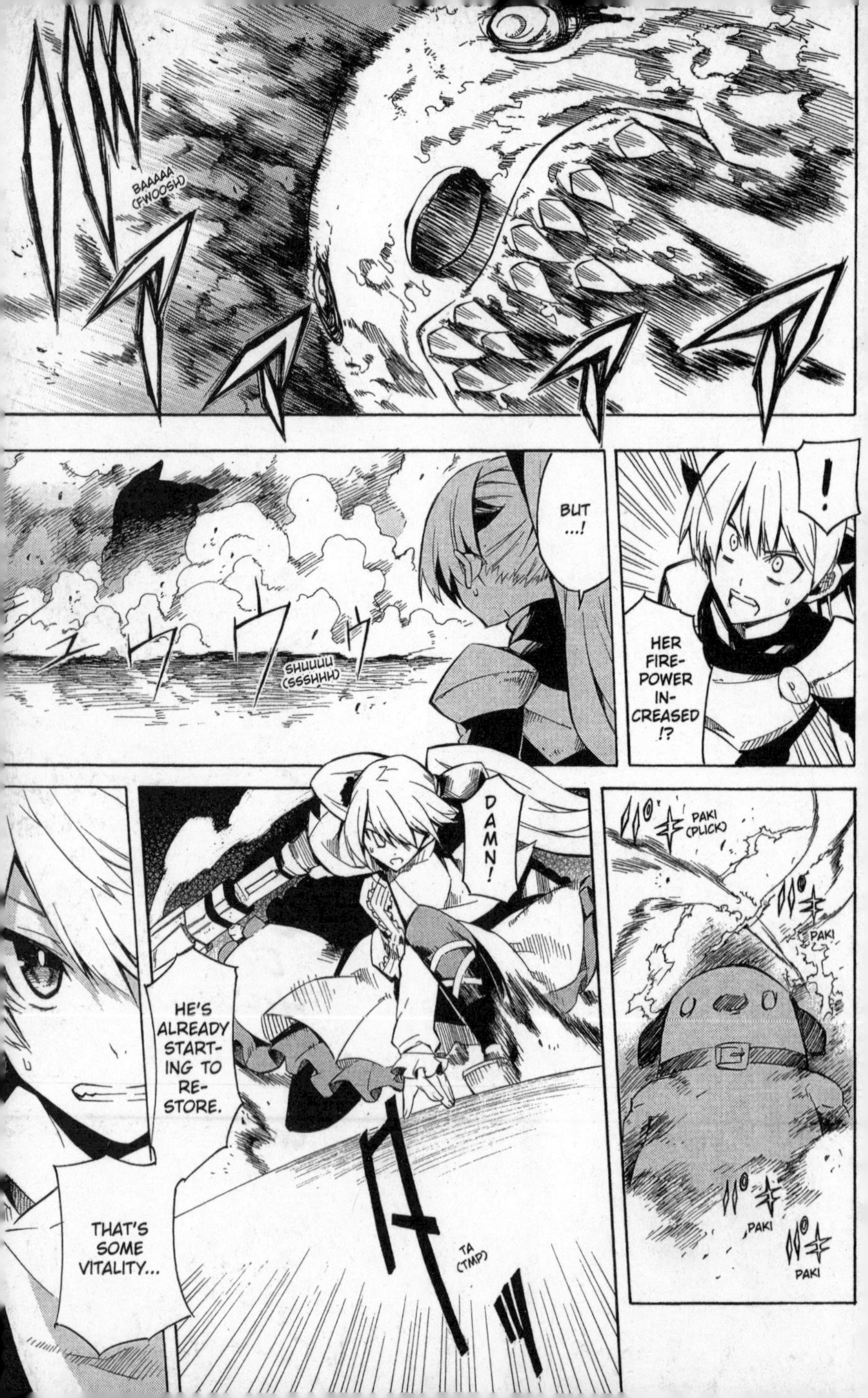
BAAAAA (FWOOSH)
!
HER FIRE-POWER IN-CREASED !?
BUT ...!
SHUUUU (SSSHHH)
PAKI (PLICK)
PAKI
PAKI
PAKI
DAMN!
TA (TMP)
HE'S ALREADY START-ING TO RE-STORE.
THAT'S SOME VITALITY...

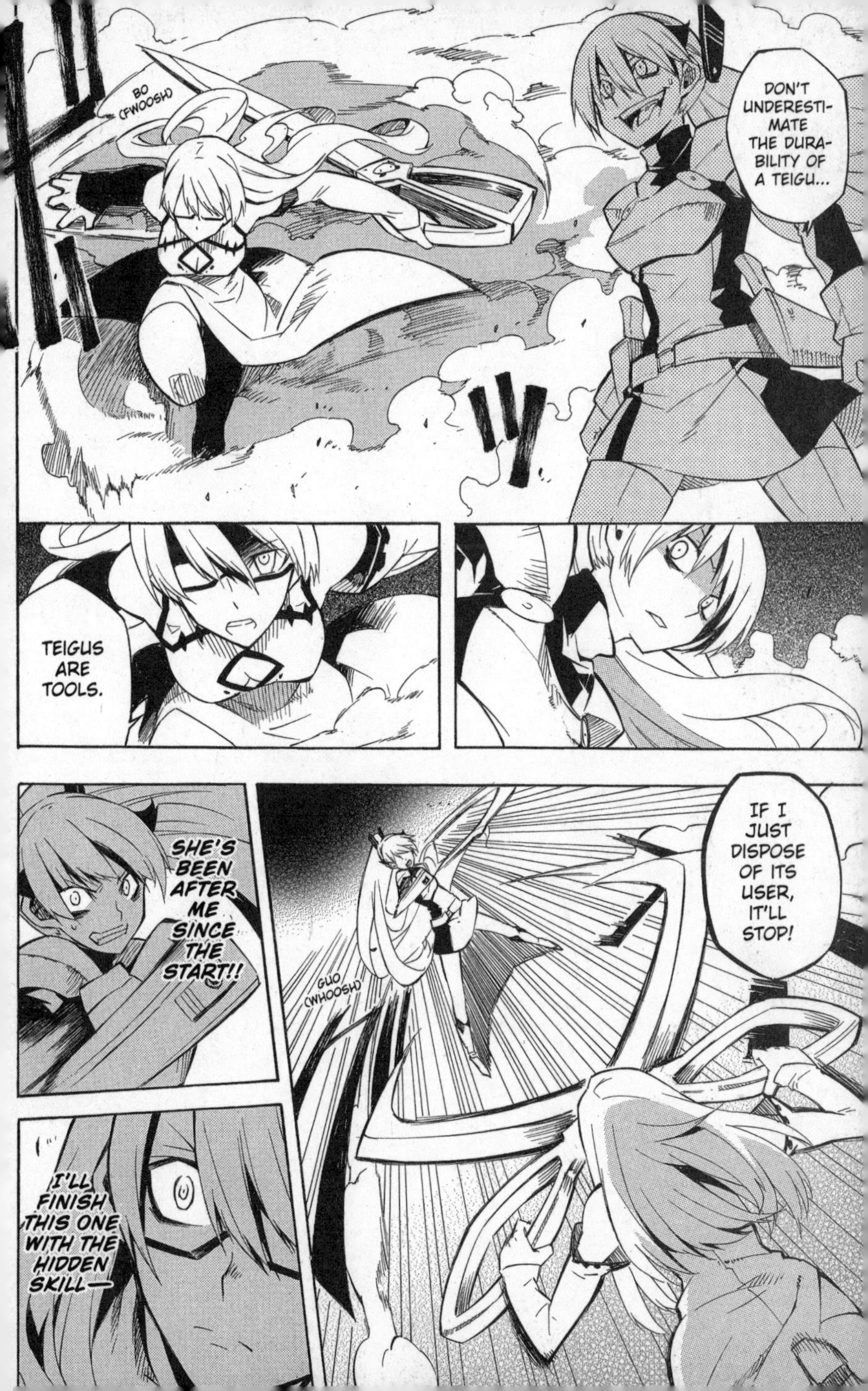
DON'T UNDERESTIMATE THE DURABILITY OF A TEIGU...
BO (FWOOSH)
TEIGUS ARE TOOLS.
IF I JUST DISPOSE OF ITS USER, IT'LL STOP!
GUO (WHOOSH)
SHE'S BEEN AFTER ME SINCE THE START!!
I'LL FINISH THIS ONE WITH THE HIDDEN SKILL—

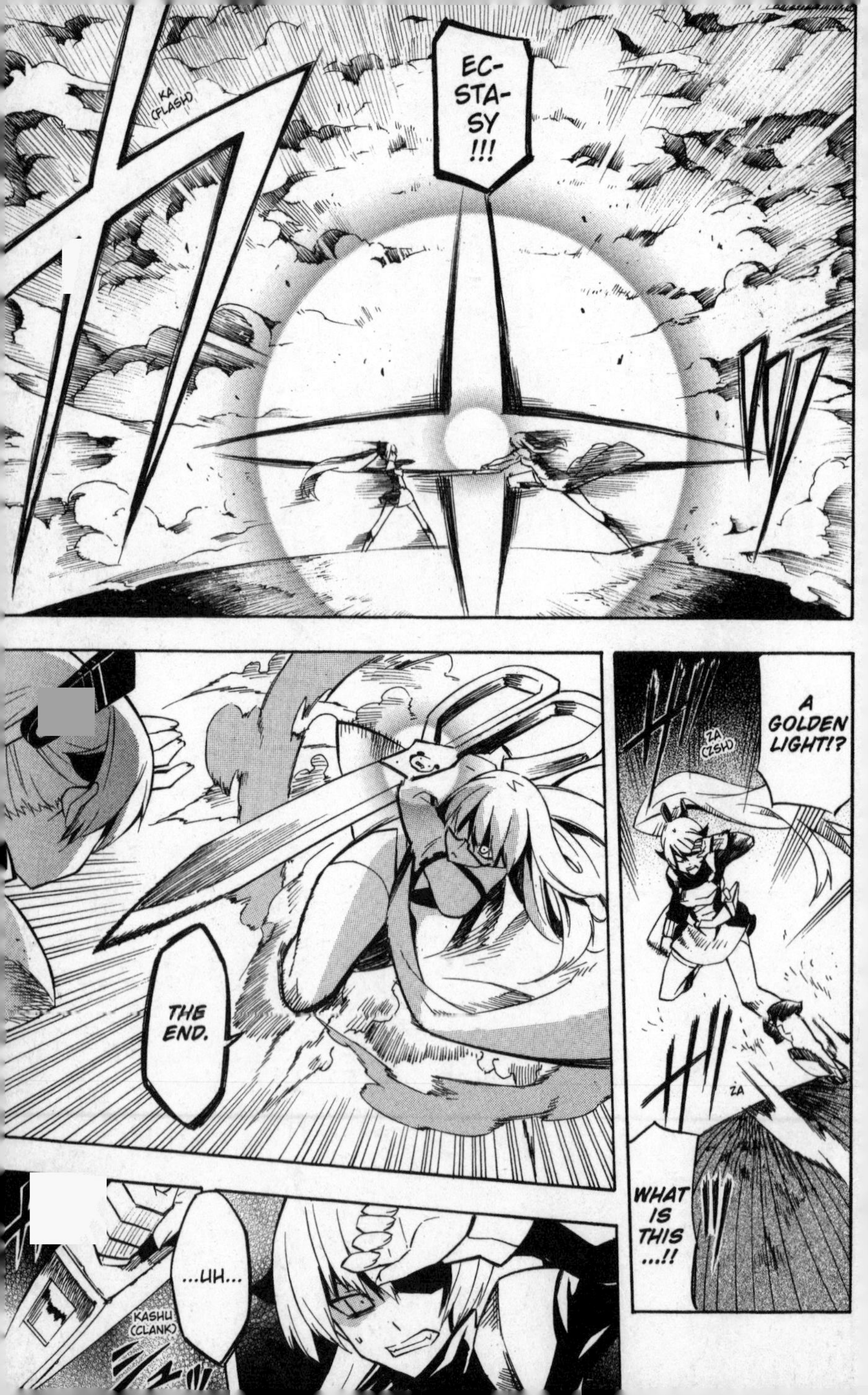
EC-STA-SY!!!
KA (FLASH)
A GOLDEN LIGHT!?
ZA (ZSH)
ZA
WHAT IS THIS...!!
THE END.
...UH...
KASHU (CLANK)

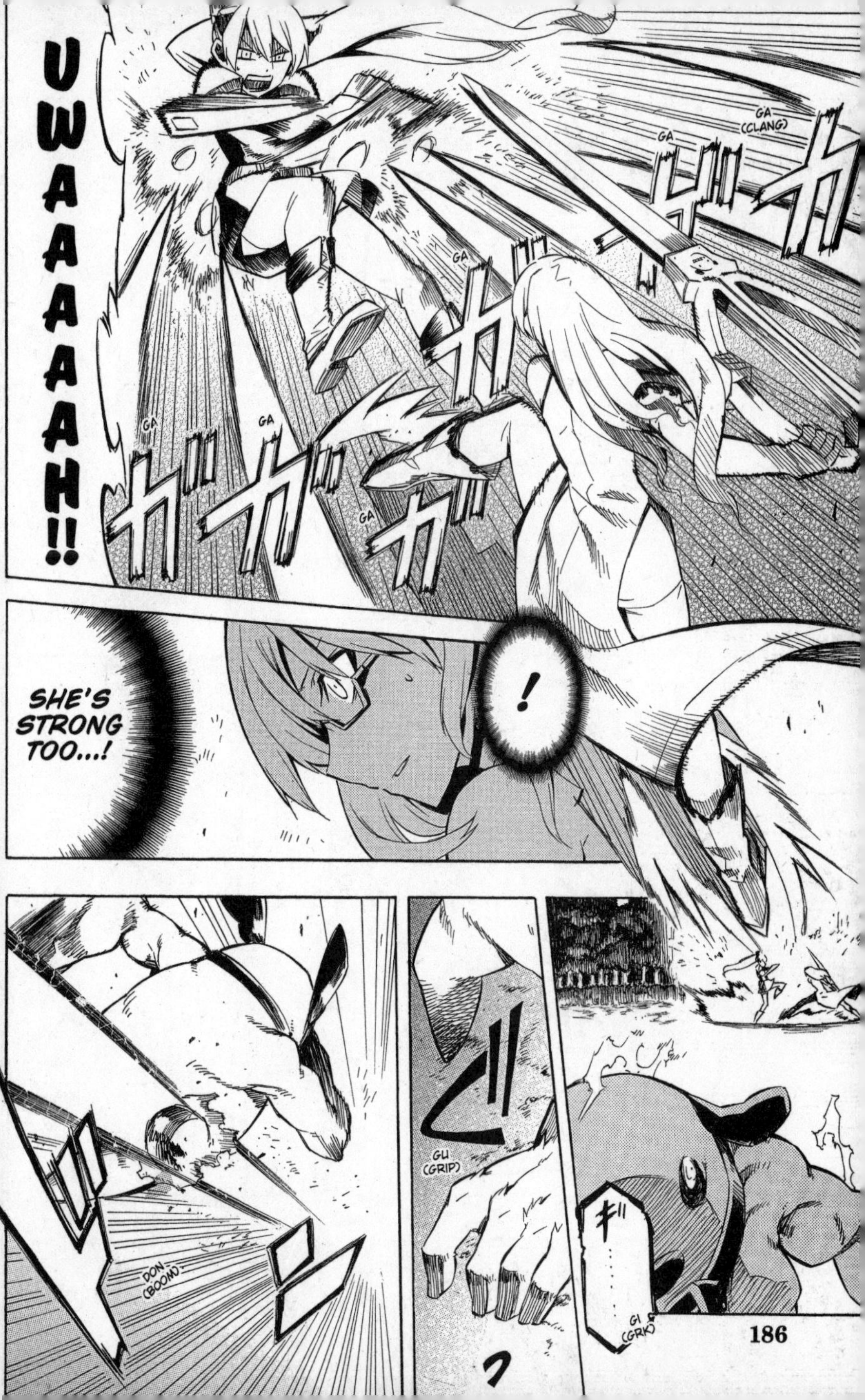

GA (CLANG)
GA
GA
GA
GA
GA
UWAAAAAAH!!
!
SHE'S STRONG TOO...!
GI (GRK)
GU (GRIP)
DON (BOOM)

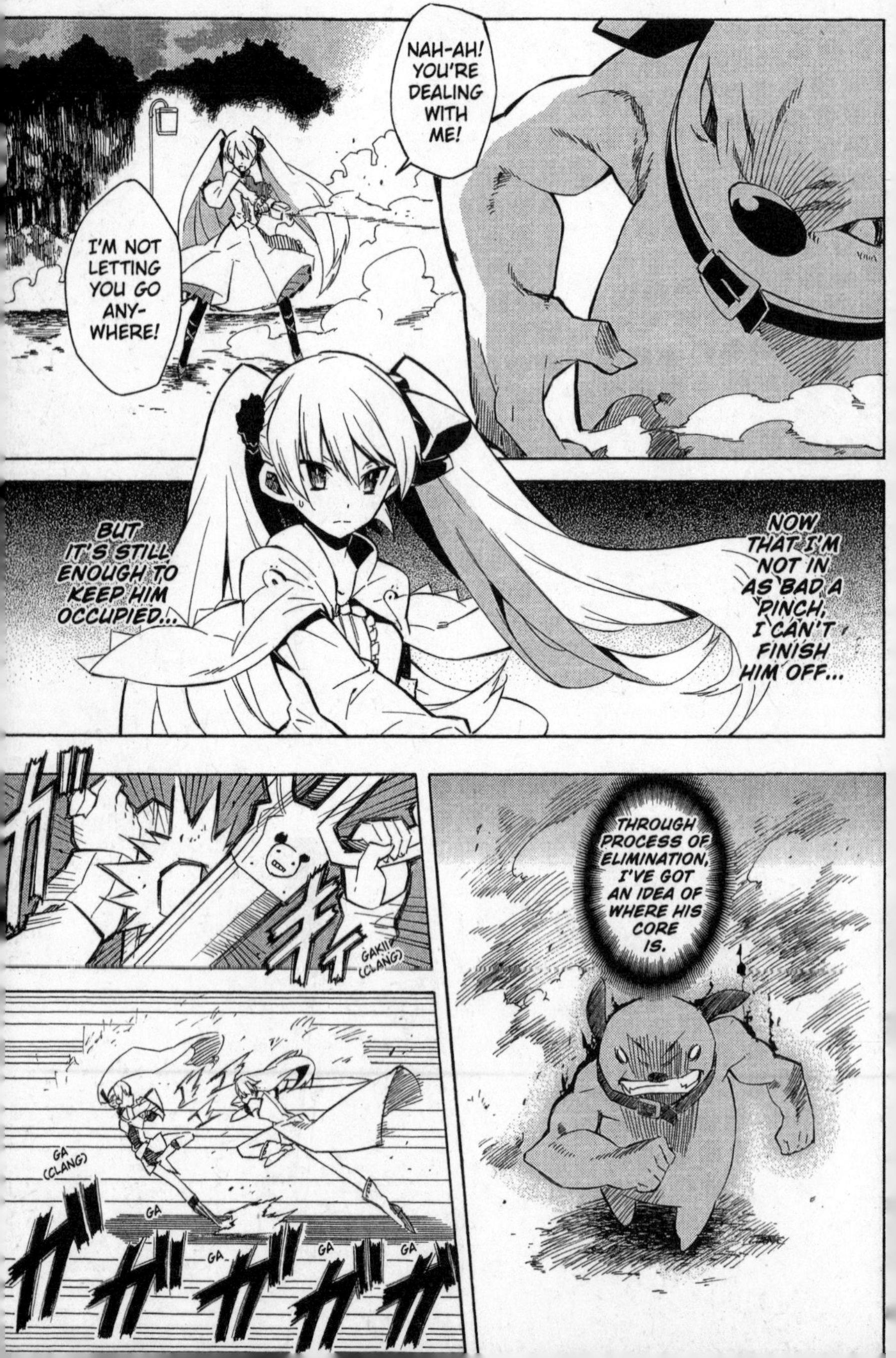
NAH-AH! YOU'RE DEALING WITH ME!
I'M NOT LETTING YOU GO ANY-WHERE!
NOW THAT I'M NOT IN AS BAD A PINCH, I CAN'T FINISH HIM OFF...
BUT IT'S STILL ENOUGH TO KEEP HIM OCCUPIED...
THROUGH PROCESS OF ELIMINATION, I'VE GOT AN IDEA OF WHERE HIS CORE IS.
GAKII (CLANG)
GA (CLANG)
GA
GA
GA
GA

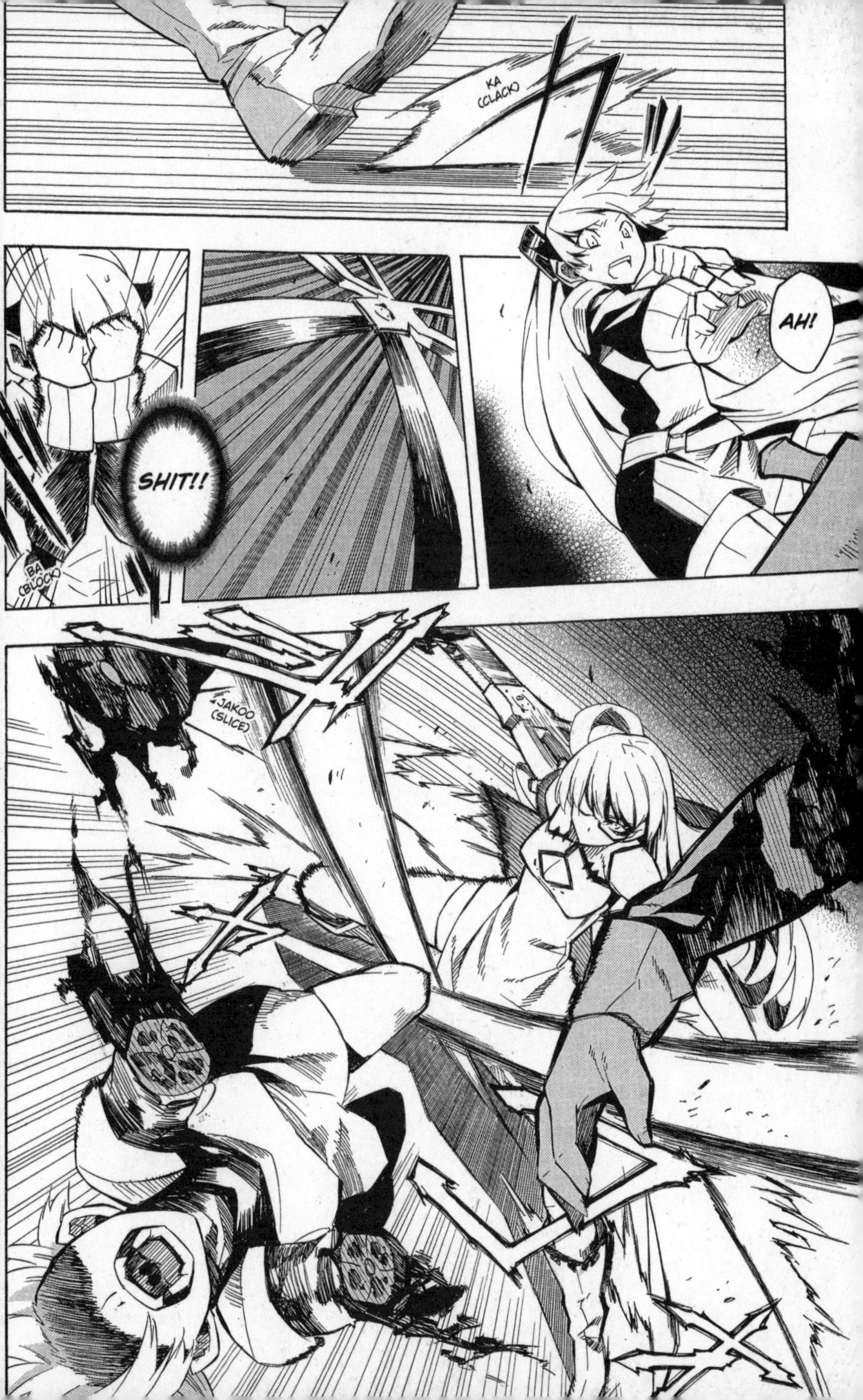
KA (CLACK)
AH!
SHIT!!
BA (BLOCK)
JAKOO (SLICE)

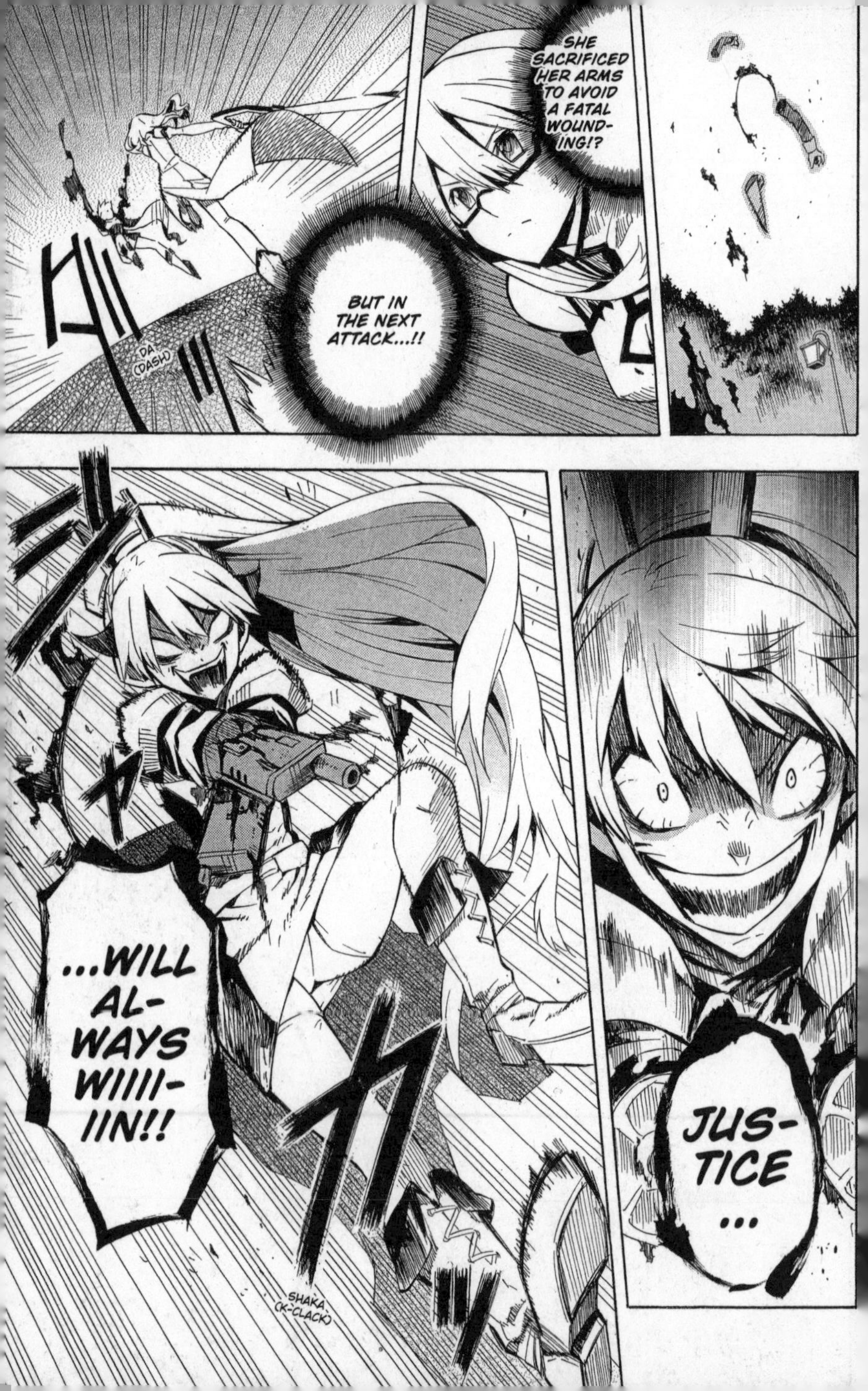
SHE SACRIFICED HER ARMS TO AVOID A FATAL WOUNDING!?
BUT IN THE NEXT ATTACK...!!
DA (DASH)
JUSTICE...
...WILL ALWAYS WIIIIIN!!
SHAKA (K-CLACK)

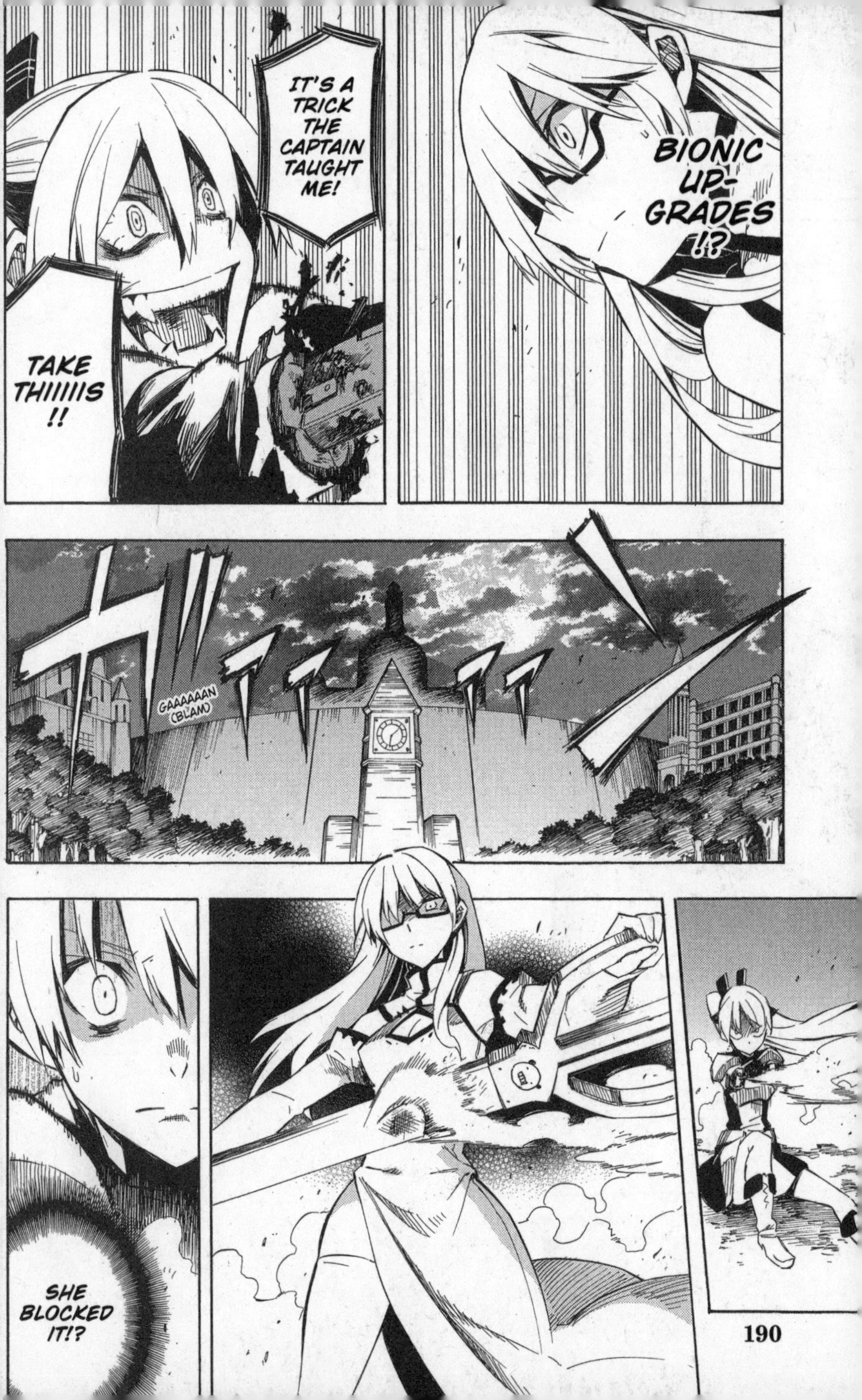
BIONIC UP-GRADES !?
IT'S A TRICK THE CAPTAIN TAUGHT ME!
TAKE THIIIIIS !!
GAAAAAAN (BLAM)
SHE BLOCKED IT!?

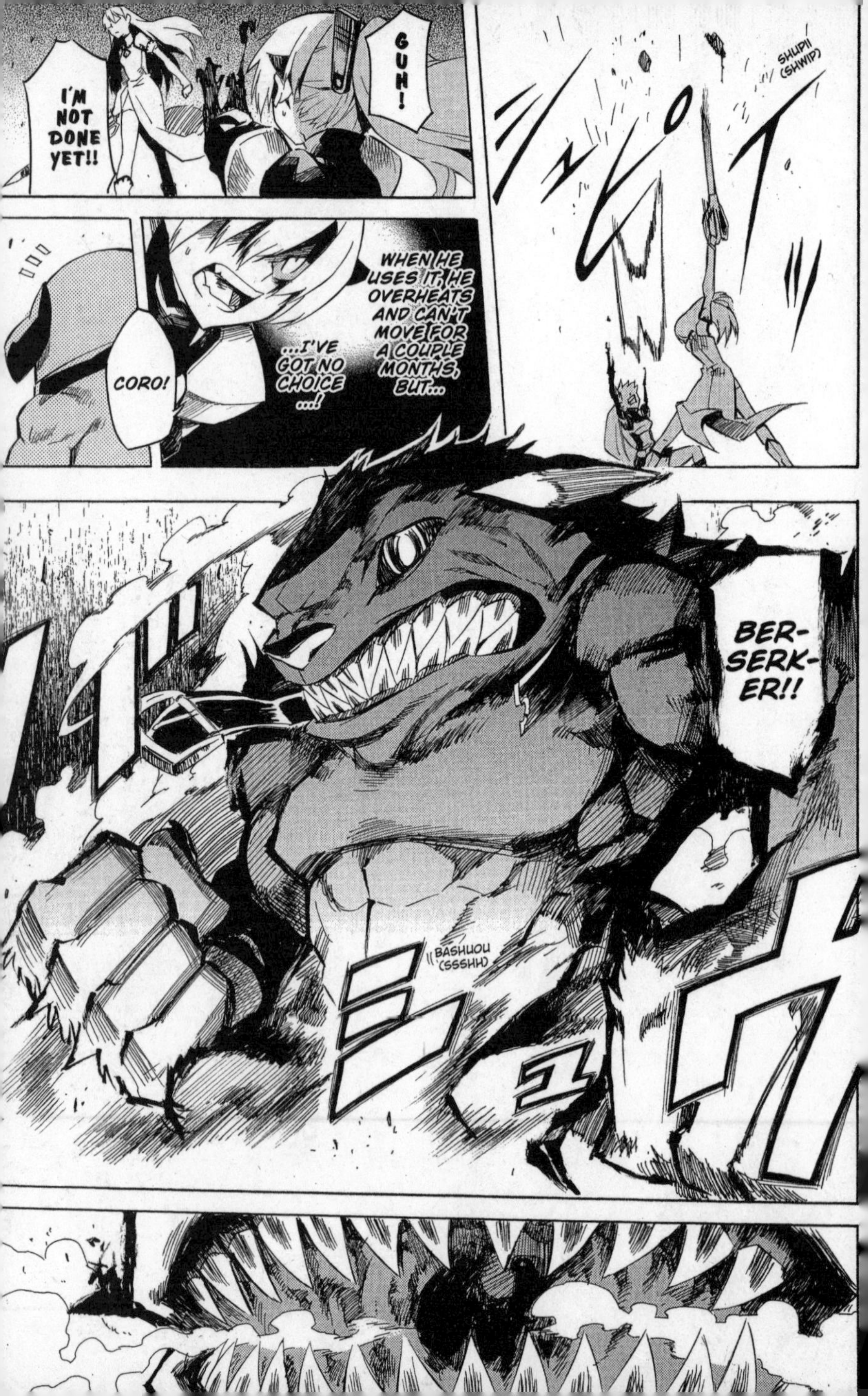
SHUPII (SHWIP)
GUH!
I'M NOT DONE YET!!
WHEN HE USES IT, HE OVERHEATS AND CAN'T MOVE FOR A COUPLE MONTHS, BUT...
...I'VE GOT NO CHOICE ...!
CORO!
BER-SERK-ER!!
BASHUOU (SSSHH)

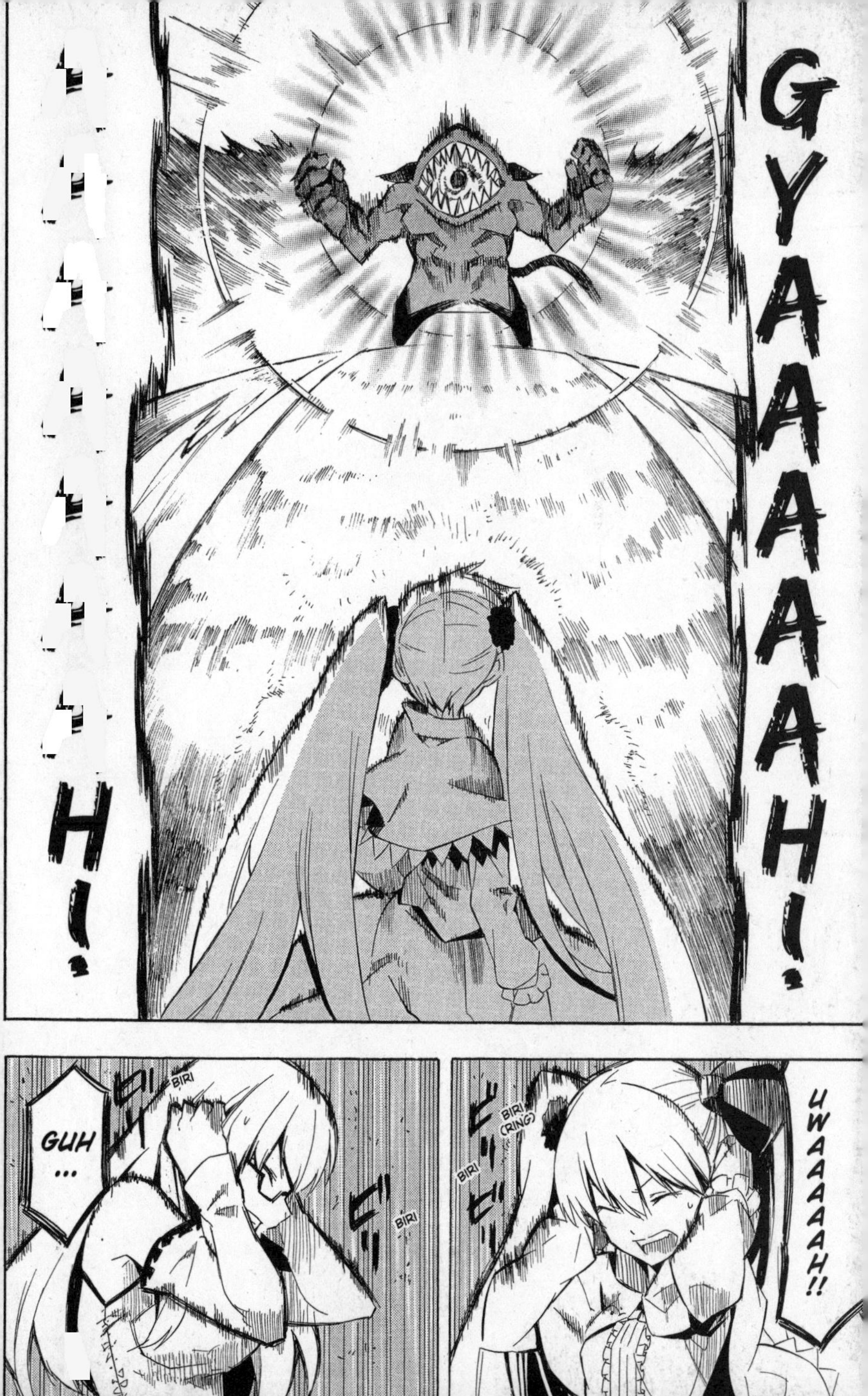
GYAAAAAH!!
H!!
UWAAAAAH!!
BIRI (RING)
BIRI
BIRI
GUH ...
BIRI

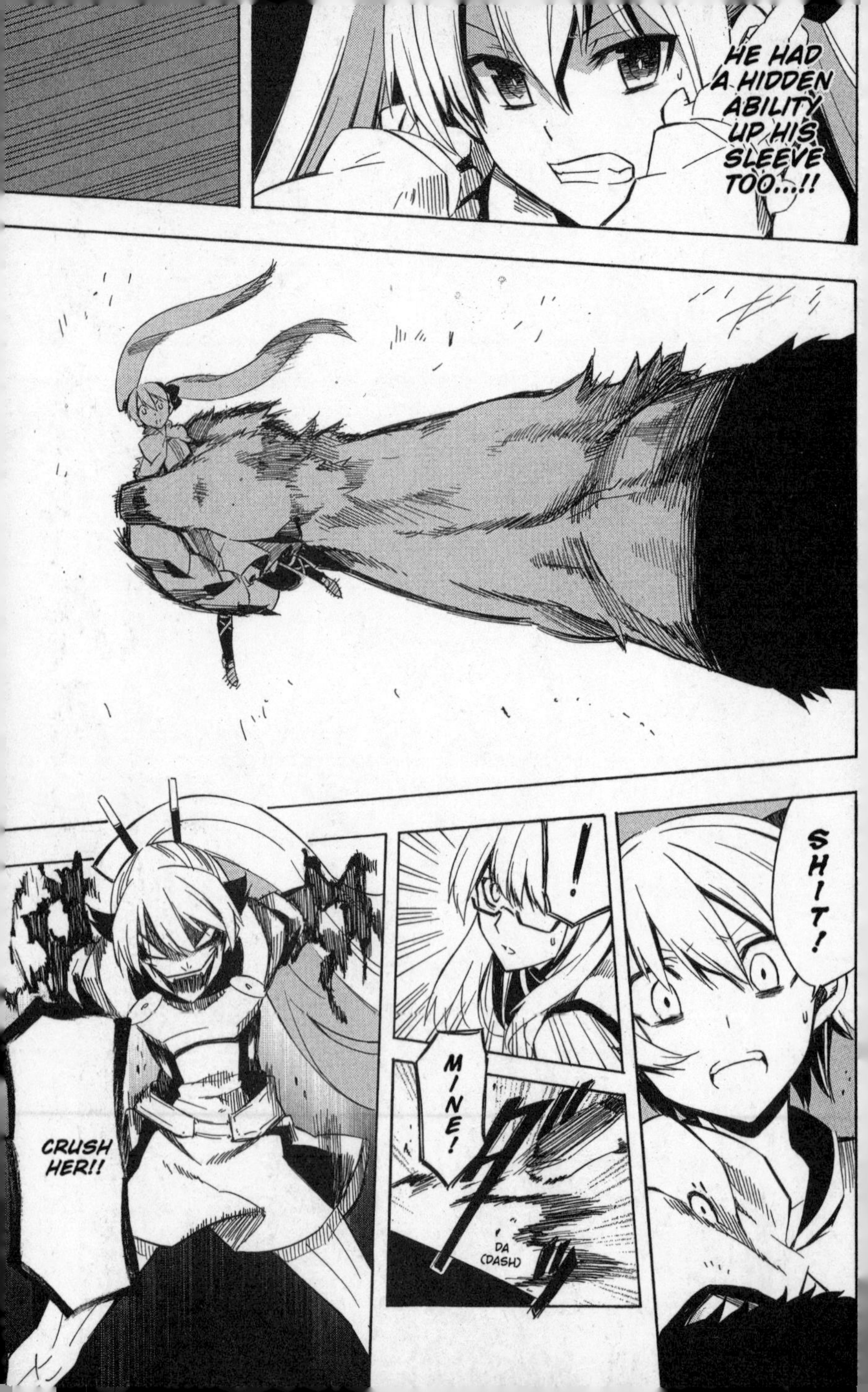
HE HAD A HIDDEN ABILITY UP HIS SLEEVE TOO...!!
SHIT!
!
MINE!
DA (DASH)
CRUSH HER!!

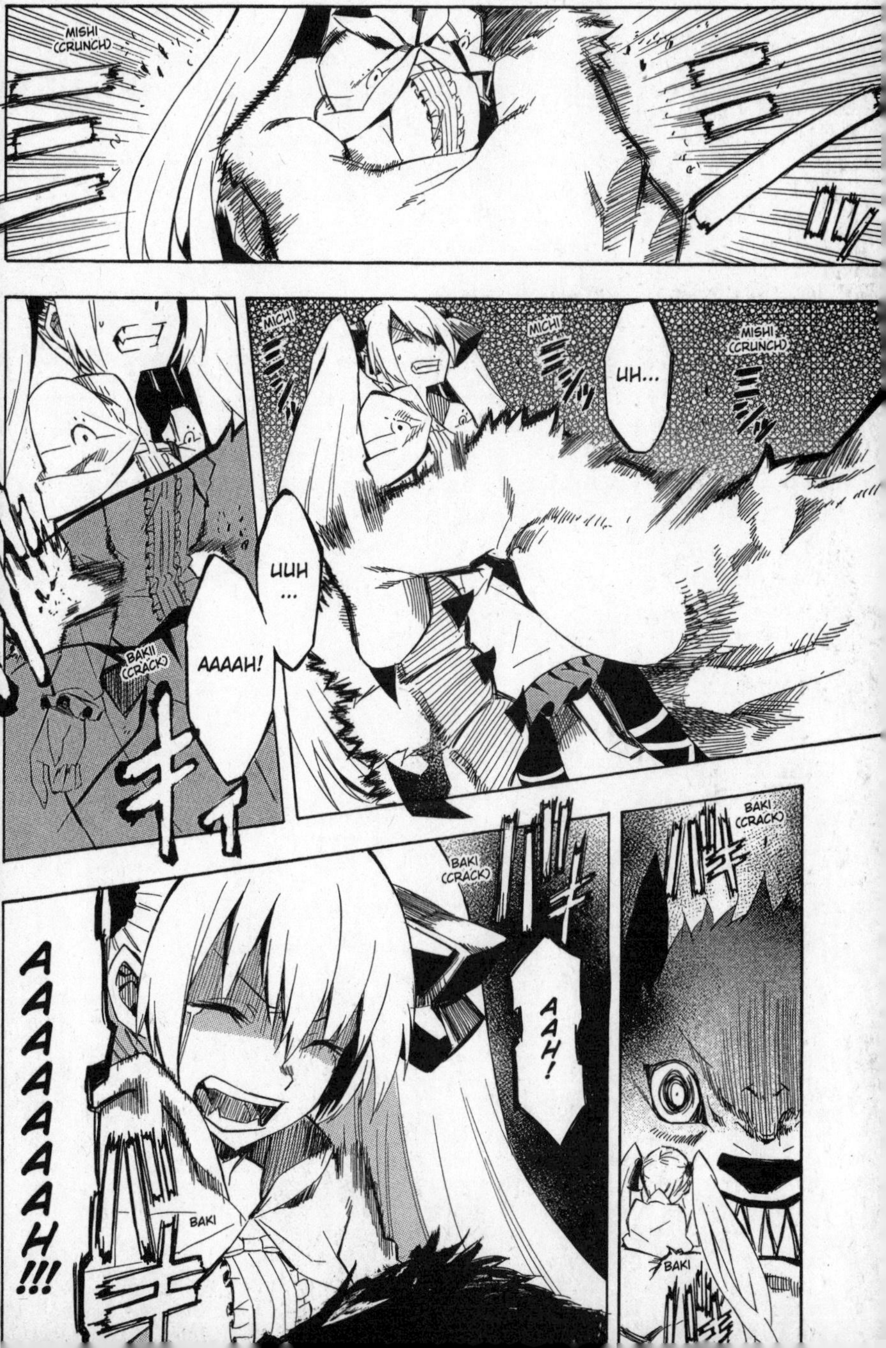
MISHI (CRUNCH)
MISHI (CRUNCH)
UH...
MICHI
MICHI
UUH ...
AAAAH!
BAKII (CRACK)
BAKI (CRACK)
BAKI
BAKI (CRACK)
AAH!
AAAAAAAAAAH!!!
BAKI

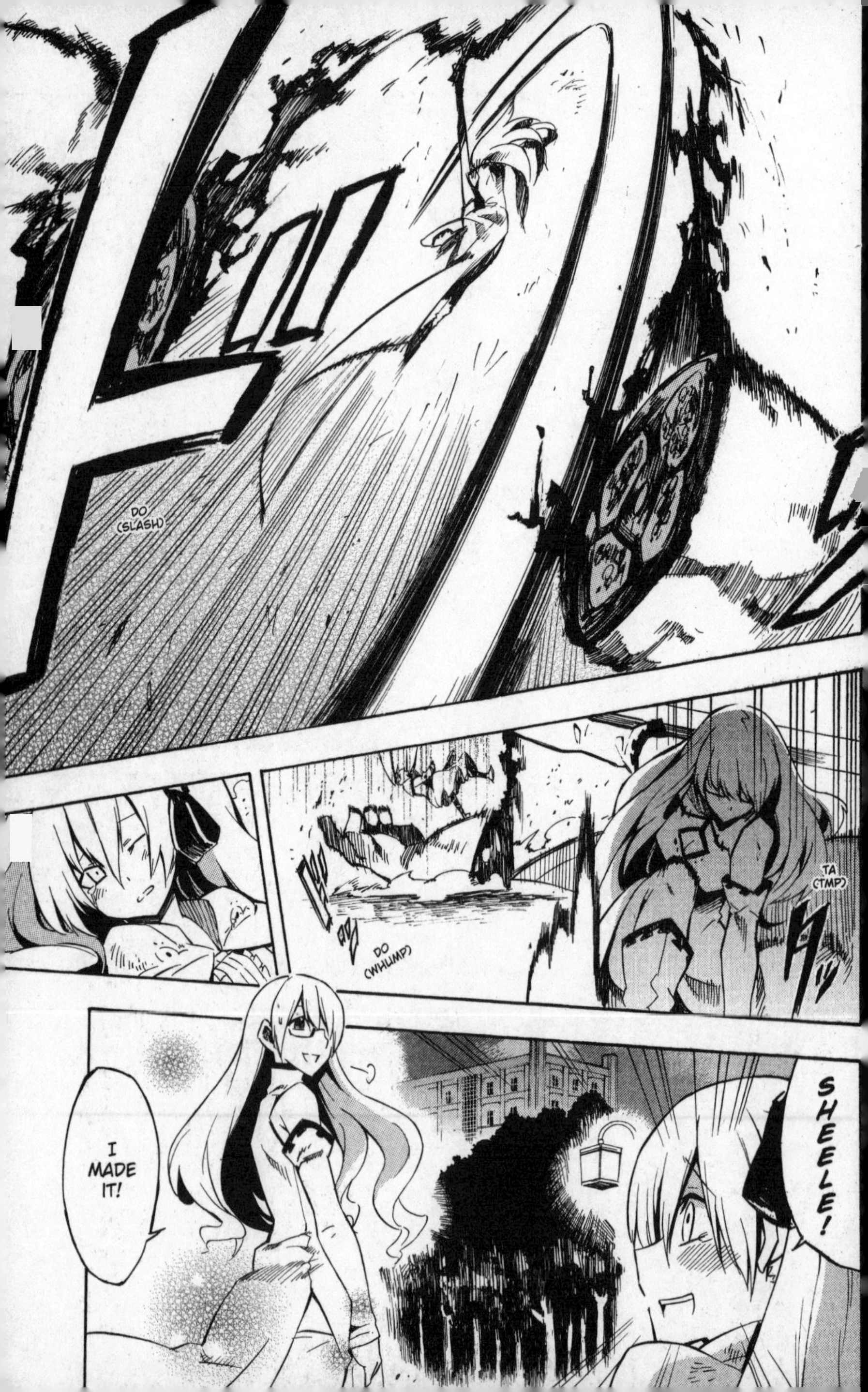
DO
(SLASH)
TA
(TMP)
DO
(WHUMP)
SHEELE!
I MADE IT!

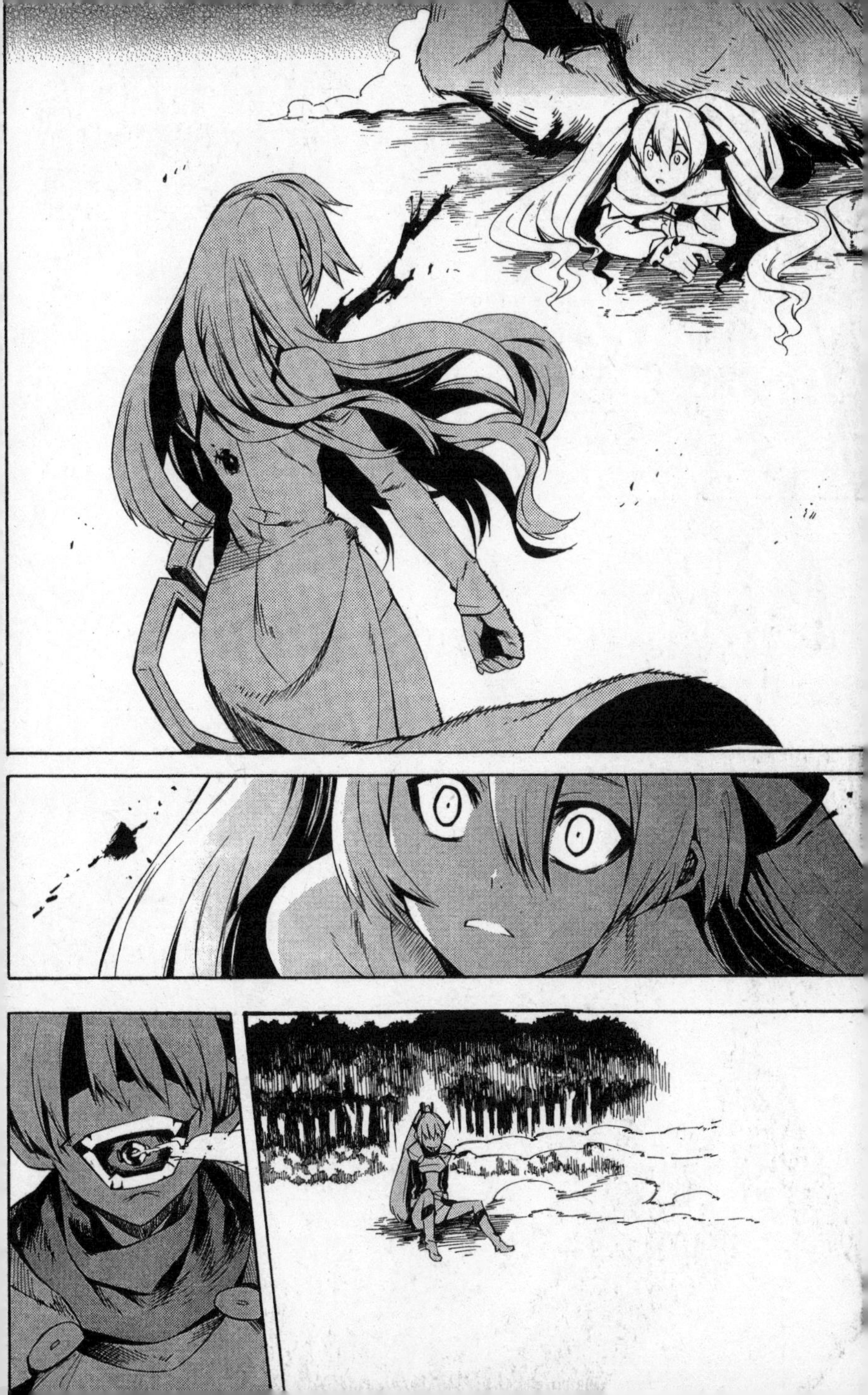

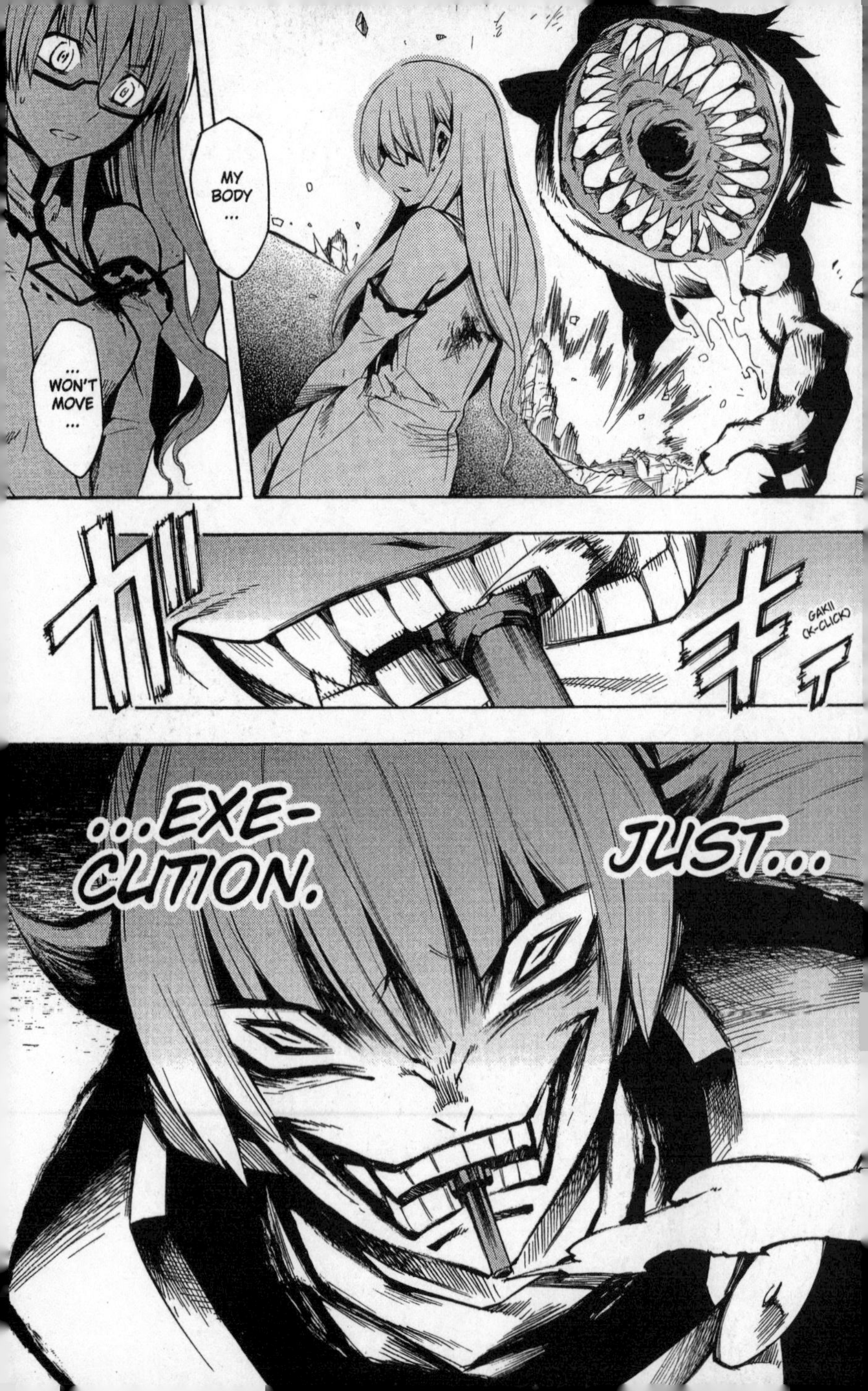
MY BODY ...
... WON'T MOVE ...
ガキィ
GAKII (K-CLICK)
JUST...
...EXE-CUTION.

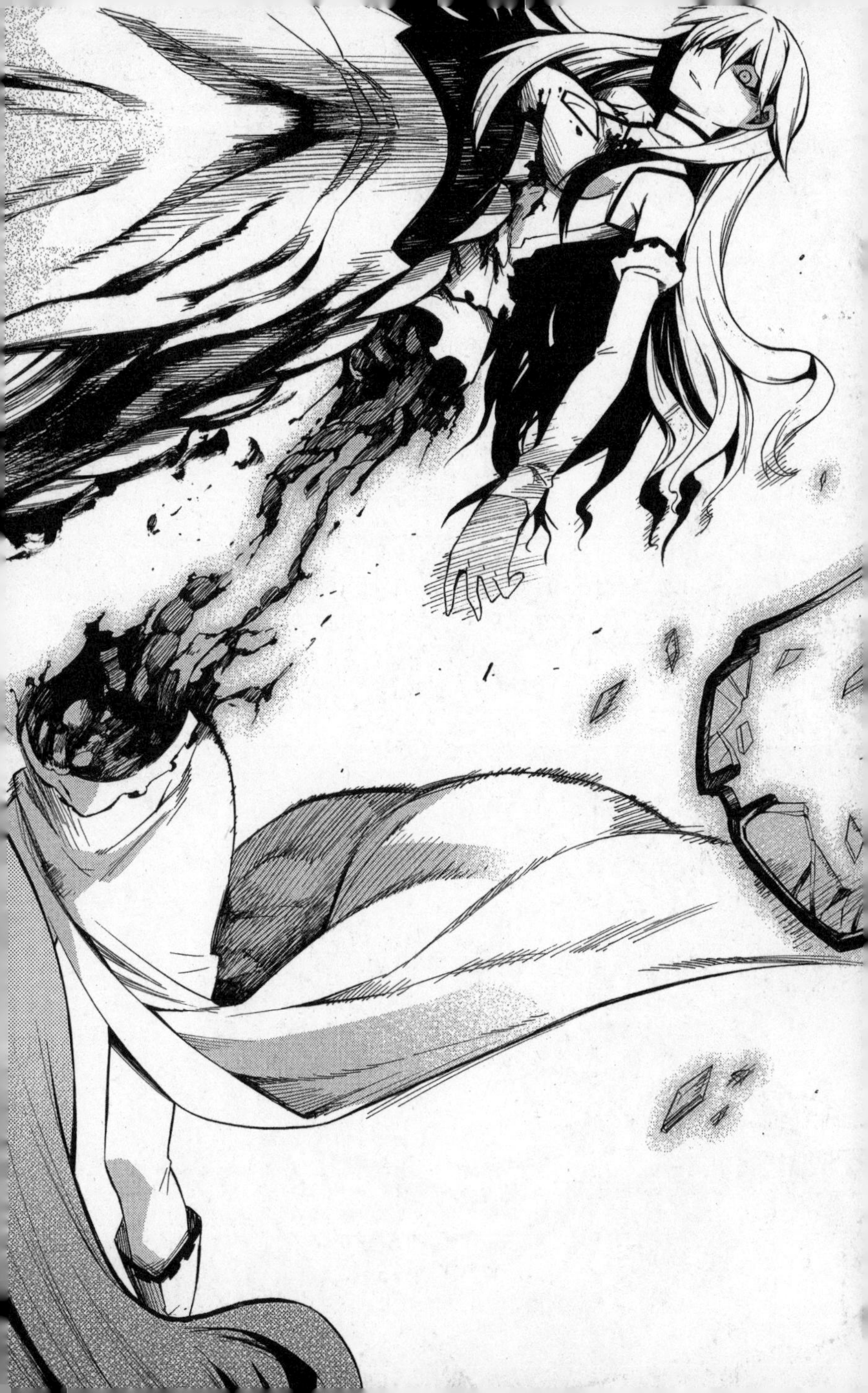

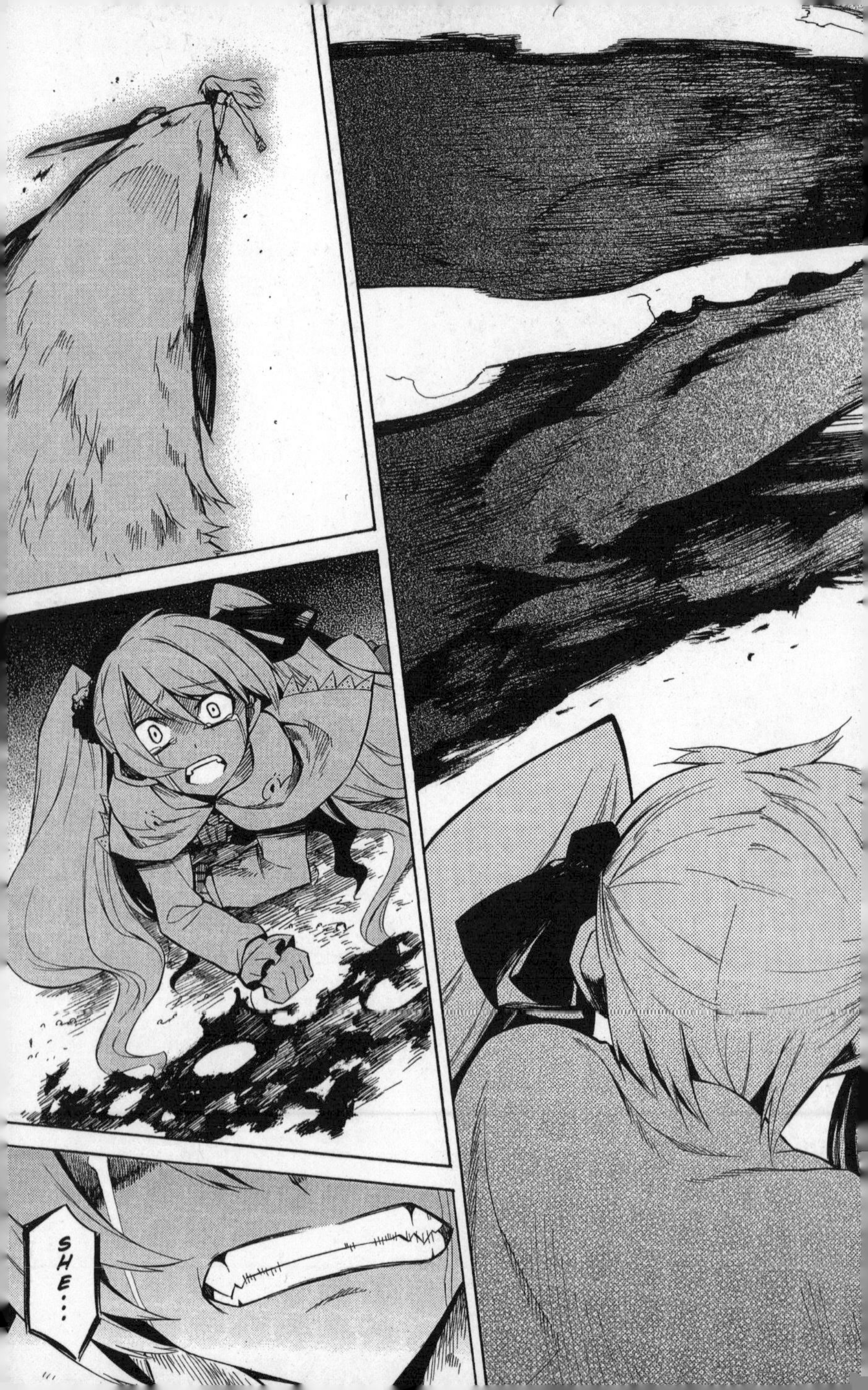
SHE...

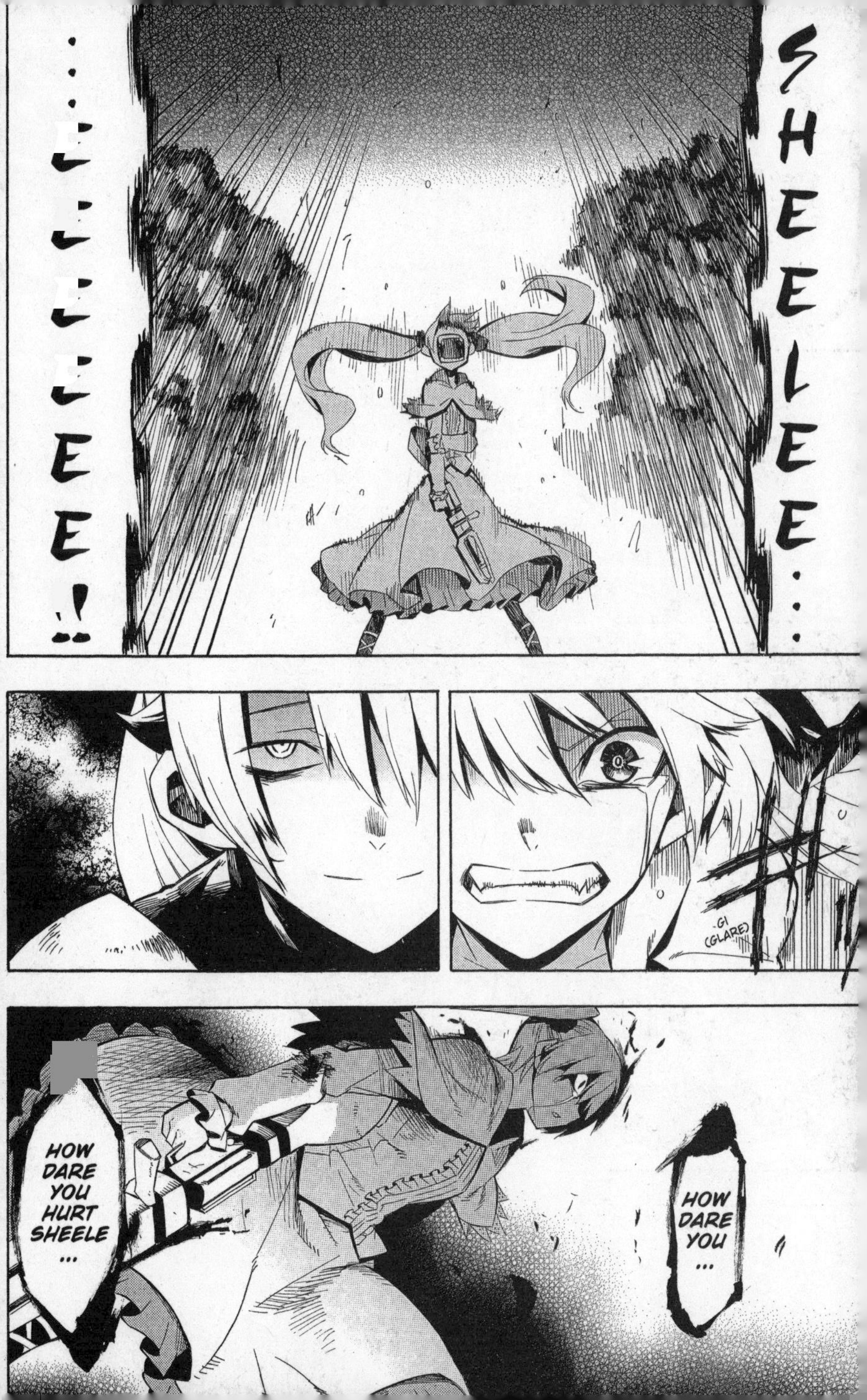
SHEELEE...
...EEEEEE!!
GI (GLARE)
HOW DARE YOU...
HOW DARE YOU HURT SHEELE...

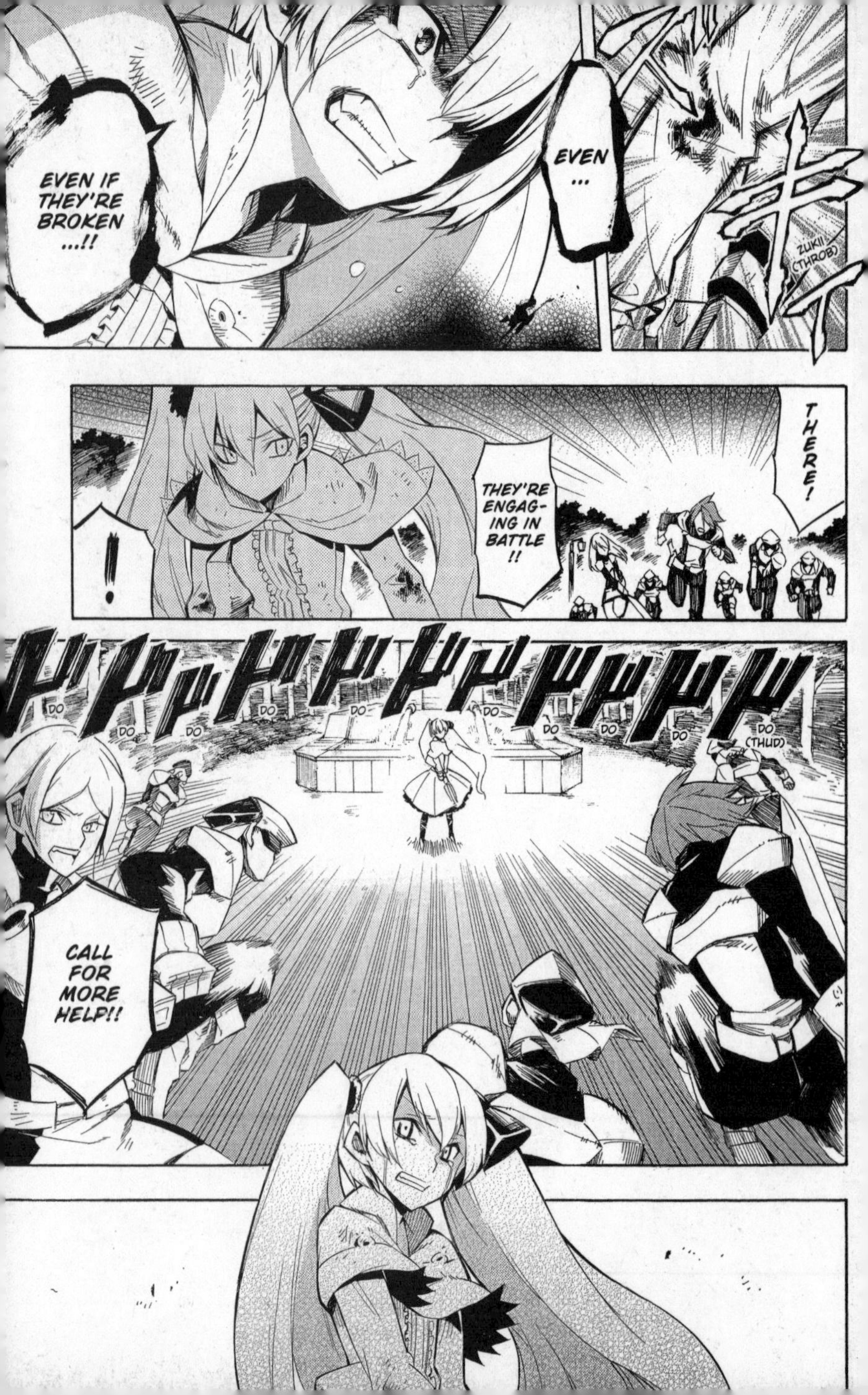
ZUKII (THROB)
EVEN ...
EVEN IF THEY'RE BROKEN ...!!
THERE!
THEY'RE ENGAG-ING IN BATTLE !!
!
DO (THUD)
DO
DO
DO
DO
DO
DO
DO
DO
CALL FOR MORE HELP!!

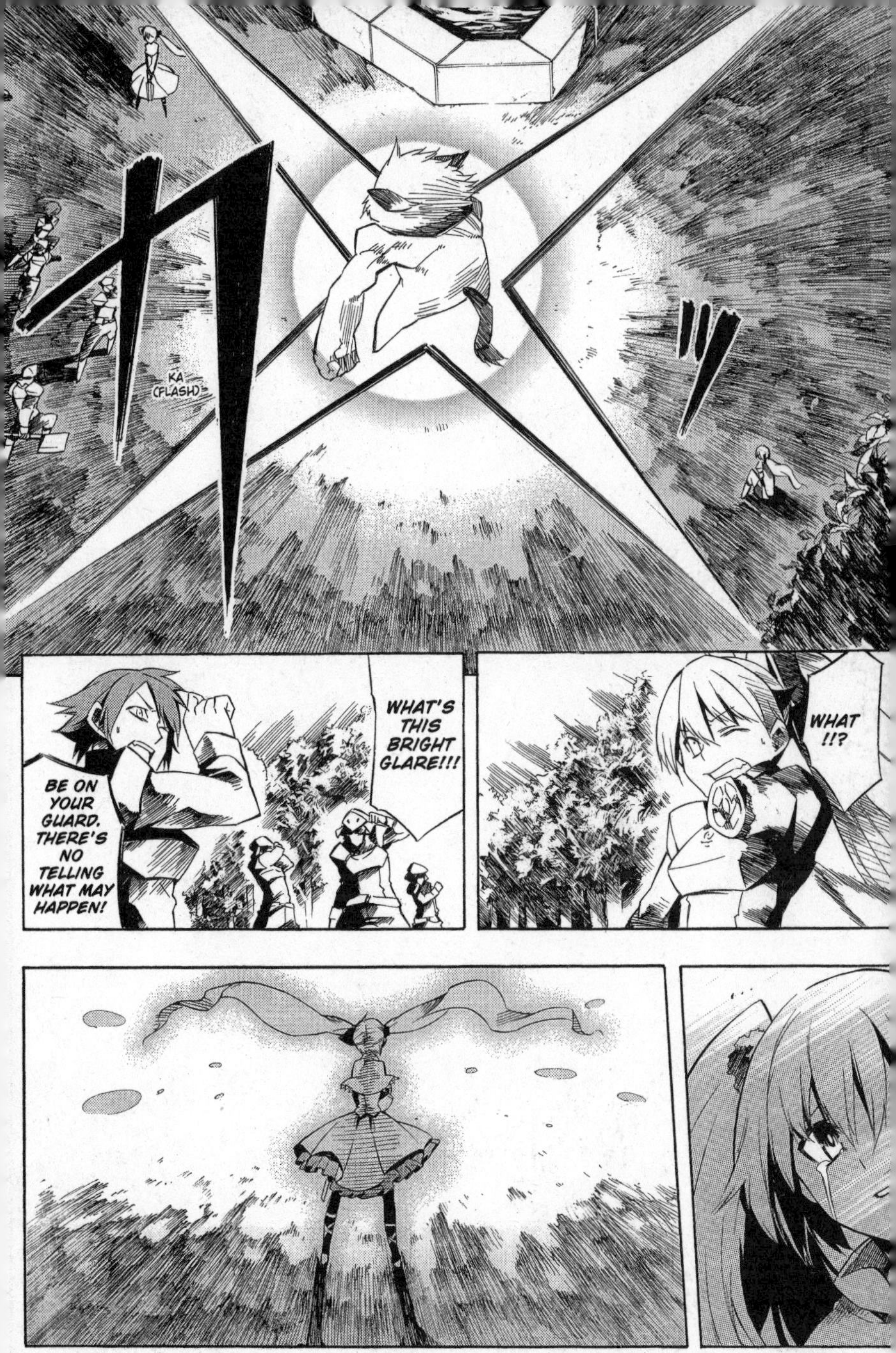
KA (FLASH)
WHAT !!?
WHAT'S THIS BRIGHT GLARE!!!
BE ON YOUR GUARD. THERE'S NO TELLING WHAT MAY HAPPEN!
...

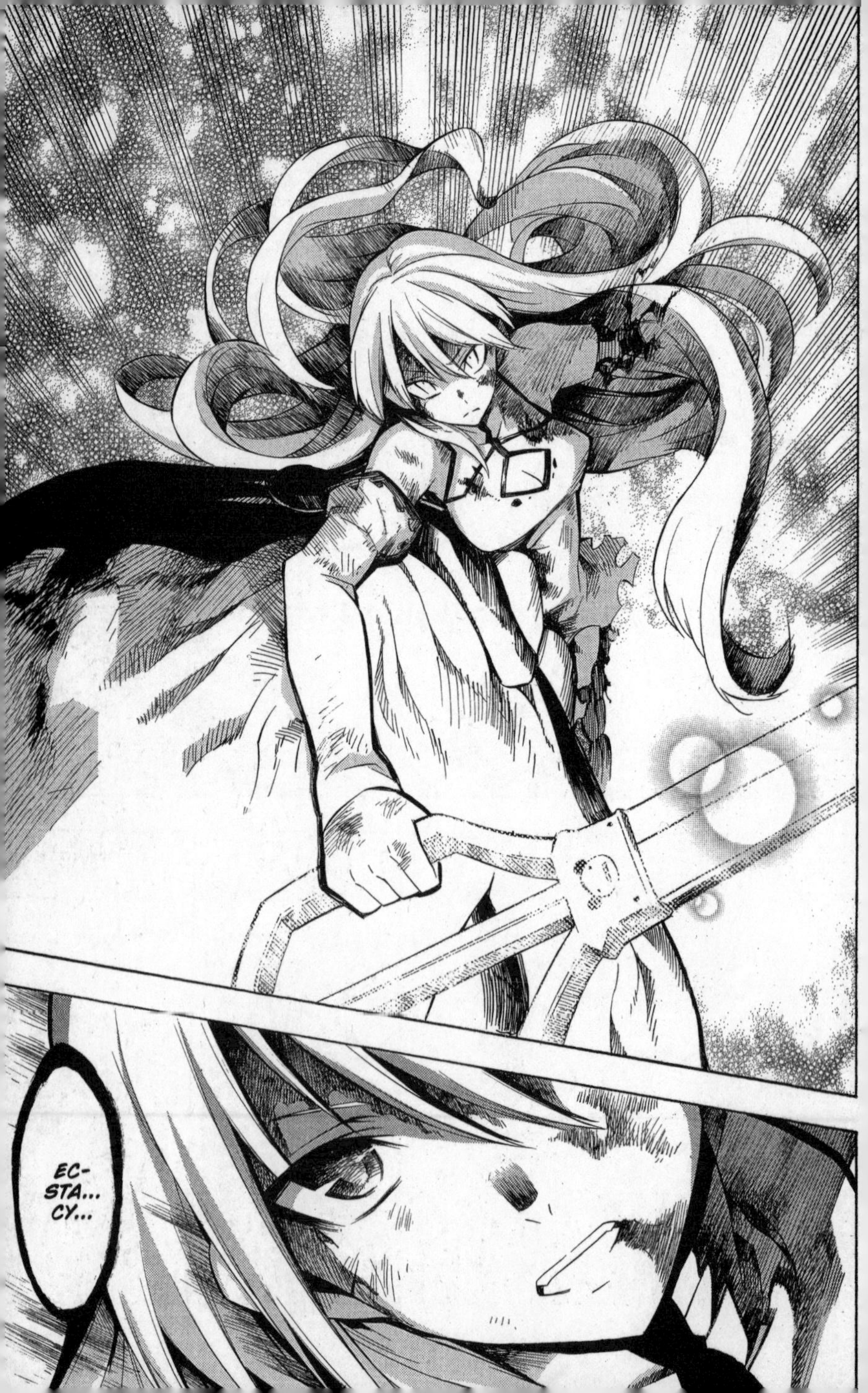
EC-
STA...
CY...

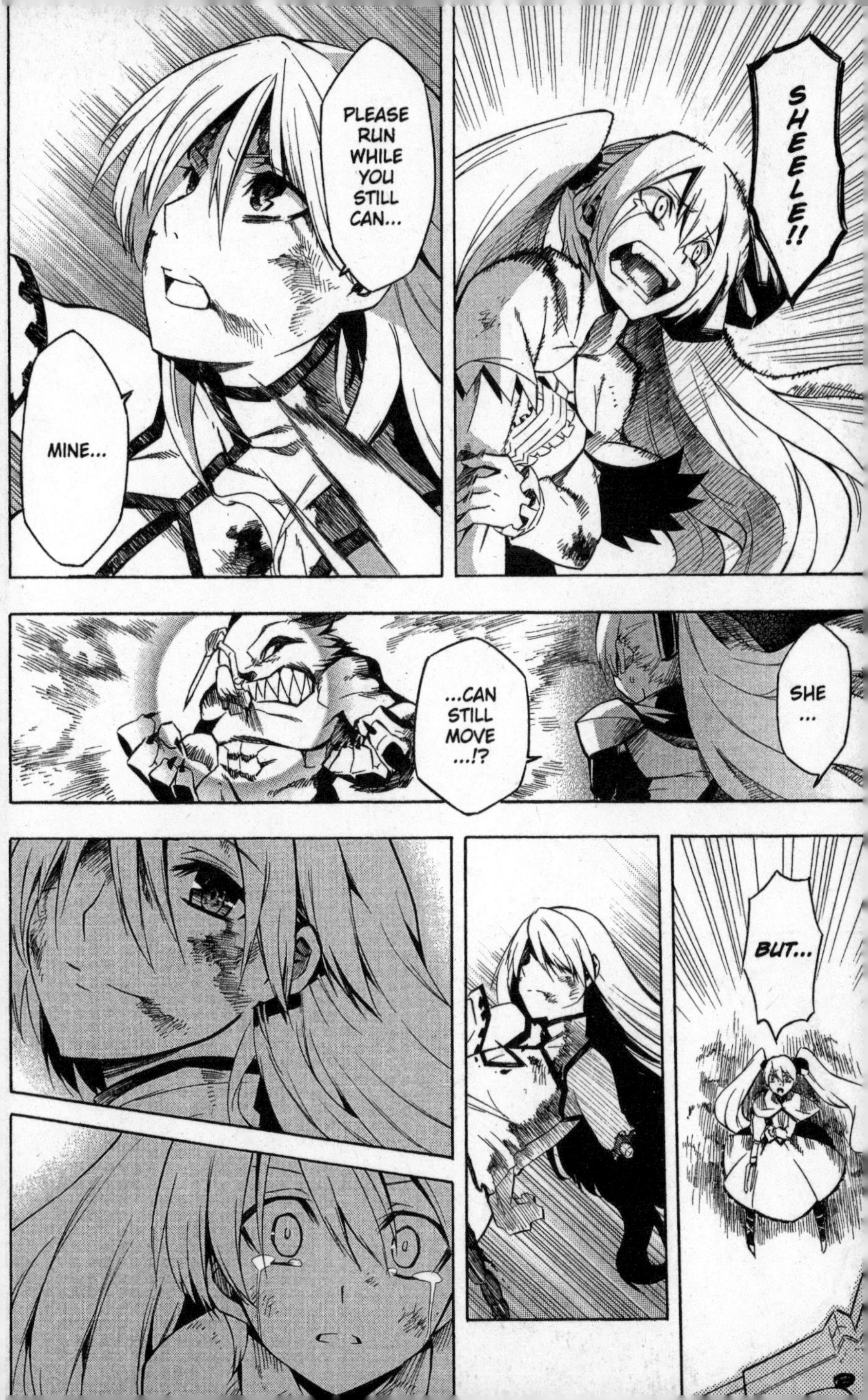
SHEELE!!
PLEASE RUN WHILE YOU STILL CAN...
MINE...
SHE ...
...CAN STILL MOVE ...!?
BUT...

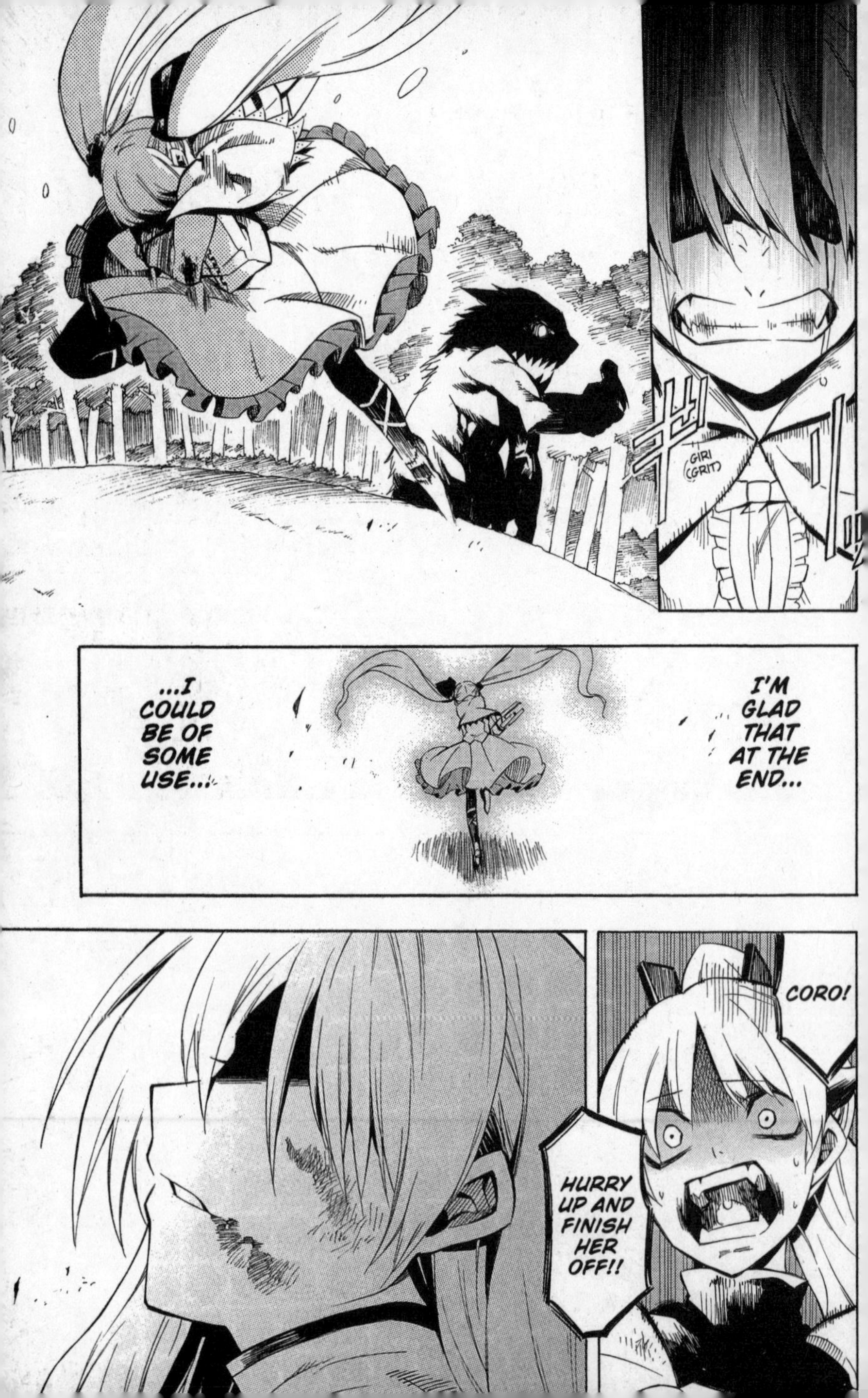
GIRI (GRIT)
I'M GLAD THAT AT THE END...
...I COULD BE OF SOME USE...
CORO!
HURRY UP AND FINISH HER OFF!!

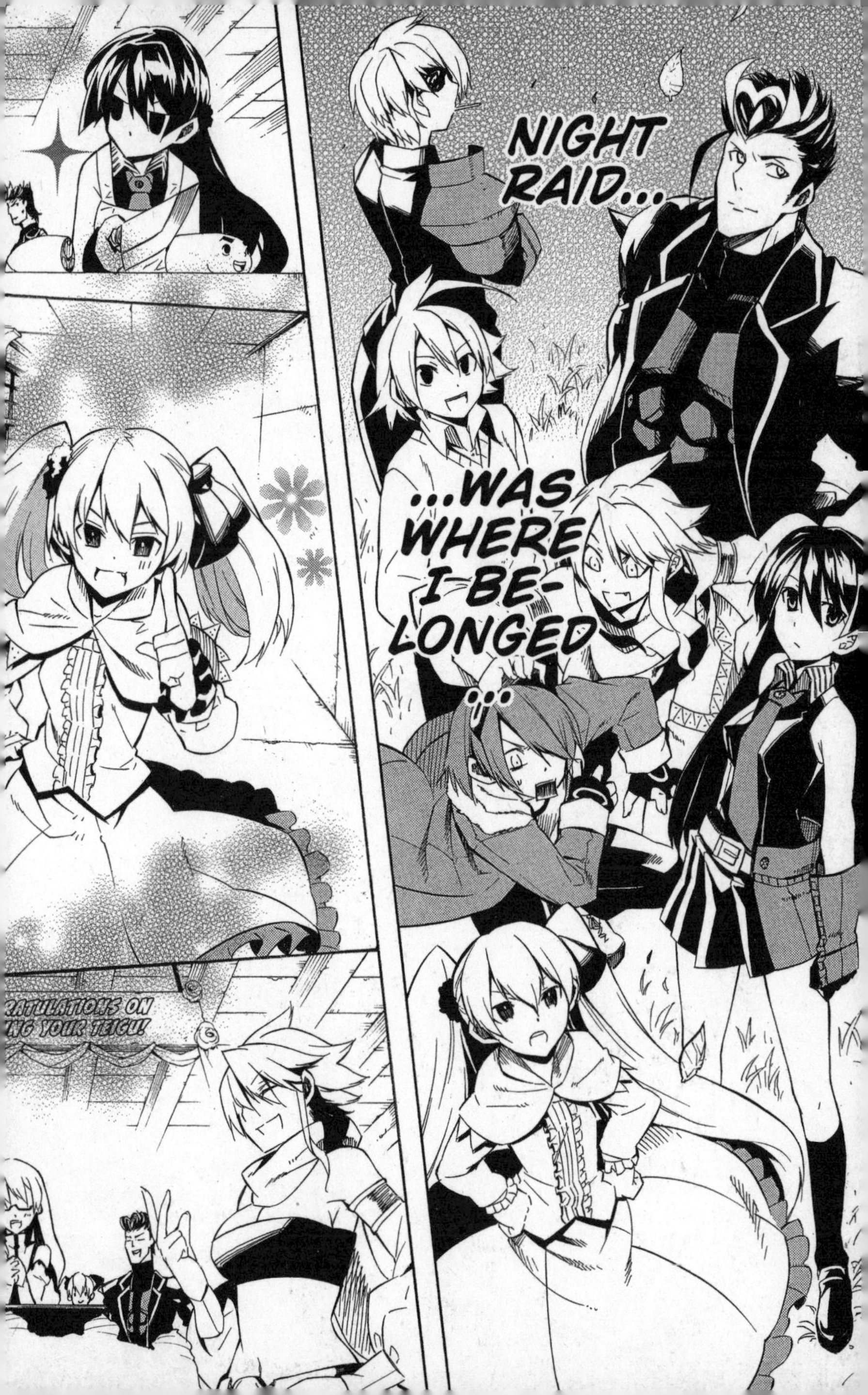
NIGHT RAID...
...WAS WHERE I BE-LONGED
...
RATULATIONS ON NG YOUR TEIGU!

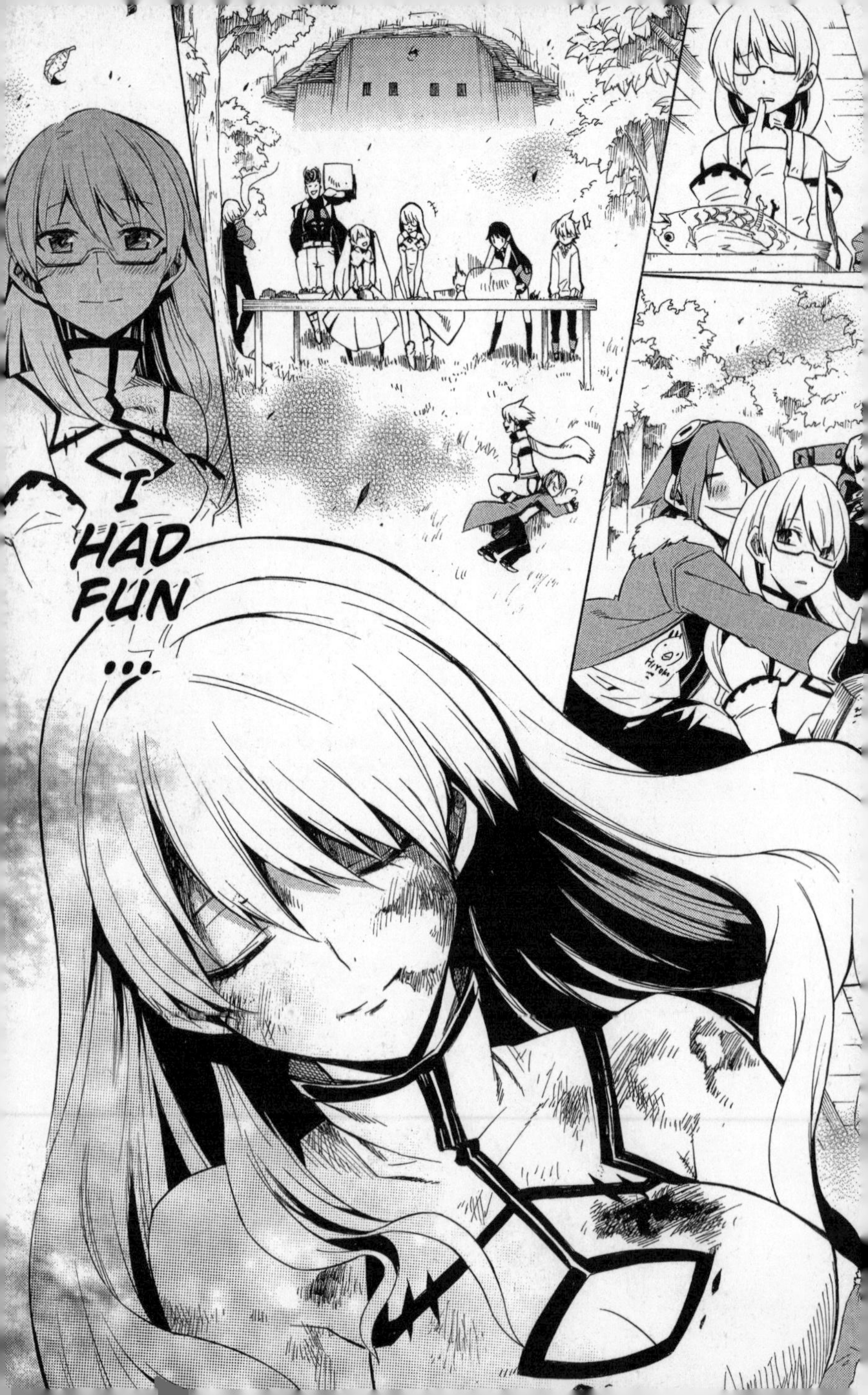
I HAD FUN ...

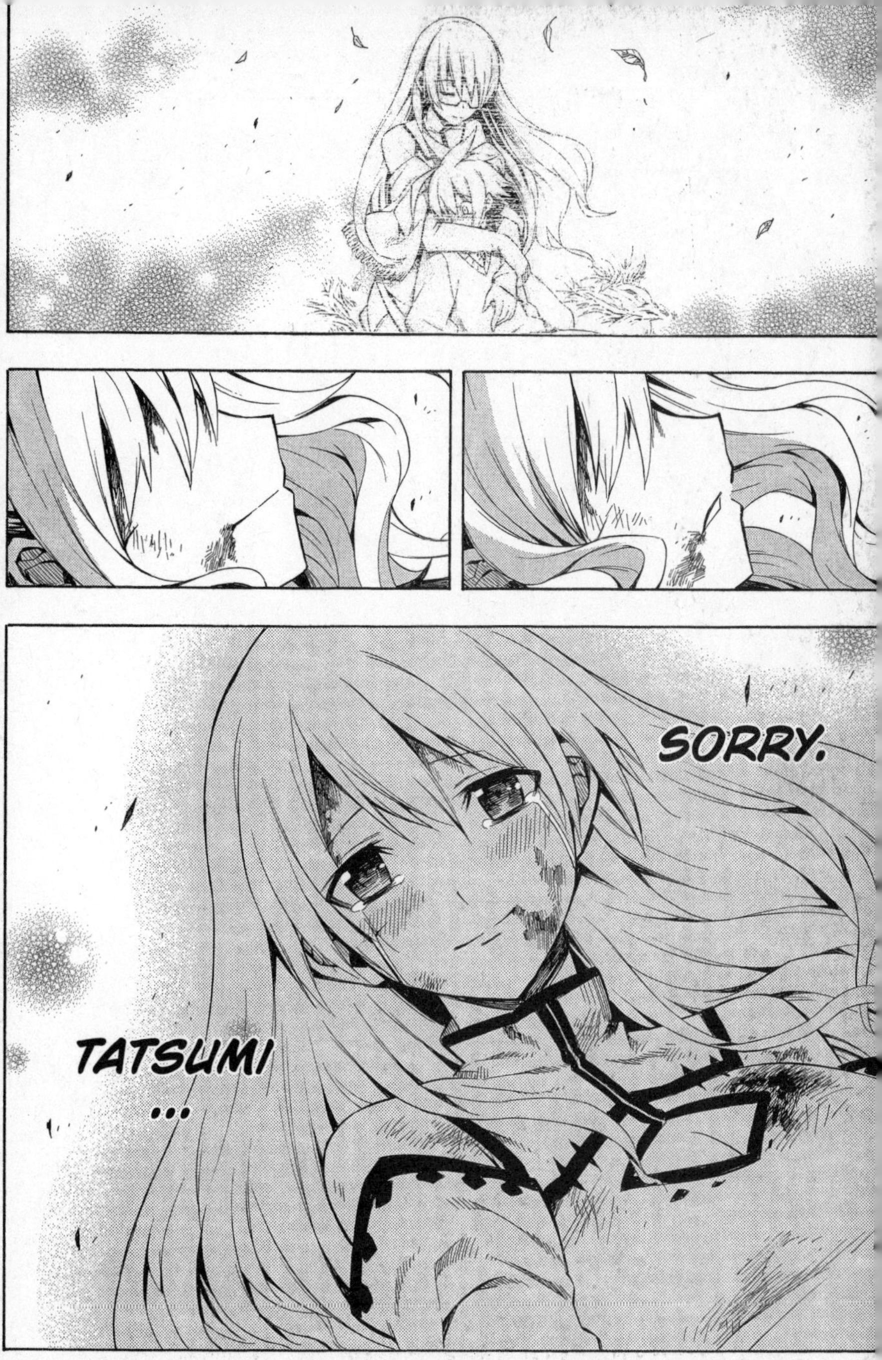
SORRY.
TATSUMI
...

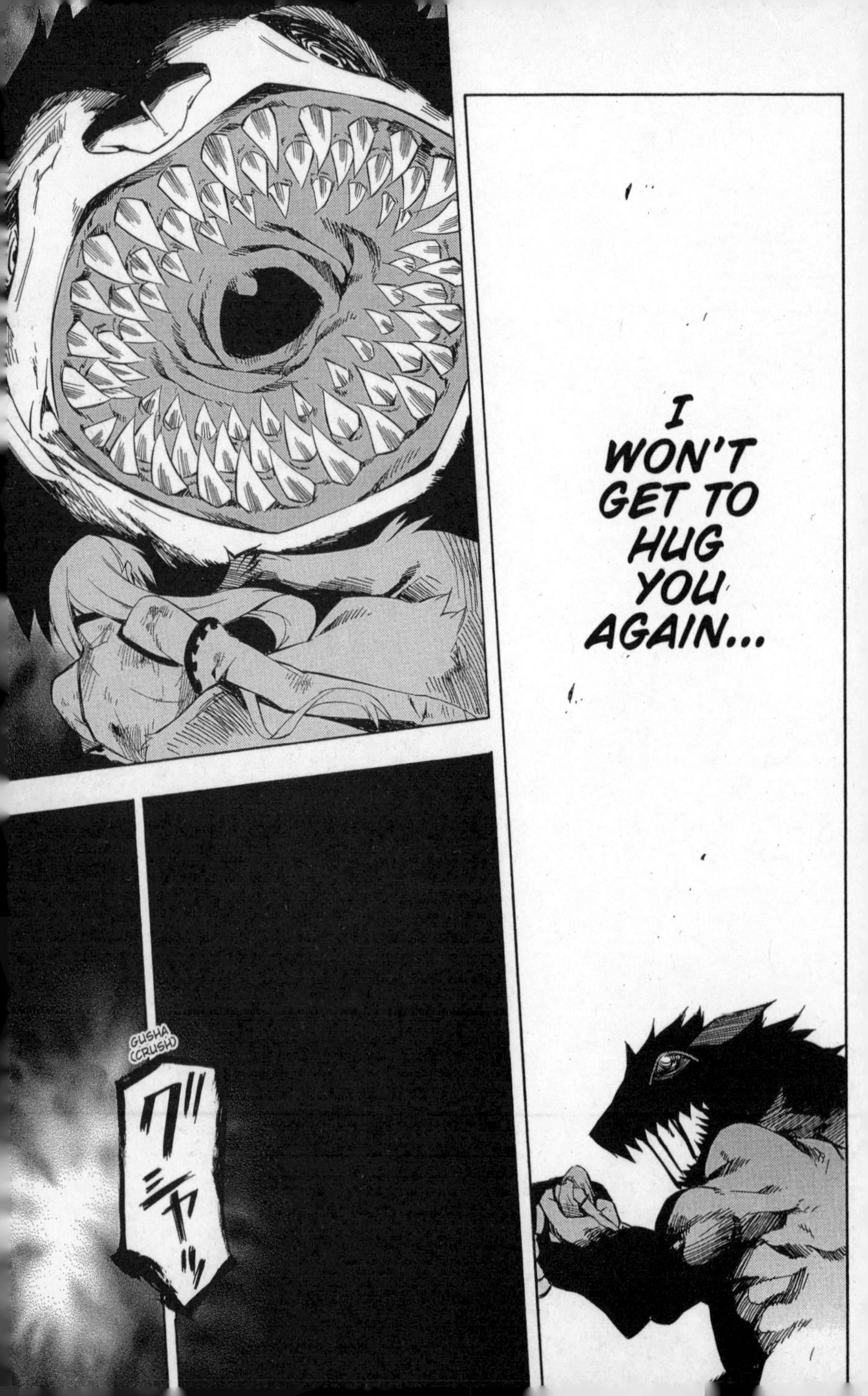
I WON'T GET TO HUG YOU AGAIN...
GUSHA (CRUSH)
グシャッ

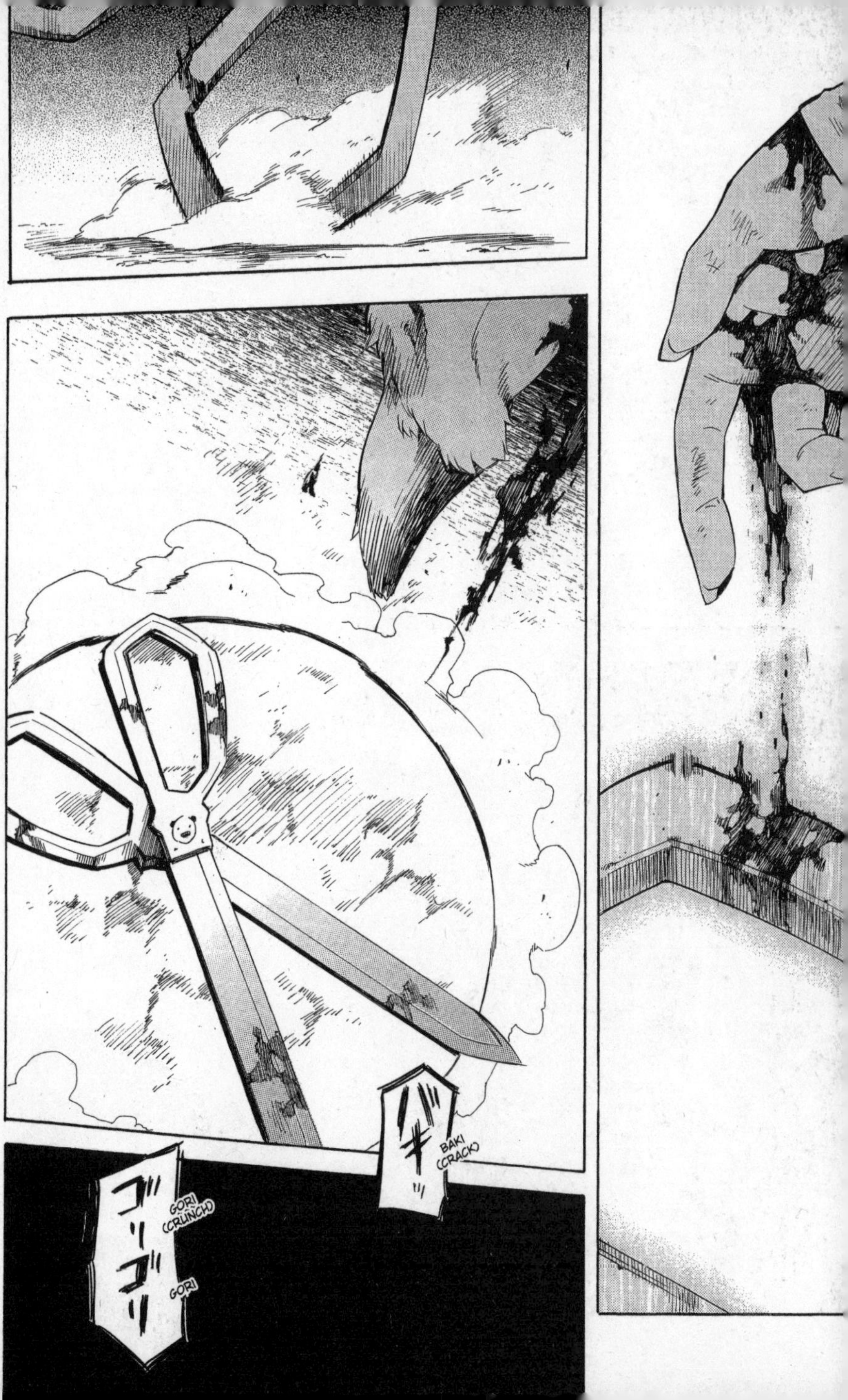

バギッ
BAKI (CRACK)
ゴリゴリ
GORI (CRUNCH)
GORI

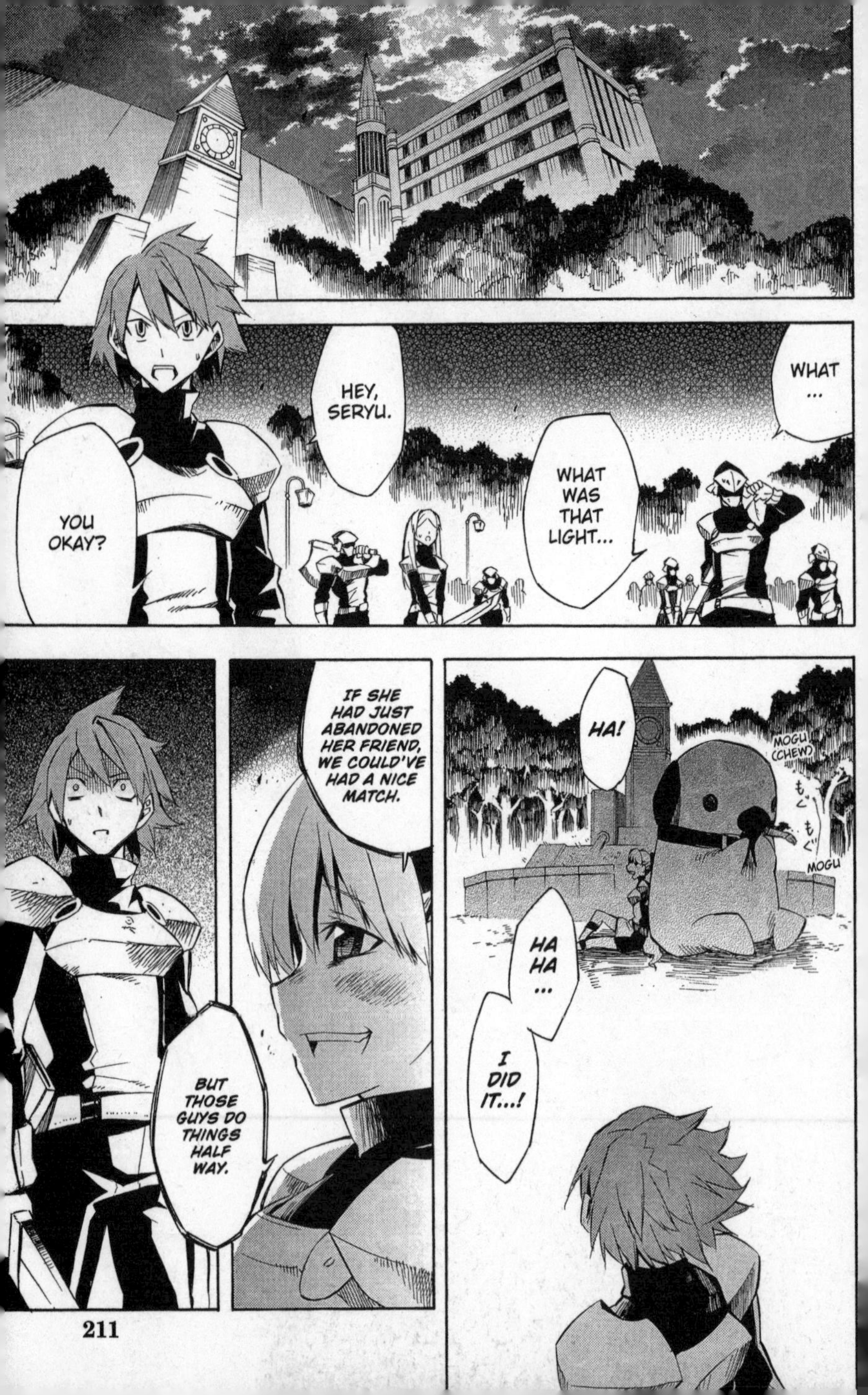
WHAT ...
WHAT WAS THAT LIGHT...
HEY, SERYU.
YOU OKAY?
HA!
MOGU (CHEW)
もぐ もぐ
MOGU
HA HA ...
I DID IT...!
IF SHE HAD JUST ABANDONED HER FRIEND, WE COULD'VE HAD A NICE MATCH.
BUT THOSE GUYS DO THINGS HALF WAY.

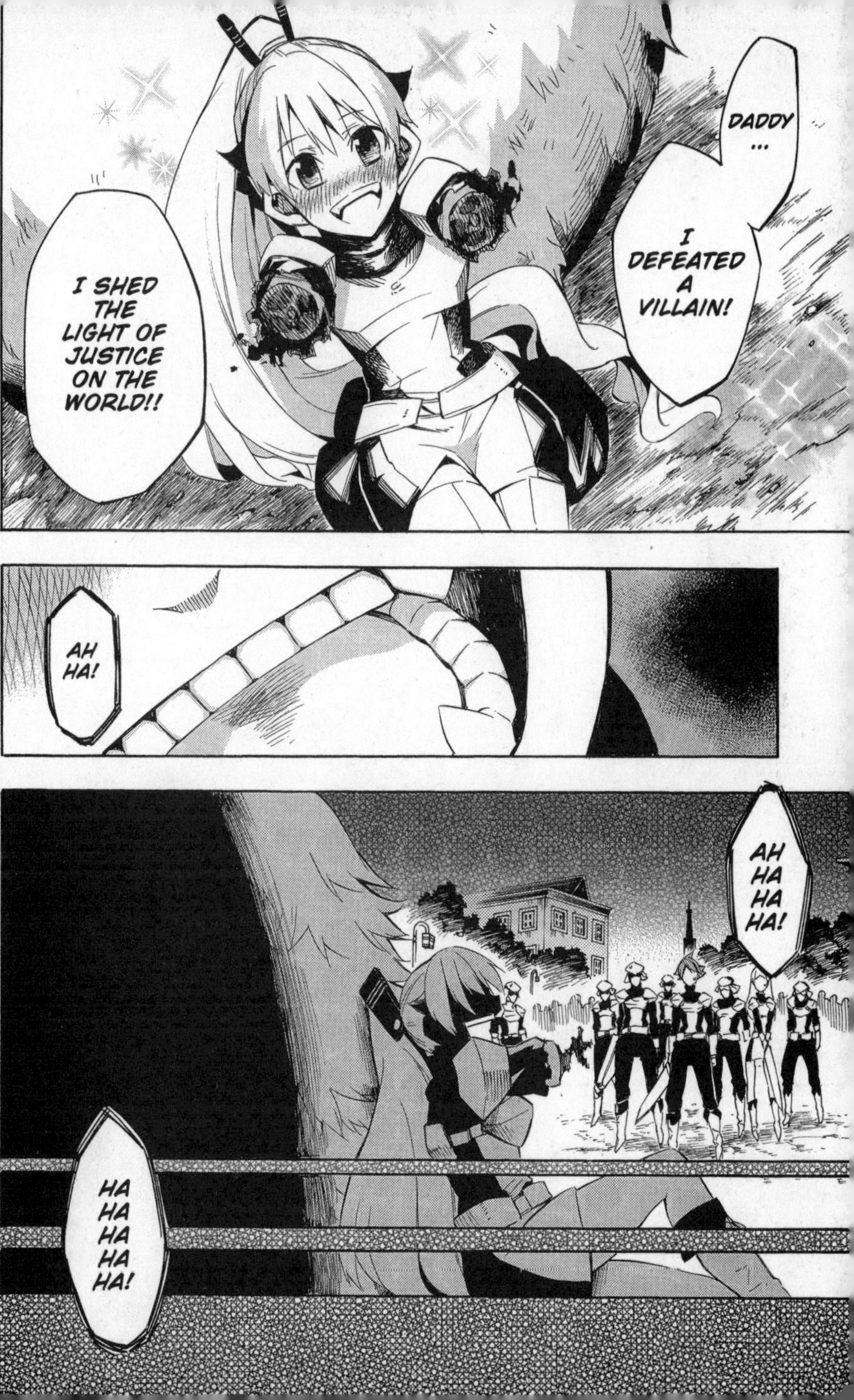
DADDY ...
I DEFEATED A VILLAIN!
I SHED THE LIGHT OF JUSTICE ON THE WORLD!!
AH HA!
AH HA HA HA!
HA HA HA HA HA!

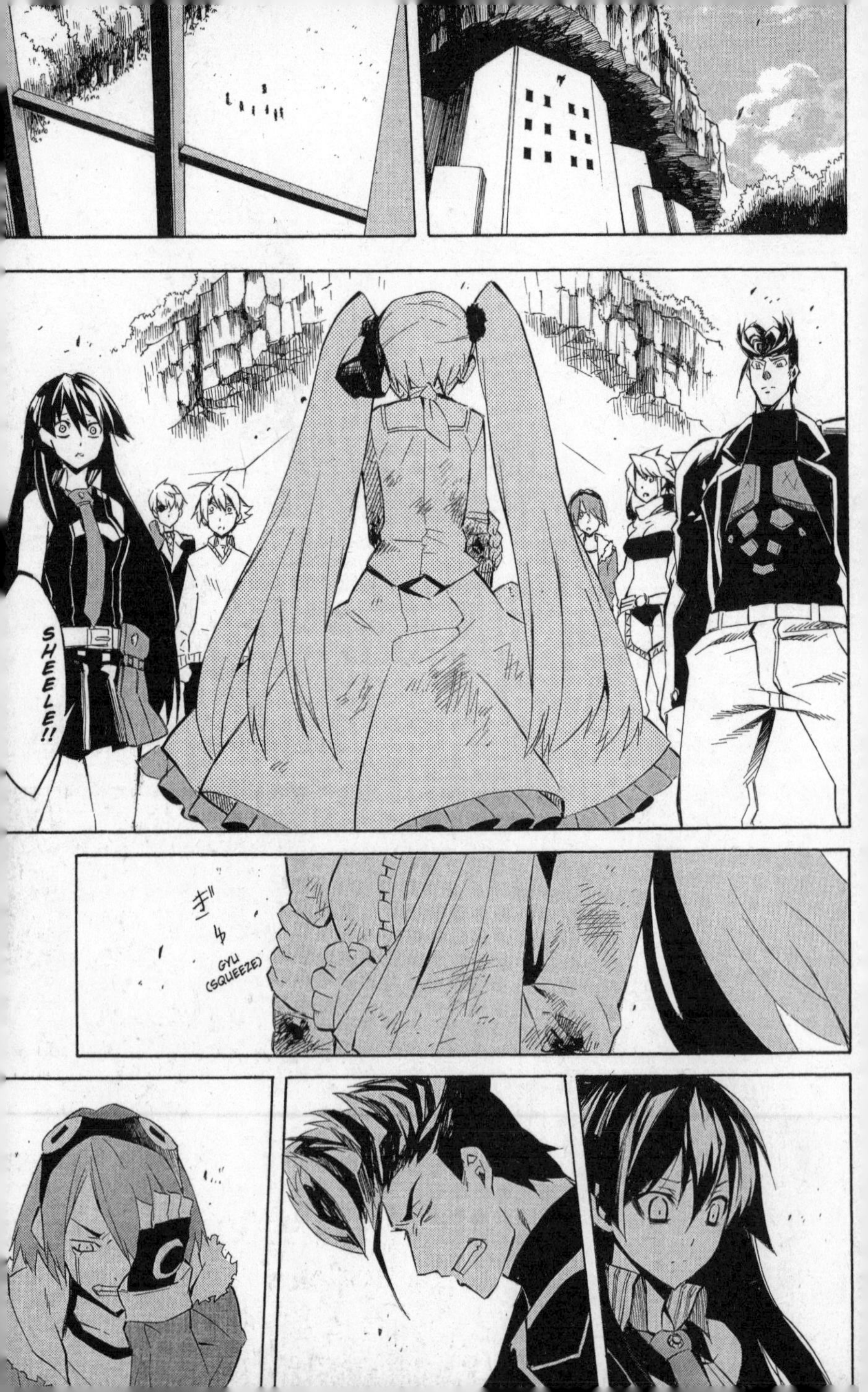

SHEELE!!
ぎゅ
GYU (SQUEEZE)

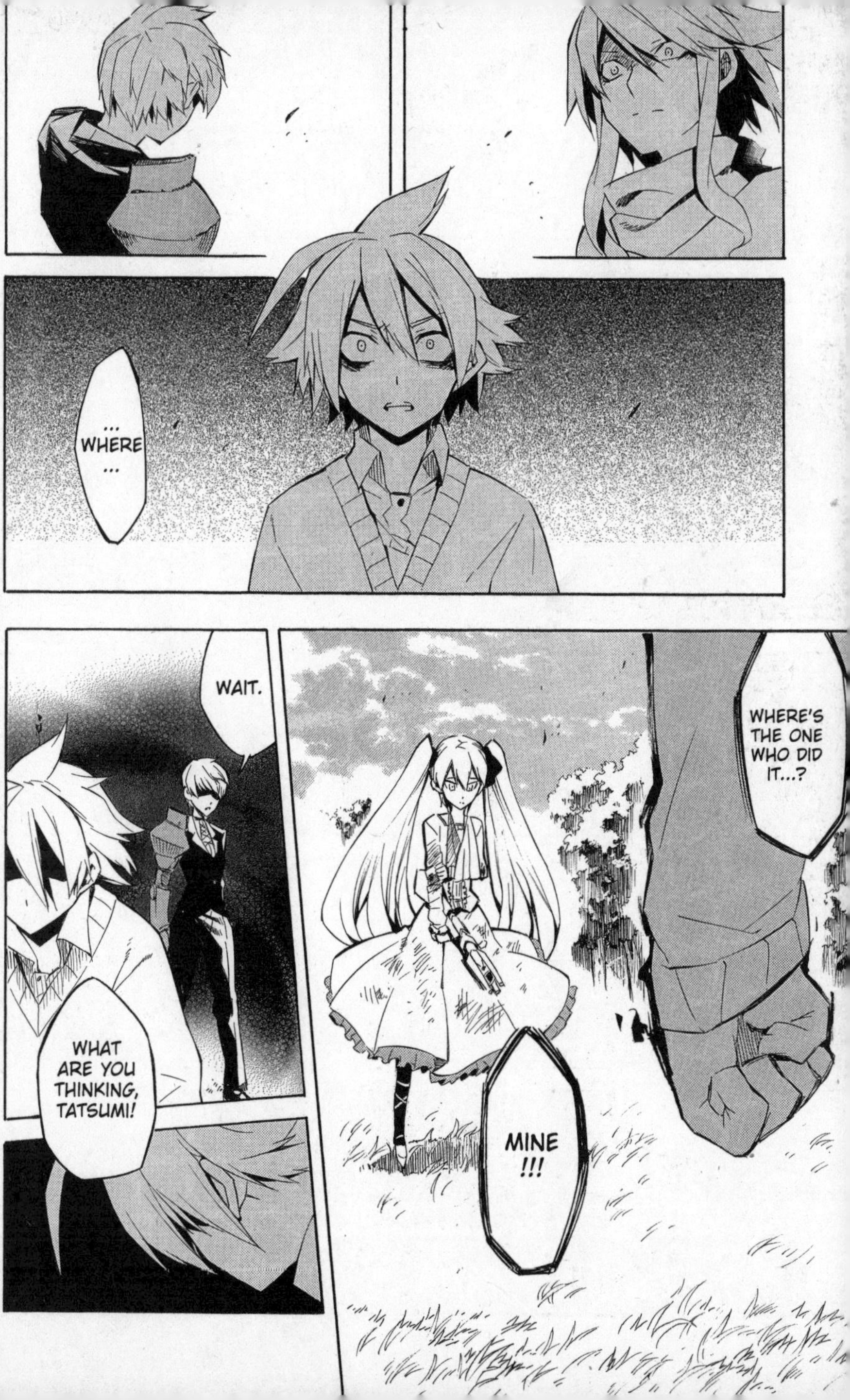
... WHERE ...
WHERE'S THE ONE WHO DID IT...?
MINE !!!
WAIT.
WHAT ARE YOU THINKING, TATSUMI!

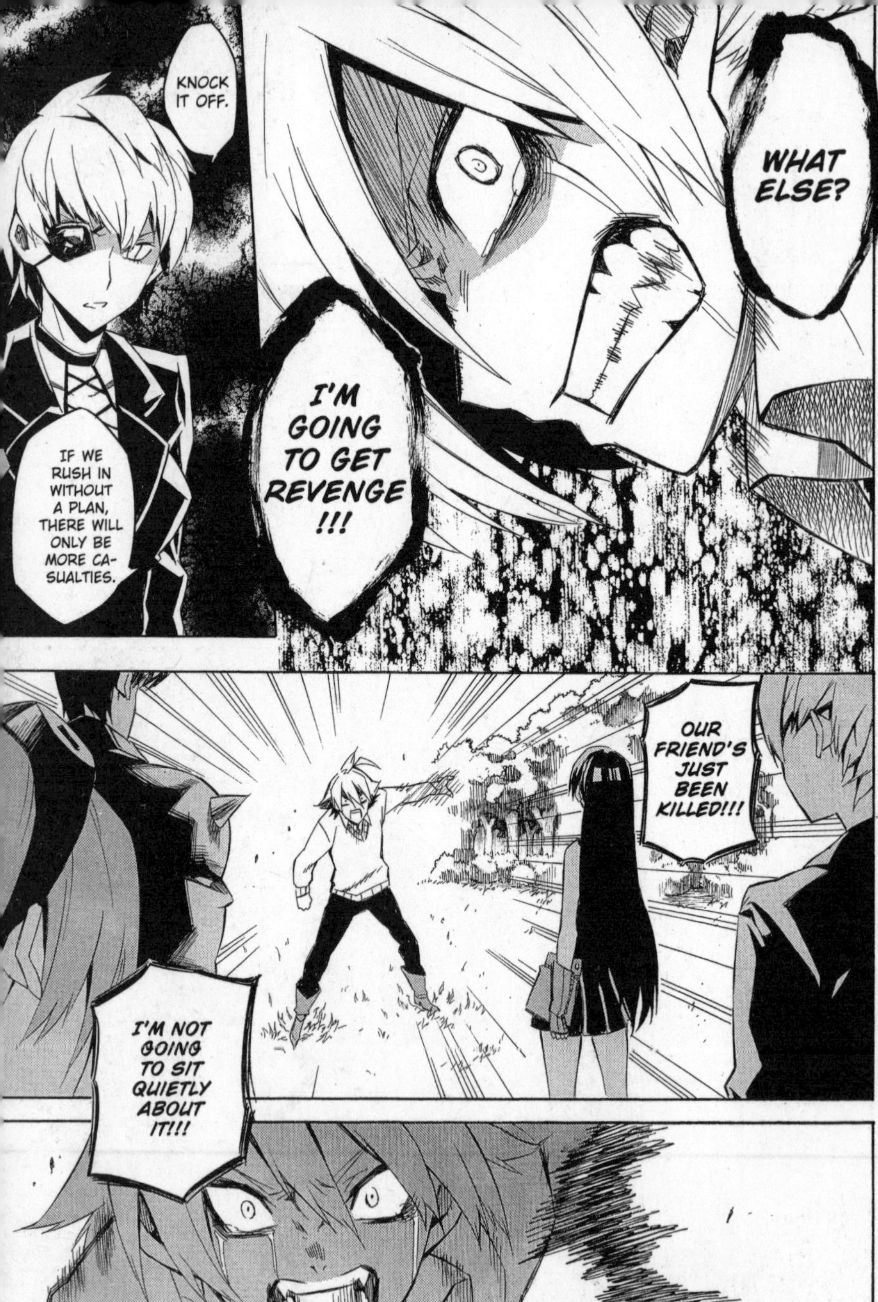
WHAT ELSE?
I'M GOING TO GET REVENGE!!!
KNOCK IT OFF.
IF WE RUSH IN WITHOUT A PLAN, THERE WILL ONLY BE MORE CA-SUALTIES.
OUR FRIEND'S JUST BEEN KILLED!!!
I'M NOT GOING TO SIT QUIETLY ABOUT IT!!!

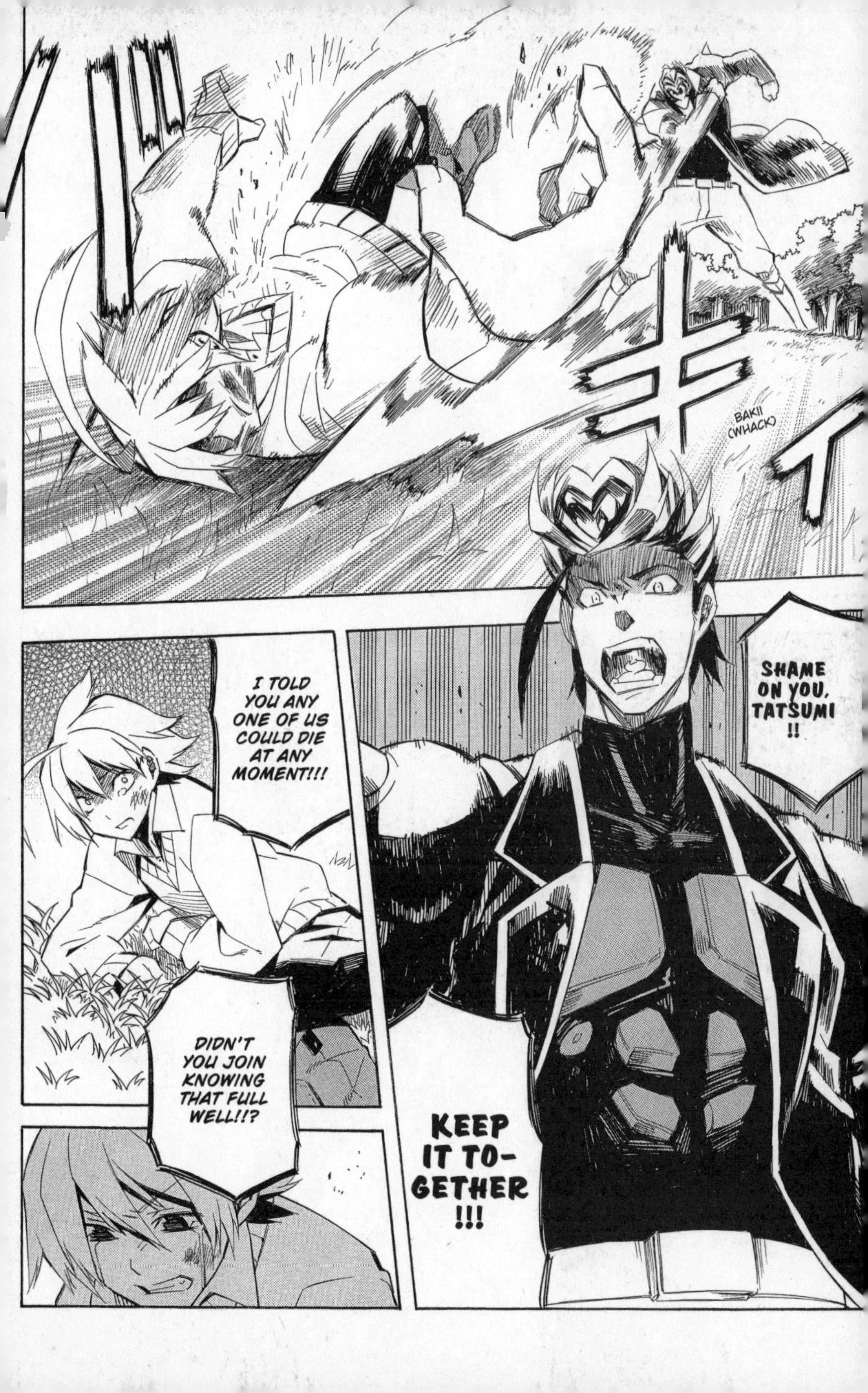
BAKII (WHACK)
SHAME ON YOU, TATSUMI!!
KEEP IT TO-GETHER!!!
I TOLD YOU ANY ONE OF US COULD DIE AT ANY MOMENT!!!
DIDN'T YOU JOIN KNOWING THAT FULL WELL!!?

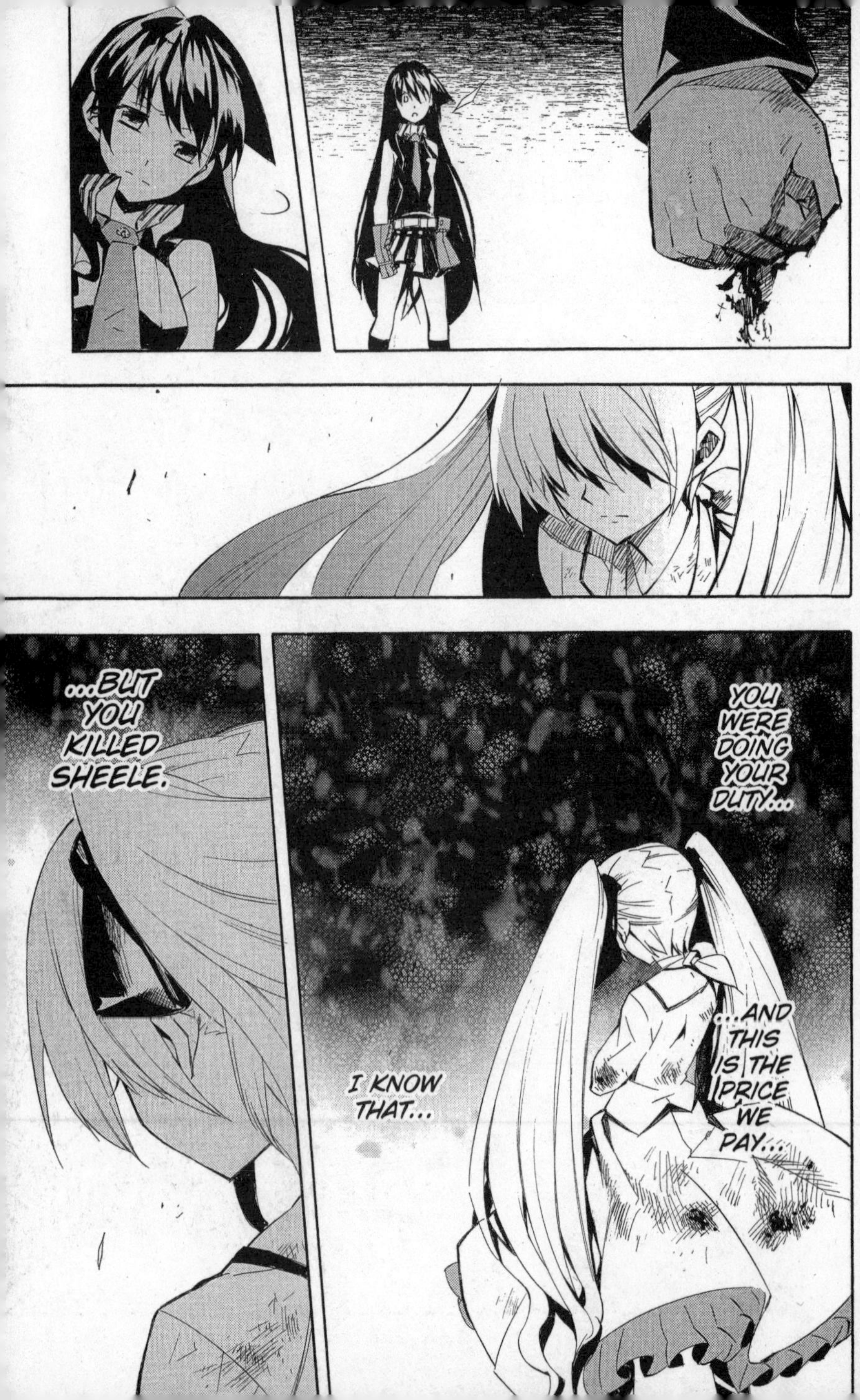
YOU WERE DOING YOUR DUTY...
...AND THIS IS THE PRICE WE PAY...
I KNOW THAT...
...BUT YOU KILLED SHEELE.

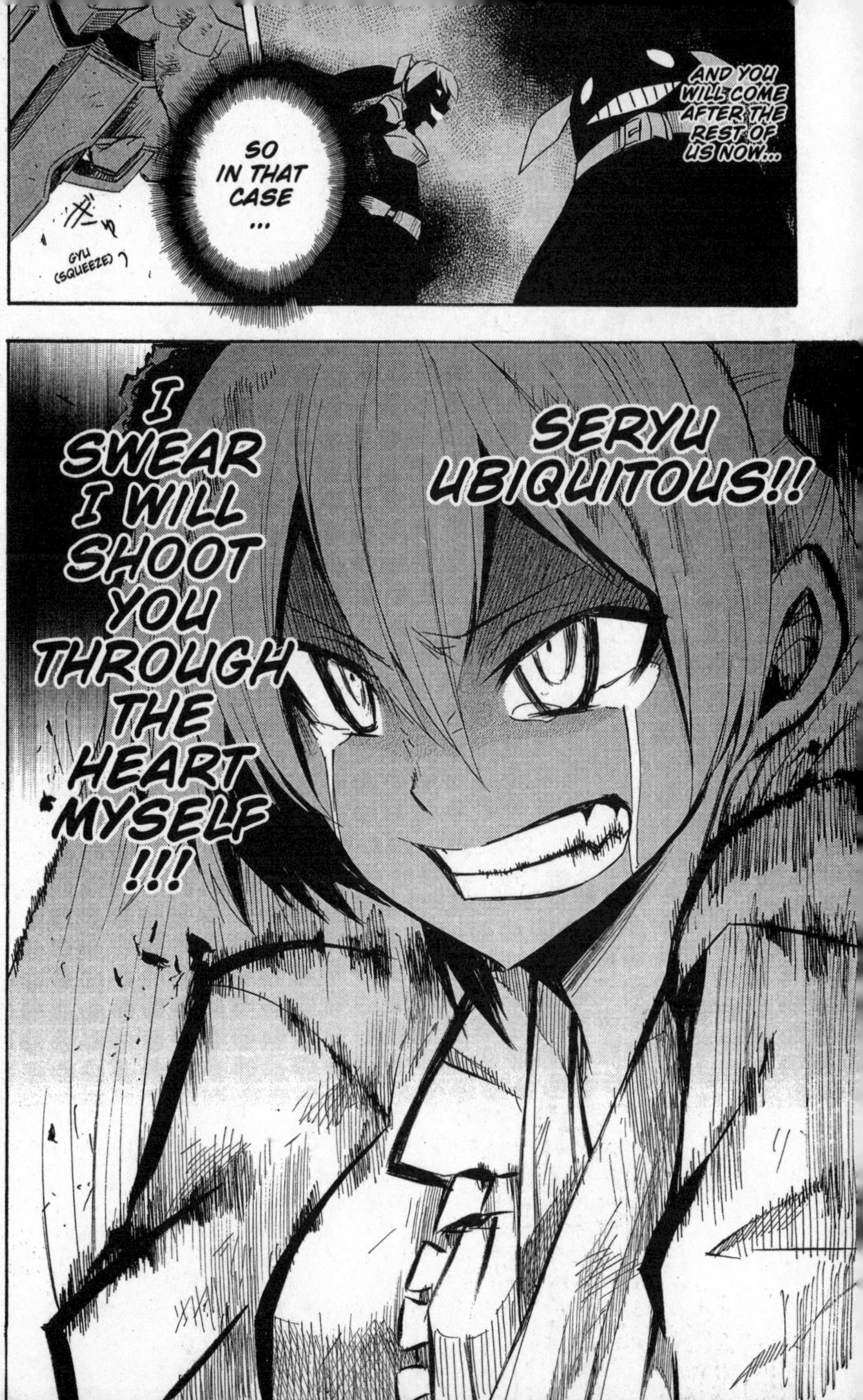
AND YOU WILL COME AFTER THE REST OF US NOW...
SO IN THAT CASE ...
GYU (SQUEEZE)
SERYU UBIQUITOUS!!
I SWEAR I WILL SHOOT YOU THROUGH THE HEART MYSELF!!!

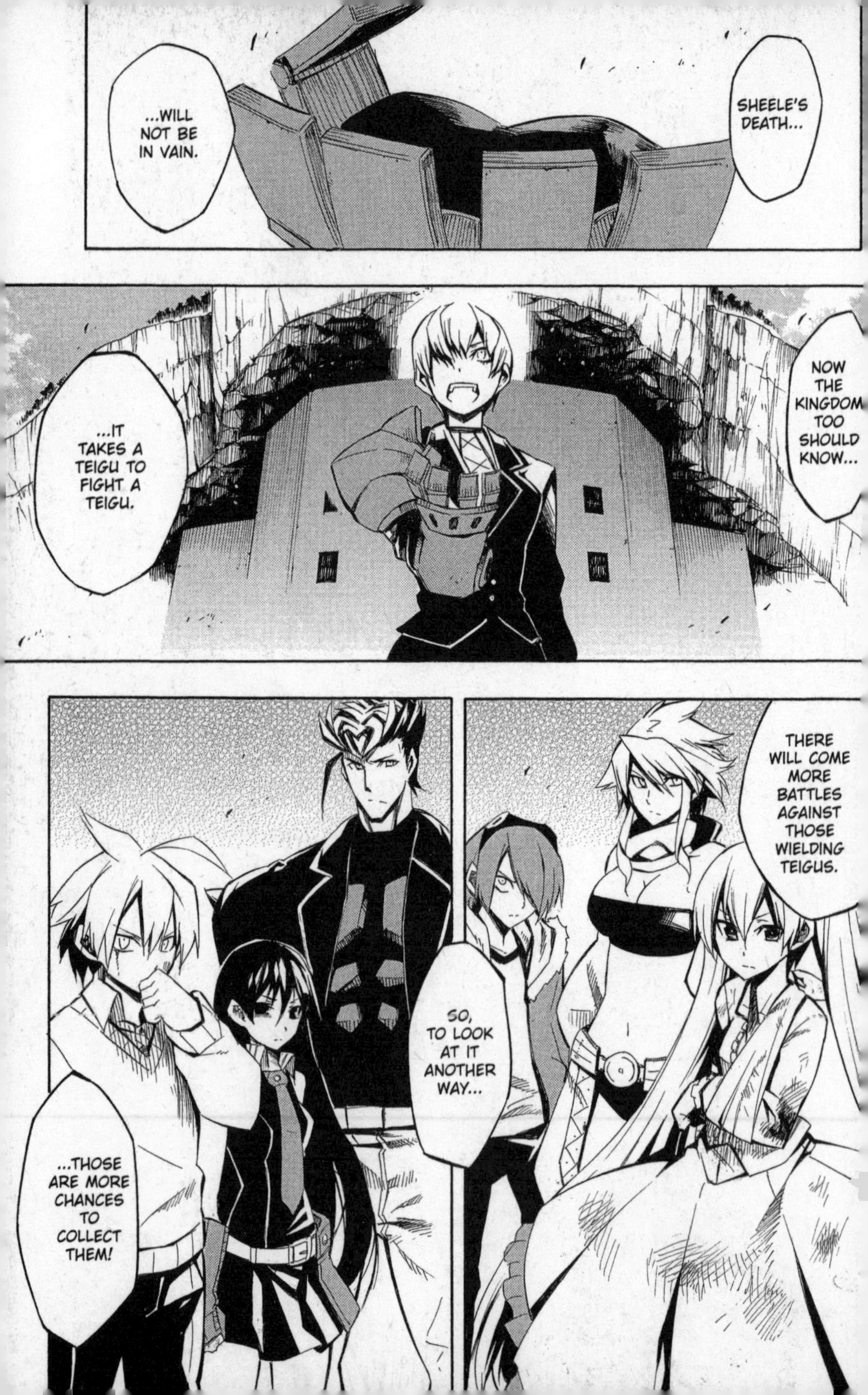
SHEELE'S DEATH...
...WILL NOT BE IN VAIN.
NOW THE KINGDOM TOO SHOULD KNOW...
...IT TAKES A TEIGU TO FIGHT A TEIGU.
THERE WILL COME MORE BATTLES AGAINST THOSE WIELDING TEIGUS.
SO, TO LOOK AT IT ANOTHER WAY...
...THOSE ARE MORE CHANCES TO COLLECT THEM!

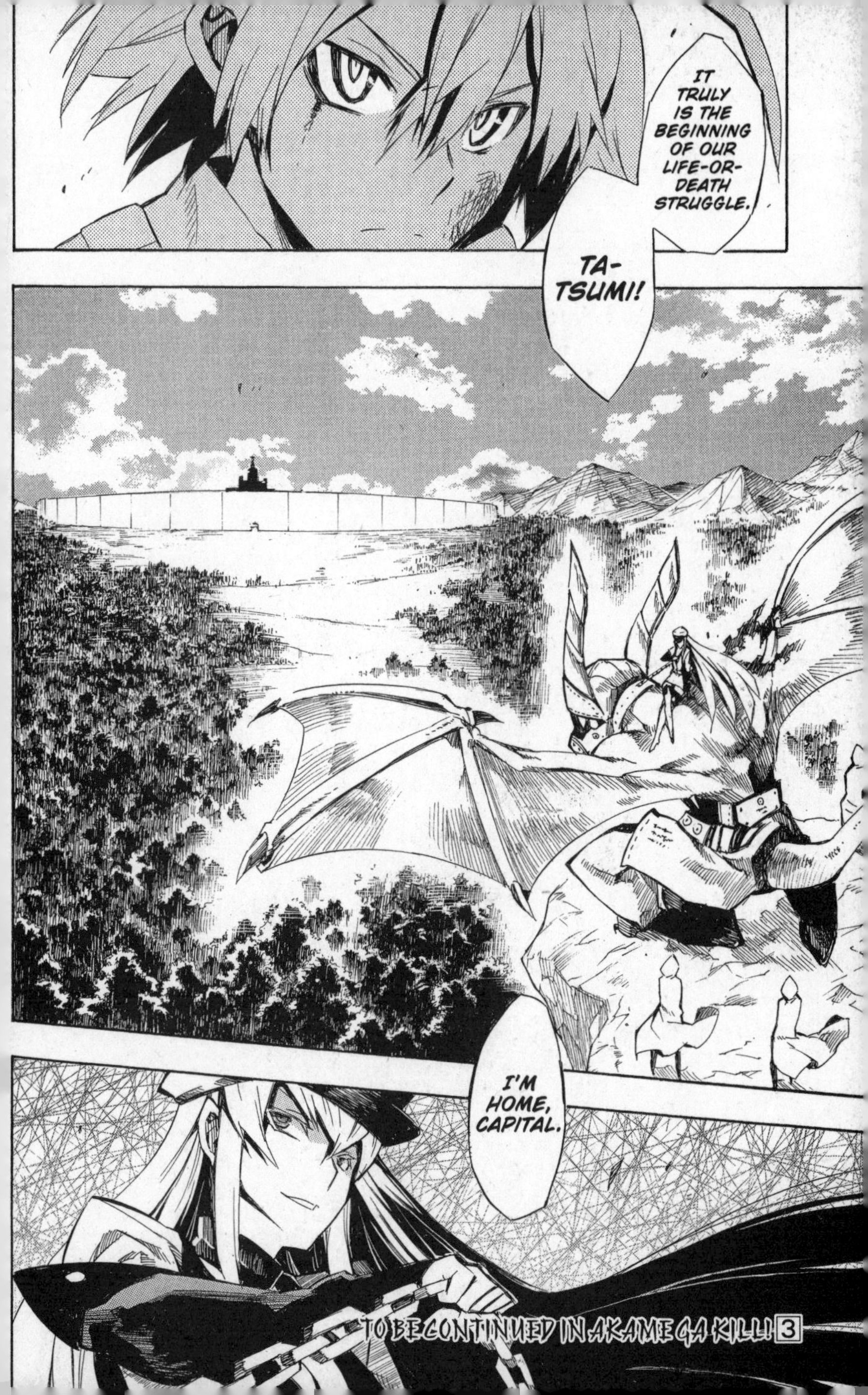
IT TRULY IS THE BEGINNING OF OUR LIFE-OR-DEATH STRUGGLE.
TA-TSUMI!
I'M HOME, CAPITAL.
TO BE CONTINUED IN AKAME GA KILL! 3

TAKAHIRO's POSTSCRIPT

Hello.
This is Takahiro from the studio
this project came from, Minato Soft.
Today I'd like to talk to you about
the work process for the manga.
Using a scene from Chapter 8,
the script looks something like this:

// Imperial Palace   Royal Hall

Messenger: "Reporting, sir! General Nakakido
and General Hemi have both deserted us! It seems
they have joined sides with the Rebel Army!!"

// The court officials murmur in concern

Official 1: "General Nakakido was a pro at war..."
Official 2: "The Rebel Army is amassing a frightening
strength..."
Official 3: "If we don't act fast, the kingdom..."
Emperor: "Order!!!"

// The officials calm down.
The emperor is being manipulated by the
Minister but has an elegance about him.

Something like that. I leave the decisions on panel layout to
Tashiro-san.
After I've submitted the script, Tashiro-san
and the editor will sometimes come to me with questions like,
"What do you think about doing this part like this?" I work in
a wonderful environment where I get to write as I please and
receive good ideas too.
Thank you always, Tashiro-san and editor
Koizumi-san.

Well, I look forward to seeing you in Volume 3.
Until then~!

Takahiro

AKAME GA KILL! 2

·Staff

KAGETSU-SAN NOZUE-SAN

TAKAGI-SAN IMAI-SAN

YAMASHITA-SAN MINAMI-SAN

FUJINO-SAN YAMAMOTO-SAN

·Special Thanks

HIROSHI KIYOHARA-SENSEI & PINE-SAN

·Original Writer

TAKAHIRO-SAN (AUTHOR)

·Editor

KOIZUMI-SAN (EDITOR IN CHARGE)

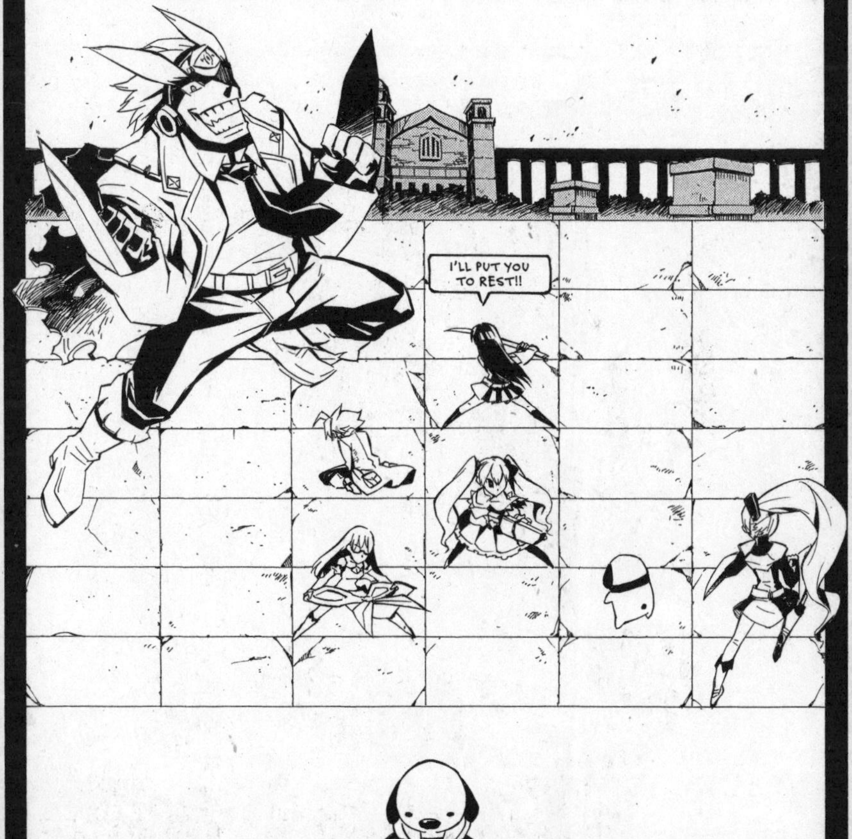
I'LL PUT YOU TO REST!!

THANK YOU VERY MUCH FOR BUYING VOLUME 2.

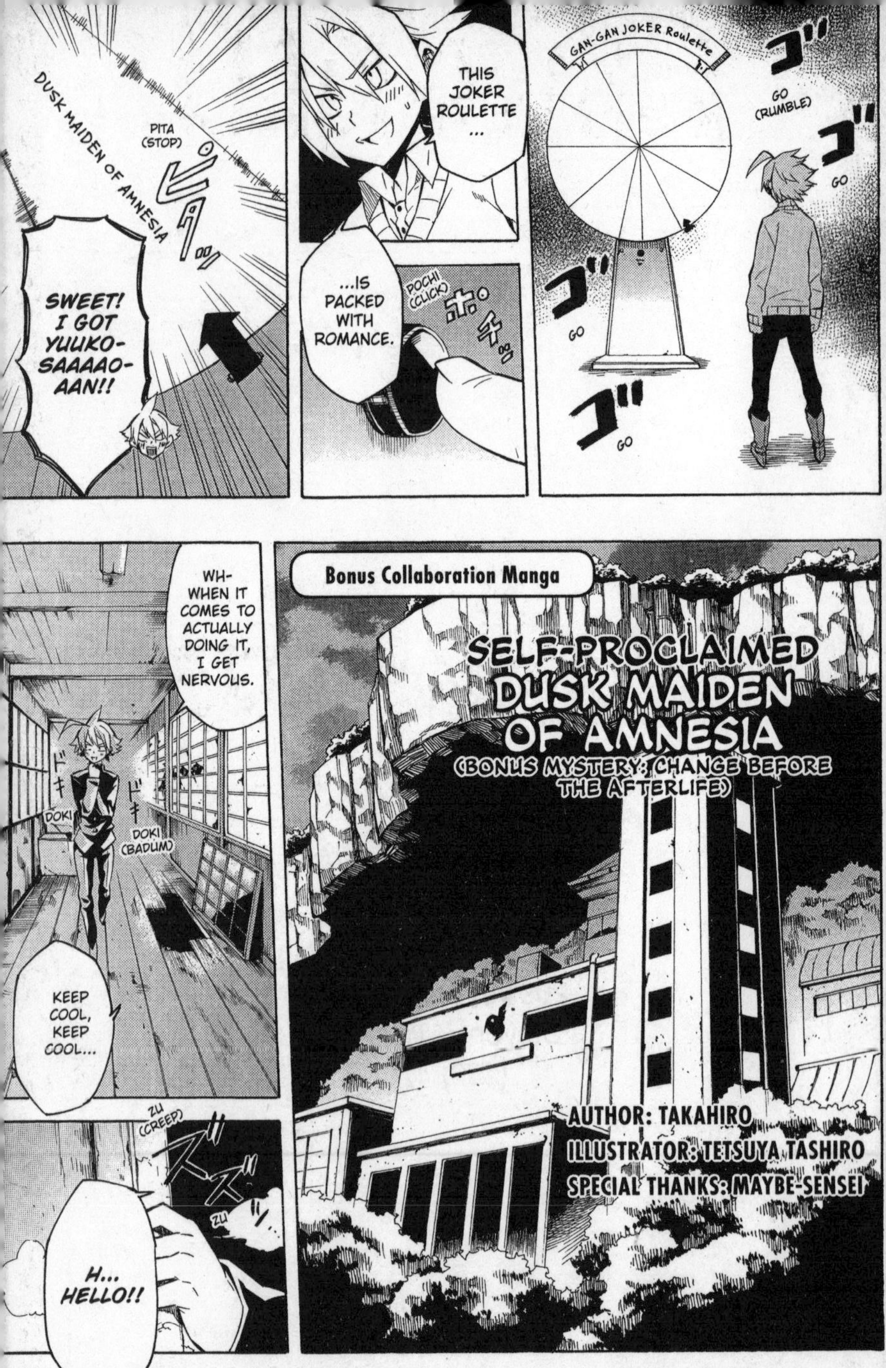
GAN-GAN JOKER Roulette
GO (RUMBLE)
GO
GO
GO
THIS JOKER ROULETTE ...
...IS PACKED WITH ROMANCE.
POCHI (CLICK)
PITA (STOP)
DUSK MAIDEN OF AMNESIA
SWEET! I GOT YUUKO-SAAAAO-AAN!!
Bonus Collaboration Manga
SELF-PROCLAIMED DUSK MAIDEN OF AMNESIA
(BONUS MYSTERY: CHANGE BEFORE THE AFTERLIFE)
AUTHOR: TAKAHIRO
ILLUSTRATOR: TETSUYA TASHIRO
SPECIAL THANKS: MAYBE-SENSEI
WH- WHEN IT COMES TO ACTUALLY DOING IT, I GET NERVOUS.
DOKI
DOKI (BADUM)
KEEP COOL, KEEP COOL...
ZU (CREEP)
ZU
H... HELLO!!

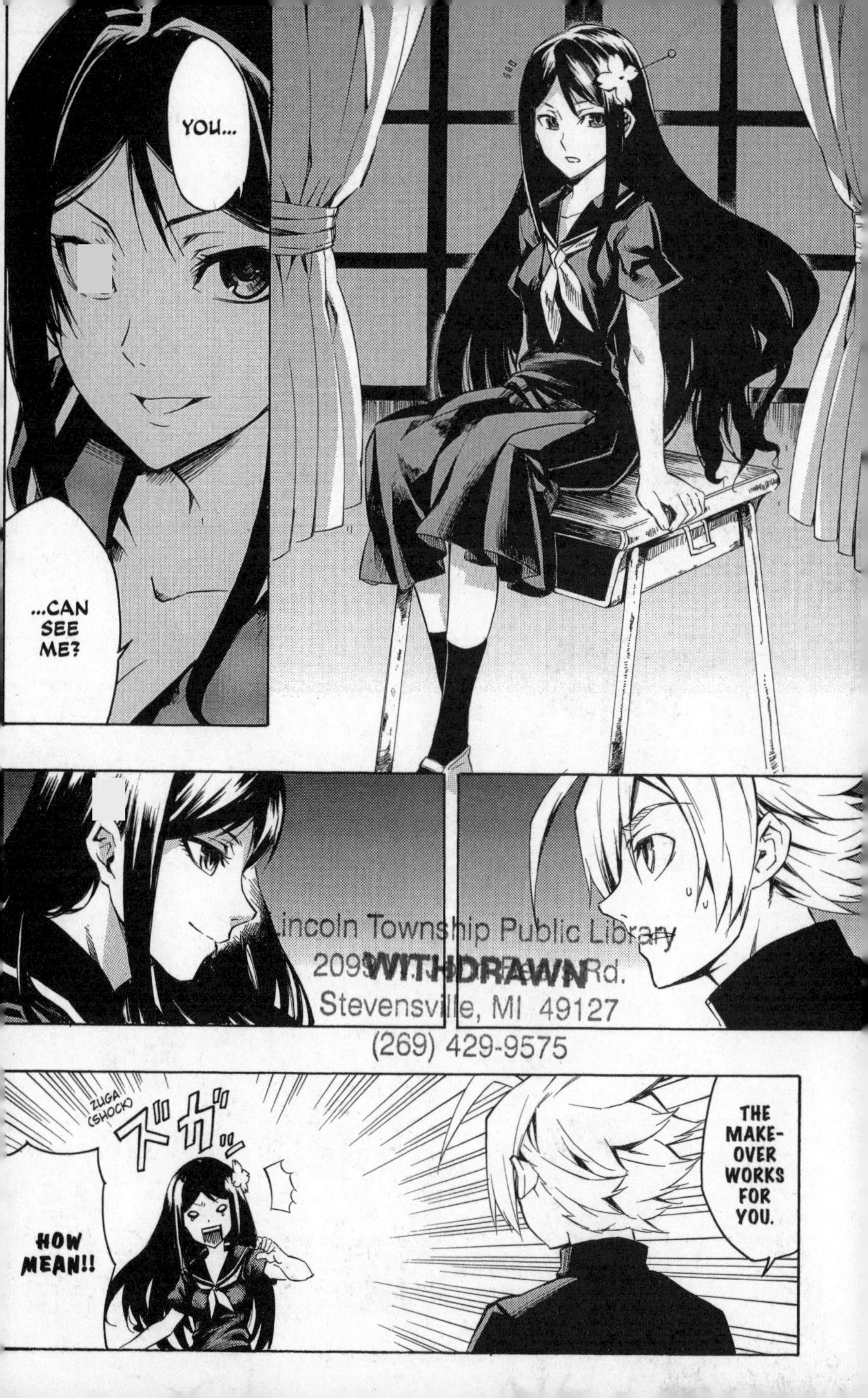
YOU...
...CAN SEE ME?
THE MAKE-OVER WORKS FOR YOU.
ZUGA (SHOCK)
HOW MEAN!!

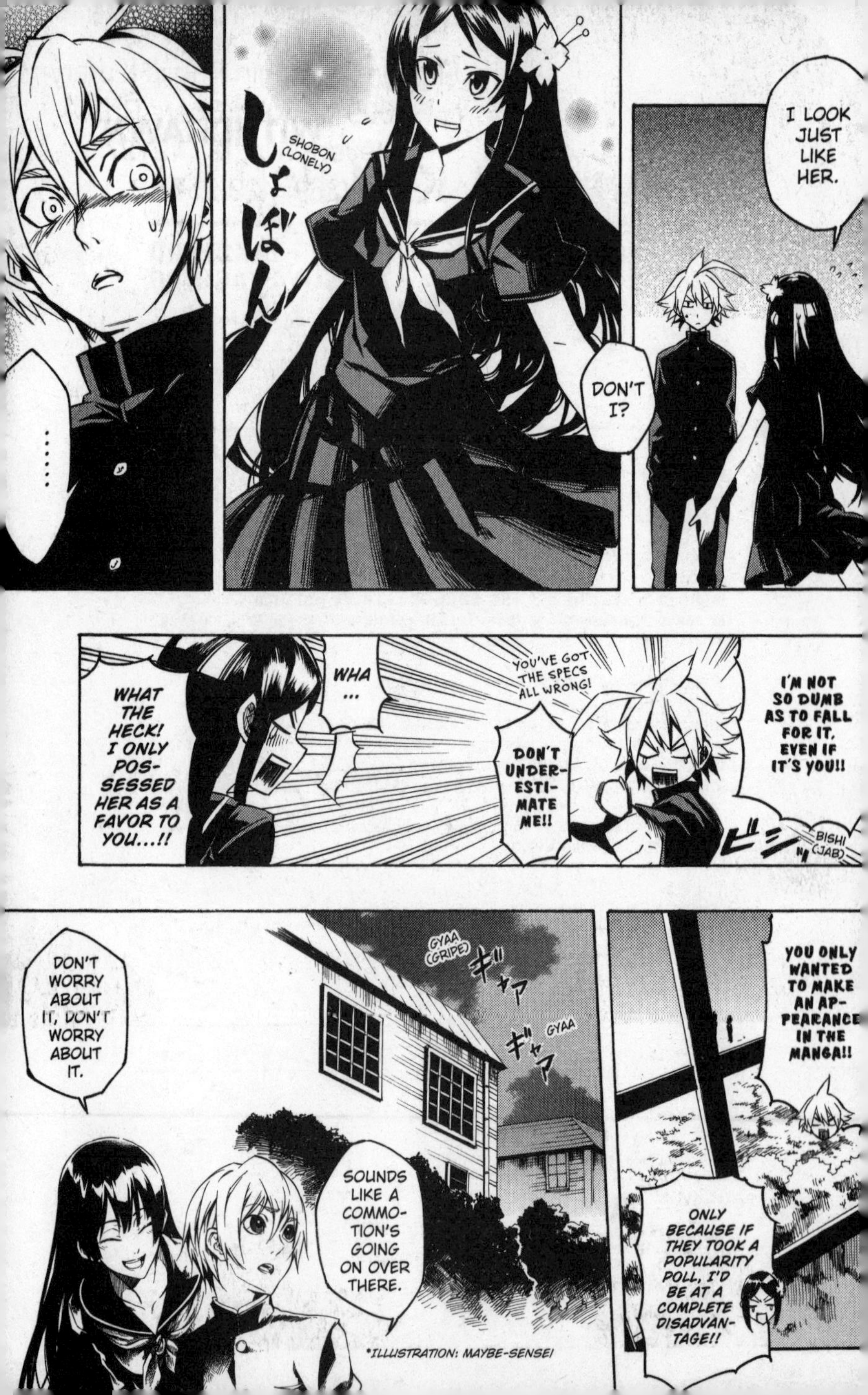
I LOOK JUST LIKE HER.
しょぼん
SHOBON (LONELY)
DON'T I?
......
I'M NOT SO DUMB AS TO FALL FOR IT, EVEN IF IT'S YOU!!
ビシ
BISHI (JAB)
YOU'VE GOT THE SPECS ALL WRONG!
DON'T UNDERESTIMATE ME!!
WHA ...
WHAT THE HECK! I ONLY POSSESSED HER AS A FAVOR TO YOU...!!
YOU ONLY WANTED TO MAKE AN APPEARANCE IN THE MANGA!!
ONLY BECAUSE IF THEY TOOK A POPULARITY POLL, I'D BE AT A COMPLETE DISADVANTAGE!!
ギャア
GYAA (GRIPE)
ギャア
GYAA
SOUNDS LIKE A COMMOTION'S GOING ON OVER THERE.
DON'T WORRY ABOUT IT, DON'T WORRY ABOUT IT.
*ILLUSTRATION: MAYBE-SENSEI

AKAME GA

Translation: Christine Dashiell • Lettering: James Dashiell

This book is a work of fiction. Names, characters, places, and incidents are the product of the author's imagination or are used fictitiously. Any resemblance to actual events, locales, or persons, living or dead, is coincidental.

AKAME GA KILL! Vol. 2
© 2011 Takahiro, Tetsuya Tashiro / SQUARE ENIX CO., LTD. First published in Japan in 2011 by SQUARE ENIX CO., LTD. English translation rights arranged with SQUARE ENIX CO., LTD. and Hachette Book Group through Tuttle-Mori Agency, Inc., Tokyo.

Translation © 2015 by SQUARE ENIX CO., LTD.

Yen Press
Hachette Book Group
1290 Avenue of the Americas
New York, NY 10104

www.HachetteBookGroup.com
www.YenPress.com

Yen Press is an imprint of Hachette Book Group, Inc. The Yen Press name and logo are trademarks of Hachette Book Group, Inc.

First Yen Press Edition: April 2015

ISBN: 978-0-316-34002-1

10 9 8 7 6 5 4

BVG

Printed in the United States of America